PROMISCUOUS KNOWLEDGE

Promiscuous Knowledge

INFORMATION, IMAGE, AND
OTHER TRUTH GAMES IN HISTORY

Kenneth Cmiel
and John Durham Peters

The University of Chicago Press   Chicago and London

The University of Chicago Press, Chicago 60637
The University of Chicago Press, Ltd., London
Published 2020
Printed in the United States of America

29 28 27 26 25 24 23 22 21 20   1 2 3 4 5

ISBN-13: 978-0-226-61185-3 (cloth)
ISBN-13: 978-0-226-67066-9 (e-book)
DOI: https://doi.org/10.7208/chicago/9780226670669.001.0001

Published with the assistance of the Frederick W. Hilles
Publication Fund of Yale University.

Library of Congress Cataloging-in-Publication Data
Names: Cmiel, Kenneth, author. | Peters, John Durham, author.
Title: Promiscuous knowledge : information, image, and other truth
games in history / Kenneth Cmiel, John Durham Peters.
Description: Chicago : University of Chicago Press, 2020. | Includes index.
Identifiers: LCCN 2019024338 | ISBN 9780226611853
(cloth) | ISBN 9780226670669 (ebook)
Subjects: LCSH: Knowledge, Sociology of. | Communication
and culture. | Communication—Philosophy.
Classification: LCC BD175 .C554 2019 | DDC 306.4/2—dc23
LC record available at https://lccn.loc.gov/2019024338

♾ This paper meets the requirements of ANSI/NISO Z39.48-1992
(Permanence of Paper).

I wish that friendship should have feet, as well as eyes and eloquence.
It must plant itself on the ground, before it vaults over the moon.
I wish it to be a little more of a citizen, before it is quite a cherub.

RALPH WALDO EMERSON

Contents

Preface

On Groundhog Day 2006 Kenneth Cmiel (pronounced Camille) collapsed in Iowa City, Iowa, from an undetected brain tumor. He died instantly at age fifty-one, leaving behind his wife and three children, countless friends around the world, several incomplete research projects and unanswered emails, a huge collection of books, and a big hole of grief. Ken, as everyone knew him, was my close friend and collaborator from the time we met by chance in the University of Iowa's main library in 1987 and discovered we were working on uncannily similar projects. From that point till his death, almost everything we wrote or read, and much that we didn't, we did in conversation.

Ken was many things—historian, family man, Chicagoan, Cubs fan, musician manqué, lapsed Catholic, lover of classic Hollywood, bon vivant, Americanist with a fondness for French thought, department chair, insomniac, human rights activist, multitasker, procrastinator, one-of-a-kind genius, and friend. Many who knew him said he was the smartest person they'd ever met. He savored contradictions and balanced contraries in both his life and his writing. His intellectual life was dazzlingly multifaceted, and in a companion volume to this one I hope to collect several of his writings and offer a brief intellectual biography.

The present book is something quite other. At some point after his death I took it upon myself to finish it in his name. His first book, *Democratic Eloquence: The Fight over Popular Speech in Nineteenth-Century America* (1990), was a pioneering intellectual history of modes of discourse in the American public sphere, and his second, *A Home of Another Kind: One Chicago Orphanage and the Tangle of Child Welfare* (1995), was a pioneering institutional history covering a century of wrangling over what to do about children with no parents to care for them. *Promiscuous*

Knowledge was also to be about his core topic, American political culture, but with a new focus on images and information and written in a more accessible style. Media history, that's my field—easy enough to round off the trilogy, I thought!

I little knew how hard it would be. I kept starting and stopping—hence the long delay. After trying three times to get it off the ground, I signed a contract with the University of Chicago Press in summer 2015. Two obvious things in particular were difficult: voice and timing.

At first I thought I could write the book in Ken's voice, but I soon discovered that you think and write very differently from another person, even a close friend, when you try to coauthor something with them—especially when you need to hold up both sides of the conversation. It's hard to steer the plow with an absentee yokemate. After several attempts at playing ventriloquist, I gave up. Still, plenty of his voice remains. Ken spiked his rough drafts for this book with brief confessional moments, often about his daily life, and I have preserved those for color and flavor. When you read "I" in the body of the text, it's almost always Ken in his own words. For the sake of unobtrusiveness, I changed most of the other *I*'s to *we* whenever it didn't matter. Even if most of the words are mine, and even if our voices sometimes move in counterpoint, the book's overall design and core concepts are Ken's.

Ken conceived this book in the early to middle 1990s and worked on it on and off until about 2002, with the last updates coming in 2004. As of November 1996, he had all the pieces more or less in place. He designed the book as a prehistory of the "swirl of image and sound" and the information overload he saw ascendant around the turn of the millennium.[1] This was the high-water mark of worries about the "postmodern" engulfment of reality by images. In the tech world, 1996 or 2002 is very long ago, and things have changed as radically in the intellectual and political realms as in the digital. Ken loved what he called *haute vulgarisation* (highbrow popularization) and wanted to write a history of the present, as he thought historians should always do. And he took the history of communication seriously, something historians rarely do.

But the present as he knew it is long gone. His emphasis on information overload as the central story of digital life remains relevant, but today we are more likely to worry about the structural pathologies of the internet: surveillance, echo chambers, fake news, racist algorithms and sexist trolling, data breaches, firewalls, *kompromat*, election tampering, the banality of social media, and the end of net neutrality. His outline and framing remain, though I have freely added material and updates (e.g., a sidebar on the "selfie") that he couldn't have written.

Ken's analysis provides a longer lineage for the wobbly status of truth that is so obvious in our time. He saw this book as a contribution to the history of truth and truthmaking, and he chose to pair pictures and facts, images and information as his protagonists. He never offered a single clear definition of *image, information,* and *knowledge,* or of *truth* for that matter, in part because he believed these terms had distinct meanings in different eras. In chapter 6 he presented promiscuous knowledge as a historical condition peculiar to the 1970s and beyond, but the entire book is about the challenge of containing the sometimes illicit copiousness of knowledge in any era. There is some fuzziness in his central concepts, productively enriched (one hopes) with the historical specificity of the examples.

Writing this book has been an act of friendship and of mourning. In its main chapters it is a multicolored history of information and images, but read with the postscript it is also a metabook, a meditation on knowledge, documents, distance, and death—on promiscuous knowledge of a different sort. This preface introduces the story of the book's writing, but the postscript is a much more extensive and heartfelt meditation on writing, death, and loss.

Ken left a torso. I've tried to make it a complete figure in ways that would honor his vision. The two excellent reviewers of an earlier version of this manuscript for the University of Chicago Press offered split advice on how to proceed. Peter Simonson suggested I draw closer to Ken's voice and vision, and Fred Turner suggested I take Ken's outline as an inspiration for structure, topic, and animating curiosity but cut loose and write the book any way I wanted. After long hesitation, I tried to take the second path but kept getting pulled back to the first. The structure of the chapters, the choice of many topics, and the overall argument are all Ken's. So are many words, taken from early outlines and drafts. Ken's legacy had a gravitational pull too strong for me ever to reach exit velocity. To break loose and write my own vision of our moment would have required a completely new starting point.

So here you have it, an experiment and a compromise—like much of the world we live in—between the living and the dead.

The result is not always what either of us would have wanted to say and is certainly not the way Ken would have said it. This book is no pretended transcript or extrapolation of his thought. If I might echo the manic commentator-narrator of Vladimir Nabokov's *Pale Fire,* to much of what follows my dear friend would probably not have subscribed, but for better or for worse the survivor has the last word.[2]

The raw materials that went into this book include one published essay ("Drowning in Pictures"), one essay draft ("From Knowledge to Information"), the draft of a talk ("From Facts to Aesthetic Exemplum"), a book review (of Steven Conn, *Museums and American Intellectual Life*), several partial drafts and sketches left on Ken's computer, his voluminous and miscellaneous book collection, which I inherited, four boxes of research materials, hours of conversation, a semester and a summer of team teaching, and years of friendship. (Ken's original documents for this book are available online at a University of Iowa website. Curious readers can compare what Ken left with what this book became at https://doi.org/10.17077/ocj3-36ob.) The process of coauthoring a posthumous book conjured up many of the book's themes—the squirrelliness of facts, the captivation of images, and the uncontainability of knowledge. Not only is the book about promiscuous knowledge, but the book enacts it in its gaps, gluts, and efforts to corral facts into larger stories.

There were particular challenges in completing each part that deserve brief comment here.

The raw material of the introduction comes from a pitch to a publisher that Ken wrote about 2002. He used the dot.com bubble of 2000 to frame the central theme of "data glut" or "data smog" (to mention two titles from the many books he consulted). Much of this pitch doesn't describe how the book turned out—it didn't end up as light as Ken wanted or as breezy—so it's not included here, but the final paragraph features Ken at his most whimsical and self-deprecating:

> My first book [*Democratic Eloquence*] had a lot of facts, too many to make it readable. The second [*A Home of Another Kind*] was pared down a bit. This, my third try, has fewer facts still. I'm trying, in my own pathetic way, to put my energy into the writing, having finally figured out that brevity makes a better read. Of course, this is part of the hype of the hypertext age: Keep it short! Add some pictures! But after having written a book on a very depressing subject last time, and working on another sober book [an unfinished project on the history of genocide and human rights] right now, I appreciate the lightness and whimsy that this culture spins at its best. On some days, I'd like to keep going this way, each project having fewer and fewer facts, until, like the well-known cat, all that's left is the grin.

Chapter 1, designed as an overview of the rise of early modern thinking about facts and images, opens with one of the most concentrated chunks of writing in Ken's own voice—an aria of wit and irony. The rest of the chapter develops notes he left on the seventeenth century. He left next to nothing about images except for a bit on the pioneering microscopist Antoni van Leeuwenhoek, though he clearly would have developed the theme of iconoclasm. And as is often the case in intellectual retrieval missions, there is a mystery text that has vanished without a trace: in about 2000 I heard Ken give a lecture on "neoclassical" and "baroque" modes of organizing knowledge that would have substantially rounded out this chapter, but it is gone except for my memory. He may have delivered it from notes that he tossed, and there is no record of it in his files or my own. This was not the only time fantasy (falsely) suggested that a couple of pieces of paper might have solved the puzzle of fitting the book together!

Whereas the sheer outrageousness of covering the entire eighteenth century in a few paragraphs at the end of chapter 1 seemed somehow reasonable, given the compression of the point, chapter 2 on the nineteenth century opened potential labyrinths at every turn. One could write an entire book about Mathew Brady's photographs, the history of playbills, popular science, or P. T. Barnum. And people have. Good books. In following Ken's narrative of the shift from the flood of factual abundance earlier in the century to efforts to corral it starting in the 1870s, I've filled in much else, and so has Gina Giotta, whose three sidebars and other contributions add resonance and detail here and elsewhere in the book. Ken drafted the sidebar on Frederick Douglass.

Chapter 3 concerns how cultural arbiters in the interwar years invented new methods of managing facts through strategies of cultural summary. It fell into place relatively quickly, unlike most other chapters. Ken already had done much of the outline, and his boxes of research folders held much material to add to the outline he left. Ken drafted the sidebar on John Dewey. The sidebar "Vietnamese Impressions," discovered at the last minute on a diskette in University of Iowa Special Collections, shows Ken's mature style at full strength.

Chapter 4 is the image counterpart to chapter 3's focus on information. Like parts of chapter 5, it is based on an essay Ken published called "Drowning in Pictures" as well as on the boxes of research material he left behind.[3] Of all the chapters, the trail was thinnest for this one, though his central argument about the onetime dominance of mythic images was clear. He left notes on Hollywood, photojournalism, the Leica, and photographers such as George Hurrell, James VanDerZee, and Weegee. I centered the chapter on 1945 as a convenient turning point. The sidebar on war photography is derived from Ken's 2005 presidential lecture at the University of Iowa, to be published in full in the compan-

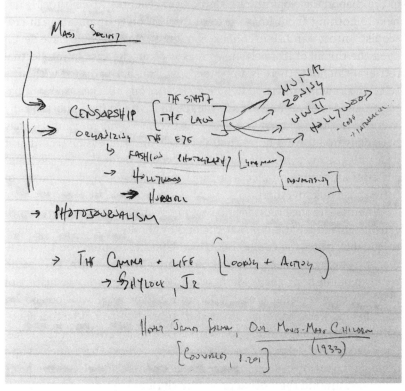

FIGURE 0.1. Kenneth Cmiel's notes on image censorship in twentieth-century America for his class The Image in America. Early 2000s. University of Iowa Special Collections, Kenneth Cmiel papers, box 2.

ion volume. The chapter finally jelled when I realized the year 1945 could pull together the curious mix of the playful and the serious, *levitas* and *gravitas*, that is so central to everything he thought.

Chapters 3 and 4 offer Ken's view of the United States in the middle of the twentieth century as a "mass culture system." The welfare state implied a sense of national solidarity, a widely supported policy of taxation as insurance for the common good, and a commitment to mitigating risk.[4] There was a more or less common faith in social planning and the power of experts to better the human condition. Aesthetics and popular culture respected crystallized essences and images as benign containers. Film, radio, television, and journalism provided programming of wide popular appeal. Mass culture, he thought, was a way to bring people together, to lessen conflict. Everyone saw and heard the same things. Ken recognized the obvious limits of the system, such as its blind spots concerning sexism and racism, though he admired the films, music, and national solidarity it produced; he simply thought we had to understand our moment in its contrasting light. As chapters 5 and 6 show, little of the settlement was still in place by the late twentieth century.

Ken left a full draft of chapter 5 as well as many notes on details. It is paired with chapter 6 as the image side of the image/information coin. These final two chapters were the hardest to know what to do with, not only for the obvious reason of datedness but also because of approach. Ken framed his history of communication here as a story of political struggles about media content in a single nation and slighted the ways technological systems work behind our backs—an approach very different from my own, but still one we can learn a lot from.[5]

Then there is the tone of chapter 5. It is told, if not as a story of decline and fall, then certainly as one of increasing confusion. The chapter catches him in a bit of a downer or at least a sober mood. It is sympathetic with culturally conservative worries about coarsened visual culture and displays little of his interest in postmodern playfulness (which comes out more in chapter 6). He knew both the heavy and the light sides of images (as in chapter 4 and other essays),[6] but this chapter ended up tilting toward the first. The kind of television he describes— one without a narrative sense, spilling before distracted viewers—hardly fits our moment of artful TV series and binge-watching. Ken nonetheless caught something. To miss the crassness of much of late twentieth-century visual culture was to not have one's eyes open. I think his worries about pornography, for instance, were apt. Here he zeroed in on the single image genre that more than any other marked the shift from mid-century mainstream attitudes. In any case, Ken didn't believe in downfall stories. Among his raw materials for this book I found this characteristic gem: "The silly argument is that the world is in decline and fall. The world has always been going to hell; it just finds different ways to do it."

Chapter 6 is an original analysis of the knowledge fights of the 1970s and the 1990s and an effort to come to terms with digital culture. Here again Ken slighted structuralist stories of technological systems for more gnarly tales of activists, lawyers, doctors, and publics. He left a decent draft, including the idea for a sidebar on *Desk Set*, and the sidebar on Bell and Lyotard is his. Some of it, such as a discussion of the latest (1990s) scholarship on the internet, I cut as no longer relevant. Chapter 6 caps off the book in proposing promiscuous knowledge as the key to the new regime.

This thought fit the minimally filtered internet and postmodern theory of the 1980s and 1990s but is still highly suggestive. The coexistence of professional knowledge and popular suspicion remains very much à la mode. After Brexit and the US election of 2016, nobody believes that digital innovation means a new age of enlightenment. Many felt betrayed by their epistemic instruments: polls, news media, data, pundits, and hunches were all wrong. The flat structure of the internet once celebrated by theorists as a great democratizing force now looks more like a strategic failure of self-defense. Instead of nationwide parliaments of the whole, we have bots, propagandists, and trolls. Anyone looking for a reason to permanently retire any lingering illusions about the innate democratic wisdom of the vox populi should consult an online comments section. In our moment, Ken's analysis of the many means by which knowledge has been shored up historically is desperately needed.

Ken saw the end of the twentieth century as the gradual dismantling, erosion, or even collapse of the mass culture system. He saw several trends: the growing gulf between politics and aesthetics in postmodern architecture, the distancing of images from everyday life in magical realist cinema, the waning support for national betterment through taxation, and the inability of a single presentation strategy to contain the social whole. Ken usually avoided an apocalyptic tone, though he had a gift for peering into the dark.[7] Reason and expertise had not collapsed; they were simply more embattled, more fluid and fractious, and perhaps more interesting. He permitted himself no nostalgia for the old regime and found it no longer viable or credible, though he didn't want to discard it and its legacy casually in favor of other untested and potentially more miserable options. He was curious about what new beast was being born. How I wish he were around to help us figure that out.

Introduction

Do we live in a time of "too much information"? In the late twentieth century, many people certainly thought so. Scientists couldn't keep up, the *Chronicle of Higher Education* told us in a cover story: "From astronomy to zoology, researchers face an unprecedented wealth of information."[1] "There is too much information," a radical-scholar activist noted elsewhere. Ours was a time of "data smog," reported a third observer.[2] We needed to spend more time in civic discussion, we were told, as if that could fend off the torrent. Researchers of all kinds were "drowning in a sea of data," noted sociologist Bruno Latour. "I too," he added, "have this problem."[3]

A chief context for the spike of such worries was the internet. Before the introduction of browsers in 1993, the internet was primarily used by academics and the military for technical purposes rather than in everyday life. In the early 1990s its popular use took off, but aggregators and search engines were still in their infancy. It was routine then to compare the internet to a vandalized library in which the books had been tossed on the floor with their covers and title pages torn off.[4] Online indexing was still primitive. The hunt for random treasures amid the tangle of linked computers was once thrilling. A colleague told me how his teenage son, about 1993, spent a couple of hours one afternoon surfing the web with a friend at the University of Iowa's "information arcade" and emerged with an exciting find—a recipe for chili.

That experience is long gone. A couple of keystrokes will get you more chili recipes than you could ever want. Ordinary users may know that the internet is a gigantic chaosmos (to take a term from James Joyce) of hardware and data, but our devices screen us from its viscera of cables and data centers. The books are no longer scattered all over the floor, and even if they are it doesn't matter because search engines know how to index their contents. The card catalog–like services of data miners such as Google make it relatively painless to find anything that exists searchably online. Metaphors of disorder or overload have given way to other worries. Muddle is no longer the dominant experience of cyberspace. We are as likely to find ourselves reeling at digital life's perversities as at its overabundance.

A change in quantity can lead to a change in quality, and the history of information overload is an important backdrop for understanding our moment's difficulty in establishing truth. Anxiety about too much information is a constant theme from at least the seventeenth century. The acceleration of formal knowledge production in the 1600s immediately raised fears of facts out of control, and the worry has not stopped since. As chapter 1 explores, the sheer opulence of nature became ever more apparent by the seventeenth century in light of European voyages around the earth, the microscope, the telescope, the new scientific societies. The number of known particulars expanded enormously. Europeans now confronted countless novel mineral substances, plant species, and animals. Investigators peered into their microscopes and had trouble deciding whether what they saw was animal, vegetable, or some cross of the two. Descartes decided at one point to stop reading reports of experiments, since they got in the way of his working out the basic principles he thought animated all knowledge. He didn't want excess facts to clutter his evolving philosophical position.

Undomesticated facts in particular have been seen as potentially disruptive. Practically any time in the past three centuries you can turn up commentators nervous about facts running out of control, upsetting order instead of serving it. A French philosopher in 1740: "A unique fact is a monstrous fact."[5] An American journalist in 1867: the number of new facts was "appalling, and utterly beyond the grasp of the intellect."[6] Philosopher John Dewey in 1939: the "increase in number and diversity of unrelated facts" led people to accept slogans over analysis.[7] Before the seventeenth century facts did not yet exist as we know them, and they may or may not be in the midst of another historical shift today.

If information has often exploded, the same is not true for images. It is relatively easy to think our way back to image-thin times. For a long time, a single daguerreotype provided the canonical image of poet Emily Dickinson, and there was much excitement in 2012 when a second image was made public after a couple of earlier false alarms (see chapter 2).[8] The image of a diffident young woman was supplemented by a more confident, sociable, and physical presence. Though Dickinson now has two portraits, most of the people who have ever lived left none. But today it is entirely different. Most people in digitally saturated societies lack an iconic image owing not to dearth but to plenty. Some celebrities today make a point of the ever-changing plasticity of their looks (Does anyone have any idea what Lady Gaga "really" looks like?), and a 2015 survey reported with dubious exactitude that the average millennial will take 25,700 selfies in his or her lifetime (see sidebar 5.3).[9] Today it would be difficult for anyone to have a persona of unattainable mystery without a massive effort.[10]

It is fair to say that there is a unique surfeit of images in modern times—the Nike swoosh, iconic sports heroes, celebrity antics, the latest mayhem. By some reckonings, over 200,000 new images are uploaded onto Facebook every sixty seconds. Eye-catching ads based on research on the psychology of attention pop up on the edges of our screens. The dominant medium for teenage boys is the visually intense world of the video game. The academic habitat has been colonized by PowerPoint. Worried middle-class parents portion out their children's "screen time."

In the late twentieth century, intellectuals argued about television versus book, image versus word, but that dualism has since been breached—if it ever was genuinely viable.[11] Digital devices present text and video promiscuously. For years we have been awash in calls to become "visually literate"—to learn more about how we see. And this isn't bad advice, given the constant barrage of pictures all around us. But these issues aren't new. The debates are ancient: Is showing something a good way to teach about it? Or does vision seduce, draw us away from any "serious" reckoning with vital issues? Plato struggled over good and bad ways of seeing. Iconoclasm was a recurring motif in the Hebrew Bible. In the New Testament the apostle Thomas had to not only see but also touch the resurrected Jesus. What would Thomas have done in our world of virtual reality, where pictures dance before us without physical contact? How would he have dealt with a resurrected Jesus who put up a website to spread the word or turned up as a sound bite on the evening news?[12]

Do we live in an age of information or of image? The answer, of course, is both. Doctors, architects, engineers, and scientists have long transcended the cliché of "information versus image." Data-visualization techniques are essential now in science, business, and government. CAT scans and magnetic resonance imaging are only recent installments in a long medical history of the graphic display of diagnostic data. The National Security Agency employs graphic designers to make its findings interpretable, though perhaps not always effectively—for a while in 2013–14 leaked NSA PowerPoint slides were the subject of widespread internet mockery for their ugliness. And it is noteworthy that on the University of Iowa campus the "Image Analysis Facility" is housed not in the School of Art and Art History or the Department of Cinematic Arts but in the Department of Biology.

This book is a genealogy of what it was once fashionable to call the "information age," in particular the changing ways we think about fact, image, and knowledge. It isn't a straightforward history of film or television, photography or photojournalism, digital images or painting. Nor is it a straightforward history of libraries (chief organizers of facts) or museums (chief organizers of pictures), though these institutions often play in the background. Rather, it comes at these issues sideways via a set of inquiries into the historical organization of information and images. We can better recognize our own presumptions by contrasting them with how information and image were discussed in the past.

This book is about information politics as a problem of communication. It is about shifting attitudes toward truth and authority—different "truth games," as Jean-François Lyotard called them. A history of the ways diverse cultures tried to manage and organize the flow of facts and pictures can tell us much about their hopes and anxieties at particular points in time, as well as about what has counted as "true." Seen in this light, the key point for understanding knowledge in the contemporary moment is not the proliferation of scientific publications, the "cloud" of data, or the contest over what counts as legitimate knowledge, but the new attitudes toward such things. Few would deny that the world today holds more information and more pictures, of various shapes and sizes, than ever before. But the question is how those heaps have been threshed and sorted, indexed and interpreted.

One important strain in modernity is the building of containers to house the information that seems in danger of overflowing. These containers—learned societies, classification schemes, disciplines, notions of taste, networks of experts, journals, encyclopedias, digests, laws, customs, schemas, search engines, and institutions such as museums, libraries, the university, and the state have all at different moments in the past few centuries served to put an untidy cognitive universe in order. The most important container is something called "knowledge," quite distinct from information. Whereas the most common theme of modernity has been information versus *ignorance*, the stability of knowledge is always threatened by both superstition *and* unruly fact. Information threatens to undermine the comforts of knowledge.

One of the containers used to house information is "image." The early to middle twentieth century saw the explosion of an image culture that was new and was central to an effort to portray knowledge to the public in an orderly way. The smooth seductiveness of the image was meant not only to house knowledge but also to build the ties of twentieth-century mass culture. The story of the late twentieth century was increasing distrust of those images. They were no longer benign stores of knowledge but altogether more devious creatures. The collapse of the culture-stabilizing image is a key argument of this book.

It is precisely at the point where knowledge moves out of its esoteric origins to some less disciplined social space that the stakes get real. Galileo and the church, nineteenth-century formal knowledge trounced by the popular press, the contemporary expert testifying to a jury, the bazaar of social media news and rumor unconstrained by editors—the point where knowledge touches the outside is the crux. Managing knowledge often means translating and popularizing. Truth claims get complicated in a variety of ways when they pass to a larger public. One special concern of this book is the erosion of firm boundary lines between formally produced knowledge and that asserted by popular or outsider forces. This erosion—not erasure—is one key to promiscuous knowledge, a mix of the popular and professional. Formal knowledge communities face newly insistent challenges. The boundaries have definitely not disappeared, but there are more boundary disputes. Promiscuous knowledge is, we will argue, a key part of our information politics, a concept that helps us make sense of things as disparate as ACT-UP's incursion into AIDS research, fights about expert testimony in courtrooms, and data leaks of nude photos or offshore finances.

The fraying of hope in the progress of knowledge and the incorporation of distrust into the system constitute a chief story of our time. Epistemic containers have had varied histories, but they all started to leak in the last third of the twentieth century, which saw increased skepticism about science and distrust of expertise. But this skepticism generates its own reaction. If there is no bedrock of fact, communitarians have worried, then our collective life is in danger. Public opinion would be ruled by sound bites, by gaps in knowledge, not by information but by the most enchanting or gruesome or outrageous pictures to cross our television or computer screens. Without the discipline of facts, political deliberation would be at risk of populist frenzy or poor judgment. But with too much deference to experts, the broad range of popular sentiment risks being ignored. Either way, we face a painful dilemma.

Today more information is generated than ever before. Things once ignored as unknowable are now the constant subject of massive surveillance, such as clouds and climate or the "likes" of populations. But no one claims this mass of facts will add up to cumulative knowledge, let alone cumulative wisdom. Yet the lack of confidence about any ultimate synthesis that is characteristic of our time does not mean we want to get rid of our knowledge regimes. It is precisely because so many people intuitively accept what might be called a vulgar Foucaultism about the intimate relation between power and knowledge that there is no substantial move away from the avalanche of information. It is too important a weapon to give up. Big data may not lead to public enlightenment, but it is certainly a rich toolbox. Few activists today may believe in the ultimate progress of knowledge, but even fewer will give up marshaling facts, arguments, and evidence. The condition of promiscuous knowledge means that we doubt the old containers of knowledge but continue to rely on the work of experts.

This book offers some contrasts to our moment. As chapter 2 shows, no one in the middle of the nineteenth century would feel moved to defend the inherent worth of facts as President Barack Obama did in a 2016 address.[13] Through much of the nineteenth century it was commonly thought that producing more and more facts advanced the democratic project. Information was supposed to kindle knowledge at the most basic popular level, where its spread would contribute to political progress and human liberation. Moreover, recent decades do not represent the first point where unfiltered information has generated a sense of crisis. In the 1920s and 1930s, cultural arbiters confronted the crisis of complexity and worried about how to better manage and disseminate the avalanche (chapter 3). To understand our own time, it is useful to chart out the earlier faith in facts, what sort of culture replaced it in the early twentieth century, and why this earlier solution is no longer tenable.

What is most characteristic about knowledge in our time is our willingness to ignore the containers of fact or to treat them cavalierly. We should understand what is unique today not in terms of new technology but as a set of new sensibilities about the flow of information and managerial practices. Distrust and suspicion reach beyond the academy into popular culture, the press, and courts of law. Librarians, museum curators, and academics—three of the chief managers of information and images—constantly navigate this divide. Formally produced knowledge is treated skeptically by elites and publics alike. But neither professional expertise nor formal knowledge has been summarily dismissed. Instead, the "information explosion" is a way for individuals to manage their own lives without the tyranny of professionals. It's not all that simple, of course, and in the closing chapter we will have more to say on this. But the basic point is this: promiscuous knowledge is the mix of distrust and dependency—on images, on facts. Rather than seeing digital culture as the apotheosis of the Enlightenment, whether as grotesque or as a glorious success, it is the triumph of fuzzy logic, of information loosened—but not freed—from one of modernity's great stabilizers: knowledge.

Our take on digital life is obviously not celebratory. There are any number of visions of silicon salvation on offer, but we've heard similar tales before. They were told with the first tap of the telegraph, the first radio crackle. They are stories spun when some communication medium is so new that utopia is believable, the buzz so hot that anything seems possible.

But with every new technology, the first moment passes. Within a few years, novelty wears off and the machine slides into the quotidian. Poverty and sin continue to haunt us. The political process falls into dysfunction and gridlock. Our bodies slowly fall apart. Then we need other tales.

We are now well past the first waves of giddy optimism about the internet as an endless supply of peace, love, and chili recipes, but utopian dreams have the whack-a-mole property of sprouting up again and again. IT industries produce ideological fantasies about new horizons in the same way that mining operations produce toxic runoff. Technofix fatuousness is as hardy a perennial as fear of information overload. This history aims to be one antidote.

This is primarily a book of synthesis. One change in recent generations is that there has been an explosion in the academy of writing about visual culture. In discipline after discipline, reticence about studying pictures has disappeared. Not only are we drowning in pictures, we are drowning in writing about pictures.

The book offers a series of contrasts between historical moments. To keep the narrative manageable, we focus on three discrete periods: the later nineteenth century (chapter 2); the 1920s through 1945 (chapters 3 and 4); and 1975 to 2000 (chapters 5 and 6). The first chapter, mostly using secondary materials, looks at these issues broadly in the seventeenth century. The last four chapters are paired. Chapter 3 treats the rise of a culture of happy condensation for facts, and chapter 4 deals with the midcentury celebration of the image as a mythic unifier. Chapter 5 covers the unraveling of faith in the image and chapter 6 the waning confidence in a manageable, progressively growing world of knowledge. Although we focus on these specific moments, we also freely mention transitions that take place outside these particular periods, including the present. The strategy is entirely pragmatic: we have chosen well-defined moments that are markedly different to highlight the comparisons. We can allude to all the transitions in between without spending excessive time describing them. With this selection of key moments we want to produce a reader-friendly text.

Some excellent historians have also written about the rise of information as part of the emergence of modernity, as part of the way a society organizes itself, or as the history of technology. Stephen Shapin, Peter Galison, Peter Dear, Barbara Shapiro, Theodore Porter, and Mary Poovey have written about the history of "truth," what gets constituted as truth, the evolution of concepts of objectivity, and the cultural practices that have an authoritative ring.

Especially helpful has been the work of historian of modern science Lorraine Daston, both on the history of "fact" and on the history of objectivity. Rather than praising or denouncing objectivity, Daston asks us to unpack its history and practices.[14] Whether she is writing about scientific illustrations of plants, glass models of flowers, or photographs of clouds, she is always acutely aware of the excesses in any attempt at realistic representation.[15] Fidelity to the unique reality of the individual case can both reveal details and obscure the general morphology of its kind. Photography, for instance, latches on to the individual flower or cloud but can never reveal the general type. Her research opens up the central concern of this book: how knowledge handles the profuseness of information and the excess of the image. Our interest in the ways truth claims become strained when they connect with the public very much follows in the spirit of Daston. For it is exactly at the point of public contact where we shift away from internal knowledge-creating communities and face the outside that anxieties arise most acutely.

In straddling that divide, the book wants to be a guide to the digitally perplexed. But it has clear limits. Chapter 1 ranges across Western Europe, but the rest of the book focuses on how questions of image and information figure in the American context, with only an occasional glance across the Atlantic—or anywhere else around the globe. It tries to tell a story, not make an airtight case. And it is a study of mainstream middle-class cultural attitudes and practices. We are very much aware of the pitfalls of this sort of history. In most chapters at least one sidebar directly addresses the problems of those outside the mainstream. The sidebars, from several paragraphs to several pages long, suggest regions of detail and argument lying beyond the main text. Setting something in a sidebar draws attention to it, makes it stand out visually. It is a way to make sure readers do not minimize the importance of outsiders. It is also a way to remind readers of the innumerable byways in the history of truth.

Warning Horatio

Facts and Pictures

There are a few stories commonly told about facts. Facts, goes one, are building blocks. They are bricks, carefully set next to each other, used to make something grander: knowledge. We patiently collect our facts, cement them together, and end up with a sturdy, elegant edifice that shines with all the strength and power of truth. This is the story of positivism.

An alternative story is this: "Facts" are not things we find, discover, or collect. They are something we make, sometimes with great toil. They do not create anything so permanent as "truth" but are social conventions used to prop up existing worldviews. The facts we highlight are defined by culture. "There are no 'facts-in-themselves,'" thought Friedrich Nietzsche, "for a sense must always be projected into them before there can be 'facts.'"[1] This is the story of what is commonly known as "social constructionism."

These stories, beneath it all, are not so very different. Think of them as the Cain and Abel stories about facts. For though they hate each other, they are still siblings. Both reduce facts to a one-dimensional supporting role. Facts are there only to buttress a larger story about the world. It is just that in one story (Cain's or Abel's? You pick . . .) these facts are "true" and in the other they're made up. In one story they build "knowledge," while in the other they play into existing worldviews or power structures. But "facts" play the same simple-minded clot in each of these morality plays.

But facts (and information) are so much more than these two stories portray. Even in the Western philosophical tradition their meaning is richly varied. Immanuel Kant used two terms for "facts," the German

Tatsache and the Latinate *Faktum,* and their meanings shifted from critique to critique.[2] Ludwig Wittgenstein famously started the *Tractatus*
by contrasting "facts" and "things." Giambattista Vico distinguished *factum* (the past participle of the Latin *facere,* "to do," close in meaning to
"deed") and *verum* (the truth), a contrast he borrowed from the ancients.
Scholars of many shades of opinion in the history and philosophy of science have shown similar complexity and nuance on the notion of fact.

It is easy to see the flatness of these two reflex stories about facts
and how they miss the multitude of ways facts work in the world. Indeed, facts are chameleon-like in fit and fruit. Facts build knowledge,
but they also keep us informed of events, entertain us as trivia, and pragmatically help us navigate our lifeworlds. Bus schedules are, or should
be, bundles of fact. Facts can be stable or unstable. Some of the stable
ones will certainly turn out to be untrue. From the twelfth century to
the seventeenth, many Europeans were dead sure that beyond the world
of Islam there was a thriving region of Christians ruled by Prester John.
More recently, and more grimly, millions were convinced that *The Protocols of the Elders of Zion,* the anti-Semitic forgery from the early twentieth
century, was "fact." It is all too easy to think of more recent examples.

Both the social constructionist and the positivist stories assume that
facts try to be cold, calculating, and neutral. But facts have a rainbow
of emotional tints. To hear someday that the Chicago Cubs have won a
World Series (a claim with a Prester John-like ring to it) would be a fact
not neutral and flat but raining down joy on their long-suffering fans.[3]
Facts can be exciting, troubling, wondrous. They can stoke outrage. We
can cling desperately to a fact ("She loves me"). Their emotion can work
behind our backs. A fact can hit you like a ton of bricks ("The test is positive").

My first book was an orgy of facts, example piled on top of example,
arranged with all the stupendous boredom of run-of-the-mill porn.
(Making that book, I might add, even less inviting to read than porn is
to watch!) Was this my own positivism peeking through? By all means
no. Even then I had no faith in the mantra. It was my own insecurity. If
I piled on the examples, I reasoned, no one could complain that I didn't
know what I was talking about. The facts in that book were coupled in
boring and unholy ways to protect me. This mind-numbing orgy of information was not rolled out in the service of positivism but was the
nervous defense of a first-time author. I was not doing science, I was
building a fort.[4]

I am not a positivist. I do not believe that "facts" are out there. I do
not believe they are simply "found" or "discovered" by researchers. The

old Latin *factum*, fact as something made, has a lot to be said for it. But I am not a social constructionist either, at least not in the way that term is often used.[5] Facts are not basically fictional (although some things we accept as fact might very well be wrong). Instead, *fact* is a "pointer word." We name something a "fact," in science, law, or everyday life, when we want to point it out, take it out of the flow of experience, and mark it for consideration. Those things we deem "facts" sit between knowledge, cultural pictures of the world, or our own metaphysical certainties, on the one side, and the dirt, dust, wood, and pain all around us on the other. They are a bridge from the latter to the former. Facts are made, then, but they are not necessarily fiction. If I go to the New Pioneer Co-op at 2:00 a.m., it will be closed. That's a fact.

Facts whose sole mission is to prop up larger stories (either "knowledge" or "social construction") also leave little room for ambiguity or confusion. Particulars get folded into their narratives as neatly as shirts at the laundry. Even as smart a philosopher as Paul Feyerabend thought at one point in his career that there were no such things as "bare facts." All, he thought, were saturated with theory; facts were "essentially ideational."[6] This classic version of social constructionism led Feyerabend to picture Galileo as using his facts to tell a story about the cosmos that was well formed right from the start. According to Feyerabend, Galileo was smart and canny, but he was not confused. The problem with Feyerabend's account is that for several years after 1610, Galileo *was* confused. He stared into his telescope, looked toward Saturn, and did not always see the same thing. Sometimes he saw three objects in a row. Sometimes he complained about his instrument. Finally he drew a planet circled by rings. For a while, Galileo wasn't sure what it was adding up to.[7]

Facts unable to fit easily into larger stories help create ambiguity and even wonder. This is not incidental to our argument. It is its core, a central starting point, and one, we might add, that owes much to Paul Feyerabend's later ruminations. Ambiguity points to the impossibility of explaining all facts by either social constructionism or positive knowledge. Facts always have the possibility of being excessive. They can escape their containers. Scientism is most wrong whenever it takes this hypertrophic form: "Science can explain everything in the universe." (Most scientists, I would venture, do not mouth this platitude.)

"There are more things in heaven and earth, Horatio, than are dreamt of in your philosophy." Hamlet's famous advice, remember, came on the heels of seeing a ghost. All my heroes have thought something like this—Epicurus, Montaigne, Walt Whitman, William James, and of a more recent vintage, Feyerabend, Ian Hacking, Italo Calvino. The key is not to hate science at all, but to preserve the vital sense of an outer limit to our knowledge. The universe is a wondrous place, so much of it happily eluding our understanding.

Images lately get just the opposite rap. Instead of being simple-minded clots, they are easy to picture as dark and complex. They are the noir of intellectual history, the femme fatale of thought. Their ability to manipulate us is taken for granted. (Usually this is ludicrously presented by intellectuals as the ability to manipulate *others*.) We are obsessive about them. They transfix us, overpower us. Worries about images roll through the culture—about televised violence, the trance states induced by video games or internet pornography, the draw of jihadist videos on disaffected young people, or the traumatic numbing that befogs the military drone operator. Pictures of a beheading or of a drowned or sobbing child can move nations. Images can induce rage, wonder, revulsion, excitement, insight, sympathy, arousal, or nausea. Pictures grab hold of reality, but they also, so we fear, grab hold of us.

The intellectuals and the preachers, on this at least, often agree. Images are treacherous and seductive, something to distrust. "The visible," literary theorist Fredric Jameson asserts in one of his more remarkable sentences, "is *essentially* pornographic."[8] But this is its own form of simple-mindedness. Images don't just trick us. They don't just obsess us. They aren't *essentially* pornographic. MRIs and CAT scans provide crucial information. I am proud, not embarrassed, to carry pictures of my kids when I'm out of town. I enjoy moments of beauty in movies. To rub all this down to the obsessive is to make the common error of mistaking the part for the whole. There are more things in heaven and earth, Fredric Jameson, than are dreamt of in your philosophy.[9]

Yet if images are seen as working darkly on us, they are also often presented as having simple messages. Pictures sum something up. They are iconic, capturing the essence of a moment in time (the photo of the Kent State massacre), a myth (Joe DiMaggio swinging), a nation (Norman Rockwell, *Freedom from Want*). (They are also expensive: these images do not appear in this book because the rights to use them would have cost $2,000. You may imagine them—or google them.) We fear their power to tell only one side of the story. But once again the idea that a picture offers a simple summary ignores Hamlet's truth. "The whole world is too much for an image," filmmaker Jean-Luc Godard noted later in his career, recognizing that no image could completely "capture" an essence.[10] As with facts, so with images: there is always the outside.

Viewers, moreover, understand the icons differently. Ah, yes, a moment in time—but playful, oppressive, or pathetic? (Consider Marilyn Monroe on the subway grate in *The Seven-Year Itch*.) The answer depends on where in the picture your eyes wander and what you make of it.

Within every photograph, as Roland Barthes once so shrewdly noted, there was always excess. For Barthes it was the detail that drew our eyes and suggested something more than the caption or the received interpretation. Photographs are full of surprises and incidents that keep their meanings dancing. Their sometimes stupidly faithful renderings can capture things that otherwise would escape.

Both information and image have multiple uses. They can be evil and beautiful, sentimental and cynical. They can be as hard as a club or as tender as a caress. And both are excessive—tumbling out of the containers we try hold them in, escaping the frames we use to manage our lives. Image and information can confirm or unsettle. Facts and pictures do make knowledge and serve as metaphors of our prejudices—but they also reveal ambiguity and confusion and persistently testify to the abundance of the world. If we pay attention, they teach us how little we know. But paying attention can also teach us how they have been made to speak in different times and places.

Wild Facts in Early Modernity

In the 1600s, the modern fact elbowed its way into European civilizations. The modern fact was a thing—a datum, a piece of information, or a specimen. It was, to use Lorraine Daston's useful phrase, a "nugget of experience." Most important, it was a nugget set free from theory. It stood on its own. Facts were "notoriously inert—'angular,' 'stubborn,' or even 'nasty' in their resistance to interpretation and inference."[11]

There had been particulars before, and a healthy debate about them was strung through thirteenth- and fourteenth-century philosophy, but for most informed commentators their value apart from some classification was minimal. Aristotle, who like all ancient Greeks had no conception of facts, disdained particulars free of larger explanations. So did his medieval disciple Thomas Aquinas. For them particulars were meant to exemplify or even embody universals. The medieval origin of our term *information* actually indicated this point of view: information was the process by which universal forms infused and gave life to the particular matter of the world.[12]

Seventeenth-century empiricists, in contrast—men like Francis Bacon, Robert Boyle, or John Locke—wanted to advance science by making more disciplined forays into the singular and unruly fact. This was one way to smash Aristotle, who was revered as "the master of those who know" (Dante) in the Middle Ages but had become the bogeyman for the seventeenth-century empiricists. They could not stand Scholastic dependence on what mathematician and astronomer Johannes Kepler derisively called the "world on paper" when the wide world outside beckoned.[13]

In broad strokes, before the seventeenth century no one believed in facts. People believed in things. "Things, like ourselves, are eminently subject to change, to growth, all the while remaining what they are. Facts on the other hand are static and immutable."[14] Such a view prevailed for much of the nineteenth and twentieth centuries. But in the seventeenth century facts were not so stable. As they entered the broader scene from the area of law, facts were flashes of wonderment, oddity, novelty. As scientific practice found ways to make them stable, facts began to take on durability and consistency. Facts "began as marvels and ended as regularities." This shift is particularly clear, as Daston argues, in the difference between someone like Robert Boyle, whose "militant empiricism" luxuriated in the irregular surprises of rare facts, and the work in the 1730s of the French physicist-chemist Charles François de Cisternay du Fay, who prized the invariant and stable quality of facts.[15] The broad tendency in European science of the seventeenth century was to pay heed to wild facts, and in the eighteenth it was to organize them into families and orders.

In European languages, the new meaning of "fact" starts to emerge in the seventeenth century. The Spanish *hecho*, Italian *fatto*, German *Tatsache*, French *fait*, and Dutch *feit* all gathered new meaning in the early modern period. The first example of the modern meaning of *fact* in the *Oxford English Dictionary* appears in 1632. The French term lost its sense as a deed (or an account of a deed) only in the eighteenth century, though this sense lives on in the term *fait accompli*, and the term *Tatsache*, a translation of the English "matter of fact," entered German only in 1756. All these terms point to the new fact as an independent bit of experience, something so stubbornly crusty in its uniqueness that human imagination could never have invented it. Facts are fickle in their indifference to human fabrication. When Raymond Chandler's private eye Philip Marlowe complained that a witness's testimony sounded like "the austere simplicity of fiction rather than the tangled woof of fact" he carried on an understanding that began in the seventeenth century.[16] Facts were odder than anything we could invent.

The ancient Greeks had no word for fact, and the Stoics seem to be the first to have had a conception of facts. Aristotle knew of *pragmata*, things present to hand, but not of *facta*, a concept it was left to the Romans to devise, and anticipations of "fact" occur in that slippery word *res*, which can mean thing, affair, lawsuit. The modern meaning of *fact* seems to have emerged from a legal context, at least in Britain.[17] In English law juries were supposed to determine the "matters of fact" and judges the "matters of law," implying a split between fact and theory. Originating in Roman law and then lost in the Middle Ages, this distinction reemerged in the thirteenth century and by the 1300s was well known to lawyers.[18] The Roman *factum* referred, as noted, to something done by humans, a sense it bequeaths to its descendant *feat*. Yet this was not yet the modern fact. When Hobbes referred to "a fact doing" in his *Leviathan*, he was using this older meaning.[19] For the medieval lawyers, "matters of fact" related to human acts and actions, and often specifically to criminal ones. The seventeenth-century fact, in contrast, stood on its own, defiant, resistant to theory or interpretation. There was more than a bit of the macho in it.[20]

Early modern philosophy came upon the innovative thought that a fact could be "natural." In Scholastic thought, things made by nature or God were necessarily true (*vera*, "true things") and things done or made by humans were contingent matters (*facta*, "things made or done"). The idea of a "natural fact" would have been an oxymoron.[21] But this is just what the empiricists were looking for. The modern fact eked out a new existence in the space between the old contrast of *verum* and *factum*: like *verum* it was autonomous from human purposes; like *factum* it was susceptible to collective procedures of assay and trial.

The new fact was linked to new ideas of "experience." Historian Peter Dear has charted the shift in the understanding of experience. In medieval Scholasticism experiences were "statements of how things happen in nature" in general. In seventeenth-century empiricism experience became particular rather than general, often including events induced by human beings in a laboratory. This practice helped to differentiate the English words *experience* and *experiment*, which are still linked in other modern European languages. The singularization of experience was especially important for freeing up the modern fact. Inquirers wanted to know the *what* rather than the *why* of nature; they wanted regular patterns, not teleological assurances.[22]

The paradigmatic modern "fact" belonged to naturalists, astronomers, explorers, cartographers, painters, and men and a few women of science. Yet it also represented a new sensibility, one that found astonishing value in collecting information. There were so many new facts. Fact and fantastic were not yet enemies. Daston, in her important work on the empiricism of the seventeenth century, has uncovered the centrality of the "strange fact" to the new science. It was the emptying of the category of preternatural, Daston argues, that was so important for the emergence of the modern culture of fact.

The fierce scramble to gather and record facts was one way early moderns handled a world newly bursting its former bounds. Double-entry bookkeeping, actuarial tables, circulating newsletters, ships' logs, collections of insects, zoological gardens, still-life paintings, cabinets of curiosities, and early museums stuffed with natural wonders—compilations of fact emerged in a host of ways.[23] In science, empire, and art the age had a logistical spirit of gathering and warehousing the things of the world. Renaissance humanists were possessed of an "info-lust."[24] The seventeenth century's rapid accumulation of scientific data deserves comparison to the way people talk about "big data" today. The jolt was equally substantial.

In the Spain of Philip II (1527–98), for instance, a new constellation of practices emerged for tracking the treasure, territory, and subjects of the imperial dominion. The Crown collected tabular, cartographic, and narrative accounts about coastlines and currents, rivers and tides, flora and fauna, florins and ducats, passengers, vagabonds, and beggars in its worldwide empire. Philip was sometimes called the king of paperwork (*el rey papelero*) because of his love of documentation. Instead of traveling around his kingdom in royal procession, as was typical of medieval monarchs, he asked his kingdom to come to him daily in mountains of documents. The rather quixotic ambition of the *casa de la contratación*, a clearinghouse in Seville, was to create a complete and constantly updated *padrón real* (royal register) of Spain's overseas dominions that would correspond one-to-one with its conquests. Seville was also the place where exotic goods, animals, plants, and minerals spilled from the New World into the old. This desire to map the world was not just a passing aim of Hapsburg bureaucracy but was central to the empiricist spirit of modern science.[25]

A recent generation of historians has tried to unsettle older notions of the "scientific revolution," which told the story of a colossal seventeenth-century transition in which the modern replaced the medieval and science conquered superstition. A few have suggested getting rid of the term altogether. After all, *scientific revolution* wasn't coined until the 1880s and wasn't in common use until after 1939.[26] Although that hasn't happened, the new science of the seventeenth century is now seen as more complicated, less fully formed than previously thought. The old and new mixed, and the new wasn't quite "our" new, its partisans not yet exactly "us." Isaac Newton cared about alchemy. Francis Bacon devoted considerable attention to monsters. The great chemist Robert Boyle, the public face of English experimental science, thought amulets containing pulverized toad and the first menstrual blood of virgins, worn when the moon was in the right phase, would counteract a string of diseases.[27]

If late twentieth-century stories of positivism and social constructionism indicate some kind of neat fit of fact and theory, seventeenth-century empiricism complicates it. Like so much else in the scientific revolution, the seventeenth-century fact was modern, but not quite. Facts roamed free of explanation—aggressively so. They straddled categories, threateningly or delightfully. At its birth, modern empiricism was sprawling, unsteady, careening. There was no good fit of fact and theory.[28]

Right from the beginning there was the fear that facts could run out of control. There was *so much* new information. Travels to distant parts of the world gradually exploded old ideas about the natural world. Who could catalog all the flora and fauna of Africa, Asia, and the New World, let alone Europe? What was one to make of armadillos, tomatoes, and cannibals? Hans Blumenberg notes the ubiquitous metaphors of "sea voyage and the discovery of unknown lands" to describe early modern knowledge, showing how difficult it was to orient oneself "in a reality for which standard measure, scope, and direction were almost entirely lacking."[29] In the *New Atlantis*, Francis Bacon imagined "the Spanish tongue" being spoken in his new academy of sciences, connecting English empiricism with the prowess in voyaging and discovery of England's rival power.[30] Even microscopic studies were understood as miniature sea voyages in droplets of fluid. Robert Hooke, the secretary of the British Royal Society, figured microscopes and telescopes as ships that brought "new Worlds and Terra-Incognita's into our view."[31]

One turning point was Francis Bacon, whose *Histories* compiled long lists of curious particulars immune to larger interpretive schemes. Bacon, the first ideologue of the "strange fact," believed the weird should be folded into new categories. He was not a simple empiric. Freaks of nature were critical even though—and perhaps precisely because—they defied easy explanation. He thought it the mission of natural philosophers to collect "deviating instances, such as the errors of nature, or strange and monstrous objects, in which nature deviates and turns from her ordinary course."[32] The fact of seventeenth-century natural science was locked on the weird. Bacon thought assembling and collecting strange facts an important part of improving the human estate. "Long after scientific facts ceased to be the anomalies and exceptions

Bacon used to destroy Aristotelian axioms and natural kinds, they retained their reputation for orneriness."[33] Nature was so multifarious, he
thought, that whatever advancements we made in knowledge, it would
always exceed our understanding. New facts were stubborn not because
they were solid, "but because they resisted explanation."[34]

Given that so many of the new facts were monstrosities, weird freaks
of nature, they proved maddeningly difficult to replicate. Instruments
were new, conventions for their use not yet established. It took long
training to see tiny creatures through a glass-bead microscope. Experimental procedures were still up in the air. Unlike our own sense of facts
as durable, seventeenth-century facts were fleeting. Thomas Sprat, the
first historian and publicist of the Royal Society, admitted that experiments were "often various and inconstant," even "in the hands . . . of
the same Triers."[35] Natural science would *never* get to the precision of
mathematics, Boyle thought. For generalities, mathematical models
were fine, but they broke down as they got closer to particulars. Chemi-
cal materials could never be free of idiosyncrasy. Since there was no such
thing as "pure" air, he reasoned, a scientist could never reach a lawlike
understanding. The atmosphere changed the way elements reacted.
Boyle loved testing hypotheses, but he hesitated at the idea of a "law of
nature," since he thought such regularities were subject to God's will.[36]
Even more, he thought the idea that God needed nature as his assistant
was potentially blasphemous.[37]

Excessive Images in Early Modernity

As the modern fact elbowed its way in, so did the modern image. If the
modern fact emerged abruptly in the seventeenth century, the equally
abrupt historical turning point for the modern image is classically the
discovery of linear perspective in the Italian Renaissance and the birth
of a new kind of realism in depiction. Artist-engineers such as Filippo
Brunelleschi and Leon Battista Alberti in fifteenth-century Florence un-
furled a new discipline of picture making in which the size of objects
varied in proportion to distance. Perspective showed how to use vanishing points and grids to represent three-dimensional scenes on two-
dimensional surfaces, and it did so with spectacular results. This story—
the Italian Renaissance marking a radical break in its interest in the here
and now—was one that the painters and thinkers of the era invented.

From Italy and Flanders came an outburst of image making that
sought to achieve geometrically inspired mimesis of the world in architectural plans, bird's-eye views of cities, maps isomorphic to their terri-

tories, and exquisite paintings. (Of course, many great painters did not follow the new rules slavishly but bent them for style and effect.) In a chronologically ordered museum of European art, you can see images start to change as you step from the fourteenth to the fifteenth century: horizons, plants, fabrics, colors, and a feeling of depth all leap from the canvas, thanks to the new medium of oil painting and the new technique of perspective. Painters looked outward to the world, not inward to spiritual realities, delighting in appearances. In quattrocento oil paintings, tiny castles seen through window frames teeter on cliffs leagues behind the people, tapestries, and tiles in the foreground, all of them rendered with craft and care in color, shape, and shading. Thanks to its Euclidian unconscious of point, line, and plane, perspective showed artists how the eye saw distant objects, not how they thought it saw them. Even in Vesalius's textbook on human anatomy, *De humani corporis fabrica* (1543), the breakthrough book of scientific illustration, the flayed bodies in incongruously classical poses stand before a deep horizon showing trees, buildings, and distant foothills. Perspective was too compelling an image-making technique to neglect even when its immediate utility was not obvious.

Amid all the geometrical discipline, however, you can also see objects that resist the grid almost as if in rebellion. Against all odds, clouds flourish under the new regime. The color, shape, and blur of clouds defy the plane, line, and point of perspective. In his *Treatise on Painting*, Leonardo asked the painter not to neglect such things as "spots on the wall, cinders of the fire, the cloud, the mud," and other ordinary sights. He observed that shadows were not always black, just as clouds were not always white, but harbored a range of colors to be noted by the observant painter. (Indeed, an influential handbook on painting from the fifteenth century, *Il libro dell'arte*, spends much time on recipes for different kinds of black.) A bit later, Erasmus of Rotterdam noted that the German artist Albrecht Dürer painted things that "could not be painted," such as "fire, rays, thunderclaps, thunderbolts, lightning flashes, and even clouds."[38] This interest in depicting sublunary things as they appear to the human eye marks a new attitude, a shift from marvels to descriptions, portents to symptoms, allegories to appearances. Alberti took it for granted that a painter would not be concerned with anything that is not visible, but earlier painters freely painted many "real" things not seen by the eye— angels, dragons, nimbi. Religious themes remained important, but there was a new crop of the this-worldly as well, an emphasis shared with rising scientific sensibilities.

In the seventeenth century an interest in appearances went together

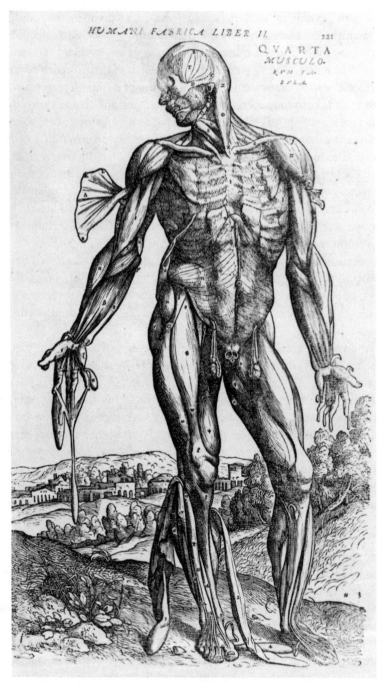

FIGURE 1.1. Andreas Vesalius, *De humani corporis fabrica* (*Of the Structure of the Human Body*), 1555. Metropolitan Museum of Art.

with new scientific theories and instruments of vision. The work of mathematician and astronomer Johannes Kepler was decisive. Perspective has a long history that goes back at least to Euclid, and Kepler's breakthrough in optics built on scientific theories developed by medieval Muslim and Christian scholars. Kepler understood that the lens in the eyeball projected a picture on the retina. He realized that the light striking our retina, like that in a camera obscura, was upside down. In the process of seeing we somehow inverted the visual input one more time to produce the upright image we thought we saw. He did not have an explanation for how the brain or mind handled the inverted image— his discoveries were in optics rather than in the neurophysiology of perception. The eye was thus not a window to the world but rather a kind of instrument actively involved in processing and interpretation. Few metaphors would have such a career in modern thought as the idea that we saw the world upside down without knowing it.

Kepler, as one recent book argues, might well be seen as a key to modernity, with his discovery of how vision works as a technical process.[39] As there were lenses outside the eye that could supplement our vision, so there was a lens inside it that enabled it.[40] Kepler made it clear that the eye was the recipient and not the projector of light (as Aristotle thought) and that the retina rather than the lens was the site of visual uptake (as Galen thought). Kepler observed that the eye consisted of a lens, chamber, and screen (the retina), like a kind of camera obscura (a term he coined in 1611, meaning "dark room"). Sensation was thus not the same as perception (to use a later distinction); the raw material of vision had to be translated into what we thought we saw. Kepler's language was ripe with painting metaphors: the image falling on the retina was a *pictura*, and the multiple rays passing through the lens he called *pencilli*, the Latin word for an artist's paintbrushes, thus connecting the work of art and the operation of vision.[41] Indeed, his use of the term *pictura* marks him being the first to understand vision as an image projected onto the retina.[42]

Vision was a topic at the heart of seventeenth-century science, philosophy, and art. There was a new fascination with light in painting, with the anatomy of the eye in medicine, and with processes of mental image making in epistemology. Fields now distinct—optics, anatomical dissection, philosophy—were pursued by philosopher-scientists such as Kepler, René Descartes, and Baruch (Benedictus) de Spinoza. Medieval thought, to be sure, was fascinated with light, but the new optics was empirical, down-to-earth, and mathematical. Seventeenth-century scholars studied rainbows, prisms, mirrors, reflections, refractions, lenses, and the compound eyes of flies. They wanted to measure and command light, not just revere it. Artists sought to fool the eye in trompe l'oeil paintings, and they often succeeded.

Lenses in the seventeenth century were something like computer code today: *the* cutting-edge technology. Descartes's *Dioptrique* (1637), a book on optics, was also a how-to manual about lenses. Descartes complained that lens making had languished too long under the care of craftspeople who were left to the hit-and-miss of lucky discoveries; he wanted to speed innovation with a deeper understanding of the principles of light. He opened his first essay by praising the most recent advance in the knowledge of nature: "those marvelous telescopes, which being in use for only a short time, have already discovered more new stars in the sky, and numerous objects above the Earth, than we had seen before."[43] Hooke and Leeuwenhoek would soon say similar things about microscopes. With a certain sangfroid, Descartes noted that if one takes an eyeball from a recently dead human, or at least a large animal, cuts off the back, and uses it to project light onto a surface in a darkened room, one will see an inverted but faithful image of the world outside. Voilà! the eye as camera obscura.[44] (Body parts harvested from cadavers have often served in both the imagination and the invention of sensory-enhancing mediums.)[45]

Spinoza made his living as a lens grinder, and this is sometimes described as the philosopher's engagement with a humble but noble craft, as if he ground lenses in the morning and wrote the *Ethics* after dinner. This picture is not altogether wrong, but lens grinding was not just any old craft like brewing, dyeing, or weaving; lenses were *the* avant-garde technology of the day. What he was doing was less handicraft labor than scientifically informed instrument design. Spinoza was steeping himself, at a world-class level, in the most radical technology of his time. He was less an otherworldly savant than a world-renowned technician and thinker. In their work on lenses, Descartes and Spinoza were among the leading technologists of the time.

The new optical technologies rearranged both the universe and our means of grasping it. One decisive effect of the telescope was to break what Hans Blumenberg calls "the postulate of visibility," the notion in medieval Aristotelianism that the naked eye could take in all there was to know. For Galileo the telescope was not simply an aid to vision, but a new kind of sense organ that displaced the natural eye as the agent of Aristotelian *nous* (mind). Hooke, the all-purpose experimentalist who as secretary to the British Royal Society served as a kind of early curator of curious facts and artifacts, put it well in the preface to his lavishly illustrated book on the microscope, *Micrographia* (1665): "The next care to be taken, in respect of the Senses, is a supplying of their infirmities with *Instruments*, and, as it were, the adding of *artificial Organs* to the *natural*." Chief among these were "Optical Glasses" such as the telescope and the microscope.[46] Media, so they say, are extensions of the human sense organs.

In seeing eyeballs and optical devices as equally instrumental, people like Kepler and Descartes helped both to denaturalize the eye and to remove apprehensions about lenses as instruments of distant perception.[47] Glass lenses had long been considered untrustworthy instruments of observation because they distorted scale, confusing relations of near and far. In the seventeenth century their dislocation (or enhancement) of the eye was reevaluated as a scientific benefit, in part because numerous strategies evolved to prevent lenticular distortion.[48] Optical-assist devices helped topple unaided vision from its lofty epistemological perch and launch what some have called "the 'idea' idea" in modern philosophy, the notion that access to the world is always mediated, that we perceive representations, not things.[49]

It is not accidental that the rise of modern philosophy, with its hard subject/object distinction, went together with a radical redefinition of what counts as an image. In his *Dioptrique* Descartes explicitly rejected the medieval notion of intentional species, which he mocked as flitting through the air into our eyes.[50] There were objects, and there were the impressions those objects made on our senses, but the idea that there was an essence found in—or even transcending—both he fiercely rejected. Reality was no longer a matter of the underlying forms that lay behind the world but consisted of the appearances that struck the senses as information.

The new optical devices went together with strange facts. And what strange new specters were opened up by this demotion of unaided vision: a cratered, earthlike moon, new stars swarming Orion's belt, the black void (was it?) of receding space, the multitude of stars that compose the Milky Way. Galileo's *Sidereus Nuncius* (1610), the pamphlet that announced such discoveries, also pioneered the use of scientific illustrations: his engravings of the moon, showing its cratered and thus imperfect surface, were among the most important images in early modern science and were often copied (and altered) in later pirated editions.[51] Such discoveries were just as strange as medieval mixed artifacts like winged salamanders, unicorn horns, or gemstones ground into medicines, but they fit into a very different intellectual framework. (One of Galileo's rivals called his telescopic findings "monstrosities.")[52]

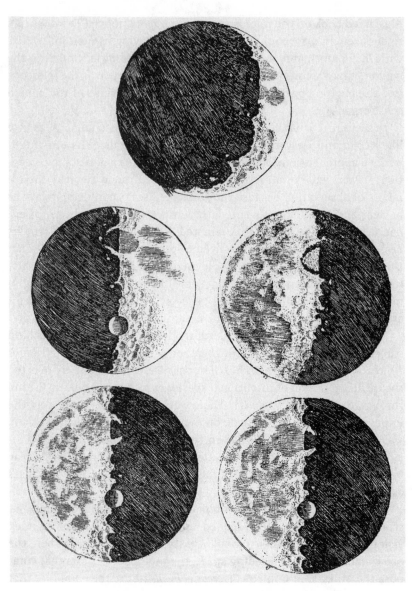

FIGURE 1.2 Galileo's sketches of the moon from *Sidereus Nuncius*, 1610.

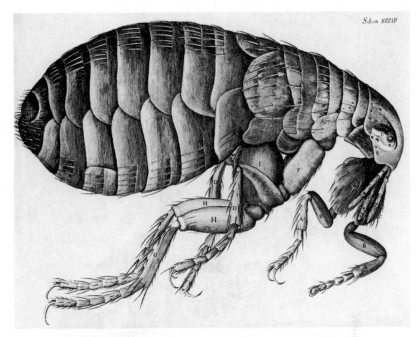

FIGURE 1.3. Robert Hooke, Engraving of a flea in *Micrographia*, 1665.
Wellcome Collection. CC BY.

The microscope was in some ways even more radical than the telescope. The telescope revealed worlds that were similar to the one we knew. These worlds, such as moons circling other planets, were certainly strange, but they were not phenomena never seen before. But the microscope opened an entirely unfamiliar world of creatures and shapes.[53] In Hooke's *Micrographia*, exquisite engravings show the wonders of the microscopic world, including a magnificent foldout of a flea, one of the most famous images in the history of scientific illustration.

The book was the first scientific best seller and the second book published by the Royal Society. In adding "artificial organs to the natural," Hooke saw instruments as repairing the natural defects of perception and even restoring the vision humans had before the Fall. Thanks to the microscope, we now "behold almost as great a variety of Creatures as we were able before to reckon up in the whole Universe itself."[54] *Micrographia* is a catalog of wondrous particulars, both artificial and biological, seen close up—needles, razors, watered silks, burnt vegetables, snowflakes, gnats, moths, spiders, flies, seeds, sponges. It was part of a wave of Renaissance scientific illustration going back to Vesalius. Ordinary things looked magically different when magnified. Hooke provided an

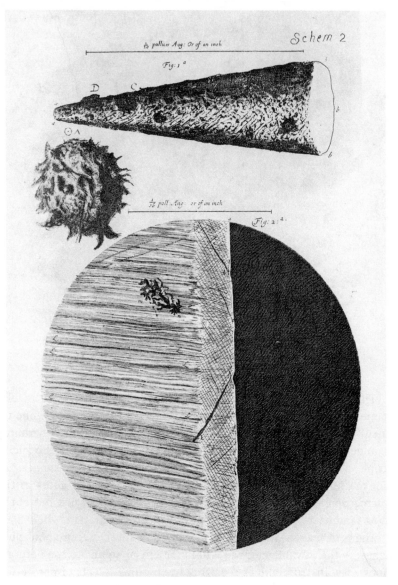

FIGURE 1.4. Robert Hooke, point of a needle, in *Micrographia*, 1665.
Wellcome Collection. CC BY.

image of a period (printer's point) that looked like a round, furry beast or a cratered asteroid, showing that our perception of print as smooth and regular was, like all perception, an abstraction from the graininess of facts.[55] The point, long conceived of as a vanishing abstraction in Euclidean geometry, when magnified looked instead, as Hooke memorably put it, like "a great splatch of London dirt."[56] There were kingdoms upon kingdoms in the small worlds invisible to the unaided eye. The microscope had revealed the minuteness and subtlety of reality itself.

What *Micrographia* did not show were microorganisms. That discovery was left to the greatest microscopist of the age, the Dutch scientist-obsessive Antoni van Leeuwenhoek, who stared into his devices for decades in his long life, seeing strange things, half animal, half plant. The son of a cloth merchant, Leeuwenhoek grew up familiar with magnifying glasses as tools for assessing the thread count of fabrics. In middle age he turned to his single-lens microscopes, which were capable of up to 500x magnification. In his almost three hundred letters to the British Royal Society, now conveniently available online in their Dutch originals and English translations, he described the *diertgens* or "animalcules" that he saw everywhere—in the rain, on our clothes, in our food—"more animals living in the scum on the teeth in a man's mouth than there are men in the whole kingdom."[57] In 1678 he saw more than a thousand "living creatures" all "moving about" in a drop of semen no bigger than "a grain of sand." (He hastened to assure his learned readers of the proper marital harvest of said liquid.)[58] What could anyone make of this, the first sighting of spermatozoa in the history of the world? Was it more audacious that he looked through a microscope or that he thought to examine such a substance at all? Such information inevitably flopped outside the Aristotelian corset.

Leeuwenhoek took samples from puddles, the beach, mud, rainwater, and snowmelt, from skin, tooth plaque, pus, earwax, and saliva. His wife and daughter seem to have willingly participated in his sometimes unappetizing experiments. He carefully watched what happened to solutions of pepper, nutmeg, cloves, ginger, and vinegar, trying to learn what gave them their pungent flavor. (As wine gauger for the town of Delft, he had reason to be interested in the science of how things taste.) He saw red blood cells but didn't understand their shape. He examined the semen of over thirty animals, including that in a testicle taken from a live rat, and his skill at microdissection allowed him to behold the semen of tiny insects such as fleas and gnats. That such minute creatures had organs of reproduction was a clear strike against the Aristotelian theory of spontaneous generation. He experimented on himself with lice, toe jam, and burns.[59] He supplied scientists throughout Europe with fresh observations. If there ever was a connoisseur of the strange fact, Leeuwenhoek was it.

Leeuwenhoek lived in Delft in a house 150 yards from that of the luminous painter Johannes Vermeer, was born in the same year, and moved in the same social circles, though there is no clinching evidence that they knew each other. Laura J. Snyder's recent book *Eye of the Beholder* nicely pairs the two figures, showing how the new techniques and technologies of seeing shaped their parallel worlds of science and painting. Where Leeuwenhoek used microscopes to form visual fields in which to see his "little animals," Vermeer used optical aids to help achieve the remarkable depth of field, color effects, and play of light and shadow that characterize his paintings. Scholars have offered detailed technical objections to Snyder's interpretations, but the use of optical devices by many early modern painters is incontestable.[60] The long-simmering debate about the role of devices in art seems fueled in part by the sense that technological enhancement is cheating. Indeed, it seems that some seventeenth-century painters feigned ignorance of the camera obscura that they were obviously using. For Vermeer and others optical aids were assets in the toolbox, not betrayals of craft. Vermeer was no slave to optics but often violated straight-up mimesis for emphasis and dramatic effect. The question whether art is cheating—or is nothing but—is an old one. Similar questions about artistry and authenticity would pop up again in the mid-twentieth century concerning documentary photography (see chapter 4).

Vermeer, of course, was only one of the most brilliant of an astonishing group of painters in the seventeenth-century Netherlands. The work of the Dutch masters—who included some women—has famously been called "the art of describing."[61] It luxuriated in the things of this world, in fruits, flowers, papers, and insects. Dutch artists loved the being and seeming of facts in all their visual variety—clouds, orange peels, shells, light breaking through windows or bouncing off glass, skin, lobsters. They also liked to depict the means by which facts were compiled and ordered—letters, maps, globes, and atlases, coins, ledgers, compasses. The philosopher G. W. F. Hegel praised Dutch Golden Era painting for its "feeling for upright, cheerful existence," "love for the apparently insignificant and momentary," "the open freshness of the eye and the undistracted immersion of the entire soul in the most confined and limited things simultaneous with the highest freedom of artistic composition, the fine sensitivity for the peripheral." Dutch painting was, he famously summed up, "the Sunday of life."[62]

Sidebar 1.1 Maria Sibylla Merian and the Art of Insects

Insects were prominent in the art and science of the Renaissance and early modernity. Bees served many thinkers as a model of how to make a sound collection of knowledge or objects.[1] Francis Bacon disdained Scholastic thinkers as spiders who spun philosophical webs out of their own substance, in contrast to industrious empiricists who gathered materials as ants do (he was drawing on a long tradition of animal fables as moral lessons). According to his first biographer, Spinoza enjoyed staging fights between spiders or throwing flies into spiderwebs, and sometimes he laughed out loud at their antics. The philosopher also observed flies and fleas under a magnifying glass.[2] Leeuwenhoek, as we have seen, constantly looked at moths, worms, mites, flies, and even smaller organisms under the microscope. So popular was insect observation that magnifying glasses were commonly known as "flea glasses." Descartes remarked on the ubiquity in the Dutch Republic of *lunettes à puces* (*Optics*, 7th discourse). Another observer, mocking the fascination with magnifying insects, complained that Oxford scholars were "good at two things, at diminishing a Commonwealth and Multiplying a Louse!" Hooke's *Micrographia* provided a foldout image of a flea; evidently a regular-sized page could not do it justice. (He was following ancient precedent in magnifying the flea.)[3] The new ability to travel with the eye into hitherto invisible realms only heightened this fascination with the insect kingdom (see fig. 1.3).[4]

Insects were among the most important subjects for painter and naturalist Maria Sibylla Merian (1647–1717). Like most female artists in seventeenth-century Europe, such as Artemisia Gentileschi, Judith Leyster, or Rachel Ruysch, Merian was born into a family of artists. Her father was a Frankfurt engraver and publisher who had won fame for his scientific illustrations and riches for his depictions of the flora and fauna of the New World. Although he died when she was two, his interest in alchemy—the transformation of one substance into another—was

1. Hawhee, *Rhetoric in Tooth and Claw*, 156–59.

2. Johannes Colerus, *Korte, dog waaragtige levens-beschrijving, van Benedictus de Spinosa* (1705; repr., The Hague: Martinus Nijhoff, 1910), 32–33.

3. Hawhee, *Rhetoric in Tooth and Claw*, 111. See also John Durham Peters, "33 + 1 Vignettes on the History of Scalar Inversion," *ELH* 86 (2019): 305–31.

4. Snyder, *Eye of the Beholder*, 103–4.

clearly passed on. Merian was fascinated by insects from an early age, and thanks to her family's ties to the silkworm business, there were plenty of caterpillars around; at age thirteen she had observed silkworm caterpillars metamorphosing into moths well before this was the widely accepted scientific consensus.

Not only were insects inherently interesting, they were also, like flowers, a safe subject for a female student and illustrator of nature. Merian, like other amateur artists, seized on the opening of the water-color medium and miniatures to develop her art, working apart from the mainstream of all-male guilds with their oil painting, historical allegories, and nudes.[5] Watercolor, gouache, and engraving were left fallow for Merian and later female natural history illustrators in the eighteenth century.[6]

Merian's first publication was a collection of flower images, *Neues Blumenbuch* (1675–80), followed by a study devoted to the metamorphosis of caterpillars and the flowers they ate (1679–83), both issued in Nuremburg. (This after being married at age sixteen to another artist and giving birth to two daughters.) In her treatment of caterpillars Merian exuberantly praises "the creator of even of these smallest and humblest little worms," and accompanying poems by the Nuremburg theologian Christoph Arnold make clear the religious stakes: if the lowliest worm could become a butterfly, so could the human worm be redeemed. In her pre-Linnaean moment, however, Merian makes no effort at an underlying logic or classification, and no architectonic scheme orders her specimens or pictures. She says she put silkworms first because they were the noblest worms and the most useful to people.[7] The worms and their plant food were arranged in baroque profusion, not in neoclassical order, scattered across the page as they were in the visual tradition she inherited from the Flemish painter and naturalist Joris Hoefnagel, among others.[8]

In 1685 Merian joined the Labadists, a utopian religious community,

5. Natalie Zemon Davis, *Women on the Margins: Three Seventeenth-Century Lives* (Cambridge, MA: Harvard University Press, 1995), 143.

6. Lorraine Daston and Peter Galison, *Objectivity* (New York: Zone, 2007), 89.

7. Maria Sibylla Merian, *Der Raupen wunderbare Verwandlung und sonderbare Blumen-Nahrung* (Nuremburg, 1679), available online at http://digi.ub.uni-heidel berg.de/diglit/merian1679bd1.

8. For this point and many others I (JDP) am indebted to Marisa Bass.

abandoning her possessions and her husband. She moved to Friesland in the northern Netherlands with her two daughters, learned Dutch, and divorced her husband, though she referred to him as deceased. After six years, apparently tiring of the ascetic strictures and turmoil in the religious commune, she moved to Amsterdam, where she won fame as an artist and naturalist and was the teacher of painter Rachel Ruysch, herself the daughter of the foremost anatomist of the time. The Netherlands was a relatively tolerant place for a woman interested in alchemical transformation: not a witch had been burned there for over a century, in contrast to her more censorious native Germany. Amsterdam, then the central market of world trade, abounded in insects and other specimens brought from around the globe. Merian was well connected with art dealers, anatomists, botanists, entomologists, and painters, and she had access to rare collections and cabinets of curiosities, but the insects were all dead, dried, and thus removed from the cycles of change that fascinated her.

To study insects in their natural habitat, in 1699 she sold many of her paintings to help finance the expedition and sailed with her younger daughter Dorothea to Suriname, a Dutch colony in South America where slaves toiled with sugarcane to satisfy Europe's growing sweet tooth. This European woman went to explore South America well over a century before the expeditions of male scientists such as von Humboldt or Darwin. As in her earlier move to Friesland, it was almost unheard of for a woman to boldly set off for parts unknown without male protectors. After two years of active botanical, artistic, entomological, and anthropological work in the Dutch colony, she could no longer take the jungle and returned to Amsterdam with sketches, watercolors, workbooks, specimens, and the aftereffects of malaria, accompanied by her daughter and, it seems, an Amerindian woman servant.

In 1705 Merian published her magnum opus, *Metamorphosis insectorum surinamensium* (Metamorphosis of the insects of Suriname), in Amsterdam.[9] It was printed in a large folio format, with sixty engraved plates. The text facing the plates provided commentary rich with zoo-

9. For helpful background, see David Brafman and Stephanie Schrader, *Insects and Flowers: The Art of Maria Sibylla Merian* (Los Angeles: Getty Museum, 2008); Heidi Reidell, "A Study of Metamorphosis," *Americas* 60 (2015): 28–35; and Kim Todd, *Chrysalis: Maria Sibylla Merian and the Secrets of Metamorphosis* (Orlando, FL: Harcourt, 2007).

logical and anthropological data such as how the local people used the plants and animals for food and medicine. The images were copper engravings, and deluxe editions were hand-colored by Merian and her daughters. These images have since become famous, joining the painstaking craft of hand-coloring miniatures with the grandeur of a printed text to be distributed among a wider public.

Every plate is closely observed and attractively composed; Merian has no fear of blank space. The central theme is her lifelong fascination with insects—caterpillars, ants, butterflies, moths—and other creatures interacting with plants. Merian shows organisms embedded in their environments, depicting leaves eaten by caterpillars and worms embedding themselves in cut fruit with sensitivity to an ecosystem. Though her images are beautiful, she does not shy away from nature's harshness: a tarantula devours a hummingbird, chains of army ants storm a plant, a banana peel wears small bruises like hieroglyphs. Moths with spooky red eyes mingle with salamanders on a bare branch covered with eggs. Her images compress many points of time into single frames, appropriate for a scientific mind interested in transformations: a guava tree is shown with bud, blossom, and fruit all at once, and animals in different stages of development such as caterpillar and butterfly, tadpole and frog, can appear in the same image. Merian was interested in nature as moving dynamically through time, not as static types pinned behind glass.

Merian's reputation was strong in her time. Both of her daughters were artists and carried on her legacy. She was esteemed as a naturalist as well as an artist: Linnaeus quoted her hundreds of times in his taxonomy of insects. She belonged to a confluence in which scientific research and the decorative arts flourished side by side.[10] In the nineteenth century she was largely forgotten. The later twentieth century revived her; her portrait showed up on German banknotes and postage stamps, redoubts of nationalist iconic images. Merian shows that a woman with will, talent, and imagination could overcome the strictures of the age to achieve stunning things. Historian Natalie Zemon Davis, in a spirit of feminist appreciation, treats Merian as a heroine who saw native people with greater empathy, "unsettled the colonial encounter," transcended the binary of savage and civilized, took seriously the testimony of native informants, learned local languages, recognized the

10. Daston, "Glass Flowers," 233.

FIGURE 1.5. Maria Sibylla Merian, plate XXIII in *Metamorphosis insectorum surinamensium*, 1705. Courtesy of Linda Hall Library of Science, Engineering, and Technology.

suffering of slaves, and even learned about ethnobotanical birth control techniques from local women.[11] Maria Sibylla Merian shows us that, like "facts" in the seventeenth century, there were also people who defied every category you could try to fit them into.

11. Davis, *Women on the Margins*, 191.

Sidebar 1.2 Still Life with Flowers

In the Rijksmuseum in Amsterdam hangs a painting from 1639 by the Haarlem painter Hans Bollongier (or Boulenger), called *Stilleven met bloemen* (Still life with flowers). It is an exuberant picture showing flowers of many kinds in a dark globular glass vase set on a table against the backdrop of an interior wall. The composition is lovely, with diverse color accents exploding outward—white, green, yellow, pink, red, and violet—against a nondescript, out-of-focus ocher background with a purplish and orange tinge as if you were looking at it through a glass of wine. What look like a few petals fallen on the table turn out on closer inspection to be a snail and a caterpillar, as well as a flower stalk, next to which a lizard recoils. (It's a comment on digitization that I [JDP] didn't notice these creatures in the original painting in the Rijksmuseum, or in the photo I took of the painting, but only in the enlarged image available online.)[1] In that uncanny way beloved of seventeenth-century Dutch painters, the vase reflects a light source, evidently a double-paned window, while also allowing us to see through the glass to the dark stalks of the flowers. The foreground of the arrangement is brightly lit, while some items are dark and indistinct in the background.

Among so many beautiful still lifes of flowers in the museum, there is perhaps no reason to single out this particular painting. At first it seems to belong to that venerable theme of Dutch Golden Age art, *vanitas*, a warning that earthly glory is fleeting. Prominent in the painting are tulips, a flower whose being still hovers, in that very Dutch way, between earthy beauty and economic commodity. In fact the painting features the "semper augustus" tulip, the most expensive variety at the time. If the legend of the tulip mania of 1637 is to be believed, people lost their heads and wallets over this very variety as prices for exotic bulbs skyrocketed, then just as suddenly collapsed. Modern researchers have cast doubt on the historicity of the *tulpenwoede*, however irresistible it is as a cautionary tale for more recent economic bubbles. The painting may be a moralizing comment on irrational exuberance; it may also be a tourist advertisement for Haarlem's floral bounty.

Despite its realistic appreciation of petal and leaf, the painting presents an impossible state of affairs. The flowers depicted—tulips, roses, anemones, and carnations—do not come into bloom at the same time

1. https://www.rijksmuseum.nl/en/collection/SK-A-799.

FIGURE 1.6. Hans Bollongier, *Still Life with Flowers*, 1639.
Rijksmuseum, Amsterdam.

of year. For all its apparent naturalist accuracy, the painting of freshly
cut flowers depicts a scene that could never have occurred in the seventeenth century. Instead it offers a kind of time-lapse composition of
distinct temporal moments, a seasonal mashup, a montage within a
single frame. The painting is improbable in culture as well. Although
the Dutch were proud to show off cut tulips in their delftware, it is not
likely that anyone would cut such precious flowers and put them in a
vase only to have them wilt. Bollongier's painting would be one of ex-

traordinary conspicuous consumption! And these are definitely living, cut blooms, not dried specimens. Bollongier has mixed many moments into a single image.

Although many observers since the mid-nineteenth century have noted in seventeenth-century Dutch painting a fidelity to appearances that seemed almost photographic,[2] the ability to collage chronology has always been the artist's advantage. The single-shot camera is hostage to the happenstance of what comes before the lens, one reason still photographers often put so much effort into setting the scene. (Some iconic American photographs of the twentieth century, such as *Migrant Mother* or *Flag Raising on Iwo Jima*, were later shown to be posed or re-enactments; see chapter 5.) Photographers, of course, can also manipulate what comes after: a double exposure is an early technique to allow for the layering of temporal orders, and digital photography blurs shooting and postproduction (see sidebar 2.3 on airbrushing). Bollongier's painting is a kind of double, triple, or quadruple exposure of botanical time. The only way to get freshly cut tulips, roses, anemones, and carnations into a single vase would be by rapid transport from diverse climates, impossible in his time.

In this regard, *Stilleven met bloemen* anticipates film, an art form whose essence is time-axis manipulation. Paintings and illustrations, in contrast to the still camera's debt to whatever the moment delivers, have a temporal and pictorial liberty that makes them ancestors of cinematic editing. Graphic artists can compress narrative happenings into a single frame that even the luckiest photographer could never arrange. Bollongier's still life is like a frozen movie.[3] This ability to narrate in a single frame is one reason illustration persists long into a photographic age. Handmade images can prune away the indiscriminate excess caught by a mechanical device such as a camera and add knowledge gleaned from other points in time. Since at least the seventeenth century, naturalist illustrators had sought to portray plant forms without being limited by the idiosyncrasies of individual specimens. They were interested in the truth of the kind, not in the deviations of any single instance. Only a lazy

2. Simon Schama, *The Embarrassment of Riches: An Interpretation of Dutch Culture in the Golden Age* (Berkeley: University of California Press, 1987), 10.

3. For the argument that early Dutch seascapes implied motion by plotting the moving eye of the sea navigator, see Bernhard Siegert, "The *Chorein* of the Pirate: On the Origin of the Dutch Seascape," *Grey Room* 57 (Fall 2014): 6–23.

or incompetent scientific illustrator would draw a single plant exactly as it appeared. "Seeing," as Daston and Galison note in this regard, "was an act as much of integrative memory and discernment as of immediate perception; an image was as much an emblem of a whole class of objects as a portrait of any one of them."[4]

Bollongier's flowers have plenty of individual quirks—the tulips and roses are presented in various states of development—but his painting is also a kind of "theoretical composite" in the sense that it pools many observations that could never appear in a single moment to an unaided eye.[5] It packs many *chronoi* into a single *kairos*. In its synthetic reach, it anticipates the summarizing power of a very different form of presentation: statistics (see chapter 3).

The still life may be faithful to the flowers in texture, shape, and color, but it arrays them in a subtle fabrication of imagination. That we see not the object, but our eyes' version of it, was the discovery of seventeenth-century opticians, physicians, philosophers, and painters. Vision was mediated, processed, and thus subject to tampering in transit. This mix of faithful copying and artificial concoction is one secret to the art and thought of the Dutch Golden Age. The picture could reveal a truth that existed nowhere but in the picture. The artist was both mirror and artificer. Bollongier offered posterity a living memory of a vase of flowers that never existed, never could exist, but still continues to dazzle. Perhaps, after all, *vanitas* and its temporary overcoming by art was his theme.

4. Daston and Galison, *Objectivity*, 104.

5. For the notion of "theoretical composite," see Peter Galison, "Judgment against Objectivity," in *Picturing Science, Producing Art*, ed. Caroline A. Jones and Peter Galison (New York: Routledge, 1998), 327–59, at 348, and Daston and Galison, *Objectivity*, 353.

Not everyone, however, loved the new world of images. The Renaissance and early modern period were marked by waves of Protestant iconoclasm, starting with breakouts in southern Germany and Switzerland in the 1520s, peaking in the 1560s, and lurching in waves across Europe until the Peace of Westphalia in 1648.[63] These conflicts form a kind of deep structure for the still lingering idea that images are idols and texts are holy, that screens breed distraction while books breed concentration. Vast treasures of religious art—glass, sculpture, and painting—were destroyed by zealot-vandals in "image storms" of iconoclasm.

Of course, to the vandals the images were not "art" at all: they were idola-
trous nothings, seductive deviations from the truth.

The Protestant-generated fear of the bewitching image went together
with the recognition of how important visual depiction was for the
new science. Francis Bacon considered common epistemological mistakes "idols," calling for strict regulation of the mind's fantasy, but he
was also excited by microscopes and telescopes and believed that "sight
has the chief office in giving information."[64] Many Dutch painters admired Bacon, and their chief theorist, Samuel van Hoogstraten, cited
him approvingly in his treatise on the art of painting. (Hoogstraten was
also a student of Rembrandt's.) The long-standing Catholic defense of
the image as a way to teach the common people—with cathedrals as
libri pauperorum, books of the poor, for instance—got a new boost in
the Counter-Reformation from the magic lantern, an early projection
technology.[65] Images, then as now, could be both threatening and infor-
mative. They could be objects of devotion or of scientific information,
spellbinding devices of mental capture or lovely illusions that invited
elucidation. Tensions around image and information from early modernity, echoing even more ancient worries, still resonate centuries later.

Trust and Order

Because of the new abundance, partisans of modern natural philosophy could wind up repeating the Epicurean chant: the universe was
more than we could know. "The subtlety of nature," according to Francis
Bacon, was "greater many times over than the subtlety of the senses and
understanding."[66] Blaise Pascal, the first of many whose heads started to
spin in the infinite space of the modern cosmos, believed our imagination is always outflanked by nature's exuberance.[67]

Loose fact, uncertain fact, detailed fact, abundant fact, strange fact—
the positivist saw fails here, because there was no firm link between fact
and explanation, and because the fact itself was so insecure. Our picture of the seventeenth century can be distorted by the later processing
of facts into discrete pellets of information in the Enlightenment and
the nineteenth century, but seventeenth-century facts were woolier. If
empiricism was sprawling, hard for humans to control, this was not a
problem. Its friends had several strategies to cope with it. In the seventeenth century the insecurity of proliferating facts was met by a string of
mechanisms designed to make truth claims more reliable. This is where
knowledge comes in.

The question of what could count as a fact was itself one key dispute.

Astrology, for instance, was consistently excluded from the empiricist realm. It did not produce facts. Other areas were more variable. Daston writes that "whole domains of experience—dreams, electrophosphorescence, musical harmonies—have drifted in and out of facticity since the seventeenth century."[68] Drawing boundaries between the factual and the fuzzy has always been one support for science's claim to produce knowledge; indeed, the term *science* comes from a root meaning "to separate" and is related to words such as *scissors, discernment,* and *shit*—that which is always set apart.

The emergence of experimental practice was a second key device for separating truth from fable. Claiming that the facts of nature could be artifacts of experimentation was a rejection of the long-standing Aristotelian contrast of art and nature. Such natural facts could be discovered only collaboratively. The progress of science thus depended on many observers whose trustworthiness had to be established. As Steven Shapin and Simon Schaffer have stressed, the new experimental science of the seventeenth century rested on a community of reliable coinquirers. Experimental philosophy required norms of intersubjective verification and trust: "In that process, a multiplication of the witnessing experience was fundamental."[69] The testimony of a single observer could never constitute a matter of fact. Facts had to be witnessed by many, and preferably (at least potentially) by all. Part of this was also the legitimation of the new scientific instruments of the age—telescopes, microscopes, clocks, scales, thermometers, and the air pump—as providing reliable testimony.[70] Communication among inquirers was itself part of the scientific process of confirmation and replication, since guaranteeing the uniformity of testimony was at the heart of the experimental method. The relative homogeneity in assumptions among inquirers of similar social position eased such exchange.

Connecting truth claims to the direct witnessing of experience and replicating laboratory results were core values of the British Royal Society.[71] The civil debate of the learned was preferred to the credulousness of the crowd. In matters of fact, according to Shapin and Schaffer's thesis, gentlemen prefer gentlemen.[72] Since gentlemen had independent means, they were "free, and unconfin'd," as Sprat said.[73] They were supposed to act impersonally and see nature as it is and not as they thought it ought to be. Even if the thesis is a bit overdrawn—other scholars have shown that the Royal Society sought out the testimony of people Sprat called "Mechanick Artists" and had members without a genteel pedigree—it is clear that seventeenth-century empirical investigation was both a social network and a set of epistemic norms.[74] Perhaps all empirical investigation has indeed been both, in wildly varied ways, ever since.[75]

A third early modern initiative to create trustworthy sorting mechanisms is the book, whose fixity was an answer to the question of trust and whose communicability lent stability to knowledge. Here the key scholar is Adrian Johns. Shapin and Schaffer had already emphasized the "literary technology" by which seventeenth-century savants cross-checked each other, especially via Boyle's idea that sufficiently detailed minutes describing procedures could afford a kind of "virtual witnessing" for readers.[76] In a similar spirit Johns shows the systematic efforts to secure the published text as a reliable uniform entity. British publishers-booksellers or stationers, as they were known—developed a practice of civil order and reliability among colleagues that ran in a kind of parallel to the genteel order among erudite scientists. This code sought to guarantee the reliability of the press, although nothing like our current idea of "copyright" existed in the 1600s. Norms among printers answered a communication question: how to trust what you only read about. The seventeenth century saw a concerted effort to develop a new level of credibility for the printed word.[77]

Norms for securing the veracity of the printed word existed outside Great Britain in this era as well. In its initial publication, the first part of Cervantes's Don Quixote (1605), for instance, was prefaced by a series of authenticating documents. First was the tasa (price), attesting that the book consisted of eighty-three signatures at the cost of 3.5 maravedis each for a total price of 290.5 maravedis (unbound). Second was the testimonio de las erratas, certifying that the printed version corresponded to the manuscript copy. The third document, called simply El Rey, grants Cervantes a license to print the book for ten years and attests to the authority of the royal officers who signed the tasa and the testimonio.[78] This elaborate documentary apparatus of economics, authentication, countersigners, and royal authorization is so foreign to us that most modern translations of Don Quixote omit it as tedious historical flotsam. In the four centuries since, we have grown used to backgrounding the techniques that legitimize print materials. But in the seventeenth century print, like the bizarre images in telescopes or microscopes or reports from distant observers, needed to be vouched for by authorized witnesses. Questions of authenticity and intellectual property grew even more interesting in part 2 of Don Quixote (1615), which built into the novel reflexive scenes of documentary authentication that exposed (and mercilessly mocked) the impostor author who was foolish enough to publish a sequel to part 1 before Cervantes finished the actual one.

Scientists, likewise, had protocols for literary presentation. As secretary of the Royal Society, Hooke had very particular ideas about how investigations should be recorded. Boyle likewise practiced an austere, sober, and painstakingly thorough prose style that is still the hallmark of scientific writing. To indulge in prose too florid, he said, would be "like painting 'the eye-glasses of a telescope.'"[79] Natural philosophers had to learn how to navigate the hazards of print publication. Without strategies to make printed documents trustworthy, there could be no experimental science. "Counterfeiting" was a major transgression for printers and experimenters alike. Publishers, scientists, writers, and royalty all took part in an effort to fight fraud or piracy of printed ideas. Practices like experimentation and publishing and institutions like scientific societies were all designed to securely ground our knowledge.

Fourth, equally important as a container of the roiling world of fact but harder to pin down, was hope for the future. During the 1600s the impure had not been fully weeded out, but confidence was strong that good progress was being made. Hooke was willing to postpone the discovery of laws of nature to some distant future. Post-Aristotelian epistemologies in the seventeenth century, it is important to stress, differed dramatically from each other. Bacon, Descartes, Locke, Leibniz, Spinoza, and others had sharp differences. They all, however, had faith that their new ways of knowing could successfully separate the true from the false.

Spinoza, for instance, thought the fictitious idea was "necessarily confused," since it "directs its attention promiscuously to all parts of an object at once without making distinctions." But ideas "which are clear and distinct," on the other hand, "can never be false." In his conviction of the necessary correspondence between subjective clarity and objective reality he was typical of the age's hopefulness about progress, a view shared not only by rationalists.[80] Leibniz, whose cosmic optimism was made both famous and foolish by Voltaire's *Candide*, thought that telescopes and microscopes made the argument for God's justice easier to believe for moderns than for ancients.[81] (Thus he pegged theological persuasion to technological progress.) The confidence that science and theology would live together happily ever after was not the least part of his optimism.

Together with faith in the future went confidence in classification. The idea that rational categories could reduce the empirical overload was to take the upper hand in the eighteenth century, but in the seventeenth century it was pushed especially by the rationalists. Descartes, though supportive of experiments in principle, complained about the clutter of too much information. He found the experiments he read about "for the most part so complicated with unneeded details and superfluous ingredients that it would be very difficult for the investigator to discover their core of truth."[82] He famously thought the best point of departure was reflection alone, and that thought, often called the *cogito*, was the bedrock on which he founded his philosophy. Descartes believed thoughts could be as hard and reliable as any other kinds of facts, a notion central to his mathematics as well. There was a necessary order among ideas, and mathematics provided a privileged model of how the ideal realm could be rigorous.

Spinoza, inflamed by this kind of insight, built his entire ethics on the principles of geometry. Just as ideas could be joined together by logical force, so could events be united by causally necessary links.[83] Leibniz, the third of the great seventeenth-century rationalists, as a later generation would dub them, used brainpower to try to order it all. His office in Hannover, like his brain, was a great data-processing center for all the knowledge of his day; he was a diplomatic hub, a post office for scientific information.

The interest in synthetic order did not mean the rationalists didn't care about particulars. They were, on the contrary, intensely interested in the profuse variety of phenomena—rainbows, artillery, optic nerves, fire, musical harmony, Chinese ideograms, Hebrew grammar. After a visit to Delft in 1676 Leibniz remarked, "I care more for a van Leeuwenhoek, who tells me what he sees, than a Descartes, who tells me what he thinks."[84] Leibniz loved facts and books and gathered them voraciously as a court librarian, as did many other intellectuals of the time. Heaps of particulars, he believed, could be accommodated in systems of rational truth, whether strategies of display, mathematics, or memory. Leibniz embraced the Renaissance idea of a theater of memory and took an intense interest in universal languages.[85] The infinitesimal calculus he invented simultaneously with Newton not only was a mathematical tool for modeling events, it was a bureaucratic device—a "state machine" one scholar calls it—for managing and organizing data.[86] It was one key organizer of wild facts that turned out to be perhaps the most important modern scientific technique for ordering a world in motion and classifying its contents. In an update of the apocryphal sign over the door of Plato's Academy, the moderns could say to anyone wanting to study any science: let no one ignorant of calculus enter here.

The Two Modernities

The idea that we could build order through discovery of natural laws grew in the eighteenth century. Galileo wrote of the "laws" of motion and the "laws" of the planets, which gave him posthumous status as

the founder of modern science.[87] Newton did not need to choose between empiricism and the calculus he had invented; both contributed
to his understanding of the basic laws of physics. By the early eighteenth
century there was a new sense of order, of balance. Locke and Newton
were the heroes, especially in France. Descartes went into eclipse, but
his spirit of *clarté* carried on. Classification became the goal. The gap
between knowledge and the marvelous started to expand (again). Facts
now became valued for their part in a grid. "In contrast to the inductive facts of the eighteenth and nineteenth centuries," Daston writes,
"seventeenth-century matters of fact were neither mundane, repetitive,
homogeneous, nor countable."[88] The new grid was elegant and organized, and it aspired to be free of mess and anomalies. The radicals of the
French Enlightenment set out to publish an encyclopedia, the genre and
testament of the ambition to order all knowledge in one central place.
The baroque profuseness of the seventeenth century gave way to the
neoclassical order of the eighteenth. One form of modernity prized the
rampant uniqueness of facts; the second sought an encyclopedic system
that would contain everything.

Sidebar 1.3 The Idea of the Encyclopedia

If ever any genre claimed to contain all knowledge, it would be the encyclopedia. The term comes from the ancient Greek *enkyklios paideia*,
which means the full circle of learning, a course of study that takes in
all the disciplines—a *curriculum*, as we say today, following the Latin
term for *enkyklios*. *Encyclopedia* did not refer to a literary genre until
the sixteenth century, though there are forerunners of the genre. It has
its ancient precursor in Pliny the Elder's *Natural History*, a thirty-seven-
book compilation of marvelous things interrupted by his death in the
eruption of Vesuvius in AD 79. Proto-encyclopedias of the Middle Ages
and Renaissance followed a vision of the organization of the universe.
Alphabetical order, modeled on the dictionary, was late in coming and
controversial: theologians complained at its arbitrariness—for instance,
putting *Angelus* (angel) before *Deus* (God).

   Undoubtedly the key encyclopedia of European history was the
French *Encyclopédie* of the eighteenth century. According to its great
student Robert Darnton, it was "the supreme work of the Enlightenment," "the summa of a great intellectual movement," and "the biggest
book of the century." Its production touched all levels of society: *chif-*

foniers begged rags and old linens from the back doors of bourgeois homes, only for the same material to return through the front doors as the *Encyclopédie*. As Darnton summarizes it, "A whole world had to be set into motion to bring the book into being. Ragpickers, chestnut gatherers, financiers, and philosophers all played a part in the making of a work whose corporeal existence corresponded to its intellectual message. As a physical object and as a vehicle of ideas, the *Encyclopédie* synthesized a thousand arts and sciences; it represented the Enlightenment, body and soul."[1]

Renaissance encyclopedias were buffers against catastrophe, storehouses of knowledge to prevent a second vanishing of classical learning, whose first loss in the so-called dark ages was painfully felt by scholars. The French encyclopedia was a bulwark against another catastrophe, not in the past but looming on the horizon: the overflow of books.[2] Denis Diderot complained that in writing the encyclopedia everything got more and more complicated and labyrinthine. In the offing was a vast accumulation of books that would have to be kept in immense buildings: "As centuries pass by, the mass of works grows without ceasing, and one foresees a moment when it could be almost as difficult to educate oneself in a library as in the universe." Instead, we needed an organized effort of workers to sift books for the true and the false, to reduce the complex and distill it into an alphabetically ordered set. Voilà *l'encyclopédie!*[3]

The *Encyclopédie* was stuffed to the gills. It wasn't all light and synthesis. It held 71,818 articles and 2,855 plates. Nor was everything expressed in what Descartes had called "clear and distinct ideas." Crystalline information was hardly the only good on offer. Its editors and authors invited games of reading between the lines. Karl Kraus's quip that works the censor can understand are justly forbidden certainly applied in this case. The real zingers, especially attacks on Christianity,

<hr/>

1. Robert Darnton, *The Business of Enlightenment: A Publishing History of the Encyclopédie, 1775–1800* (Cambridge, MA: Harvard University Press, 1979), 4, 15, 454, 521, 522.

2. Chad Wellmon, *Organizing Enlightenment: Information Overload and the Invention of the Modern Research University* (Baltimore: Johns Hopkins University Press, 2016), chap. 3.

3. Denis Diderot, "Encyclopédie," in *Encyclopédie, ou Dictionnaire raisonné des sciences, des arts et des métiers,* 5:640A; https://artflsrv03.uchicago.edu/philologic4/encyclopedie1117/navigate/5/2355/.

were tucked away in obscure entries. Reading the encyclopedia was an education in the art of skepticism, in not taking things at face value. Nor was the project consistent across all its volumes. Some articles defended the tax exemption on aristocrats and others vehemently criticized it. And even as a physical set of books it wasn't a consistent entity; it existed in six distinct versions, plus other pirated versions that pillaged and reprinted it. If its spirit was synthesis and order, its body was a grand, wonderful mess.[4]

Many are the uses of encyclopedias. The radicalism and totality of the genre was irresistible to many modern thinkers. Almost all nineteenth-century Romantic nationalists used encyclopedias and dictionaries to celebrate and consolidate the language, culture, and heritage of marginalized peoples dominated by empires. (Nationalism and philology have had a long and rocky marriage.) In a similar spirit, W. E. B. Du Bois worked on an *Encyclopedia of the Negro* in the 1930s, and in his nineties he moved to Ghana to work on an *Encyclopedia Africana* to parallel the *Encyclopaedia Britannica*. Neither ever appeared in the form he planned.

Philosophers too liked the genre for its promise of unified knowledge. Hegel styled his entire philosophical oeuvre as an encyclopedia, picking up a theme dear to German thinkers around 1800.[5] In the early 1890s the ex-Hegelian American pragmatist John Dewey briefly dreamed of a utopian newspaper to be called *Thought News* that would operate like a daily updated encyclopedia. The idea never tasted ink for a number of obvious reasons. (About the same time, the early Sears catalog called itself a "merchandise encyclopedia.")[6] The Vienna Circle philosophers Rudolf Carnap and Otto Neurath embodied their vision in a series of publications called the International Encyclopedia of Unified Science. One of the last publications in the series was Thomas Kuhn's *Structure of Scientific Revolutions* (1962), a text that drove a very important nail in the coffin of the logical empiricist dream of unified science. There is something about the encyclopedic genre that flirts with its own undoing.

In its stretch for totalities, the genre harbors something surreal. Jorge Luis Borges saw in the encyclopedia the best genre for repre-

4. Darnton, "Introduction: The Biography of a Book," in *Business of Enlightenment*, 1–34.

5. Wellmon, *Organizing Enlightenment*, chap. 3.

6. "How Goods Are Ordered by Mail," *Black Cat*, no. 37 (October 1898): xix.

senting philosophical idealism's drive to build and furnish imaginary worlds.[7] The genre also has a clear paranoid streak, the sense that everything is relevant and has potential meaning. (Paranoia is the inability to turn off the faucet of interpretation.) More recently, Wikipedia has been the subject of debates about just how detailed an all-encompassing log of the universe should be, with a heated discussion among its German-language editors, for instance, on whether the screw on the left rear brake pad of a bicycle belonging to one Ulrich Fuchs merits an entry. (Fuchs contributed the entry as a provocation or thought experiment.) If space is no object, what principle can exclude an entry?[8] Wikipedia, the online monument to open-source Enlightenment, belongs in the long totalizing and absurdist lineage of the encyclopedia (see chapter 6). In its occasional howlers and its efforts to police form and content without an authorized panel of experts, Wikipedia is a chief index of promiscuous knowledge.

For the idealist and the paranoid alike, the encyclopedia is an irresistible temptation and sometimes an abyss. Bottomlessness is one challenge, arbitrariness another. Alphabetical order yields slightly absurd juxtapositions: ethics, Ethiopia, ethnology, ethyl alcohol, or nose, nosology, nostalgia, Nostradamus, nostrum, notary, notation. Unlike ancient, medieval, or Renaissance encyclopedias, the modern versions present their content according to no overall ordering system besides the alphabet, though their very existence is moved by faith in the synthesis of knowledge. In a remarkable shift, Wikipedia functions well without any fantasy of progress toward a grand synthesis, and its online existence dispenses with any need for alphabetical order. Every encyclopedia carries with it the legacy of the cabinet of curiosities. Surrealism and totality are the two faces of the encyclopedia.

That we get surreal results when we try to encompass the world might provide a useful hint about the nature of things. Perhaps the lesson is that the project of encompassing the universe is surreal. Or perhaps it is the universe itself that is surreal.

7. Jorge Luis Borges, "Tlön, Uqbar, Orbis Tertius," in *Labyrinths: Selected Stories and Other Writings*, trans. James E. Irby (New York: New Directions, 1964), 3–18.

8. James Gleick, *The Information: A Theory, a History, a Flood* (New York: Pantheon, 2011), 384–86.

Especially important for the history of classification was Linnaeus's (Karl von Linné, 1707–78) organizing what we still call the animal kingdom into a treelike order. In his *Systema Naturae*, published in twelve editions from 1735 to 1768, the Swedish botanist unfolded a branching hierarchy for plants and animals and developed the system of binomial nomenclature that is still in use. Linnaeus was selective in the features he focused on. He did not want the classification gummed up with traits irrelevant to the underlying system. If botanists focused on color, for instance, he feared they would posit ninety-three species of tulips when there was only one. Trained observers like himself would avoid mistaking mere variation for genuine speciation. As Daston notes, "a Linnaean taxonomic description of an organism is deliberately laconic."[89]

In its efforts to filter the noise of observation, to look beyond the anomalies of wild facts, Linnaeus's system was admittedly artificial. It was designed to make a manageable grouping of natural varieties. It made use of shortcuts, classifying plants by their arbitrary sexual characteristics rather than by deeper but less visible relations. There were some built-in inaccuracies, and Linnaeus knew the scheme didn't handle all exceptions well. Cleaner lines could mean a worse fit, but a tighter fit could mean a more jumbled presentation. As his contemporary the French *philosophe* and *encyclopédiste* Denis Diderot noted, no human system can completely banish arbitrariness; only God's system could do that.[90]

Linnaeus's system, a compromise, met resistance especially in France, but it took hold in the Netherlands, and in the nineteenth century it became the dominant scheme in Europe for classifying organisms. It is a system designed for cognitive convenience. Its aim was not to delight in the oddness of natural facts but to create plausible orders for use. Its Enlightenment ambition (to classify all life) was tempered by a touch of pragmatism (to find the best fit). Perhaps one of its most subtly portentous acts was to declare human beings a species, classed among the primates, and thus part of the animal kingdom. This move, in 1735, was one step toward the shock of Darwin.

The new museum of the eighteenth century likewise radically reorganized its contents along categorizing lines. The British Museum, founded in 1753, was originally based on a private collection, a vast array of items organized by type rather than by cultural origin or historical period. The original collector, Dr. Hans Sloane, had an antiquarian interest in his diverse objects and instruments, but the museum took a more systematically scientific approach to cataloging its contents. If cabinets of curiosities were meant to astound, the new museum boasted

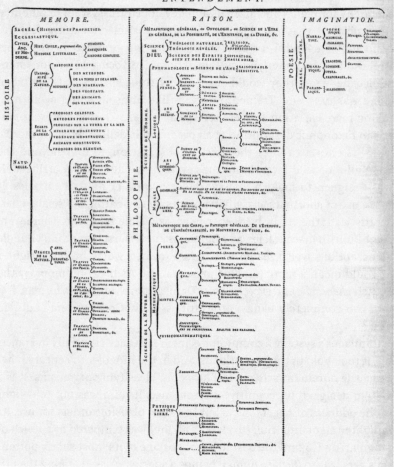

FIGURE 1.7. "Système figuré des connaissances humaines," in *Encyclopédie,
ou Dictionnaire raisonné des sciences, des arts et des métiers, etc.*, ed. Denis Diderot
and Jean le Rond d'Alembert. University of Chicago: ARTFL Encyclopédie Project,
Autumn 2017 edition, ed. Robert Morrissey and Glenn Roe.

of its thoroughness *and* taxonomies. In a similar spirit, King George III, an accomplished amateur natural scientist and collector, organized his Roman coins chronologically by emperor and shelved his books by subject. The point of neoclassical classification was to make insight and overview easy, not to celebrate the obstreperousness of wild facts. The order and light of eighteenth-century philosophy, architecture, gardening, natural history, music, and painting also extended to modes of organizing knowledge.[91] "Human reason," Kant announced in his *Critique of Pure Reason*, "is by nature architectonic." Whether or not true by nature, it certainly was true in the culture of his time.

Sidebar 1.4 Cabinets of Curiosities

In the Middle Ages collections were the monopolies of kings, but in the fourteenth and fifteenth centuries lesser nobility and urban elites got in on the action. Awe at natural marvels could serve the religious function of appreciating God's creation, and collections started to include a wider range of natural objects, being held privately by both Crown and church. One of the most notable belonged to John, Duke of Berry (son of King John II of France), who owned "an ostrich egg, a snail shell, seven boars' tusks, a porcupine quill, a giant's molar, a large serpent's jaw, a coconut shell, a number of pieces of red coral, a white bearskin, and at least three whole unicorn horns."[1] Exotic, natural, and magical objects mingle.

The seventeenth century's sprawling empiricism in facts and images has continuities with late medieval collections, especially in cabinets of curiosities, proto-museums that flourished in European courts in the late sixteenth and seventeenth centuries. The term *cabinet* blurs the distinction between two main kinds of collections—exquisitely crafted pieces of furniture holding treasures (*Kunstschränke*) or rooms overstocked with curious items (*Wunderkammern*). Both held everything wondrous made by art or grown by nature that could be presented to prince, priest, or king in a display of conspicuous consumption of taste and erudition. They were usually arranged in a marvelous miscellany, including such things as "coral, automata, unicorn horns, South American featherwork, coconut shell goblets, fossils, antique coins, turned ivory, monsters animal and human, Turkish weaponry, and polyhedral

1. Daston and Park, *Wonders and the Order of Nature*, 86, 88.

crystals."[2] They could hold Roman coins, molted snakeskins, eggs of exotic animals, even human body parts. Peter the Great, for instance, paid a great sum for an elaborate cabinet of curiosities assembled by the Amsterdam anatomist Frederik Ruysch, which included human internal organs embalmed with a secret potion, including "delicate parts" adorned with lace by his artist daughter Rachel. (Many of his preparations persist to this day.) These cabinets were meant to stupefy and startle, to inform and impress.

Cabinets of curiosities had three leading features. First, their items had to be not only rare but precious. Second, the items often blurred and toyed with the boundary between artifice and nature, either by being of ambiguous origin or juxtaposed with objects of a contrasting origin. Third, the items all had to be enough unlike each other to produce a visual spectacle of fertility and variety.[3] The cabinets aimed to wow the ignorant and impress the connoisseur. They also could stir the faithful: "ecclesiastical" cabinets were designed to provide religious edification by demonstrating God's fecundity.[4] Such cabinets were a cultural practice parallel to Baconian empiricism, with its drive to collect "everything," as he said, "that is in nature new, rare, and unusual."[5]

Cabinets of curiosities were a microcosm of the world, an ordered chaos, a diversity designed to be caught in a single gaze. Bacon described them with characteristic eloquence: "in small compass a model of the universal nature made private."[6] A *Kunstkammer* was like Leibniz's "monad" inasmuch as it was a mirror of the entire universe (Leibniz himself commended such collections as a good way to discipline the fancy and learn to observe more exactly).[7] It was also a catalog

2. Ibid., 266.

3. Lorraine Daston, "The Factual Sensibility," *ISIS* 79, no. 3 (1988): 452–70.

4. Stephen T. Asma, *Stuffed Animals and Pickled Heads: The Culture and Evolution of Natural History Museums* (New York: Oxford University Press, 2003), 112.

5. Shapin, *Scientific Revolution*, 90.

6. *Gesta Grayorum* (1594), quoted in Oliver Impey and Arthur MacGregor, "Introduction," in *The Origin of Museums: The Cabinet of Curiosities in Sixteenth- and Seventeenth-Century Europe* (Poughkeepsie, NY: House of Stratus, 2001), 1.

7. Horst Bredekamp, "*Kunstkammer*, Play-Palace, Shadow Theatre: Three Thought Loci by Gottfried Wilhelm Leibniz," in *Collection, Laboratory, Theater*, ed. Helmar Schramm, Ludger Schwarte, and Jan Lazardzig (New York: de Gruyter, 2005), 266.

of commodities. The principle of miscellaneity in a profuse and dazzling setting would persist as one of the main modes of presentation well into the nineteenth century, in well-stocked curiosity shops, apothecaries, museums, and even, distantly, the department store.[8] It showed up again in the early years of the World Wide Web.

8. John V. Pickstone, *Ways of Knowing: A New History of Science, Technology, and Medicine* (Chicago: University of Chicago Press, 2000), 67.

Here, then, were the two modernities. One was sprawling, empirical, thrilled by wild facts rather than stressed about their place in a larger scheme. The other was nervous about excess, comfortable with order. The one was baroque, in love with quirkiness and strangeness; the other was neoclassical, in love with clarity and light. Kant's philosophy was the great synthesis of the two, with its jumble of perceptions on the one hand and a priori categories on the other. The first modernity was interesting, unreliable, a bit voracious, carrying the danger of gluttony, of getting fat on a diet of rich new facts. Where would it lead—to empirical gout, perhaps? No wonder Descartes, looking over from the second, order-loving version of modernity, rolled his eyes. More than the stereotypical Gallic shrug, it was disdain for the merely empiric.

The rage for order and the hunger for wild facts, the desire to prune back the shrubbery and the love of blossoms, would continue to grapple for the upper hand.

* 2 *

Victorian Culture and
the Diffusion of Learning

During the nineteenth century, the Western world was filling up. New wonders dazzled at every turn—the railroad one day, anesthesia the next, the light bulb on still another. On top of this, everything could now be produced in numbers that boggled the imagination. Clothes, furniture, bibelots, glassware, daguerreotypes, books, wax fruit, dried flowers—the sheer quantity of things now cluttering a life was stunning. These marvels touched a surprising swath of the population—to different degrees, of course. The working class was left out in shocking ways. Clearly the bourgeoisie had the best of it. By the last decades of the century, their homes' interiors reached saturation point, brimming with stuff. (It would take the invention of throwaway culture to provide an escape valve for all the buildup.)[1] But ordinary people and elites alike collected such objects as botanical specimens, insects, natural history trophies, scrapbooks, photographs, commonplace books, and even signatures of the Founders.[2]

Among the many things that Victorians, including American Victorians, filled their world with were facts. In this age of quickly proliferating heaps, among the things proliferating most quickly were facts. The amount of information circulating in 1840, 1870, or 1900 might astound a reflective observer today. Whole new sciences surfaced with each new decade, and with them went new social identities such as *scientist, sociologist, psychiatrist,* and *photographer,* all terms coined in the nineteenth century. Statistics were kept with a zeal and on a scale dwarfing previous efforts. Over the course of the century all sorts of things that used to be moralized fell under the regime of knowledge—cholera, homosexuality, and the human memory, to name just three. New graphic techniques, foremost among them photography, helped bring into the scientific domain hitherto elusive phenomena such as clouds, weather, heat, vowels, blood pressure, and animal locomotion, and new printing techniques spread news by word and picture in quantities and to classes never yet seen.

Concerns about the wildness of facts arose throughout the later nineteenth century because there had been a burst of new knowledge creation and a substantial jump in the number of people involved in assessing truth. Compared with the seventeenth century, a much larger and more diffuse public was now creating and disseminating knowledge. The love of facts had become popular.

Historians can easily think themselves back to an "information thin" time. The natural universe has always overflowed our sensations, but the cultural thickness of fact has ebbed and flowed. Two hundred and fifty years ago there was not the mass of statistics that engulfs us today. There were not the research universities, think tanks, bureaucracies for health and science research, industries bent on combing big data. There were not the elaborate means for diffusion that we have in the mass media or the public school. There were certainly not the popular press, the news media, or the World Wide Web. To be sure, 250 years ago there were pockets of thick information among aristocratic collectors of curiosities and books, scholars and encyclopedists, statesmen and merchants. Thick information has existed in different times and places among literate elites and even ordinary people in the penumbra of print culture.[3]

The nineteenth century is an especially interesting time in the long history of information and image. Because facts were held to be the stuff of "knowledge" proper, the forces of sobriety pursued them with a zeal uncommon in history. Although there were skeptics such as Leo Tolstoy and Friedrich Nietzsche, faith that new knowledge would contribute to collective advancement was the dominant strain, a belief shared by souls as diverse as Herbert Spencer, Karl Marx, Frederick Douglass, Elizabeth Cady Stanton, and William Graham Sumner. The popularization of knowledge in the nineteenth century was often associated with passing on huge quantities of information in the most widely read publications. Information about relatively technical matters was not left to specialists; there was no thought of sparing the public the burden of detail. This was a thick culture of fact. In practice "diffusion" meant a world crowded with facts—in stark contrast to the culture of digest and summary that emerged in the early twentieth century (discussed in the next chapter).

The spread of information to increasing numbers of people was thought critical to the progress of civilization and democracy. The idea that the emancipation of humanity was tied to the growth of knowledge, a grand story that Jean-François Lyotard considered the very definition of modernity, was at high hum in the mid-nineteenth century. But Cartesian and Linnaean concerns about the unruliness of information, "facts out of control," or "appalling facts" also resurfaced in a new guise. This popularizing of the Enlightenment reopened questions about the authority of truth and who could participate in its discovery. The question whether science was only for gentlemen, with their privilege in class and gender, was now more complex. Women, children, artisans, slaves, and former slaves all came into contact with knowledge and its making. Controls for truth claims were more ragged.

To many observers at the time, the mid-nineteenth century was a confusing situation of promiscuous knowledge, intermingling formal and popular idioms at a new level. Just as the seventeenth and eighteenth centuries launched a variety of practices and institutions for securing truth, so new truth games arose in the nineteenth century. It was one of the most prolific of all centuries in inventing and naming new kinds of knowledge. We may think the internet unleashed the flood, but people in the nineteenth century lived through equally dramatic waves of knowledge in search of new containers.

The Thick Flow of Fact

One source for this thick culture of fact was ideological. In the United States, the founding era was dominated by aristocratic attitudes. Distrust of popular will was built into the US Constitution—think of the Electoral College, still controversially in place, or the indirect election of senators, abolished by the Seventeenth Amendment in 1913. A founder such as James Madison imagined private interests being harnessed for public good, faction counterbalancing faction to produce a stable polity and even, at best, public virtue. By the 1820s and 1830s a democratic and market revolution associated with Andrew Jackson's faith in the common man was in full force. Private interest leaped out of its noble cage. People had to be entrepreneurs not only in business but in culture, faith, and every aspect of their lives.

Visiting the United States in 1831, the French aristocrat Alexis de Tocqueville immortalized this culture of the individual thrust into the world without the old supports. As he famously wrote, "Not only does democracy make every man forget his ancestors, but it hides his descendants, and separates his contemporaries from him; it throws him back forever upon himself alone, and threatens in the end to confine him entirely within the solitude of his own heart."[4] In the culture of Jacksonian individualism, people had to trust their own ability to figure things out—and also to doubt the palaver hawked by others and perhaps even by themselves. Facts were one answer to the vacuum of trust and orientation left by the disappearance of the old regime of aristocratic oversight.

A second source for this thick culture of fact was an information revolution in the United States in the early years of the century. Several fine works of scholarship have traced the explosion in the growth and diffusion of information in the eighteenth and early nineteenth centuries.[5] Increased public schooling, the penny press, the ideology of self-help, gender equality in literacy for large portions of the population, the rising number of books and pamphlets printed, a bigger and more mobile population, the post office—all these things made for an extremely rich information environment by the middle of the nineteenth century.

Let us just mention a few facts. In 1800 it was very tough to get print material from one part of the United States to another. Travel by waterways and carriage was expensive and risked damage to the paper goods conveyed. By 1830, post offices had proliferated from 75 to 8,450, more than a hundredfold increase and five times as many as in France. Per capita travel between Boston and New York increased fourfold from 1794 to 1834, and overall travel volume between the two cities went up roughly twentyfold. In 1800 there were, on average, one hundred dictionaries published per decade. By 1840 there were three hundred. In 1780 no one had a dictionary of the English language; by 1860 everyone did. Newspaper circulation increased tenfold from 1800 to 1840. From 1818 to 1880 the American Bible Society distributed over thirty-two million Bibles in the United States.[6] An information-hungry society needed paper in the same way an industrializing society needed coal: the output of paper in the nine decades from 1809 to 1899 rose over five hundredfold. Paper media constituted an essential infrastructure for the thick culture of fact. Poet Walt Whitman found heaps of printed matter one more item to be celebrated in his catalogs of democracy, praising "the huge editions of the dailies and the weeklies, the mountain-stacks of white paper piled in the press-vaults, and the proud, crashing ten-cylinder presses."[7]

It was not, of course, that a high-pressure spigot of fact was the only way to communicate with the public in nineteenth-century America. There was the drama of wild oratory, the strange fantasy world of advertising, the carnivalesque effervescence of certain crowd actions, the dramatic hoaxes of the penny press, the fiery enthusiasm of religious revival

Table 2.1 Paper produced in the United States, 1809–99 (in 1,000 metric tons)

Year	Paper
1809	3
1819	11
1829	no data
1839	34
1849	71
1859	115
1869	350
1879	410
1889	848
1899	1967

Source: B. R. Mitchell, *International Historical Statistics: The Americas, 1700–2005*, 6th ed. (New York: Palgrave Macmillan, 2007), 408.

meetings. The culture of copious facts was not the only story; there were competing epistemologies.

Sentimental culture, for instance, was also important. Charles Dickens's novel *Hard Times* (1854) used the words *sentiment, fancy, feelings, art*, and *morality* explicitly in opposition to the word *facts*. He described the schoolmaster Gradgrind as "a kind of cannon loaded to the muzzle with facts, and prepared to blow them clean out . . . at one discharge" onto his students, like "little pitchers before him, who were to be filled so full of facts."[8] Though Gradgrind was a parody, he was a recognizable type. Against Gradgrind's fact obsession, sentimental culture took sympathy, not information, as the engine of progress and the basis of democratic solidarity. Abolitionism ran on the fuel of sympathy for slaves suffering at a distance. Facts were not the only story, but they were an essential one.

This popularization of knowledge by passing on large quantities of information was tied to what historian Neil Harris has called the "operational aesthetic," the desire to load mountains of fact into a popular package and to reveal the technical processes of how things worked. Harris quotes a British visitor: "Every American believes himself to be the repository of extensive information; within him is the pent-up source of knowledge; his amiable spirit of benevolence prompts him to let it flow forth for the enlightenment of his benighted fellow-citizens, and the outer world of darkness generally."[9]

Sidebar 2.1 Frederick Douglass and Facts

If the diffusion of knowledge was uneven in its reach to white women, to African Americans it extended hardly at all. Indeed, even free African Americans in the North had reason to be skeptical of the bolder claims of "progress" by people like Horace Greeley. Some of the most furious northern racism erupted when whites faced free blacks trying to improve themselves through education. Outright legal rejection happened early in the century, and in some places blacks were excluded from public schools. By the 1850s this practice was replaced by separate schools with pathetic funding. Northern whites would calmly say that African Americans were "incapable of being cultured beyond a certain point," that the republic's morality depended on providing education for Caucasians, not on granting charity to Negroes. African Americans and white abolitionists fought such attitudes but had few successes. Before the Civil War it was against the law in many southern states to teach slaves to read. In the North it was different, but not much better.[1]

Yet the idea of diffusion was such that free African Americans could make use of it anyway. Learning informally and not being deterred by hardship were parts of the Yankee credo that especially appealed to blacks facing Yankee racism.

Frederick Douglass fits the bill perfectly. For him self-improvement, hard work, and freedom were bundled together. As it was for Greeley, his first key book was Bingham's *Columbian Orator*. As a young slave in Maryland, he had sneaked around to learn to read; later he persuaded some white boys too young to grasp the intricacies of caste to teach him to write. After escaping slavery and ending up in Newport, Rhode Island, he first worked at the brutal, backbreaking lifting jobs that unskilled laborers still performed in the nineteenth century (work requiring "good wind and muscle," as Douglass said). He eventually found employment at a brass foundry, working the bellows in a miserable, blisteringly hot room "over a furnace hot enough to keep the metal running like water." In his 1855 autobiography Douglass points out that the situation was not conducive to learning—as if we had to be told.

Still, Douglass would not be denied. He managed to "[nail] a newspaper to the post near my bellows, and read while I was performing

1. Leon Litwack, *North of Slavery: The Negro in the Free States, 1790–1860* (Chicago: University of Chicago Press, 1961), 113–52, at 115.

the up and down motion of the heavy beam." At the top of this page in his autobiography is the rather understated heading, borrowed from the title of one of the better-known books on self-education, "Knowledge under Difficulties."[2]

As an abolitionist speaker, Frederick Douglass wanted to provide his audiences with an ethical framework, not just with information. This met resistance. "Let us have the facts," his white handlers told him; "we'll take care of the philosophy." The white editor of his 1855 autobiography *My Bondage and My Freedom* told readers that the book was not a work of art but "a work of FACTS—Facts, terrible, and almost incredible, it may be—yet FACTS, nevertheless."[3] As Douglass stepped onto the stage, William Lloyd Garrison whispered that he should just tell his story unvarnished. But Douglass quickly became bored with that: "I could not always curb my moral indignation . . . long enough for a circumstantial statement of the facts." Indeed, the moment came when his moral ruminations were unbelievable to some of his white northern audiences, who apparently could not believe that a former slave could be so subtle.[4]

For Douglass, facts carried on the late medieval sense of incriminating materials collected for a trial in court. His facts were meant to indict an iniquitous system of human degradation. Presented in bulk, facts were necessary devices for listeners' education and persuasion. But his imagination still broke through, arranging the facts and putting them into a larger order of critical judgment. His status as a man fully in control of his rational and moral faculties—which was so central to his performance as living proof of the indignity and absurdity of slavery—required him to transcend the cataloging of facts, however horrid in themselves.

These stories about Douglass reinforce two messages. First, they emphasize the mid-nineteenth century's linkage between facts and knowledge: the former is important but is only the prelude to the more important compendium known as knowledge. But second, they suggest how the neutrality of fact/knowledge talk masked common racial coding.

2. Frederick Douglass, *Life and Times of Frederick Douglass* (Hartford, CT: Park, 1881), 212–13. The book quoted, by George L. Craik, was called *The Pursuit of Knowledge under Difficulties.*

3. "Editor's Preface," in Frederick Douglass, *My Bondage and My Freedom* (New York: Miller, Orton, and Mulligan, 1855), v.

4. Douglass, *Life and Times*, 218–19.

Blacks were incapable of knowledge, it was often thought. They could move only in the antechamber—the domain of fact—if that. Douglass refused to stay there and showed the supposed epistemic divide to be one of power.

There is one other way Douglass stepped outside the antechamber of facts: in his use of photography for self-fashioning. His image is one of the most recognizable among all nineteenth-century figures—the three-quarter view of a well-dressed, bearded black man with a leonine salt-and-pepper mane and sternly intelligent expression, looking off into the middle distance. When Google dedicated a doodle to him on February 1, 2016, the iconic image was unmistakable.

For Harris, P. T. Barnum was the apotheosis of Tocqueville's observations about the loss of the old supports for the individual. Barnum's showmanship both performed and preyed on the combined lack of metaphysical guidance and thirst for mechanical knowledge that possessed American, especially Yankee, souls from the 1830s through the 1850s.[10] His "Great American Museum" in New York City, open from 1841 until 1865, was very much in the tradition of the cabinet of curiosities but without the aristocratic coloring. The overall message was not order and classification but dazzle and abundance, and its motive was profit, not instruction. Its ties to the theater, the circus, and other commercial mass entertainments were clear. The museum presented "a world of spectacle, disorder, and carnival."[11] Barnum boasted of vast quantities of "curiosities," whose number varied as occasion required, including "TWO LIVING AZTEC CHILDREN, the LIVING WHAT IS IT, the WHITE NEGRO SISTERS, THIRTY MONSTER SNAKES, the AQUARIAL GARDEN, LIVING HAPPY FAMILY, WAX FIGURES, and 950,000 CURIOSITIES, from all parts of the world," and bragged of an endorsement by "Prof. Aggasiz" [sic], the Harvard naturalist, his sometime friend.[12] The masters of humbug have no shame in invoking experts if it bolsters their cause.

Barnum provided a kind of intellectual exercise for an age wavering in faith. He claimed never to intentionally deceive his audience, but rather to educate and intrigue them: he would offer the public a fraud with one hand and plant hints about its possible authenticity with the other. In ad copy about his "Feejee mermaid," a stuffed monkey and fish mounted to look like a single body, he asked: "Who is to decide when doctors disagree?"[13] Part of the attraction was not only the outlandish displays but the mental stimulus of being put through the process of faith, doubt, and finally revelation of how the trick was done. Barnum figured out how to make money on both ends of this transaction. People paid first to be duped and then to have the deception explained.

Or perhaps they paid for the pleasure of thinking themselves immune to duping. Henry James wrote that as a child he and his brother William visited Barnum's museum "just in order *not* to be beguiled, just in order to enjoy with ironic detachment and, at the very most, to be amused ourselves at our sensibility should it prove to be trapped and caught." The museum could also be dull and, like Disneyland, involve long waits, but the "aches and inanition were part of the adventure." Its point in the cultural hierarchy was ambiguous: for Henry James, Barnum's museum was an "initiation" into a higher world of curiosity and "free play of mind," a gateway drug to the more expansive vision of culture associated with Matthew Arnold. And Henry astutely noted the affinity of his brother William's outlook to Barnum's—the interest in wild facts, in the borderlands of fraudulence and authenticity, in shrunken heads and outré specimens.[14] The lecture hall, posters, bottled mermaids and bearded ladies, and French acrobats were part of a cornucopia of attractions that overloaded the mind. Barnum perfected the art of disseminating many plausible and implausible propositions at once and challenging viewers' wits to see through it all. He fit the mood of democratic uncertainty, of a consciousness pulled by many things to believe and doubt. (As many have noted, the contradictory tweet storms of President Donald J. Trump—Who is to decide when doctors disagree?—belong in the Barnum lineage.)

The lengthy descriptions of whaling and sailing in Melville's *Moby-Dick* and the problem-solving murder mysteries and ciphers by Edgar Allan Poe provide final examples of the operational aesthetic. Poe was a great hoaxer but also a dedicated exposer of imposture. *Moby-Dick* is chock-full of miscellaneous learning, and few novels have ever brimmed so encyclopedically. Like many midcentury novels, its readers required both stamina and a willingness not to be bored by detailed description. The nation seemed populated by gawkers ready to look, be tricked, and then be let in on the hoax, eagerly interested in the rich technical detail of how it was done. But it was populated with bottom-up lovers of facts as well, ordinary people who collected stereographs and photographs, botanical specimens and locks of hair and put them into albums and cubbyholes. They were often the same people, credulous and curious at once. Theirs was a copious culture, fond of accumulations of all kinds.

Copious Culture

The key ingredients for the Yankee system were (1) a thick flow of fact, as much information as possible, (2) widely diffused to different sorts of people (3) who would use their own judgment to decide what mattered. In this regime of truth, facts were important but not almighty. They had to contribute to "knowledge." That it is "knowledge that pushes a civilization forward" was a theme repeated again and again in countless forums in the United States and elsewhere.

To a hard-edged Yankee newspaperman like Barnum's friend Horace Greeley, the simultaneous filling up of the world with things and with facts was part of a single package. It was called progress. In the middle decades of the century, Greeley was the editor of the best-known newspaper in the United States, the *New York Tribune*. Always ready to give an opinion, and to be sure of it, rarely in history have temperament and career matched as well as they did in Greeley's case. By his own count, as of 1860 the *Tribune* sold more than 300,000 copies daily, not counting a weekly Midwest edition that brought his wisdom to the farms of Ohio, Indiana, Illinois, Wisconsin, Kansas, and Iowa.

Greeley epitomized midcentury Yankee ideas about knowledge. He loved facts, was ecstatic about useful learning. Greeley prepared for his tenure as the nation's most influential and notorious opinion giver by working hard and learning as much as he could. He had only intermittent formal schooling, but school was a small part of his education. He pored over elementary textbooks at home, studying Caleb Bingham's *Columbian Orator* until the pages frayed.[15] He declared war on the mistaken platitudes in Lindley Murray's grammar of the English language, perhaps the most famous schoolbook of the day. Compared with our time, books were rarer but more potent. A few of them could provide an entire education to a Greeley, an Abraham Lincoln, or a Frederick Douglass. But Greeley was also out of bed at dawn to "ride horse to plough" and apprenticed to a Vermont newspaper at age fifteen. Such experience taught him a lesson he tried never to forget—that "this is a world of hard work." As an adult, even while he derided the uselessness of so much contemporary schooling he never failed to sing of the beauties of practical knowledge. Not "from *our* panting ranks will ever arise the cry that solid and symmetric Learning is a boon to be rejected or lightly prized!"[16]

To get a feel for how information was valued, it is worthwhile to look at the book Greeley put together in 1853 to promote and explain the New York Crystal Palace exhibition—itself an important influence on the development of American museums and a great example of midcentury technical display. Greeley thought the beauty of the exhibition was that "every possible artistic, scientific, and industrial production can be seen there, and seen and adjudged by competent persons." The book has no pictures. It is stuffed with minute descriptions of dozens of products and technologies on display at the exhibition. Guns, saddles, hats, techniques of wool production, boots, porcelain, glass, preserved food, soaps, perfumes, silk, statuary, cotton production and products and more are discussed with what later generations would see as an oppressive amount of detail. No technicality was spared.

Take Greeley's account of the latest breakthrough in plow technology:

> The beam is five feet long, and the whole length from end of handle to point of beam nine feet. These are made of the best of tough oak and ash timber, all the rest of the plow being made of refined cast-iron, the cutting-edges cold-chilled in the mould till they are harder than tempered cast-steel. This is called the deep-tiller sod-plow. It is intended to turn a furrow from nine to thirteen inches deep and fifteen to seventeen inches wide; and such is the perfection of its construction that it can be done easily by two yoke of oxen, such as are in common use all over the New England states. If the soil is very stiff and hard, an extra yoke is added. At the end of the beam there is a cast iron wheel, by which the required depth is gauged. The draft is from a rod attached to the beam at the standard and leading under the beam through a guide, by a screw upon which the rod can be raised or lowered four or five inches, varying the line of draft.[17]

And so on. We've mercifully provided only about half the description. And this plow was just one of the dozens of products lovingly detailed in the 386 pages of text.

So impressed was Greeley by the Crystal Palace exhibition that he devoted over a hundred pages of his newspaper to it. He editorialized about the politics of the exhibition, of course, but he also sent reporters to render its wonders in magnificent detail. Some twenty essays were published in the *Tribune*, each filled with extraordinary descriptions of some of the most significant inventions of the day. These essays relish the particular, lingering on technical workings. It is impossible to imagine any newspaper of our day doing this sort of reporting or anyone reading it with much interest. More generally, many literary forms in the nineteenth century celebrated duration, repetition, and slow time.[18] Victorian novels that try the patience of students today once riveted whole nations. People once genuinely liked copious culture. Today such detail persists in the instruction manuals that come with our cars, laptops, or telephones, but nobody sees them as bastions of democratic social progress or as good things to read.

A similarly copious practice of collection can be found in the Baedeker guides of the day. These travel books provided the same enormous detail as Greeley, a level of minutiae overwhelming compared with the best-selling bourgeois travel guides of our time such as the Eyewitness or Lonely Planet series. Karl Baedeker had started producing German-language travel guidebooks in the early 1830s. When he died in 1859, from overwork, his three sons took over the business. Looking to expand, they began publishing translations. The first English-language Baedeker appeared in 1861. Dozens were published in the following decades. This was easily the most common and companionable guide available to a Brit or an American traveling in Europe or the Near East and, by the early twentieth century, in Africa or Asia.[19]

To stare at a page of an early Baedeker guidebook is to be drawn into a world outside the realm of visual comfort. The type pushes to the edges of the page. There is a minimum of white space. The type is horribly tiny, usually four- or six-point. Sometimes the pages feature even tinier print for special material. How many bourgeois travelers went blind thanks to the Baedeker sons is a point worth pondering. The only concession to visual ease was to put subject headings in boldface. But if these books did not delight the eye, they were crammed with facts. Thousands of facts were jammed into each little package, the typical Victorian Baedeker being a bit short of 4.5 by 6.5 inches. Imagine it cumulatively: page after page in a tome ranging from 350 to 450 pages blending practical guidance, historical background, and excessively detailed travel routes through the country. In this mix of flat information and dogmatic aesthetic judgment, in that minuscule type, information very clearly dominated. Baedekers were written for people who craved facts—and travelers clearly loved the books. They are an index of an information culture we have lost. The aches and inanition were part of the adventure. Today a Google search can yield thousands or millions of hits, but the point is to rank relevance, not to take it all in. Google's job is to filter the heaps of fact, not to smother us with them.

A Baedeker guide tried to inform you about nearly every nook and cranny you might wander into. It was as much a real-time tour guide as a guidebook. Based on the thick descriptions of routes and scenery, it seems that people were expected to simultaneously read the book and observe their surroundings. It was not a reference book but a travel com-

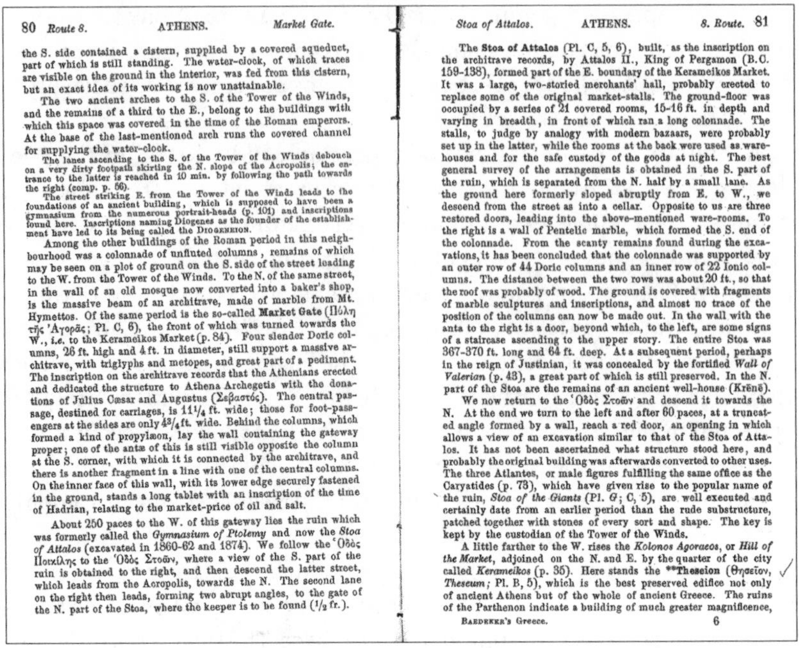

80   Route 8.   ATHENS.   Market Gate.

the S. side contained a cistern, supplied by a covered aqueduct, part of which is still standing. The water-clock, of which traces are visible on the ground in the interior, was fed from this cistern, but an exact idea of its working is now unattainable.

The two ancient arches to the S. of the Tower of the Winds, and the remains of a third to the E., belong to the buildings with which this space was covered in the time of the Roman emperors. At the base of the last-mentioned arch runs the covered channel for supplying the water-clock.

The lanes ascending to the S. of the Tower of the Winds debouch on a very dirty footpath skirting the N. slope of the Acropolis; the entrance to the latter is reached in 10 min. by following the path towards the right (comp. p. 56).

The street striking E. from the Tower of the Winds leads to the foundations of an ancient building, which is supposed to have been a gymnasium from the numerous portrait-heads (p. 101) and inscriptions found here. Inscriptions naming Diogenes as the founder of the establishment have led to its being called the DIOGENEION.

Among the other buildings of the Roman period in this neighbourhood was a colonnade of unfluted columns, remains of which may be seen on a plot of ground on the S. side of the street leading to the W. from the Tower of the Winds. To the N. of the same street, in the wall of an old mosque now converted into a baker's shop, is the massive beam of an architrave, made of marble from Mt. Hymettos. Of the same period is the so-called Market Gate (Πύλη τῆς Ἀγορᾶς; Pl. C, 6), the front of which was turned towards the W., i.e. to the Kerameikos Market (p. 84). Four slender Doric columns, 26 ft. high and 4 ft. in diameter, still support a massive architrave, with triglyphs and metopes, and great part of a pediment. The inscription on the architrave records that the Athenians erected and dedicated the structure to Athena Archegetis with the donations of Julius Caesar and Augustus (Σεβαστός). The central passage, destined for carriages, is 11¼ ft. wide; those for foot-passengers at the sides are only 4¾ ft. wide. Behind the columns, which formed a kind of propylaeon, lay the wall containing the gateway proper; one of the antae of this is still visible opposite the column at the S. corner, with which it is connected by the architrave, and there is another fragment in a line with one of the central columns. On the inner face of this wall, with its lower edge securely fastened in the ground, stands a long tablet with an inscription of the time of Hadrian, relating to the market-price of oil and salt.

About 250 paces to the W. of this gateway lies the ruin which was formerly called the Gymnasium of Ptolemy and now the Stoa of Attalos (excavated in 1860-62 and 1874). We follow the Ὁδὸς Ποικίλης to the Ὁδὸς Στοᾶς, where a view of the S. part of the ruin is obtained to the right, and then descend the latter street, which leads from the Acropolis, towards the N. The second lane on the right then leads, forming two abrupt angles, to the gate of the N. part of the Stoa, where the keeper is to be found (½ fr.).

Stoa of Attalos.   ATHENS.   8. Route.   81

The Stoa of Attalos (Pl. C, 5, 6), built, as the inscription on the architrave records, by Attalos II., King of Pergamon (B.C. 159-138), formed part of the E. boundary of the Kerameikos Market. It was a large, two-storied merchants' hall, probably erected to replace some of the original market-stalls. The ground-floor was occupied by a series of 21 covered rooms, 15-16 ft. in depth and varying in breadth, in front of which ran a long colonnade. The stalls, to judge by analogy with modern bazaars, were probably set up in the latter, while the rooms at the back were used as warehouses and for the safe custody of the goods at night. The best general survey of the arrangements is obtained in the S. part of the ruin, which is separated from the N. half by a small lane. As the ground here formerly sloped abruptly from E. to W., we descend from the street as into a cellar. Opposite to us are three restored doors, leading into the above-mentioned ware-rooms. To the right is a wall of Pentelic marble, which formed the S. end of the colonnade. From the scanty remains found during the excavations, it has been concluded that the colonnade was supported by an outer row of 44 Doric columns and an inner row of 22 Ionic columns. The distance between the two rows was about 20 ft., so that the roof was probably of wood. The ground is covered with fragments of marble sculptures and inscriptions, and almost no trace of the position of the columns can now be made out. In the wall with the anta to the right is a door, beyond which, to the left, are some signs of a staircase ascending to the upper story. The entire Stoa was 367-370 ft. long and 64 ft. deep. At a subsequent period, perhaps in the reign of Justinian, it was concealed by the fortified Wall of Valerian (p. 43), a great part of which is still preserved. In the N. part of the Stoa are the remains of an ancient well-house (Krēnē).

We now return to the Ὁδὸς Στοᾶν and descend it towards the N. At the end we turn to the left and after 60 paces, at a truncated angle formed by a wall, reach a red door, an opening in which allows a view of an excavation similar to that of the Stoa of Attalos. It has not been ascertained what structure stood here, and probably the original building was afterwards converted to other uses. The three Atlantes, or male figures fulfilling the same office as the Caryatides (p. 73), which have given rise to the popular name of the ruin, Stoa of the Giants (Pl. C; C, 5), are well executed and certainly date from an earlier period than the rude substructure, patched together with stones of every sort and shape. The key is kept by the custodian of the Tower of the Winds.

A little farther to the W. rises the Kolonos Agoraeos, or Hill of the Market, adjoined on the N. and E. by the quarter of the city called Kerameikos (p. 35). Here stands the **Theseion (Θησεῖον; Theseum; Pl. B, 5), which is the best preserved edifice not only of ancient Athens but of the whole of ancient Greece. The ruins of the Parthenon indicate a building of much greater magnificence,

BAEDEKER's Greece.   6

FIGURE 2.1. *Baedeker's Greece: Handbook for Travellers*, 1889.

panion—and a testy one at that: "The boatmen are insolent, there is no tariff and great confusion prevails," *Baedeker's Greece* (1894) informs us about steam travel between Brindisi and Corfu. "The *Harbour* is unimportant," states the Baedeker guide to Cannes without further explanation.

If they told you what to ignore, the guidebooks also directed travelers' paths in museums, baldly mapping the spaces and cataloging their (often mundane) contents like forerunners of audio guides in museums today. *Baedeker's Greece* comments about the National Museum of Archaeology in Athens: "Here also are vases in human form or in the shape of human (negro) and animal heads: 2076. Graceful female figure with wings; 2060. Aphrodite emerging from the shell; fine black ram's head, varnished. A number of well-executed human feet.—CASE 55. Vases of late form in black, with white ornamentation.—CASES 56, 57. Small toilet articles.—CASE 58."[20] Together with the museum's endless glass cases carefully stocked with rows of numbered artifacts, *Baedeker's Greece* shared a copious mode of presentation.

Yet if loaded with fact, a Baedeker offered nothing in the way of orientation. Each guide was a haystack of particulars. These books came without overview, summation, or mood; there was no wit or whimsy.

Of course the traveler was not supposed to commit all these facts to memory. Rather, the books were there to help people make their own summaries. Baedeker senior declared that his guides were meant to save travelers from "the unpleasant tutelage of hired servants and guides." They helped the traveler stand "on his own feet," putting him where "he may receive his own impressions with clear eyes and lively heart."[21] Channeling that thick river of fact would free travelers to make their own judgments.

Essential to the thick culture of fact was figuring it out on your own. Americans wanted to dare to know for themselves, to be free of tutelage. Popular science was a key aspect of the faith. Even naturalists in Dubuque, Iowa, took as their mission the diffusion of science to a wider public.[22] The eminent and the ordinary alike were obsessed with piling up granaries of information. The founding editor of *Popular Science Monthly* announced that "the primary question is, What are the facts, the pertinent facts, all the facts, which bear upon the inquiry?"[23]

This democratic theme was voiced by Barnum, Greeley, and the Baedekers. This combination of copious fact and individual assessment was common in midcentury Yankee culture. Facts were prized possessions, the foundation of those sciences that were steadily becoming more powerful, the basis of informed judgment about distant civilizations, and the source of wisdom for popular rule. As the world swelled with information, serious people of all kinds evinced a willingness to pursue detail in ways our age lacks the patience for.

Ralph Waldo Emerson, for instance, eagerly pored over the floral catalogs of natural historians such as Linnaeus and Buffon and saw their "dry catalogues of facts" as grist for the imagination. Facts were not dusty: "A Fact is the end or last issue of spirit." He thought that a fact could be "true poetry."[24] Henry David Thoreau similarly sought to bridge facts and spirit. He went to the woods in search of facts, and his diaries can spill over with an almost indigestible load of observations. He was squarely in the natural history tradition of Alexander von Humboldt, with its bottomless appetite for assembling small bits of the cosmic order. Thoreau was doing more than banking perceptions. "The fact will one day flower into a truth," he said, disdaining those "mere accumulators of facts" who never bring them to blossom.[25]

In the Victorian thick culture of fact, "facts" or "specimens," simple bits of information, had a specific role. They were the beginning of learning but not the end. Words like science, knowledge, and learning referred to the larger principles and relations stemming from fact and reflection upon it. The steady and uncritical use of the phrase "laws of knowledge"

in these years suggested the order inherent in knowledge and the importance of being more than a simple empiric, more than a gatherer of facts.
Facts were not random, or at least they shouldn't be random. Nor should
they have a life of their own. They were drops in the river of knowledge,
nourishment for science and parasitic on it at the same time. Unlike our
own time, there was a deep confidence that knowledge was adding up
to something bigger.

The view that a thick river of fact could grow into laws of knowledge was clear in the period's philosophy of science. Two of the most
important works in Victorian philosophy of science, William Whewell's
Philosophy of the Inductive Sciences (1840) and John Stuart Mill's *System of
Logic* (1843), favored gathering massive observations without forfeiting
a key role for reason. "The Idea," wrote Whewell in the second edition,
"can never be independent of the Fact, but the Fact must ever be drawn
towards the idea."[26] Despite their disagreements, both favored accumulations tempered by logic. Charles Darwin, the greatest of all natural
historians, followed in their inductivist footsteps, believing that knowledge grew through the collection and cataloging of an immense number of specimens. He delayed publication of *The Origin of Species* to study
the classification of barnacles for eight years, and his last book was a
study of earthworms. After a life spent poring over specimens, Darwin
complained in old age that he had lost the aesthetic delight he had once
taken in poetry, painting, and music; he felt he had become "a kind of
machine for grinding general laws out of large collections of facts."[27]
His theory of natural selection—a slow process of crucial innovations
emerging fortuitously as the side effects of random gropings—was an
echo of his research practice.

For the *scientist*—a term Whewell coined in 1833—the thick culture
of fact could be found in the increased compilation of statistical knowledge in Europe and North America, something historians such as Ian
Hacking and Theodore Porter have spent time exploring. Statistics
emerges in the eighteenth century as early actuarial tables and efforts
of states to oversee themselves, but there was, as Hacking has noted, a
veritable "avalanche of printed numbers" in the 1820s and 1830s.[28] The
takeoff curve was steep. In 1815, for instance, there was a cross-Channel
squabble between British and French doctors about whether there were
more suicides in London or in Paris. Surely there were more suicides in
London, said the French physician Esquirol, pointing to the notoriously
foul English weather. (French doctors of the era liked to think of suicide
as a peculiarly English illness, just as English doctors liked to call syphilis *la maladie française*.) The records, riposted the English doctor Burrows,

showed more suicides in Paris in the previous recorded year. Neither side had enough data to clinch the argument.

But over the next ten to fifteen years, abundant numerical evidence was collected about suicides and many other "facts" that had never before been investigated. Unfortunately, more data did not resolve apparently simple questions such as comparative national suicide rates. The debate grew even more complicated as questions of season, method, and motive arose.[29] Though a surfeit of data did not always bring an abundance of insight, the hearty appetite for facts was not easily satiated. Early statisticians trusted that their harvests of data would eventually be sorted out. The motto of the Statistical Society of London, founded in 1834, was *aliis exterendum*—to be threshed out by others. Massive statistical efforts soon took hold in the United States as well.

Similar attempts to gather and order heaps of fact were found in positivism. Auguste Comte, its inventor, represents the ambitions of nineteenth-century diffusion. One of his slogans was *savoir pour prévoir pour pouvoir*—"to know to predict to control." He wanted to order knowledge according to nature itself. Linnaeus knew that his scheme used artificial conceptual shortcuts, but Comte's ambitions were greater. Against what he saw as a dangerous tendency of the human mind to impose unjustified order on the world by positing gods and metaphysical abstractions as causes, Comte wanted classification to emerge naturally from the things themselves. He spurned a priori systems. Biological taxonomy, even more than botanical, was the great model for his positivist philosophy. He had confidence in building intellectual systems robust enough to handle the vast harvests of fact.

The British philosopher, sociologist, and former railway engineer Herbert Spencer, whose systematizing ambitions were as overweening as those of Comte, also used biological metaphors to corral herds of facts. "The noise of facts resounds through all his chapters," said William James, explaining Spencer's great appeal to late nineteenth-century readers. (James himself found Spencer rather soulless.)[30] Spencer's trust that knowledge could be ordered into an organic, almost physiological whole was very different from the outlook of seventeenth-century empiricists, for whom the uncontainability of facts threatened any larger system of order. Spencer's "system" fed on facts like a steam engine fed on coal. There was nothing he couldn't swallow and digest. For him as for Comte, knowledge belonged in a large branching tree, growing organically out the animal, vegetable, and mineral kingdoms, except that he added the additional element of evolutionary dynamism. The whole universe, Spencer declared, was inexorably moving from homogeneity

Sidebar 2.2 The Census

Gina Giotta

The growth in complexity of the US census illustrates the explosion of information in nineteenth-century America. The framers of the Constitution had mandated a census every ten years as a centerpiece of the representative system. Without a count of the population, two key, symmetrical functions of the state—taxation and voting—would be impossible (as would mustering armies). James Madison announced in the *Federalist*, no. 54: "It is agreed on all sides, that numbers are the best scale of wealth and taxation, as they are the only proper scale of representation." From the beginning, the United States has been in the business of government by empiricism.

But the first censuses were remarkably relaxed by our standards. They left vast patches of life untallied and uninvestigated. The inaugural census of 1790 asked a mere six questions pertaining to the age, sex, and citizenship status (race) of each member of the household, as did the equally modest censuses of 1800, 1810, and 1820. Although a number of learned societies and prominent political figures—among them Madison and Thomas Jefferson—petitioned Congress during these early years to extend the scope and function of the survey so it might serve as both a basic tool of apportionment and an ongoing record of the nation's exceptional progress, federal lawmakers rejected the idea. They reasoned that the proposed expansion (which was to include inquiries about such private matters as income, occupation, and disability) would be impossible to square with the standing mandate that census results be publicly posted in each community as a guarantee against recording error (and fraud). Citizens were encouraged to study the report and, if need be, amend any mistakes associated with their households (which served as the unit of analysis until 1850, when it was replaced by the individual). Shame served as a disincentive to omit or misrepresent facts. In ultimately choosing to retain the publicity mandate instead of enlarging the survey, Congress certified its preference for factual accuracy over factual breadth. At the dawn of the nineteenth century, information quality—rather than quantity—was still the order of the day.

By 1840, however, the seed planted by Jefferson and his pluralist ilk had begun to blossom. Congress discontinued the tricky quality-control practice of posting census tallies and embraced the multipurpose census by adding an unprecedented five new inquiries to that year's schedule—

a move that nearly doubled the number of questions asked in the previous five censuses and swelled the final report by some nine hundred pages.[1] For the first time in its largely unvaried history, the census would enumerate the number of idiots, the insane, and the illiterate among the general population. It would also finally detail the employment status of respondents in seven predetermined occupational classes.

But far from disclosing the splendor of the American political experiment (as proponents of an enlarged survey had argued it would do), the mountain of facts generated by the census of 1840 only worked to expose the United States as a nation disproportionately composed of mentally and physically defective people. Though most agreed that the distressing results reflected gross errors in collection or reporting rather than the reality of the situation, few could concur on the root cause of the exaggerations. Some blamed racist enumerators who were said to have skewed the results when they willfully mischaracterized all nonwhites as "idiot" or "insane," while others suggested that the bloated character of the survey complicated its execution.[2] Whatever the source of the debacle, the solution was not to revert to the small census that worked, but to devise new ways to ensure that the big one would. Facts were not the problem; it was their collection that needed improvement.

Key among these upgrades were better tables and tabulating methods, a printed schedule supplemented for the first time by printed instructions, additional oversight at every level, and actual statisticians on the government payroll. The census of 1850 was to be, in one senator's words, "a more perfect collection of facts." It would demonstrate that facts could be tamed and made to work for the nation rather than against it. More important, this overhauled population machine was to lay the foundation for a survey that would grow every ten years in accordance with the burgeoning information zeitgeist. By 1860 it would be the "most complete census of any nation," two decades later it would grow to "encyclopedic proportions," and by 1890 it would boldly declare the unruly frontier—like facts more generally—totally domesticated.[3]

The census even found its way into American intellectual history by

1. Carroll D. Wright, *The History and Growth of the United States Census* (Washington, DC: Government Printing Office, 1900), 911–12.

2. See Patricia Cline Cohen, *A Calculating People: The Spread of Numeracy in Early America* (Chicago: University of Chicago Press, 1982), 175–204.

3. Wright, *History and Growth*, 52, 58, 41.

Table 2.2 Length of successive censuses, 1790–1890

Year	Pages
1790	56
1800	74
1810	180
1820	188
1830	163
1840	1085
1850	1158
1860	2879
1870	2406
1880	19,305
1890	21,428

Source: Carroll D. Wright, *The History and Growth of the United States Census* (Washington, DC: US Government Printing Office, 1900), 911–14.

inspiring the famous frontier hypothesis of Frederick Jackson Turner. Speaking at the World Columbian Exposition of 1893 in Chicago, Turner gave fresh expression to a myth of American self-consciousness that had been gestating since the Puritan errand into the wilderness: that the nation's identity had been forged on the westward-receding frontier. The immediate occasion for Turner's remarks was that the census had just declared the frontier closed.

Although the 1890 census gave Turner the impetus to compress the complex mass of American history into a neat synthesis, it also inspired the rise of a new device for organizing information. The 1880 census had taken eight years to tabulate. No one was quite sure what to do with the 1890 census, even more vast in its data hoard. In 1889 Herman Hollerith, an employee of the Census Bureau, patented a method of using punch cards to analyze data mechanically. It took his new technique just one year to process the data yielded by the 1890 census. In the 1890 census, Turner saw one frontier closing; but Hollerith saw another frontier opening up: computerization. In 1896 he founded the Tabulating Machine Company, which in 1924 would become International Business Machines (IBM).

to heterogeneity, just like any organism in its development, and who were governments or do-gooders to stand in the way of cosmic progress? Spencer was not the last to view his preferred vision of political economy as endorsed by nature itself.

Detail and Veracity in Photography

The camera added to the supply of facts. Lady Elizabeth Eastlake, British art critic and historian, directly connected the two in an 1857 essay, stating that photography was "made for the present age, in which the desire for art resides in a small minority, but the craving, or rather necessity for cheap, prompt, and correct facts [resides] in the public at large."[31]

Daguerreotypy was the first photographic process available to ordinary people. It produced a single image on a metal plate, soon outmoded by faster, more reproduction-friendly wet-plate techniques. Early observers noted the worlds of astounding detail revealed by the new technique. An early appreciator of the work of Frenchman Louis Daguerre, for whom the process is named, noted that the typical image was stark enough to reveal "an accumulation of dust in a hollow moulding of a distant building."[32] Such detail was as curious and disturbing then as it is today. (Because we are used to the more diffuse images produced by paper-based prints, daguerreotypes can appear uncannily sharp to our eyes.) Sitters were often shocked by the amount and quality of the detail that surfaced in their portraits, and they frequently questioned the legitimacy of the often unflattering mechanical revelations. The airbrush arose as one technique for taming the overflow of visual detail. The camera's fidelity to what appeared before its lens was both magnificent and stupid. It reproduced wrinkles and blemishes without discernment or taste. But it also opened up unprecedented new sights.

Many were excited about the extension of our eyes into uncharted parts of nature. Edgar Allan Poe wrote that such detail opened up new paths of understanding. A daguerreotype, he intoned, with perhaps faux enthusiasm, was "*infinitely* more accurate in its representation than any painting by human hands. If we examine a work of ordinary art, by means of a powerful microscope, all traces of resemblance to nature will disappear—but the closest scrutiny of the photogenic drawing discloses only a more absolute truth, a more perfect identity of aspect with the thing represented."[33] Looking at a painting close up showed us nothing but the painted remnants of the artist's craft; a daguerreotype, in contrast, yielded a small sample of zoomable reality.

The notion that the camera enjoys an essential realism remains an

Sidebar 2.3 The Airbrush

Gina Giotta

Perhaps the cruelest fact to confront nineteenth-century Victorians was their own ugliness. On their first visit to the local daguerreotypist, many were shocked to discover that the camera's eye was considerably sharper than the eye of the painter. Troubling details that would likely have escaped the portrait artist (or been politely suppressed) were registered with striking clarity by painting's mechanical counterpart. Veiny hands, lazy eyes, and crooked noses were just some of the previously invisible physiological "facts" that now daunted paying customers accustomed to receiving a flattering likeness. "There is a wonderful insight in Heaven's broad and simple sunshine," says the daguerreotypist Holgrave in Nathaniel Hawthorne's *House of the Seven Gables* (1851). Daguerreotypy "brings out the secret character with a truth that no painter would ever venture upon, even could he detect it. There is, at least, no flattery in my humble line of art."[1]

While those like Holgrave who were interested in exposing the corruption of the painter and the vanity of the bourgeoisie delighted in this particular eruption of detail,[2] most found it insufferable. Portraits were meant to function as a sort of decorative permanent record, and few were eager to embellish their lavish parlors with images that memorialized personal flaws. Others were less practical and more existential in their distaste for photographic detail, refusing to accept the truth claims about them forwarded by the new technology. According to trade press reports of the day, these photographed subjects were especially inclined to become violently ill or angry at the sight of their blemished faces and malformed bodies, and they frequently asked that the offending photograph be destroyed on site, like a damning piece of evidence. If the daguerreotype truly was, as Oliver Wendell Holmes described it, a "mirror with a memory," it seemed to many to belong in a funhouse.

This, of course, was bad news for fledgling photography studios.

1. Nathaniel Hawthorne, *House of the Seven Gables* (Boston: Ticknor, Reed, and Fields, 1851), 101.

2. Evangelicals were among the early advocates of daguerreotypy, which they saw as supporting their larger project of moral uplift. For them, God quite literally was in the details. For a representative example of this rhetoric, see "Picture Pausings, No. II," *Christian Watchman*, May 15, 1846.

Though many daguerreotypists wanted desperately to maintain the integrity of their already dubious "art," it wasn't long before they found themselves capitulating to the demands of an evidently narcissistic clientele. Within a year of the daguerreotype's appearance in 1839, a number of mechanical picture makers quietly began adding paints, brushes, and etching tools to their professional toolbox. Besides permitting them to add splashes of color, such tools allowed photographers to "retouch" the tiny sparks of contingency that—despite careful makeup, posing, and lighting—frequently managed to materialize in the finished product.

This early campaign to discipline photographic detail in the bourgeois portrait, along with the development in the 1850s of cheaper and faster processes like the tintype, helped to guarantee the rise of mechanical portraiture in nineteenth-century America. Abraham Lincoln, reflecting on a photograph that Mathew Brady took of him in 1860, in which Brady straightened out his left eye and erased some wrinkles, declared that it "made me president."[3] (This was the first in a long line of media-deterministic quips about electoral fortunes.) Such smoothing of photographic blemishes consequently helped to ensure the emergence of what some contemporary scholars have described as "picture factories," or massive assembly-line affairs capable of producing as many as four hundred portraits a day.[4] Although these studios tended to be cheaper—catering as they did to an expanding middle class rather than the elite—most were still able to provide the time-consuming (and now standard) service of retouching thanks to a strict division of labor among studio employees and the incorporation of new technologies designed to promote their productivity. In addition, the wet-plate technique encouraged retouching by allowing manipulation of both the positive print and the negative.

Chief among these productivity-enhancing technologies was a pen-like mechanical instrument called an airbrush. Developed in the late 1870s, the airbrush satisfied the large studios' twin demands for speed and for precision by minimizing the need to stipple the surface of the

3. Christopher Benfrey, "Theater of War: The Real Story of Mathew Brady's Civil War Photographs," *Slate*, October 30, 1997, www.slate.com/articles/news_and_poli tics/photography/1997/10/theater_of_war.html.

4. Marshall Battani, "Organizational Fields, Cultural Fields and Artworlds: The Early Effort to Make Photographs and Make Photographers in the 19th Century USA," *Media, Culture, and Society* 21, no. 5 (1999): 601–26.

negative with hand tools before retouching. (The wet-plate process already allowed retouching of either the negative or the positive print.) Because the device could distribute ink over the offending detail in very tiny, calibrated droplets, the negative did not need to first be "roughed up" to ensure that the heavier strokes of the paintbrush would remain discreet in the exposed—and potentially enlarged—print. By eliminating all contact with the canvas, the traces of the retoucher's labor could be largely effaced, as could the signs of human intervention in the purportedly "objective art" of photography.

As an unassuming adjunct to the camera, the airbrush helped sustain on a massive scale the polite fiction that had grown up around portrait photography. It ensured that the mechanical pictures produced for genteel customers matched those excessively complimentary ones swirling about their heads. On a grander scale, though, the airbrush ensured the rise of a cohesive, edifying visual grammar of middle-classness marked by a lack of somatic irregularities. As retoucher's manuals of the day suggest, everything from noses to hands was to be well formed, unmarked, and—in the case of hands—"worked entirely smooth in almost every instance."[5] During a time when such outward signifiers were increasingly being read as legitimate clues about character, sanity, and guilt or innocence, the practice of standardizing the celluloid body in accordance with prevailing visions of normalcy was as much about securing one's place in the social order as about satisfying one's vanity.

Tellingly, this postproduction regimentation of privileged bodies angered phrenologists and physiognomists, who felt that retouching cheated them out of a certain knowledge of the world and the people who circulated in it. As one such practitioner of the former pseudoscience laments in a late nineteenth-century journal article subtitled "Made-Up Faces," "Little is left of the original face in these photocounterfeits, making any analysis of a conventional photo-portrait impossible."[6] Such was, perhaps, the tacit point of retouching.

5. "Hints on Retouching," *Photographic News: A Weekly Record of the Progress of Photography*, July 9, 1875, 329.

6. H. S. Drayton, "Phrenotypes and Side-Views, No. 13," *Phrenological Journal and Science of Health (1870–1911)* 104 (1897): 10–12.

enduring point in commentary about photography; so does the counter-point that the camera has special power to trick and deceive. Perhaps with a touch of joshing insight, Poe voiced two enduring themes in discussions of photography: its positivist mimicry of things as they are and its metaphysical or fantastical revelation of realities otherwise inaccessible. The photographic image presented an inexhaustible mine of truth about reality but also a potential for illicit multiplication of fakes. The photograph's destiny as a kind of promiscuous knowledge takes place between these two poles.

Ralph Waldo Emerson, however, would see things even more subtly. He described the torturous experience of sitting before a daguerreotypist in a journal entry dated October 24, 1841: "And in your zeal not to blur the image, did you keep every finger in its place with such energy that your hands became clenched as for fight or despair, and in your resolution to keep your face still, did you feel every muscle becoming every moment more rigid: the brows contracted into a Tartarean frown, and the eyes fixed as only they are fixed in a fit, in madness, or in death?" Even if subjects could control their facial muscles well enough to smile for the protracted exposure times, descriptions such as Emerson's suggest there was little to beam about during the process. (Anyone who has felt a smile freezing into a rictus while waiting for the shutter to click can relate.) Photography would have to be instant before it could be fun.[34]

Emerson, as it happened, considered himself unphotogenic, and so did his friends. When he sent a daguerreotype image to his Scottish friend Thomas Carlyle in 1847, Carlyle wrote back that it was "altogether unsatisfactory." He wrote that Emerson seemed to be "smiling on me as if in mockery, 'Dost know me friend: I am dead, thou seest, and distant, and forever hidden from thee;—I belong already to the Eternities, and thou recognisest me not!'" (Recording media always invoke the Beyond.) If Poe's account of the mechanical image was a parody of naive realism, Emerson thought his face's resistance to portraiture revealed something of greater significance. Nature was not to be captured passively by the camera, since it was always in flux. Images were not apart from but part of natural process, and the camera was not a fixer of nature's firmness but a revelator of its flux. "Everything," Emerson said, "is medial."[35]

Emerson's view of photography as participating in nature's inherent restlessness would not be in the mainstream of intellectual reflection on photography. Oliver Wendell Holmes Sr., in one of the century's most important essays on photography, followed the realist line of seeing the new pictures as samples worthy of infinitesimal inspection: "One may creep over the surface of a [photographic] picture with his microscope

Sidebar 2.4 Emily Dickinson and Vision

When Thomas Wentworth Higginson, the abolitionist preacher who edited the first collection of her poetry, published posthumously, wrote to Emily Dickinson to request a photograph, she wrote back refusing: "Could you believe me—without? I have no portrait, now, but am small, like the Wren, and my Hair is bold, like the Chestnut Bur—and my eyes, like the Sherry in the Glass, that the Guest leaves—Would this do as well?" She could spot a rival when she saw one. This astonishing description essentially pits poetry against photography for the right to depict the self. Should a person be portrayed in words or images? Poetry, after all, recorded the delicate transitions of things. It provided images too. Would this do as well?

Her first query to Higginson recalled the question posed to an earlier doubting Thomas: Could you believe without seeing? Dickinson's stunning self-description, in fact, not only was meant to outclass a mere picture—which she did in part by providing something contemporary photography could not, color—but was also a white lie.[1] A famous image of Dickinson exists, a daguerreotype from about 1847, and it is not as impressive as her description to Higginson. It shows an awkwardly posed, slightly fish-eyed young woman without giving any evidence of the piercing intellect and wit so clear to anyone who knew her in person or in her poetry. It has become the canonical Dickinson image. It is possible that she and her family quite disliked it, as one does of photographs.

More recently another daguerreotype has been found of an older, more self-confident Dickinson seated with her arm around another woman, Kate Scott Turner. No one has decisive proof that this is Dickinson, but there is no reason not to think so. She is less slight and awkward and is almost smiling, remarkably so given the constraints of sitting for the technology. One could take a thousand words from this picture—Dickinson is not frail, sickly, young, or delicate, but rather is healthy, in charge, almost imposing. We can't help but invest these two pictures with longing and meaning—something perhaps less common in a time of digital images everywhere (as already noted in the introduction).

What Dickinson would have thought about her photographic after life is not clear. She loved vision, but she understood photography as, among other things, an upstart competitor of her art. (She was anxious

1. Cynthia Griffin Wolff, *Emily Dickinson* (Reading, MA: Addison-Wesley, 1986), 163, 256.

FIGURE 2.2. Emily Dickinson daguerreotype, c. 1847.
Amherst College Archives and Special Collections.

about her troubles with eyesight from the 1860s on and even worried
that she might go blind.) Like poetry, photography was a way to rob
memory of its loss. Death for her was marked by the failure of vision:
"I could not see to see." Photographs kept on seeing and showing after
their subjects were dead. In this there was something odd or perhaps
indecent.[2]

In a poem from late 1862, Dickinson spun out a variety of photo-

2. See Eliza Richards, "'Death's Surprise, Stamped Visible': Emily Dickinson,
Oliver Wendell Holmes, and Civil War Photography," *Amerikastudien/American
Studies* 54, no. 1 (2009): 13–33.

FIGURE 2.3. Emily Dickinson and Kate Scott Turner Anthon daguerreotype, 1859. Courtesy Jeff Green and Amherst College Archives and Special Collections.

graphic themes, which may have been inspired by her reading of Oliver Wendell Holmes Sr.'s series of three essays on photography in the *Atlantic*.

> The Inner paints the Outer –
> The Brush without the Hand –
> It's Picture publishes – precise –
> As is the inner Brand –
>
> On fine – Arterial Canvas –
> A Cheek – perchance a Brow -

The Star's whole secret – in the Lake –
Eyes were not meant to know.

The first stanza quoted posits a correspondence between face and feeling. It fits the "cult of sincerity" and specifically rejects makeup, suggesting that an unpainted face is more authentic, since it can be colored by the inner feelings rather than by contrivance. But the stanza can also be read as a comment on photography. Photography, called "nature's pencil" by pioneering photographer Henry Fox Talbot, is a brush without the hand whose picture publishes precise.

The second stanza quoted takes us into the metaphysical depths. A face is an arterial canvas, but so is a photographic plate. So is vision itself, when we see the network of blood vessels in our retinas against the world as an afterimage. The reflection of the star's light on the surface of a lake is published, but what is published is a reflection, and one whose secret can also be read, as Adam Frank notes, as the pun hole/whole. What is published is an absence. Photography is figured here as a transgressive effort to gain knowledge that forever remains inaccessible—the inner brand. Poetry reveals by hiding, but photography hides by revealing.[3] There are some things eyes were not meant to know.

3. Adam Frank, "Emily Dickinson and Photography," *Emily Dickinson Journal* 10, no. 2 (2001): 1–21.

and find every leaf perfect, or read the letters of distant signs." A "frightful amount of detail," he thought, was photography's yield. "Theoretically, a perfect photograph is absolutely inexhaustible. In a picture you can find nothing which the artist has not seen before you; but in a perfect photograph there will be as many beauties lurking, unobserved, as there are flowers that blush unseen in forests and meadows." This was, of course, less a description than a metaphysical hope. Certainly no camera has ever depicted all levels of magnification with equal fidelity, but the idea that a device could do so helped differentiate the new craft from painting. Making a point that anticipates later students of photography such as Walter Benjamin and Roland Barthes, Holmes praised the camera's power to capture "incidental truths" that were often of greater interest than the main subject. "The more evidently accidental their introduction, the more trivial they are in themselves, the more they take hold of the imagination."[36]

FIGURE 2.4. Louis-Jacques Mande Daguerre, *Paris Boulevard*, 1838 or 1839.

There were real limits on what could be photographed. The infinite depth of detail praised by intellectuals was of structure, not motion. Long exposure times made photography a solemn and stately medium that was rich at depicting whatever endured and poor at catching whatever moved. This was clear in one of the first daguerreotypes. One morning in 1838 or 1839 Daguerre pointed his device at a busy Paris intersection for ten or fifteen minutes. His camera seems to have been placed in an upper window of a multistory building, making this founding image a kind of aerial photograph. Because of the long exposure, the image wiped the world clean like a pre-Socratic philosophy, saving what endures. None of the carriages, peddlers, and pedestrians that streamed through the Boulevard du Temple that day survived its gaze. The busy street looks like an empty riverbed. The teeming city became a ghost town. The unmoving buildings, trees, landmarks, and other objects insensitive to time appear on the plate, but horses and people were spirited away. A man having his shoes shined who stood still long enough to soak his way into the stubborn emulsion is the sole figure left behind. The camera had brought the Rapture to Paris.

Daguerreotypy and its successor, the wet-plate process, made a jumpy image culture technically infeasible. Early landscape photographs would be marred by a blank sky—the slow movement of clouds and the relative brightness of the sky would leave nothing but a bright blur. (Daguerre's image features a blank sky with what looks to us like an eerie nuclear glow—not a cloud in sight.) For both skies and city streets, photography was not only the modeler of the world but its selective eraser. And portraits necessitated the discipline to sit still, as Emerson noted. Exposure times lasting ten to thirty seconds (and as long as two to fifteen minutes when Daguerre introduced the process) required that sitters remain completely still. Medieval-looking iron neck braces and head clamps ensured the requisite immobility by "fixing" bodies in position while light fixed their likenesses on polished silver plates. (A brace can be seen, barely, in a Brady portrait of Lincoln.)[37]

"Nervous" sitters (or "patients," as some trade journals called them) proved particularly difficult. Children were photographed when they were sleeping—or dead. Some sitters were powdered with flour or made to endure the heat from multiple mirrors directing sunlight onto them from strategic points around the perimeter of the studio. Unlike the more casual "snapshot" culture that that would emerge at the end of the century with the appearance and marketing of Kodak cameras, early photographs were characterized by a motionless solemnity. To our more modern eyes the unsmiling and eerily crisp images of the time can seem haunted, strange, and wonderful.

The dream of instantaneous images existed well before the technological possibility. Holmes foresaw action photography. "The time is perhaps at hand when a flash of light, as sudden and brief as that of the lightning which shows a whirling wheel standing stock still, shall preserve the very instant of the shock of contact of the mighty armies that are even now gathering."[38] Holmes's dream of stroboscopically aided battle photography had to wait at least until the Spanish-American War of 1898 and World War I. Midcentury photography may have been faithful to statics, but it treated dynamics as a blur.

Mathew Brady's Civil War pictures, for instance, did not show any action. They showed the war's results, such as human remains in a desolate landscape. For the first time, war was memorialized not by saga, painting, or sculpture but by photographs that depicted the unvarnished results. War, violence, and death were old themes in the visual arts, but Brady's pictures depicted something new: unheroic death, grunts killed in the new scale of industrial warfare. He showed death, but not dying, simply because photographic technology of the time was not mobile or fast enough in shutter speed to record the events of battle. "Let him who wishes to know what war is, look at this series of illustrations," intoned Holmes in 1863. The idea that the camera could transmit the essence of war, however incompletely, has been in place since then.[39]

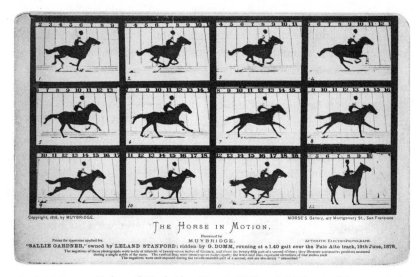

FIGURE 2.5. Eadweard Muybridge, *Horse in Motion*, 1878. Library of Congress, Prints and Photographs Division, LC-DIG-ppmsca-06607.

In contrast to the late twentieth century, when images were associated with flux, in the nineteenth century the image was a means of stopping time. The camera's ability to freeze movement increased in the 1870s, though scientific stop-motion images go back at least to 1830s efforts at modeling the anatomy of human locomotion.[40] The eccentric British photographer Eadweard Muybridge famously obtained newly fast exposure times in the late 1870s while working for Leland Stanford in California. Muybridge rigged a setup of successive trip wires to take pictures of motions too quick to be discerned by the human retina, such as the movements of horses. His camera's eye proved something no painter or scientist had been able to see before—that all four of a racehorse's hooves went airborne at some point when trotting or galloping. Finer and finer intervals of time yielded themselves to vision. His silhouettes of the mare in motion analyze a fluid event into many still images like cinema in reverse. The image reproduced here is an albumen print that he seems to have retouched to make the horse a solid body; he insisted, however, that the negative had not been doctored. He did, obviously, splice in the final image, which is clearly out of sequence: what horse could come to a full stop from a gallop in one twenty-fifth of a second? Part of the recent fascination for Muybridge must be attributed to the way his work, like digital photography, always asks us to wonder if the evidentiary power of the photographic image is enhanced—or ruined—by art and artifice.[41]

Getting the camera to track motion was difficult for both technical and human reasons. In the 1870s, using the camera to track the transit of Venus across the sun yielded disappointing results for astronomers eager to harness the medium's capacity for accuracy. In the 1880s, scientists like Ernst Mach were experimenting with exposure speeds in the ten-thousandths of a second and were able to see sights no one had ever seen before. The company EG&G took microsecond photos of nuclear explosions in the years after World War II, with astonishing results (see chapter 4). The trend toward ever smaller slices of time continues: by the early twenty-first century, scientists were making images of events that occurred in sextillionths of a second, and recent scientists claim to have developed a camera that can capture the movement of light.[42]

Unlike facts, in the middle of the century photographs were not understood with terms for disorder, chaos, or randomness. Instead, observers were struck by the absence of movement and the proliferation of detail. (Despite the breathlessness of some commentators, many detail-oriented image-making practices predate the camera. The "cult of individuating detail" can be seen, for instance, in eighteenth-century anatomical atlases.)[43] Photographs were generally understood to freeze time, to capture moments for science, pleasure, or family pride. Lady Eastlake noted that photography had become "a household word and a household want; is used alike by art and science, by love, business, and justice."[44] From the preparation that went into sitting for a mechanical portrait to the care required to properly handle the delicate keepsake upon its completion, early photographs were treated a bit like relics. One observer thought the daguerreotypists of the day were "limning faces at a rate that promises soon to make every man's house a Daguerrean Gallery." Once, having your portrait done was an aristocratic privilege, but now the sunbeam could "catch" and "fix" likenesses for all, held to be even more beautiful when the daguerreotypist had a feeling for art.[45]

The camera's ability to make images without the intervention of human hands made it a more faithful source of knowledge for some. Pictures could be collected like natural specimens or objets d'art. Holmes foresaw an infinite supply of photographic images. A photograph, he thought, was form stripped of matter. Sounding a bit like the digital prophets of the late twentieth century who lauded the infinite bandwidth of fiber optic cables, he frothed that because matter was heavy and expensive while form was light and cheap, people would be able to collect beautiful images as hunters mount and collect the game they kill. This enormous gathering of "skins," as he called them using a natural history term, should be "classified and arranged in vast libraries, as books are now." It would be free to all, whether artists, scholars, or mechanics.⁴⁶

Despite such dreams, photographs did not circulate through everyday life as they do today or did in the mid-twentieth century. Brady's Civil War photographs could be seen in his New York City gallery, but the media for the mass circulation of images—circulating libraries, billboards, photojournalism, film, newsreels, television, and the internet—lay in the future. Pictures were once relatively rare and immobile. In the nineteenth century the image did not bear as much cultural freight as information did. It was not until the twentieth century, for instance, that historians considered pictures sources of historical evidence, perhaps because in the nineteenth century images could not yet enter into the shaping of events.

Anxieties about the overflow of images and their impact on the world started only in the late nineteenth century and were later in coming than anxieties about information. Few people worried much about the proliferation of pictures until the development of mass amateur photography.⁴⁷ The first box camera came in 1888, and Eastman started marketing rolls of celluloid film in 1889. Quick and easy handheld cameras led to a boom in popular photography, and quicker shutter speeds enabled unposed shots. Soon the tabloids were printing pictures of eminent people in unflattering poses.⁴⁸ Persistent academic legend has it that the first essay on the legal right to privacy, written by Samuel Warren and Louis Brandeis in 1890, was spurred because Warren, a Boston blueblood, was upset about the intrusiveness of social columns in the popular press. The proliferation of images meant not only their multiplication but also their intrusion into what Warren and Brandeis called "the sacred precincts of private and domestic life."⁴⁹

The image genie was out of the bottle and, like unruly facts, it would need containing. In coming chapters we will see how that happened and how it burst out of its bottle again in the late twentieth century. But for most of the nineteenth century images were still helpmeets. Photography had not yet taken on its history-making power.

Taming the Tide of Information in the 1870s: Three Takes

By the mid-nineteenth century, the popularization of the Enlightenment created huge anxieties about the public face of truth. Not everyone was content with the open spigot of fact, as the rest of this chapter shows. Certainly as early as the 1830s, and especially by the 1870s, cultural elites feared the uncontrolled flow of information. The spread of books, newspapers, and education had created whole groups of people who had bits and pieces of knowledge but lacked the discrimination to put them all together. Tolstoy was not alone in his complaint about "our conceited age of the popularization of knowledge—thanks to that most powerful engine of ignorance, the diffusion of printed matter."[50]

Others warned against unbridled empiricism: In 1830 John Herschel, the British inventor-scientist who would coin the terms *photograph* and *snapshot*, wrote, "We must never forget that it is principles, not phenomena—laws, not insulated independent facts—which are the objects of inquiry to the natural philosopher."[51] Whewell and Mill, as we have seen, played similar notes. What if the rush of "fact" spilled out of the riverbed, flooding the civilization or destroying the order of systematic learning? After all, as one popular writer said in the 1850s, each science needed "an immense number of facts."[52] And the rush seemed to get faster and faster, the flow ever more overpowering. The "vast" heap of "facts" forming "the body of the various sciences" was expanding with such "marvellous rapidity," it was reported in 1867, that there were getting to be too many facts to handle. This friend of science admitted that the job of learning them now seemed "appalling."[53]

This comment ushers us into the preoccupations of the post-Greeley generation. New metaphors came into play: facts as a rush and flood instead of a stately flow; knowledge threatening chaos instead of defeating it. Our cognitive lives were being led by a kind of sorcerer's apprentice, with all the facts dancing back and forth, slopping those buckets of water everywhere, wildly out of control. Knowledge had meant progress, and progress meant order, the gradual unlocking of secrets, both of nature and of the soul. Could learning now be morphing into a monster of disorder? Could it really be right that the number of facts was "appalling"?

Along with facts out of control, what if evil people stole those facts and brewed them for their own designs? Deception was the major anxiety bred by the mid-nineteenth century cult of copiousness. Snake oil salesmen, flimflam artists, painted ladies, confidence men, and nostrum-dispensing "doctors" presented themselves not as opposed to the growth of knowledge, but as possessing special access to it. They paid tribute to the culture of thick fact by couching their pitches in terms of the latest discoveries.[54] Barnum, of course, was a great example of this mode. His strategy was to create fields of undecidability where ordinary people could not tell whether to believe or doubt.

Of course there were some idealists who believed that cosmic order developed automatically. Thomas Hill, president of Harvard in the 1860s, thought that progress in science meant the universe could be read as a vast historical archive. In the night sky he saw "a living dance, in whose mazy track is written the record of all the motions that ever men or nature made. Had we the skill to read it, we should there find written every deed of kindness, every deed of guilt, together with the fall of the landslide, the play of the fountain, the sporting of the lamb, and the waving of the grass."[55] In the most apparently random events there lurked a cosmic design. "Order reigns in the universe," agreed the future US president James A. Garfield in 1869. Recent advances in statistics, he thought, confirmed that "the world is a cosmos, and not a chaos." His ontology of cosmic order went together with an epistemology of moral progress: "Light is itself a great corrective. A thousand wrongs and abuses that grow in the darkness disappear like owls and bats before the light of day."[56] The light of knowledge meant the liberation of humanity.

In consecutive years in the early 1870s, three projects appeared, each attempting to manage fact run rampant. They were far more effortful than Hill's cosmic record or Garfield's banishment of nocturnal creatures. They came from high-minded elites sometimes called mugwumps, concerned about the torrent of information spilling into the culture and celebrated by Greeley's populist vision. These cultural forms, all of them invented at this time, remained staples until the late twentieth century. None of these projects wanted to thin out the parade of facts being communicated to the public. Their energy went into keeping the thick rush of fact going while putting it in some order. If facts were celebrated almost without restraint in the antebellum period, after the Civil War several brakes and containers were invented.

In 1871 Little, Brown published a fat tome of just more than a thousand pages. If you'd told the publishers that this was a landmark event, that this book would be a prototype for countless imitators around the world and that its descendants would still reign supreme at the close of the twentieth century, they might have looked at you as if you were mad. There was nothing "pretty" or well written in this book. It was more a compilation than an original work. And the prose was as deadly dull as the title—*A Selection of Cases on the Law of Contracts*. This was the first legal casebook ever published. Its author was the new dean of the Harvard Law School, Charles C. Langdell.

Before the 1850s, reports of previous law were limited. Court reporters like the young Charles Dickens in England wrote out reports that could be published. The system did not place a premium on the flow of case law; instead, the law and facts were summarized very briefly. Yet by the 1850s and 1860s this system fell apart. The market revolution, first of all, pulled whole peoples into the capitalist vortex, dramatically increasing the amount of litigation. Second, the system of American federalism meant that dozens of jurisdictions had separate laws that might collide. Finally, in 1856 West Publishing Company opened for business, issuing the case law for the whole nation. Suddenly massive numbers of cases were available for perusal. By the end of the next decade some jurists were aghast at the proliferation of printed material. The sheer quantity of published case law confused lawyers and judges instead of helping them. How could anyone keep up with this tidal wave of legal print? Who could make sense of it all?

Langdell could. He said the most striking thing he encountered when trying to figure out how to teach law was "the great and rapidly increasing number of reported cases in every department of law." Yet while the specifics were multiplying, if law was considered a "science" there still were "principles and doctrines" that ordered the multiplying cases. *A Selection of Cases on the Law of Contracts* was simply page after dreary page of hundreds of cases. Like a Baedeker, and unlike twentieth-century legal casebooks, it avoided any prose that might help orient readers. Instead there were bare section headings (Mutual Consent, Consideration, Conditional Contracts), each followed by from thirty to almost two hundred pages of case law. He used the medium of print to combat excess printed materials, fighting fire with fire.

Langdell thought students learned basic principles by raw immersion in the particulars. But the casebook had a twist not found in a Baedeker. It was Langdell's particular cruelty to want students to figure out the principles for themselves. The particulars were put in order, with Langdell providing the frame. No explanation. No hints. Just the incessant drone of legal opinion. This was a new compromise—the thick flow of fact remained important, students were still supposed to wade through it, but an organizer built the order they were supposed to intuit. Selection was the key.

The next year a group of entrepreneurs put up money to introduce a magazine having the same properties as Langdell's casebook. This was *Popular Science Monthly*, another mugwump effort to popularize knowledge. The editor was the social Darwinist Edward Livingston Youmans, fresh off a European tour during which he met a who's who of scientists and proposed international cooperation in scientific publishing.[57] Sometimes called the John the Baptist of science, Youmans was in love with the exploding production of knowledge but feared that its diffusion was "very imperfectly organized." The newspapers did much good in informing the American public about science, he thought, but they were hit or miss. And while nearly every school now covered a "little science," such teaching was generally superficial.[58]

While Langdell worried that the explosion of case law might bring on chaos, Youmans worried that the spread of half-knowledge might open space for deception and evil. Telling the story of a flimflam artist who visited Peoria, Illinois, Youmans reported that this "stranger and Yankee" turned up claiming he had discovered a mix of water and oil with seemingly magical properties. Nine gallons of the brew would "run a steam-engine for thirty days, heat twelve furnaces, or light a whole city with gas." Needless to say, the promoter claimed it could be done at a fraction of current costs. The town leaders bought it. After all, why shouldn't it be true in this century when there was even a machine that could make pictures of people! A joint-stock company was duly set up, but it lasted only long enough for the hoax to be discovered and the "inventor" to disappear, as Youmans sarcastically put it, to "enlighten and warm some other region."

Half-knowledge had consequences. *Popular Science Monthly* started publishing in May 1872 to fight this problem by presenting the latest research "to the generally-educated classes." It promised not only a "mass of the simpler facts," which after all were just the building blocks of science, but also help in cultivating "scientific judgment," a talent that might save the public from the bigger frauds coming down the pike. These two functions—copious accumulation and instruction in how to filter the informational dross—capture the mugwump tweak of the project of managing the information tide. Youmans aimed to enable the progress that comes through discovery. He stated his faith in two words: "Knowledge grows."[59]

In the following year still another cultural landmark underscored the new tone. In the fall of 1873, a young product of the densely evangelical "burned-over district" in western New York was working in the college library in Amherst, Massachusetts. It was here that Melvil Dewey, still an undergraduate, invented his famous system for organizing books on library shelves. Dewey aimed not to reduce the material that flowed to the public, but to organize it in some useful, practical way.[60] It was part of his more general mission of saving labor. Born "Melville," he changed his name to "Melvil" as part of his interest in spelling reform. For a while he also tried "Dui" but gave up when his employers at Columbia University Library refused to recognize the spelling. He was also, predictably, a staunch advocate of the metric system, believing that American schoolchildren lost years in learning English spelling and weights and measures. Nothing in Dewey's biography suggests that he worried unduly about either chaos or cheats. He was simply a problem solver, an improver.

Previously most libraries had stored books in rough order of acquisition rather than by author, title, or subject. This meant that only a librarian familiar with the history of the library or a reader intimately acquainted with literature would be able to find books in this system based on seniority. Dewey's system made searches transparent to everyone, opening up the stacks and allowing readers to search by subject, with no prior knowledge of authors or titles. Like business innovations of the late nineteenth century such as the mail-order catalog, his system was designed to increase circulation.[61] His library classification system divided knowledge into classes (by hundreds), divisions (by tens), and sections (by ones). Its genius was that a call number told both what the book was about and where it was shelved. The Dewey decimal system entailed a complete redo of the architecture of libraries. There were nine great classes, special libraries as he called them, plus one—the 000s— that was left open for "generalities."

Dewey did not divide the world as we would today, showing the time-bound character of containers of knowledge. The 200s, devoted to "theology," left only the 290s for "non-Christian religions." The 400s on "philology" included only European languages, and the 800s on literature similarly left only the 890s for "other languages." Neither theology nor philology would rank among the top nine domains of knowledge today, nor would knowledge be so ethnocentrically conceived, if anyone even dared try to organize everything into a single scheme. The most ambitious bibliographic agent of our time, Google, lacks the slightest pretense of organizing the contents of the internet library. Unlike Dewey, Google is all index and no shelving, all finding and no filing. Google searches say nothing about what data center holds a given document or what paths the confluence of bits took to come together on your screen; its aim is not to enlighten ordinary people about the underlying structure of the internet but to deliver information to users while mining the data users unwittingly provide.

Dewey's effort to organize all knowledge into a single system was part of the no longer widespread faith that facts might be ordered in the same way that living beings fell into taxonomies. But the Dewey decimal system lived on into a very different era. In the next century, while research libraries gravitated to the Library of Congress classification, which developed a few decades later, Dewey's system was still the norm in public libraries. In the 1960s I learned the Dewey system in Oak Lawn, Illinois, and in Chicago. Today my children have learned it in their public library in Iowa City, Iowa.

Dewey knew his scheme was not philosophically rigorous: "Theoretical harmony and exactness has been repeatedly sacrificed to the practical requirements of the library."[62] He was responding to a crisis. Books were piling up at the Library of Congress and elsewhere, and they needed to be organized. Like Linnaeus and the French encyclopedists, he knew that a practical system might occasionally have to sacrifice rigor.

Dewey's system met an urgent need. Some, like Walt Whitman, celebrated the abundance of print for its democratizing spirit: "Everybody reads, and truly nearly everybody writes."[63] Piles of newsprint could be quickly reabsorbed into the ecologies of daily life, but it was a different story for institutions interested in long-term archiving. In 1876 the Harvard Library—then as now the biggest university library in the country—had 227,000 volumes. (Compare that with about 17 million volumes today.)[64] Ordering the collection was a problem even at more modest institutions, but it was particularly acute at the Library of Congress. The Copyright Act of 1870 required that two copies of every book published in the United States be deposited in the Library of Congress. (Publishers today still submit the two copies to two distinct addresses, separated by two zip codes. If books are misaddressed they can, as a recent publisher warns in a memo, "be lost forever until the end of time.")[65]

The Copyright Act led both to the growth of the modern Library of Congress and to unprecedented accumulation. In a speech given on the Senate floor in 1879, Senator Daniel Voorhees, a Democrat from Indiana and an advocate for a renovated Library of Congress, painted a grim picture. Lack of space had left 95,000 volumes out of the Library's total of 375,000 scattered on the floor, in corners, nooks, and unknown places. It was as if Diderot's fear of a library as confusing as the universe had come true. The constant shuffling of homeless books damaged them. Even worse, there was no space for the 120,000 pamphlets and 6,000 bound volumes of newspapers, some of them complete runs going back to the eighteenth century, which were "mostly packed together like dry goods in a crowded store, one piece on top of another." Maps and charts, "a huge fund of knowledge," were heaped about like so much leather, their intelligence of no use to anyone. This disorder was a national "reproach and a shame," said Vorhees, inasmuch as "the principal value of a library consists in the readiness with which you can find what you want."[66] (Voorhees was instrumental in securing the library its first dedicated building, now known as the Thomas Jefferson Building, which was finished in 1897.)

The Dewey decimal system was invented to sort knowledge. The system was porous, but it was not intended to be. A piece of crank history could get filed alongside Gibbon. Trashy novels were a problem for nineteenth-century librarians. If Dewey didn't worry about chaos or cheats, he did worry about quality. He fought against including "sloppy" and "vulgar" books in libraries. He wanted to raise standards, to keep only the most solid knowledge on the shelves. He saw his mission, and the "proper" use of his classifying system, as redrawing the line between the formal and the whimsical. He was fighting one kind of promiscuous knowledge. He was not only a technocrat coping with quantity but also a cultural arbiter deciding quality. He disciplined the thick flow of knowledge but also ensured that it would continue to swell.

The decade of the 1870s was remarkable for its efforts to clean up a world increasingly messy with loose bits of fact. Montgomery Ward sent out the first mail-order catalog in 1872—at a single page, a mere shadow of things to come. The *Congressional Record* was established in 1873 as a supposedly verbatim transcript of the proceedings of each legislative day in both houses. It superseded several competing publications staffed by independent reporters who paraphrased whatever they thought of interest. The first Chautauqua—an outdoor adult education movement that combined elements of religious revival, circus, lyceum, and fair— was held in upstate New York in 1874 and served as a medium of popularization in America through the 1920s. The International Postal Union was founded in 1875. Brigadier General Henry Martyn Robert first published *Pocket Manual of Rules of Order for Deliberative Assemblies* in 1876, devoted to regulating parliamentary discussion, and it still governs the procedures for many meetings today. Johns Hopkins, the first American research university, was founded in Baltimore in 1876, modeled on the University of Berlin. In 1879 Oxford University Press agreed to publish *A New English Dictionary on Historical Principles*, the vastest accumulation of words ever undertaken. "A thousand readers are wanted," wrote James Murray, the founding editor of what became known as the *Oxford English Dictionary*, in a call for an early massive distributed research network.

This moment of infrastructural innovation included management not only of information but also of space, time, and matter. The Russian chemist Dmitri Mendeleev conceived the periodic table in 1869, simultaneously with several lesser-known scientists. (The index card was one sorting device Dewey and Mendeleev had in common.) In the

1870s the Canadian engineer Sandford Fleming started his campaign to organize the globe into time zones, a system established at an international conference in 1884. The first International Meteorology Congress met in Vienna in 1873 to discuss a global weather-observing network. Barbed wire, a container technology essential for domesticating late nineteenth-century frontiers in America and elsewhere, was patented in its final form in 1874. The time capsule, a literal container of unruly information for a future point, was invented in 1876.[67] Thus began the era characterized by Robert Wiebe as "the search for order," an age, as he noted, that "could only be comprehended in bulk."[68]

Misgivings about Copious Culture

Not everyone in the 1870s liked populist bulk. Nervous elites such as Charles Eliot Norton, James Russell Lowell, and E. L. Godkin all moved away from an earlier interest in the spread of knowledge. Refining taste was far more important than spreading information. High culture among elites was one way to reduce the relevant flow. Reading classics would manage the cornucopia of information.[69]

Norton, professor of art history at Harvard from 1875, for instance, complained in "A Definition of the Fine Arts" (1889) that the increasing number of poets and artists in American society was something "rather to be deprecated than encouraged." A recent volume of British poetry was "an intolerable deal of sack to every half-pennyworth of bread." Even though some good had come with "the wide diffusion of intelligence in the community and the vast mental activity implied by its material progress," it was still clear to him that "the nobler elements of the life of the imagination do not abound in it." He feared that the diffusion of intelligence raised the quantity but lowered the quality. Like many others before and since, he saw himself as a lonely voice in a materialist America forgetful that the fine arts were "the only real test of the spiritual qualities of a race."[70]

From a very different point on the compass, Anthony Comstock enacted another device for managing the profusion of data flows in the 1870s: surveillance and censorship. Norton worried about bad taste; Comstock worried about diffusion itself. In 1872 he founded the New York Society for the Suppression of Vice. "The Act for the Suppression of Trade in, and Circulation of, Obscene Literature and Articles of Immoral Use" of 1873, later known as the Comstock Act, gave the Post Office special powers of search and seizure and made him a special agent in it (a position he occupied until 1915). The act targeted perhaps the most important medium of diffusion in the nineteenth century—the post office.

To be sure, Comstock didn't so much invent a categorizing technique of lasting importance as fortify the rich American tradition of prurient prudery.[71] He aimed to serve as a gatekeeper of content. The mugwumps worried about the promiscuous mixing of the serious and the fraudulent, but Comstock's anxiety was promiscuity itself, something he saw embodied in the post office's endless circulation of illicit materials. He had no confidence in lay judgment: "Let the nude be kept in its proper place, and out of reach of the rabble." He wasn't worried so much that a dime novel might nestle next to Shakespeare as that vices could run rampant through the mail. Comstock did not want to control the flow of information, he wanted to cut it off. There were certain kinds of knowledge he didn't want anyone to have, certainly not the young. He was horrified at information and images out of control, "the natural harvest of seed sowing of corrupt publications and pictures."[72] New media often provoke repressive reactions.

Comstock wanted to stop the hemorrhage altogether, but mugwump editors, museum curators, and educators continued to support the thick and copious flow of information, guided and organized by their own capable hands. They were interested in passing knowledge along to outsiders. Langdell spoke to apprentices or the public, not to lawyers or judges. *Popular Science Monthly* was for the interested amateur, not the professional scientist. The Dewey decimal system aimed to give any reader a synoptic view of a library's holdings at a single glance. A year after Adolph Ochs bought the *New York Times* in 1896, the motto "All the News That's Fit to Print" came onto the masthead. It almost perfectly reflected mugwump ideas about the dissemination of knowledge. While most commentary over the years has focused on the first three words ("All the News"), just as important are the last four, which express elite efforts to mediate knowledge at the same time it was disseminated. The key contact point was with nonexperts. This was a communication problem: the faith was that orderly diffusion would secure truth.

Perhaps the clearest articulation of the doctrine of how to channel the thick culture of fact came from Spencer's American disciple, sociologist Lester Frank Ward. Writing in the 1880s, he argued that universal laws should keep the spread of facts under control. He complained that academic specialists could hoard facts in the same way rich people hoarded money, as if casting a sideways glance at the grotesque disparities of wealth in the Gilded Age. Such specialists forgot the purpose for acquiring facts in the first place—intellectual growth and organization.

"An accumulation in excess of one's powers to systematize may constitute an impediment to progress," he wrote. The best research would discover overarching principles that united the sciences instead of getting
bogged down in heterogeneous details. All students, he thought, should
learn the scientific method, which he considered an "irresistible weapon
of knowledge and material prosperity."[73] The flow of information remained thick to allow for the best of the democratic system—personal
judgment. But now there were arbiters who would protect the system,
filter the facts, so that errant judgments would not stray far from the
truth.

Museums

A final place to see the art of comprehending in bulk is the new culture of ordered informational abundance in museums. After Barnum's
museum burned to the ground in 1865 in a spectacular fire, the first of
several fires to ruin his underinsured edifices, the *Nation* criticized it
for failure to serve the "thousands of these earnest amateur students"
who eagerly sought out knowledge of natural science without the benefit of formal schooling. The museum was too much of a welter of oddities "without scientific arrangement, without a catalogue, without at-
tendants, without even labels." The jumble of oddities that might have
charmed aristocrats in the seventeenth century was not appropriate for
the democrats of the nineteenth. The *Nation* went on to call for a real
museum—"a place of public instruction as well as of public enjoyment,"
perhaps to be located somewhere near Central Park, as if anticipating
the American Museum of Natural History.[74]

The *Nation*'s complaints mark a shift in the vision and mission of later
Victorian museums. The 1870s and 1880s were the takeoff moment for
American museums, thanks to a widespread bourgeois desire to upgrade
educational institutions, boosters' dreams of creating cities to rival
those of Europe, and the obscene piles of newly accumulated capital in
the bank accounts of the wealthiest urbanites. The call for abundance in
collection but order in arrangement lay behind the post–Civil War wave
of museum foundings: the American Museum of Natural History (1869)
and Metropolitan Museum of Art (1870) in New York City, the Museum
of Fine Arts in Boston (1870), the Philadelphia Museum of Art (1876), and
the Art Institute of Chicago (1879). The wave moved west to places like
San Francisco in the 1890s and continued throughout the early decades
of the twentieth century. Compared with later tastes, these museums
were thick with images and objects; the culture of happy summary (see

Sidebar 2.5 Department Stores, Remote and Proximate

Gina Giotta

The late nineteenth century saw the rise of the department store in the United States: Macy's in New York, Marshall Field's in Chicago, Wanamaker's in Philadelphia. The techniques of display and philosophy of exhibition they used were close to those of museums, though perhaps even more invested in visual appeal. (Marshall Field and John Wanamaker were both active in museums as well.) The aim was to entice women with both luxurious fantasies and creature comforts (such as an attentive sales staff, escalators, and nice bathrooms—some of the first public facilities designed especially for women). The store's invitation to "browse" but not necessarily buy rested on techniques of display designed to make looking both easy and fun. In this way the department store shopper was akin to the museumgoer and the tourist in being encouraged to look at a surplus of sights and be instructed and delighted by their cumulative force.

Department stores were designed as places of visual delight—as "dream worlds," in the words of Rosalind Williams. They were stages for a democratic form of decorative art designed to lure rather than to last.[1] Electric lights were deployed to good effect starting in the 1880s, and mirrors expanded the space (and also helped staff keep an eye on potential shoplifters.) Shoppers were supposed to conduct themselves with an attitude of respectfulness, just as the staff was well mannered and well groomed. The prices were fixed, eliminating the need for haggling, previously a given in dry goods shopping. Further blurring lines, some department stores even displayed works of art. Wanamaker, an avid collector, had strong ideas about how to hang paintings (not too many at once!).[2] The goods amassed were meant to be educational in their own way. Customers could assess goods on their own, echoing Greeley's call that things should be "adjudged by competent persons," but they also had access to the expert advice of the staff on hand.

1. Rosalind H. Williams, *Dream Worlds: Mass Consumption in Late Nineteenth-Century France* (Berkeley: University of California Press, 1991).

2. This paragraph is based on Neil Harris, "Museums, Merchandising, and Popular Taste: The Struggle for Influence," in *Cultural Excursions: Marketing Appetites and Cultural Tastes in Modern America* (Chicago: University of Chicago Press, 1990), 56–81.

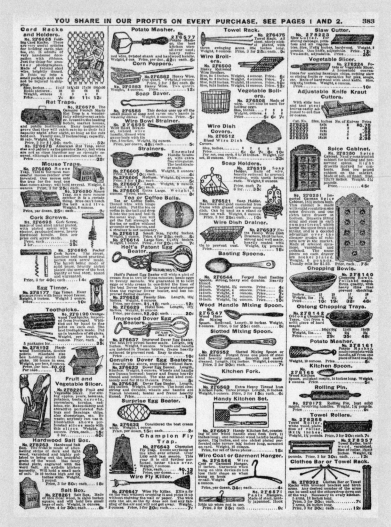

FIGURE 2.6. Vintage kitchen utensils in the Sears, Roebuck catalog, 1907.
Courtesy of Julie at the Old Design Shop.

As a print-based analogue of the department store for more isolated rural people, the Sears catalog showed off its vast wares in mass-
produced pages rather than glass display cases. Like its more stationary urban counterpart, the catalog swelled with images of everything
from bicycle whistles and ear trumpets to iceboxes and clip-on bangs. It
claimed to offer everything for the home and everyone in it, and it could

ship any trinket in its sweeping inventory. As one 1898 advertisement had it, the catalog was "a vast department store boiled down, so that you can sit down at your desk or table in your own home, and select just such goods as you want, and everything is made so plain by large, hand-some, clear illustrations, plainly written descriptions and prices in plain figures."[3] (The same arguments have been made for shopping online.)

For most of the catalog's rural readers, the crude lithographs that populated its pages offered a first glimpse of a new and abundant con-sumer culture growing up in city centers around the nation. As an illus-trated encyclopedia of consumables, the "book of bargains" was at once a throwaway catalog and a coveted visual reference book of the world. It promoted the consumption of goods but also—and perhaps more significantly—of images. By the turn of the century, when it sur-passed Montgomery Ward as the nation's largest mail-order business, Sears was effectively distributing more images to more people across the nation than any other single source. It stripped away the department store aura of glamour and exoticism and instead placed its bets on abun-dance—a strategy that by 1892 found the catalog dedicating 140 pages to watches alone. If the world was filling up in the nineteenth century, its contents were brought together by Sears in all their stupefying variety. Toothpicks, rolling pins, egg timers, oblong chopping boards—here was copious culture in all its miscellaneous glory.

3. "How Goods Are Ordered by Mail," *Black Cat* 37:xix.

chapter 3) stands between us and them. But compared with antebellum museums, they were meant to instruct rather than to dazzle or stupefy the average viewer.

Later nineteenth-century museums were, as Steven Conn argues, organized around the notion that knowledge was embodied in objects. Curators understood the world as imbued with an order that might be uncovered by classifying things. The characteristic Victorian museum display belonged to what Conn calls an "object-based epistemology." Mu-seums were packed with rows of glass display cases, as in the quotation above about the Athens museum in *Baedeker's Greece*. They could be filled with dozens of variations on a particular object gathered from around the world, each item marked with a distinguishing label. The particu-lar objects could be almost anything—fly, fish, hammer, hat. What was important was the classification. The row aesthetic—cases and cases of specimens displayed in row upon row—was meant to reveal the stories embedded in objects to untrained observers in what Conn calls "naked eye science." Museums aspired to be nothing less than encyclopedias of the world's evolution.

One of Conn's more intriguing insights is that late nineteenth-century museums were sites for new knowledge to be *made* as well as displayed. Curators felt that museums were places for research, where new orderings would take shape; their institutions actively competed with universities as sites of knowledge creation. In other words, museums were far more important to the culture than they are at present. In the contest for knowledge, the universities won. Knowledge came to be seen as embodied in books, not things. And museums came to be seen at best as popularizers of knowledge or at worst as hopelessly out of touch with the latest research. The museum has since become a place for the transmission, not the production, of knowledge, with all the dangers that involves.

Later Victorian museums put a premium on the proliferation of objects, but they aimed to make the eye into an organ of knowing rather than of delectation or dazzlement. If today we reflexively categorize visual culture as seductive, attitudes in late nineteenth-century museums were strikingly different. Those Victorian display cases were sober, responsible, and to our eyes resolutely boring. Attention to visual demonstration had very different implications then than now. Museum-goers today still occasionally run across leftovers of this system of glass cases and rows. Modes of presentation we now view as dusty and dull were at the time avant-garde strategies of display based on a vision of what knowledge was.[75]

Consider an 1874 natural history curator who thought decoration such as rocks or flowers in a display of birds a waste of precious space. "Artistic grouping of an extensive collection is usually out of the question. . . . Birds look best on the whole in uniform rows, assorted according to size, as far as a natural classification allows."[76] Not yet having resolved the problem of off-site storage, museums had a high display-to-holdings ratio, without aesthetic packaging. The copious style of museum presentation had affinities with the cabinet of curiosities in its overwhelming abundance. But if the cabinet of curiosities was blissfully miscellaneous, rows of specimens were meant to echo "natural classification." The copious style was a loose synthesis of baroque and neoclassical modes of ordering knowledge, many unique objects plus principles of knowledge. Even in museums of fine art, creating a pleasing visual effect was not a prime concern. Paintings crowded each other on the walls with little background space, often in several rows atop each other in a way that looks immeasurably busy to our eyes.

The copious museum style would start to give way in the early twentieth century. Curators, as we will soon see, wanted to relieve visitors' eyes and minds and present them with an attractive summary of knowledge. The dominant mode of knowing throughout the nineteenth century—the celebration of heaps of fact left open for democratic assortment and absorption—was slowly running out of steam.

* 3 *

The Culture of Happy Summary,
1920–45

In the early twentieth century, particularly from 1920 to 1945, one very important strategy for managing facts was the effort to summarize complex wholes with a single image, number, example, graph, or minimum of words. This is what we term the culture of happy summary. Abridgment, in all its forms, was seen as an antidote to information overload. We call it "happy" because of the sense that nothing significant was lost by these abridgments, that they merely crystallized denser truths. And this culture of summary was a crucial means through which mid-twentieth-century mass culture constituted itself. Without summary, a self-conscious mass culture cannot exist. This culture included both pictures (treated in the next chapter) and modes of information (treated here). It can be contrasted with the late twentieth century, sometimes called the "information age," when larger cultural summary became suspect (treated in chapters 5 and 6).

We generally think of the years between the wars as brimming with ever-increasing masses of information. From the 1920s to the 1940s, however, American cultural arbiters made a full-scale effort to cut *down* the amount of information passed to the public. This is different from the later nineteenth-century effort to *channel* the flow. Victorian attitudes toward the dissemination of knowledge eroded significantly. Both the populist vision of people like Horace Greeley and the mugwump vision of well-ordered knowledge of *Popular Science Monthly* or Melvil Dewey fell on hard times. Increasingly, the facts came to be distrusted as too unruly, too ready to exceed our categories—even as more facts were called for. Increasingly, there were experiments with new ways to address the public. The thick culture of fact and process gave way to something new.

The culture of happy summary aimed to relieve ordinary people of the burden of sorting. In the 1880s, Lester Ward argued that there were only two ways we could get smarter. We could wait for the brain to evolve, which would take centuries, or we could accumulate facts and organize them into larger frameworks. In the short run, for him there was simply no other option. Ward argued that every citizen should learn to be a scientist by understanding experimental inquiry from the inside out. By the early years of the twentieth century, science had grown so much more complicated that this advice had become unrealistic. Quantum physics, for instance, was anything but intuitively available to common sense. The new popularization was a rejection of Ward's Victorian assumptions about the everyday accessibility of scientific knowledge. Not everyone could follow the technical details. We would get smarter not by cramming our heads with scientific truths but by reducing the information flow. The emphasis was on what classical rhetoricians called *exempla* rather than *copia*—vivid instances instead of stacks of evidence. Insight came through pruning, not bulking up.

As early as the 1890s a few intellectuals were complaining about the untamed overflow of information and the culture's inability to order or contain it. Karl Pearson and Henry Adams were two examples. Pearson, a British biometrician, invented new statistical techniques to manage masses of information, and Adams, an American historian and man of letters who wrote that he had had his "historical neck" broken by the new accumulations of energy and power, sought a law of acceleration to explain it all. German sociologist Georg Simmel similarly worried about how modernity exacerbated the perennial gap between "objective" and "subjective" culture—between how much material was available and how much an individual could know or experience.[1] Such complaints about information explosions mushroomed over the next decades. By the 1920s they had become common. Indeed, the popularity of Adams's *Education* in the twenties (in 1907 it was privately printed in only a limited edition) was one sign of the sense that "the facts" were getting out of control.

None of these complaints aimed to get rid of an information culture. Indeed, the 1920s and 1930s were real growth years in the production of statistical knowledge. Economic information in particular exploded during those decades. Information on things like gross national product and national unemployment appeared for the first time.[2] Intellectuals felt very comfortable with the growth of knowledge. Walter Lippmann was not alone when he called for information bureaus to help shape public discussion in the United States.

It was not opposition to amassing information that was new but the growing sense of its complexity. The cliché of "complexity" was not new at the time, of course. It has been around perhaps forever, and it certainly was common in the latter half of the nineteenth century. The world seemingly is always getting more "complex." But that assertion has different consequences at different times. In the nineteenth century, despite scattered worries that knowledge and information might be out of control, the charge of "complexity" did not translate into a new approach to public communication or a new attitude toward popularization. The thick flow of fact featured accumulation without being overwhelming. But in the early twentieth century it did feel overwhelming. This change took decades but was centered in the 1920s and 1930s.

What was new was the belief that complexity had to be streamlined. Information was to be handled differently than before. A wide variety of figures, most of whom might disagree on much else, began to argue that the mass of empirical data had to be boiled down for the public, simplified into a core. What William James called "the blooming, buzzing confusion" of sensory experience was so complicated that information had to be packaged not in all its confusing details but as a distilled essence. A striking image might capture a social totality. The ancient rhetorical trope of synecdoche—the part for the whole, "sail" standing in for the ship—became the preferred device to minimize the crush of information and display truth to the public. The dominant mode of popularization shifted from dense particularity to summaries of conclusions.

Cognitive shorthand was taken not only as legitimate, but as necessary. The notion of "stereotype," invented by Lippmann in 1922, at first did not imply a negative generalization about other people. It was a potentially useful epistemic shortcut, a way to slash through the thick brush of sensation; it was a notion that clearly owed something to the pragmatism of James, with whom Lippmann studied at Harvard. Gestalt psychology, whose heyday was the 1930s and 1940s, made summary into one of the basic acts of the human mind. Kurt Koffka opened his *Principles of Gestalt Psychology* (1935) by complaining about scientists' overreliance on fact-finding. His introduction included an eight-page polemic against "facts." There had to be a coherent theory to sum it all up, he argued. His now discredited "law of Prägnanz" claimed that the tendency to grasp information simply and elegantly was biologically rooted. We could grasp wholes as well as parts: wholes were themselves perceptible. No less than in Einstein's physics, our eyes and ears operated in "fields." The central argument of Gestalt psychology, that we grasp things as wholes and not by accumulating particulars, is a summary of the culture of summary itself.

The story of early twentieth-century culture is often told as one of cultural fragmentation. There were the breakthroughs of quantum physics, Fauvism and cubism, montage in cinema, psychoanalysis, and air travel, and there was the dull, grinding chaos of the trenches in World War I. It was unquestionably a period of tremendous dislocation. But it was also a period that invented new "shock absorbers," as Lewis Mumford called them, for coping with the assaults of modern life.[3] This chapter tells how fragmentation and anxiety were dealt with through new techniques of simplification and summary. Modernity is not only the breaking up of culture, but its consolidation into digestible packets and summaries. Streamlining is as important a theme as fragmentation.

Summarizing Popular Knowledge: Print

It is amazing to see the variety of places a move to summary surfaced in the 1920s and 1930s. One source was a series of new approaches to the popularizing of science and medicine. Whereas nineteenth-century popularization tried to discuss a science "systematically," a rising tide of complaints suggested that systematic knowledge was not what people were getting. The editor of *Modern Medicine* argued in 1920 that knowledge of science among the general populace was "fragmentary, unrelated, and, for the most part, acquired through spectacular accounts of the Sunday newspaper." Clearly not all summary was good! Such disconnected reporting of science information had contradictory results, leading the public to a sort of "mysticism" about science and "the absence of any definite knowledge."[4]

Instead of centering on process and system, the emphasis would be on results. Here was no dream à la Lester Frank Ward of making every citizen a scientist. Instead, the public should be given the practical cash value of science. As science itself appeared to be more and more complex and confusing to the layperson, scientific popularizers increasingly reported on applied science. The same was true of medicine. As John Burnham notes, during the 1930s "popularizers tended to shift from diffusing systematic knowledge to teaching about the products and consequences of medical science."[5] The move to summary, aesthetic exemplum, and synecdoche was *not* done in the name of getting rid of modern scientific culture; they most often worked in tandem.

Another expression of this shift could be found in legal culture. While not an immediate concern to the general public, there was the growing fear that the legal system was being overwhelmed by case law. The explosion of published cases was making it hard for lawyers to keep up. Again, the particulars were becoming so numerous that they threatened order. According to Elihu Root, "the confusion, the uncertainty was growing from year to year." This was the same problem Langdell had tried to solve in the 1870s, but the 1920s had a different answer. The American Law Institute was created in 1923, dedicated to compiling "Restatements of the Law." Instead of providing the raw material, as Langdell had done, committees of notable attorneys summed up (or "restated") the basic principles of contracts, torts, and so on, reducing the empirical complexity of case law by creating generalizations for lawyers to consult. The restatements were enormously influential in following decades.[6] The American Law Institute synthesized and summarized; Langdell's casebook put all the originals in one place with only the barest guidance.

Another striking example was the appearance, during those decades, of what was called "interpretive reporting." Interpretive reporters questioned the assumption that thick loads of information were vital to public information, an assumption central to journalists as different as Greeley and various nineteenth-century editors of the *New York Times*. Instead, interpretive reporting emphasized summary. In 1931 the *New York Sun* changed its weekend format by producing summaries of news instead of fact reporting. This launched a trend. In the next years the *New York Times, Washington Post*, and Associated Press were among those following suit. Herbert Brucker, in *The Changing American Newspaper* (1937), argued that "the increasing complexity of the world" made the new reporting imperative. Facts by themselves were just confusing. Interpretive context was necessary.[7]

One of the harbingers of the new style was *Time*, first published in 1923. *Time*'s publisher, Henry Luce, certainly believed that the "complexity" of modern life opened a niche for the new magazine. The jauntiness of *Time*'s prose, a trademark for decades, was designed to mark a sharp contrast with information-dense papers. Luce hoped that his news magazine would be a concise and breezy summary of the news for busy people in a busy world. *Time* was not a compilation of objective facts, which Luce didn't believe in anyway. He aspired to offer an interpretive picture of the whole. It was one early twentieth-century response to the nagging of confusion and overload. Gardner Cowles Jr., the Iowa publisher who launched *Look* magazine in 1937, reflected that "the most notable publishing successes of the last decade have all been publications which condensed their contents more than their predecessors." He was thinking of *Reader's Digest, Time,* and the *New York Daily News,* all of which he praised for abbreviating and thus improving "long-winded" material.[8]

Reader's Digest, launched by DeWitt Wallace and Lila Acheson Wallace in February 1922, was different from interpretive reporting but shared its spirit of information reduction. Digests of current writing were certainly nothing new; Benjamin Franklin started one in 1741 (it didn't last a year). *Littell's Living Age,* a weekly founded in 1844, helped nineteenth-century Americans navigate the thick flow of fact. What was new was the scale and success of the enterprise. Historian Daniel Boorstin says *Reader's Digest* ushered in "a new era of abridgements," spawning a host of imitators such as *Writer's Digest, Catholic Digest, Protestant Digest, Science Digest, Negro Digest, Children's Digest,* and even *Quick Digest.* It offered a service to the reader, not to the author, whose work could be mercilessly chopped. Its aim was to summarize the full cornucopia of print for busy readers. "It is not possible for the average busy person to read even a hundredth part of the best books, periodicals and journals, or to discern them readily in the mass of mediocre or worthless matter that comes pouring from the presses of America and Europe," noted a rival in 1930.[9] The Wallaces aimed to help people "in a fast-moving world" get at "the nub of the matter." A former editor called the magazine a "distillery" that "boils verbal water over a series of editorial flames until there's nothing left but the highest proof stuff."

Part of the periodical's selling point was the implication that the editors had searched high and low through all contemporary writing (though it would eventually resort to planting articles in other publications in order to claim them for digesting). It presented a reassuring panorama of everything you needed to know. Headlines would often ask questions forwarded by the article, while subheads would frequently answer them (in case you didn't want to read the whole thing). (A snide tone—as in the sentence you just read—has always been part of elite commentary about *Reader's Digest.*) One reporter described DeWitt Wallace as looking "at the universe constantly through the wrong end of the telescope. . . . He has no delusions of grandeur. He has, if anything, delusions of smallness."[10]

Even print advertising fell under the sway of deemphasizing information. This may seem a peculiar claim to make, since advertising long had powerful traditions of sleight of hand and fantasy inconsistent with the culture of fact. Yet there was always a competing "plain style" of advertisement, one that gave lip service to "just presenting the facts" so that consumers might make informed judgments. It was especially influential for a brief time early in the twentieth century. This was a textually dense style, full of prose explaining the superior virtues of a particular product. Not so much a part of earlier styles of popularizing knowledge as a simulation of them, these ads disappeared by the end of the 1920s. As historian Roland Marchand notes, "The cumulative experiences of a decade in radio had crushed the vision of advertising as a broad educative force." More seductive appeals to the flavor or essence of a product increasingly replaced elaborate word discussions.[11]

In literature too there were efforts to declutter. In 1922 Willa Cather called for housecleaning the novel, whose furnishings she found had grown to be overstuffed. A great drama, she argued, didn't need heaps of realistic details: it needed four walls and a great passion.[12] Modernist literature could be grand and synthetic—think of two works from 1922, T. S. Eliot's *The Waste Land* and James Joyce's *Ulysses*—but it had no patience for sustained description on a Victorian scale. It was leaner and jumpier.

The more utilitarian genre of the travel guide also deemphasized the stuffed-with-facts quality of its predecessors. In the 1920s Baedeker guides were described as "stuffy and unstimulating," not as "human" or as "exciting literature." Baedeker's "passion," one writer granted in 1922, was "for facts," but the thick flow of fact no longer provided sufficient orientation.[13] *The* American Guide series, started in 1935 by the Federal Writers' Project as part of the New Deal, was designed in opposition to the spirit of Baedeker. American Guide authors welcomed local color and photography, literary writing, and frankly promotional language. The Baedekers wrote about places like methodical taxonomists; the FWP authors aspired to write like poets. They spent their "waking hours on the hard, new job of getting all the relevant facts about a community into a few paragraphs or pages, of making sure that the facts were honest and accurate, of disciplining those facts so that they would march in order and tell a story."[14] The last thing the Baedekers did was "discipline" their facts; they simply piled them up. By the 1930s, a good guide had to cut through the clutter. It had to tell a story, hopefully with some poetry and pictures to sweeten the facts.

Various efforts to popularize literature and humanistic learning in the interwar years also reflect the larger trend. The Book of the Month Club, founded in the mid-1920s, hoped to reduce the confusion of so many books published by separating the wheat from the chaff. As a 1927 advertisement in the *New York Times Book Review* put it, "You know that, out of the thousands of books published, there are only a few you are interested in. You want the outstanding ones. But what are they?" The club would do the sorting for you. In 1930 the book publishing industry launched a campaign for middle-class households to acquire new equipment for managing print's proliferation: bookshelves, one of several innovations of the time meant to organize paper goods at home and the office.[15]

Print culture saw not only the simplifying of content but the streamlining of form. In journalistic design the twentieth century saw an enormous "aeration" of the newspaper page. Nineteenth-century print could be as dense and forbidding as a Baedeker guide. White space now became part of the layout. Visuals had been increasingly frequent from the 1880s, thanks to the rise of halftone printing, and typefaces became larger and bouncier, especially in the famous screaming headlines of the tabloid press.[16]

The material of printing itself—typography—was also subject to aerodynamic reform. Efficiency expert Frank Gilbreth, now remembered chiefly as the father in *Cheaper by the Dozen*, complained that the written alphabet was "full of absolutely useless strokes."[17] Designers of typefaces called for eliminating flourish and ornament. Though first designed in the 1830s, sans serif type had little currency until the 1910s, when it was used for the iconic signs of the London underground. After the First World War, Swiss and German typographers influenced by the Bauhaus movement adopted sans serif type. They liked it because it lacked any nationalist aura, matched the machine spirit of the age, and was clear and impersonal. Others followed in turn, including advertisers, who appreciated its readability for large-format letters. Serifs represented the outmoded, the bureaucracy, the dead past; sans serif type stood for modernity and speed.

Advocates of the new typeface gave several reasons for its superiority. A spelling reformist in 1914 saw abolishing serifs as a matter of health: "Being, as I suppose, survivals of the natural marks resulting from the entrances and exits of the writer's pen, they are now mere vestigial relics of organs long since disused—matter in the wrong place, harbouring the microbes of eye-strain headache and presbyopia."[18] Beauty was once the overriding factor in type design, said one artist in 1928. But now, "because of the manifold claims for our attention made by the extraordinary amount of print, which demands the greatest economy of expression," clarity was more important.[19]

Not everyone liked the plainer typography. In Germany in 1933 Joseph Goebbels outlawed sans serif type, calling it "a Jewish invention." He relented later when it became clear that the gothic Fraktur type he and other Nazis favored was hard to read on aircraft and in other military settings. Even the Nazi propaganda machine had to bow before the very modern pressure of quick reading under duress.

Summarizing Popular Knowledge: Museums

Museums were one of the most important places where the new attitude toward information appeared. During the first decades of the twentieth century, museums lost faith in the Victorian mission. They turned away from organizing their collections around objects. It became an axiom in advanced museum circles during the 1920s and 1930s that the amount of material presented to the public should shrink. The constant complaint was about overstocked displays in both art museums and museums of natural history. As we have seen, nineteenth-century art museums covered their walls with paintings, and museums of natural history laid out cases and cases of specimens next to each other; both can be seen in the 1822 watercolor by Titian Ramsay Peale of the museum maintained by his father, Charles Willson Peale. In both kinds of museums there was meant to be an abundance of particulars. Up to about 1870 in the United States, as noted in chapter 2, the museum was more a "laboratory of research" than a school or theater for the public; universities and museums once actively competed as sites of knowledge creation.[20] Popular visual appeal was left to advertisers and showmen. And although it was not until after World War II that the changes were in place, there was a long germination period in which Victorian display techniques were attacked; even by the late twentieth century, museumgoers could occasionally find remnants of the old copious system. At every point, the new culture of representative sampling led the attack. A curator at the Metropolitan Museum of Art in New York City summarized the shift in thinking in 1928: the exhibition as "a collection of static objects" was outmoded; instead, it was "the museum's task to train the eye."[21]

In reformist literature of the 1920s and 1930s, extant museums sound like an utter drag. They were "body wearying and soul stupefying" buildings designed for the sole delight of scientists with no thought given to the "average intelligent person," "casual visitors," or children. They were gloomy "tomb-like places" that left their visitors with a "limp-rag weariness." Museums were divorced from daily life, were useless as an "educational tool," and lacked a "friendly and helpful relation" to ordinary people. They should take a hint from libraries and movies. Public libraries were accessible, community-based, and staffed by people eager to share information, and they had made their peace with such diverse media as "journals, maps, pictures, pamphlets, clippings, music records, and movie films." They had started to explore the arts of visual instruction pioneered in movies. Visual delight in learning, some reformers concluded, should be exploited so that museums could rightly be called

FIGURE 3.1. Titian Ramsay Peale II, Interior Front Room of Peale's Museum, 1822. Detroit Institute of Fine Arts.

"Institutes of visual instruction." The museum, in short, "ought to be a place which would give a synopsis."[22]

In *Technics and Civilization* (1934), Lewis Mumford commented on shifting practices in museums of technology. The Conservatoire des arts et métiers in Paris he thought "a mere storehouse," and the Deutsches Museum in Munich was "exhaustive" (this was not a compliment), for its collections had "a little overreached themselves in bigness." In such a museum, Mumford thought, "one loses sight of the forest for the trees." On the other hand, he praised Chicago's new Museum of Science and Industry for its dramatic reconstruction of a working coal mine and thought the industrial museum of Vienna had "educational value without being overwhelming."[23] An American biologist on a tour of European anatomical museums in the same period shared Mumford's reaction: "I never saw such quantities of junk on exhibition in all my life. The museums over there remind one of Dickens' Old Curiosity Shop."[24] The friends of the new museum held no reverence for an abundance of objects. Rooms were less cluttered; dramatic simulacra and the telling example were favored. Too much information just confused people. Abridge the presentation artfully, make it lively, and all would be well.

Another impetus for streamlining museum displays came from industrial psychology. Psychologists in the 1920s and 1930s left few aspects of museums unstudied: they considered the glare and reflection of glass, labeling, lighting, layout, and traffic patterns, along with the nature of learning more generally. They measured the average time visitors spent before displays and the average number of displays they examined. By the 1930s they were convinced that the nervous system could not handle excessive stimulus. "Museum fatigue" was a real condition. Just as progressive educators led by John Dewey cautioned against rote memorization, museum curators argued against too many specimens or paintings. What they called for instead was thematic unity in presentation, a summary of the whole to replace the psychologically debilitating dependence on a multitude of examples. In this they anticipated the postwar focus on "stress" as a central factor in physical and mental health.[25]

As early as 1887 Franz Boas worried about the clutter and organization of ethnological museums. Such institutions generally organized their material typologically. Spindles from various cultures were put together, as were eating utensils, shoes, musical instruments, stools, and every other sort of artifact. To one Victorian curator, Otis Mason, this was logical, since so many people with so many specialized interests came to view the artifacts—soldiers, potters, musicians, artists. All these visitors "desire to see, in juxtaposition, the specimens which they would study." Exhibits had to be grouped to appeal to the "greatest diversity of mind."[26] Such attitudes well reflected the nineteenth-century sense of popularization. As much information as possible had to be presented to the public so that people could explore the matter for themselves without superintending guidance.

To Boas, however, such decontextualized groupings were a mess. He argued that exhibits should be organized by cultural origin. Each artifact had to be understood as part of a greater but particular whole. Museum exhibits should not be bundles of artifacts but should show the life of a single group. Tribal distinctiveness, according to him, might be shown by specially chosen artifacts. The part, in other words, might represent the whole.[27] Boas was turning toward a concept of what later anthropologists would call holism—the idea that every artifact or practice, whether a door lintel or a bride-price, should be understood within a unique cultural context.[28] This idea would dominate twentieth-century anthropology.

Boas's thinking about museums was transitional. He thought most museumgoers just wanted entertainment. To appeal to the majority, exhibits had to contain a few artifacts dramatically displayed, leaving such casual viewers with a single overriding message. Exhibits would contain less, but they would more carefully direct the visitor. Boas might have thought most viewers were casual and needed guidance, but he also saw the museum as a place where more serious scholars would do research. He himself had gotten insights from staring at clusters of artifacts at museums. This led to a tension between his desire to reduce the complexity of exhibits for the general public and a desire to have massive numbers of artifacts available for ethnologists to study. The collecting wave of ethnographic museums at the turn of the century further complicated this picture. At the American Museum of Natural History (AMNH), where Boas worked from 1896 to 1905, any chance of streamlining displays was defeated by the lack of storage space for new acquisitions. The new material continued to clutter the exhibit rooms.[29]

Boas's views were transitional in an even more important sense. His ideas about simplified organization did not take hold at the time, one of the reasons he left museum work in 1905. (He also felt somewhat overwhelmed between his two jobs at the Museum of Natural History and at Columbia University, where he was building the new field of anthropology in North America.) Indeed, one turn-of-the-century observer found it "somewhat revolutionary" to divide museums into two parts: an anthology for the public and copious matter for the scholar.[30] But for later generations this division would become routine. Research would hide from public display, just as public libraries would split from research libraries. The culture of representation would triumph.[31]

This was especially the case with museums of natural history. The shift toward the epitome and away from the array had begun as early as the 1890s, but the mid-1920s saw dramatic movement away from the rows of specimens that were the norm in the 1880s.[32] The new model was the diorama. The diorama blended a painted backdrop and other natural effects (grass, rocks, sand, depending on the setting) with taxidermy or models for the figures in the foreground. The combination was supposed to create a compelling, lifelike representation of animals or native peoples. Dioramas explicitly substituted dramatization for categorized specimens. They relieved spectators of the burden of sorting and sifting. They were exercises in popularization, not in firsthand research.

Dioramas started small in the late nineteenth century with people like Carl Akeley at the Field Museum of Natural History, then known as the Columbian Museum of Chicago. He was a taxidermist whose first break came when P. T. Barnum chose him to mount Jumbo after the elephant was killed by a locomotive in 1885. Akeley later made several expeditions to Africa, including one in the company of Theodore Roosevelt, and died there in 1926, possibly of the *Ebola* virus. He was a key mover in the popular display of natural history—and a villain for later critics of cultural summary (see chapter 5).

The long-awaited African Hall (1936) at the American Museum of Natural History in New York City was eventually named in Akeley's honor. This hall, along with the AMNH's Hall of Asian Mammals (1930), was a turning point in diorama technique. Instead of being placed in discreet corners, dioramas now dominated the hall. They could be one to two hundred feet wide, sometimes up to two stories (forty feet) tall, with lighting well calculated to add to the effect—suggesting light at different times of the day, for instance. The hall itself was dimly lit, and the light came from within the dioramas, so there was no glare on the windows. Dioramas had a documentary flavor but owed a lot to two other leading display techniques of the early twentieth century: the cinema and the shop window.[33] The animals were posed so as to show themselves to the viewers without acknowledging their presence. The image we present here from the Yale Peabody Museum of Natural History is typical in that the bears and seagulls deal with each other or their environment, not with the viewer; they decorously refuse to break the fourth wall. The scene is designed to be a day in the life, not a spectacular dramatic event. Actual rocks and tundra in the foreground blend almost seamlessly into the painted backdrop. Dating from the 1950s, the Yale diorama is in the second generation of the Akeley tradition and traces a direct lineage to artists working at the AMNH.[34]

The final chapter of John Rowley's *Taxidermy and Museum Exhibition* of 1925 was the turning point in theory. Rowley, who worked at the American Museum of Natural History and later at the Oakland and Los Angeles County Museums of Natural History, was an expert in taxidermy but even more of a genius at illusion. He set standards for animal poses: nothing dramatic. "Very clever illusions" he thought were better cultivated by "quiet attitudes" than by violent scenes of action and conflict. He believed the observer's eye should determine foreground composition and background space. Rowley eliminated the ceiling and aestheticized the diorama in a way no museum designer had done before. Better effects were gotten by oil-painted backgrounds than by photographic reproductions of the animals' habitats.[35] Dioramas were meant to provide visual delight and wonder—notions very, very absent from nineteenth-century museums.

Unlike rows of cases in earlier museums, the diorama was supposed to create a Gestalt, a larger sense of the animal's actual life. The old style, Rowley complained, presented the visitor with "a conglomeration of

FIGURE 3.2. "Alaskan Tundra," 1950s. Used with permission
of the Yale Peabody Museum of Natural History.

objects." Instead, "an exhibit must tell a story." Dioramas radically reduced the number of specimens. Creating an overall lifelike and dramatic picture was more important than providing lots of examples. A
diorama did not imply a classificatory schema that would cover related
specimens. Viewers were not left to their own devices but were guided
in their understanding. His aesthetic norm summarized the culture of
summary: "Simplicity should be the rule rather than the assemblage of
too great a variety of objects. . . . To get the best effect from any one thing,
it must be massed."[36] Prefabricated narrative rather than individual inquiry was the truly democratic mode.

By midcentury the change from bulk to story, from clutter to visual
delight was complete. The director of the AMNH could boast in 1951 that
the museum had left the old ways behind. "The natural history museum
used to be a cold and dusty place, poorly lighted, with a labyrinth of rows
and rows of glass cases full of Indian arrowheads, ancient iron imple-
ments, and beaver pelts, from its entrance to the exit." Now the museum
was "comfortably warm and well lighted" and was shifting its approach
"from amassing dead animals and artifacts" to showing living plants and
animals in interaction with their habitats.[37] The new ecological thinking that informs this statement was itself a kind of holistic summary, a
vision relevant both to natural systems and to display practices.

Summary also offered political advantages. Curators could be above the fray. Margaret Mead, who was associated all of her professional life with the AMNH, eventually becoming the curator of ethnology in 1946, thought museums could be as "value-free" as social science. They served a propaganda-weary public best by avoiding the tactics of promotion that had taken over many other institutions. "Because the staffs of Museums have insisted on saying: 'Is this true?' instead of asking: 'Will this make a hit?'—they have kept the people's trust." Visitors to museums could enjoy the democratic liberty of using their own senses. "For an hour or so they have been able to trust their eyes and let their minds rove over materials which have not been arranged to impress, to convert, to push them around, but merely to tell them as much of the truth as is now known, and that quietly." Mead combined the older ideal of do-it-yourself inquiry by individuals with confidence that an expert arrangement of materials could tell the truth with no ax to grind.[38] The culture of condensation at its best was an oasis between the screech of advertising and the thrum of political propaganda. Truth's foe was not representation but rather money and power.

The decluttering moved at a slower pace in art museums than in museums of natural history. In the 1920s they were still dominated by the nineteenth-century display aesthetic. But by the middle of the decade the same complaints were becoming a steady drumbeat. Rooms stuffed with paintings were increasingly decried as cluttered and shapeless. In 1926, for example, Forest Cooke attacked museum organization in the *Century Magazine*, complaining among other things that museums were devoted to the quantitative instead of the qualitative.[39] Cooke was one of a string of writers in the 1920s and 1930s who attacked art museums for being stuffy, old-fashioned, and out of touch. More dramatic visual display was called for. And the presentation of information was minimized.

All this was tied to the museum's job of educating the public. Since an art museum should "endow the uneducated with an abiding sense of the good, the beautiful and the true," one commentator noted in 1927, it should "not chronicle art as a fact but enact it as an event." Instead of five thousand examples of Japanese objects, for example, there might be a "Japanese room" dominated by one painting that set the theme and gave meaning to accompanying objects included as detail.[40] One idea was to create period rooms, an innovation of the 1920s. Period rooms would combine different arts (painting, furniture, tapestry, crafts) from a particular moment. Items were to be grouped not by similarity but by common historical origin, an analogue to Boas's ideas of holistic grouping by culture. Like the diorama, they were supposed to create a single mood. Another strategy was grand stylistic tours: paintings in the rococo period, followed by a neoclassical room, then a Romantic room, and so on. In general, the number of pictures on the walls of fine art museums declined. Modern curators began talking about having a central piece in a room to set the tone, with fewer pieces surrounding it to create a single ambiance.

When the Museum of Modern Art opened in New York City in November 1929, it adapted the new display aesthetic known as the "white cube" style. The museum set an international standard for exhibiting contemporary art. This was not the first time precious objects had been isolated from their surroundings for close viewing, but the white cube won a reputation as a uniquely modernist initiative. The ideal was plain white walls and a polished wood or carpeted floor, with evenly lit paintings hung in a single row with plenty of space between them. The feel was less of a plush sitting room than an austere artist's studio or a laboratory. It was to be a neutral, even sacred space for contemplating isolated works, set apart from the glare, decoration, and distractions of a materialistic consumer culture. Its design embodied the ideology of art as pure form rather than as historical or political document. The floor plan also played down contextual concerns by grouping works in a rough chronology rather than by national origin, as if to tell the story of modern art's autonomous unfolding according to its own inner logic. There was also a drive to reduce the biographical and historical information about the paintings. Visitors were encouraged to lose themselves in the art as such without the fuss of excess information. Artists called some of their works "untitled" for this very reason.[41]

One result of the influential research of Edward Robinson, a Yale psychologist, was the decision by a large number of art museums in the 1930s to move to a single row of paintings, matched to visitors' sight line. The modern visual display aesthetic reduced the number of paintings one was supposed to be exposed to. It also reduced the color stimulus. In 1870 a museum expert could confidently assert that "Pompeian red" was "the most agreeable of all hues as a background to pictures."[42] (This color is still found in museums such as the National Gallery in London.) By the 1920s, American art museums were turning to inconspicuous off-white backgrounds, which German museums had been using since the end of World War I. The broader world was being filled with ever increasing color—in plastics, schools, hospitals, factories. Technicolor brought color to movies in the 1920s and 1930s, most famously in *The Wizard of Oz* (1939), just as lacquer and enamel paints brought new colors to cars in the same period. The *Saturday Evening Post* had its first cover in color in

1926. But art museums turned away from all this.[43] White backgrounds helped differentiate museums from the rest of the culture.

Efforts to study and mollify the sensory barrage were not restricted to museums. In the factory, the discovery of the "Hawthorne effect" in the 1930s—that workers' productivity responds when a sense of community is created, even if it is the community of subjects in an experiment—was a serendipitous by-product of research on the sensory conditions of industrial labor, especially lighting. Industrial psychologists started the experiment by varying the sensory stimulus in the factory but discovered instead that social life has power to filter unpleasant conditions. This idea that team solidarity aids productivity would grow wings in later management theory, but the Hawthorne effect was at first a discovery of how social relations could counteract stressful stimuli. In elevators and doctor's offices, efforts to create a calming rather than jarring experience gave us Muzak, one of the many "shock absorbers" Mumford saw cropping up in response to the buffetings of modern life.

Culture in this period had a front stage and a backstage. The use of pass-through mechanisms showed an acceptance of the functional differentiation of expert and lay audiences—something that unraveled in the later twentieth century. The curator had access to all the specimens, but the public saw only the diorama. Rowley's *Taxidermy and Museum Exhibition* put it well: "The modern museum demands two classes of collections—a research or study collection which is solely for the use of the student or specialist for comparison and scientific research; and an exhibition or display collection for the general public." Artists and modelers had become just as essential to the success of a museum as scientists. The mistake of the old row-style museum display was to mix the dense data experts needed with the sparkly stories the public wanted.[44] Experts cooked up displays from the raw data they alone had access to. The public library was for citizens and the research library was for scholars. One gave assistance at the reference desk; the other gave access to the stacks. British physicist Arthur Eddington contrasted the scientific "showroom" with the "workshop."[45]

Many developments hid the mechanism from public view. To use more recent language, user-friendly interfaces proliferated, leaving the hardware to experts. The icebox, which had required frequent replenishing by hand and offered a clear understanding of its operation, was gradually replaced by the electric refrigerator from the mid-1920s on, when General Electric sold the first mass-market refrigerator. The first electric starter for a car was installed in Cadillacs in 1912, and by 1920 it was standard in American automobiles. The old hand-crank mechanism had a wicked kickback that could break a wrist or jaw; the new starter required nothing but the twist of a key. Crystal radio sets—built from scratch and tuned by constant adjustment by a skilled operator during the aughts and teens—had all but vanished by 1930, when mass-produced radio consoles were becoming the norm. Even in industrial design there was a front stage and a backstage.

For a Horace Greeley, demanding know-how advanced democracy. For the culture of happy summary, in contrast, popular education hid the details in synthetic packages and framing devices. There were dissidents, such as leftist playwright Bertolt Brecht, who believed that popular political education lay precisely in exposing the apparatus, but many of his contemporaries saw democratic potential in hiding the machinery.

The clean lines of high modernist aesthetics and design found beauty in summary. The unadorned buildings of the international style, Piet Mondrian's crisply rectangular, primary-color paintings, Wittgenstein's supremely austere early philosophy, and Arnold Schoenberg's twelve-tone compositions stripped away superfluities like the serifs on typefaces. Georgia O'Keeffe's paintings were so immediate in their appeal that some observers found them "wished upon the canvas." O'Keeffe hid the work of painting, like her fellow "precisionist" artists, one of whom remarked in 1939, "Today it seems to me desirable to remove the method of painting as far as possible from being an obstacle in the way of consideration of the content of the picture."[46] The growing hostility to ornament and detail in high culture was not that different from the new interest in statistical sampling and the concept of culture. All provided a way to shape and present an essence by shaving off incidentals. Gone was the overstuffed late Victorian aesthetic. (The lush drips and splotches of abstract expressionism, celebrating the medium of paint for its own sake, would soon rebel against this asceticism.)

Organizing Expert Knowledge:
Intellectuals on Libraries in the 1940s

Backstage, a growing sense of glut and crisis loomed. By the late thirties and forties a host of writers began a new phase of discussion on the prospects and problems of knowledge and information. These debates were less about popular forms of presentation than about the internal organization of knowledge. Scientists, librarians, and social scientists dominated. The discussion was not about a postmodern or postindustrial social order or the origins of an information age, as it would be in the 1970s, or about the liberating effects of digital technology, as it would be in the 1990s (see chapter 6). Knowledge and information, in this discussion, were crucial to the "completion" of the industrial world: they were the epitome of modernity, and even for experts they had to be organized. The confidence that experts and governments working together could plan and organize knowledge offers a strong contrast with our own moment.

In the late 1930s a number of writers started commenting on the phenomenal growth of formal knowledge in the modern world. Science, social science, engineering, humanities—in all fields there had been an explosion of knowledge production. The institutional changes beginning in the 1880s had been profound: the creation of the modern research university, the consolidation of the PhD as an expert credential, the rise of corporate laboratories, the massive actuarial tables produced by insurance companies, the ever-increasing research done by national governments, and the emergence, especially in Europe, of government-sponsored research centers. Intellectuals in the late thirties and forties were trying to assimilate the meaning of this massive change in the level of knowledge production. They were convinced that the trend would continue. As sociologist William F. Ogburn stated in 1937, there was now "some evidence to indicate that knowledge grows according to the exponential law." The increase "is not a straight line going up, but a curved line growing by increasingly large amounts."[47] The same principle that once scared Malthus—geometric growth—had moved from populations to information.[48]

Participation in World War II by scientists of all sorts only intensified the belief that research and knowledge production were crucial to the modern world. The development of the atomic bomb was the most famous mobilization of scientists, but they played a part in the development of radar, the mass production of penicillin, the cracking of codes, the analysis of Nazi propaganda, and the psychological adjustment of soldiers. This belief that knowledge and information were crucial cut across the political spectrum. J. D. Bernal, the British Marxist crystallographer who wrote pioneering work on the sociology of science in the 1930s and 1940s, observed in 1945 that the "experience of the war has taught a very large number of scientists the vital place of an efficient information service." The patrician Yankee Republican Vannevar Bush wrote in the same year, "Progress in the war against disease depends upon a flow of new scientific knowledge.... Similarly, our defense against aggression demands new knowledge so that we can develop new and improved weapons." And between these political poles, Franklin

Delano Roosevelt established a commission (with Bush in charge) to explore how the science generated by the war effort could continue once the war ended.[49]

Those interested in issues of knowledge and research were contemplating what it meant for industrial societies to be awash in formally produced knowledge. This was new. In the past, the classic tropes had been enlightenment versus ignorance, knowledge versus superstition. Such a view, dating back to the seventeenth century, remained crucial to the commentary on science in the 1860s and 1870s. By the 1940s, however, the question was how to manage the copious research being produced by a multitude of universities, corporations, and governments.

It was common to hear that the research had grown so extravagantly that it had outstripped any capacity to organize its results. We faced, as one commentator put it, "documentary chaos." In 1945 the editor of the *Atlantic Monthly* defined the problem as "making more accessible our bewildering store of knowledge." Vannevar Bush argued that "the difficulty seems to be, not so much that we publish unduly . . . but rather that publication has extended far beyond our present ability to make real use of the record." Bush's essay, now a fixture on course syllabi as prophetic of digital media, argued that a complex civilization required mechanizing its record. Smart machines would make our lives more enjoyable by giving us the luxury of forgetting things, since we had a ready way to recall them.[50]

Libraries were overwhelmed. For public libraries, the late 1920s brought the urgent question of updating and culling books. According to a British librarian, this was not a problem twenty years earlier.[51] Indexing was an imperfect art, to say the least. The abstracting of research was even worse. Researchers simply didn't know what their colleagues were doing. A cautionary tale warned of research duplicated because a researcher just didn't know what had already been done. The war, once again, exacerbated the problem. Thousands of pieces of government research were written up for the first time as "technical reports" to move them along more quickly (and in a few key cases more secretly) than published articles. But how could anyone keep track of this research? According to Fremont Rider, in one of the more widely circulated of the "knowledge problem" texts during the war, librarians were watching the "veritable tidal wave of printed materials yearly, monthly, *hourly*, mount higher and higher." (We've seen such worries about print engulfing the world in Diderot and Melvil Dewey.) Libraries could never keep up, Rider said, but it was far more than a library problem: "We seem to be fast coming to the day when, unless it is afforded the most expert sort of bibliographical service possible, civilization may die of suffocation, choked in its own plethora of print."[52]

Nonexistent in the debates on this problem was discussion of the computer, nor was there mention of the breakthroughs in the "information theory" of Claude Shannon or the cybernetics of Norbert Wiener. Sometime in the 1940s mathematician John W. Tukey coined the term *bit* (from *binary digit*) as the new minimum quantum of information. As science broker Warren Weaver observed in his now famous 1949 essay in *Scientific American*, the term *information* was used in information theory "in a special sense that must not be confused with its ordinary usage."[53] Yet in 1945, when J. D. Bernal published *Information Service as an Essential in the Progress of Science*, he was using the term *information* in exactly that "ordinary" sense. It referred to relevant facts, nothing more.

Not only was the computer absent, but this literature focused on a very different "breakthrough" technology—microfilm. Microfilm had been developed in the early 1930s. Many of these writers saw microfilm as the most important single way the scientific cornucopia could be managed. It would reduce costs, could easily be sent through the mail, and would solve the space crunch in libraries. There were numerous schemes to expand microfilm usage in these years. The one most widely watched was the Bibliofilm Service, a private, nonprofit organization that served as a national clearinghouse to microfilm research and make it available to whomever needed it. It began microfilming in the library of the US Department of Agriculture in 1934. By 1937 it was also working in the collections of the Army Medical Library and the Library of Congress. The service grew impressively in the next few years. In 1939 the *Saturday Review of Literature* waxed enthusiastic: a researcher of "all subjects for which printed or manuscript materials are needed" could now, thanks to microfilm, find them effortlessly and use them "in the peace of his study with all his notes about him at a fraction of the expense which the European tour would have cost."[54]

Microfilm as a panacea remained a steady theme in the early 1940s then faded in the early 1950s, only to live on in research libraries through the new millennium. The organizational solution was as important as the technology. Most important for writers in the late thirties and forties was integrating research into some more comprehensive social planning. Research and knowledge production were only one part of a more comprehensive belief in a planned society. There had to be better coordination of research—scientists and governments had to think seriously about social needs and move science to address them.

"Planning" at that time could attach itself to a variety of political viewpoints—conservative, social democratic, and communist. Vannevar Bush, representing the first, called for better coordination of research in one of the most widely read reports of the day. He wanted a conservative form of planning, one that spent a lot of money for military and medical research, had the federal government do the funding, but left considerable leeway for scientists themselves to make decisions about it. Bush's experience with the Manhattan Project during World War II convinced him of one thing: throw a lot of money at the experts and they will solve the problem. His 1945 argument for better coordination between science and government was one important catalyst for the creation of the National Science Foundation five years later.[55]

Further to the left, sociologist Robert Lynd also called for more research and planning. Lynd can best be described in American terms as a left-leaning liberal. He was sympathetic to European social democracy. For Lynd, writing in 1939, research had to solve social problems, but social scientists had turned into mindless fact gatherers. There was no coordination to this mindless empiricism. Lynd argued that social scientists needed to ask better questions, questions about the *real* problems people faced. (Here he echoed his Columbia colleague John Dewey.) That was the only way social science would do anything useful. He too called for planning, but unlike Bush he did not automatically think the experts would get it right. "Our problem is to discover how control can be used to enhance vital freedom to live creatively at points important to the human personality, by eliminating current wasteful freedoms that operate in fact to limit these more vital freedoms."[56]

Finally, J. D. Bernal also called for planned research. In 1939 Bernal was comfortable citing the power of the Soviet Union's five-year plans and contrasting them with the disorganization of capitalist science. Bernal thought science should be in the service of human needs. While a progressive government might set the agenda, he thought, it was also important for the whole system to be flexible.[57]

Bush, Lynd, and Bernal, despite political differences, were all enthusiastic about planning. None of them raised questions about the difficulties of coordination. All thought that better coordination would lead to better science. Bernal and Bush both used the image of the encyclopedia. In perhaps the only essay in this literature to suggest an important role for the computer, Vannevar Bush argued that the new machines had the potential to create "wholly new forms of encyclopedias." Bernal asserted that the encyclopedia should be "a coherent expression of the living and changing body of thought; it should sum up what is for the moment the spirit of the age." Although that was the case for the eighteenth-century encyclopedia, he claimed, its contemporary descendant had "degenerated into . . . a mere mass of unrelated knowledge sold by high-pressure salesmanship." More organized research would correct the problem.[58]

Lynd thought similarly. Modern social science, with its superficial sense of "order," missed the fluidity of our experience, the "vast sea of uncertainty" most people lived in. But Lynd did not relish this chaos. To have order in society, Lynd argued, science must be used to make some order in the social world. Only if it was used for socially beneficent purposes could there be any order. And while Lynd did not use the term *encyclopedia*, he did argue that social planning was tied to intellectual synthesis. The order of society and the order of knowledge were homologous.[59]

For these authors, better coordination of research not only would lead to a better world, it would lead to better and more synthetic science. Planning science would improve public welfare and end the "documentary chaos" of the age. It would make formal knowledge as coherent as it had been in the (no doubt mythical) past. We could write a new encyclopedia of knowledge. Planning would complete the Enlightenment project, aided by new devices of information storage and recall. It was one more midcentury answer to how to build a dike against the floods of information. For the public, there was summary and popularization; for the experts, there was planning and microfilm.[60]

Condensation as a Truth Game

The crisis of knowledge management among experts that became clear during World War II had roots in the earlier discovery that abridgment was needed not only in the public presentation of information but in the creation of knowledge itself. Summary and factual abridgment became an important "truth game" in their own right. There were a number of turns in academic culture that attempted to corral "the facts" into something much tighter than the opulent and sloppy world of unrestricted empiricism. One was logical positivism, which presented itself as the antithesis of "empirical positivism" and found a highly hospitable environment in the United States in the 1930s as its advocates fled Nazism. Some refugees took up professorships in midwestern universities where their leaner, meaner doctrine productively hybridized with native strains of positivism. Hardheaded logic might cut through the unrelated sprawl of facts to uncover the core of ascertainable truth. Logic guided a limited empiricism to build solid but revisable general-

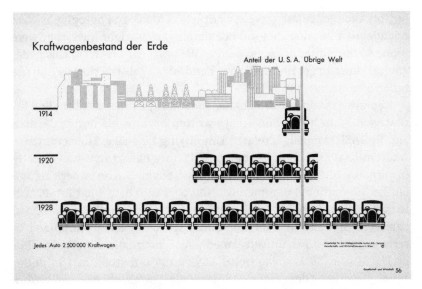

FIGURE 3.3. "Kraftwagenbestand der Erde" (1931). Otto and Marie
Neurath Isotype Collection, University of Reading.

izations, a theme expressed in A. J. Ayer's English-language manifesto
for the movement, *Language, Truth, and Logic*, published in 1936.

Abbreviation lay at the core of another expression of logical positivism: Isotype. Otto Neurath, a core member of the Vienna Circle, also was
active in museum work and collaborated with others on innovations
in graphic display. As curator of the Social and Economic Museum in
Vienna, founded in 1924, he developed a system of graphic representation of quantitative information that proved influential and is still used
in modified form. The system, which he and Marie Reidemeister, his collaborator and later wife, eventually called Isotype, used pictures to represent arrays of data. Neurath explained that one automobile icon, for
instance, could represent 2.5 million vehicles. The image included here
shows the exploding inventory of automobiles on earth from 1914 to
1920 to 1928, with the United States decisively leading the entire world.

Neurath's willingness to think on this scale shows the extent of the
abridgment he thought his "pictorial statistics" could make possible. As
a Marxist, he thought museums had the mission "to show social processes, and to bring all the facts of life into some recognizable relation
with social processes." Smart abbreviations were one way to cut through
the fog shrouding capitalist societies. They were essential for popular
pedagogy and consciousness raising. He considered such graphic displays "a popular version of logical positivism." Isotype could both order

sensory experience and serve as a critique of ideology. Photographs were not adequate because they did not simplify in the right ways; they were prone to the clutter of excess detail. "We have," he wrote, "in this pedagogical effort, to get rid, on the one hand, of pure abstraction and, on the other, of crude facts."[61]

Neurath explained his thinking about the pictorial display of quantitative data in books and essays written both in his native German and in BASIC English, a related simplifying language. The acronym—International System of Typographic Picture Education—was directly inspired by BASIC, which was also an acronym: British American Scientific International Commercial. Isotype was to data what BASIC was to language. Invented by British scholar C. K. Ogden in the 1920s, BASIC consisted of an eight-hundred-word English vocabulary intended to serve as a pared-down universal medium of communication. A coauthor of *The Meaning of Meaning* (1923), Ogden not only took part in philosophical debates about communication but also sought to make it work more efficiently. Even language itself could usefully be condensed and purified.[62]

Sidebar 3.1 Facts for Tough Guys

Facts, and nothing but the facts, were of intense interest to two distinct masculine genres between the wars: detective fiction and positivist social science.

The hard-boiled detectives of *Black Mask*, the pulp mystery magazine of the 1930s, had a different relation to clues and evidence than did the more middle-class fictional detectives of the day. Gender and nation played a role as well as class. Many, but not all, of the writers for *Black Mask* were men; all were American; and all rebelled against the genteel mores of detective fiction that developed in Britain in the 1920s with the first great wave of mystery writers including Agatha Christie, Dorothy Sayers, and Josephine Tey. The London Detection Club was founded in 1928 as a guild of these and other influential writers of the genre. The club laid down rules such as avoiding ghosts or other supernatural crutches, steering clear of lower-class criminal elements such as gangs, leaving a trail of clues that readers could rationally reconstruct without hunches, intuition, or other leaps, and honoring "the king's English."

All these rules were gleefully violated by the *Black Mask* writers.

Their texts belonged to a more artisanal world where know-how, street smarts, and personal fortitude counted for more than the fussy deductions of Christie's Hercule Poirot or the dilettante inquiries of Sayers's Lord Peter Wimsey, who solved one case, for instance, using a point of French grammar.[1] The *Black Mask* writers were more interested in the knowledge possessed by cops and coroners than by aesthetes and aristocrats. Enormously inventive with language, they drew on slang and tough talk rather than educated or literary patterns of speech, and they spoke anything but the king's English. No one could outdo Sam Spade or Philip Marlowe in wisecracks. "We didn't exactly believe your story," says Spade to Brigid O'Shaughnessy in Dashiell Hammett's *The Maltese Falcon* (1930). "We believed your two hundred dollars."[2] And these authors claimed a realism that the British ladies and gentlemen lacked. Raymond Chandler in his polemical essay "The Simple Art of Murder" thought such writers "too little aware of what goes on in the world."[3] *Black Mask* offered tough guys whose unmistakable misogyny went together with their more general misanthropy. They didn't really like anybody.

Black Mask detectives engaged with the world, often at the price of their own safety. They often made a worse mess of things—and of themselves—the deeper they went into the labyrinth of a case. Asked whom he worked for, Chandler's Philip Marlowe once answered, "I just fumble around and make a nuisance of myself. Often I'm pretty inadequate."[4] Here was no white-glove objectivity. The private dick was on a first-name basis with the details of the world—clothes, furniture, interior design, guns, tobacco, and drinks—and had a gift for sizing up people instantly. The facts *Black Mask* detectives noticed were often the relevant plain bits that others, blinded by their learning and class privilege, could not see. Their knowledge was not the kind you got in a classroom. Perhaps they knew the rawness of things so well precisely because they had abandoned any trust in ideals. Despite his feelings for

1. Dorothy L. Sayers, "The Entertaining Episode of the Article in Question," in *Lord Peter: The Lord Peter Wimsey Stories* (New York: Harper and Row, 1972), 22–34.

2. Dashiell Hammett, *The Maltese Falcon* (San Francisco, CA: North Point Press, 1984), 44.

3. Raymond Chandler, *The Simple Art of Murder* (New York: Vintage, 1988), 11.

4. Raymond Chandler, *Playback* (New York: Ballantine, 1958), 164.

her, Sam Spade tells Brigid O'Shaughnessy that he won't "play the sap" for her. The worst thing in his moral code would be to be taken in. Cynicism was a protection.[5]

In social science between the wars there was an interest in the raw fact, but it was not in the name so much of a real grasp of things on the ground as of distance from the cognitively confused world of "value." Following sociologist's Max Weber's distinction between instrumental and substantive forms of rationality, empirical social scientists of the 1920s and 1930s claimed a damn the torpedoes ethic about science's duty to find facts about even the most delicate or sensitive topics. They were motivated by what they called the fact-value distinction. Robert Park, leader of sociology at the University of Chicago at the department's zenith in the 1920s and 1930s and former personal assistant to Booker T. Washington, once said that sociologists should study race relations with the same detachment biologists use with the potato bug. Park well knew that race was more an inflammatory topic than potato bugs, but he thought we should find the facts before the arguments started; indeed, finding the facts would change and improve the nature of the argument. (To be fair, Park's own ethnographic, neighborhood-based style of sociology is not the best representative of a hard-boiled social scientific ethic.) If social scientists had the inner steel to avoid judgment and the proper method to gather the real facts, they might change society positively. Social scientists had the ultimate aim of delivering truth and justice to a world that had elaborate means of avoiding both.

Such withholding of judgment could reach the heights of destructive asceticism. Sociologist George Lundberg wrote in 1929, "It is not the business of a chemist who invents a high explosive to be influenced in his task by considerations as to whether his product will be used to blow up cathedrals or to build tunnels through the mountains."[6] Lundberg was not hoping to comfort penitents like Alfred Nobel, who endowed the prize in his name after making a fortune on dynamite; he was exhorting graduate students in the social sciences to show a ruthless

5. On this genre, see the very helpful Erin A. Smith, *Hard-Boiled: Working-Class Readers and Pulp Magazines* (Philadelphia: Temple University Press, 2000); also Cmiel, "On Cynicism," 90–91.

6. Quoted in Robert K. Merton, "Science and the Social Order," *Philosophy of Science* 5 (July 1938): 321–37, at 329.

indifference to social sensitivities when they did basic research. Science was the discovery of facts, and scientists had to be on guard against the perception-clouding power of values. No less than the detectives of *Black Mask* magazine, sociologists had to avoid swooning before lofty ideals. They couldn't play the sap. The *American Journal of Sociology* was a couple of rungs higher on the class ladder than *Black Mask* magazine, but there was something hard-boiled about them both. A fact in one realm could be a kick in the gut; in the other it could be a statistical plot that did damage to our favorite prejudices. On the street facts were tangled into complex webs; in social research they were organized into generalizations. Both detection and social science recognized the thick messiness of facts, and they sought different ways of streamlining them into clear conclusions without being taken in by wishes or norms.

There was the occasional link between the two worlds. One avid reader of *Black Mask* magazine was the philosopher Ludwig Wittgenstein, whose later thought proved so suggestive for students of social life (and much else). His handicraft approach defied the age-old norm that the philosopher should be aloof from the world of things. He left his native Vienna to study aeronautical engineering in England before turning to philosophy. Wittgenstein was a gifted designer and architect who made beautiful doorknobs and radiators with the same care he used untangling the intricacies of language, logic, and mathematics. He was fascinated with tools and the works of men. Wittgenstein diverted his most serious disciples from careers as professional academics to become doctors or carpenters. He himself worked with great efficiency as a medical orderly during World War II. He sometimes thought that philosophy was the corruption of an honest life. He was no less self-torturing than most private eyes.

Wittgenstein was once memorably compared to James Bond for his knack for getting himself into conceptual jams that allowed him to show his extraordinary skill as an escape artist.[7] But he is sometimes just as close to Spade or Marlowe or their colleagues, with his grounded intelligence, air of asceticism, and possession of hard-won tragic truth about the knottiness of the world. Wittgenstein was not a social scientist in the usual sense. Rather, he can be viewed as a detective who looked deep into the logic of human wickedness and tried, with astonishing interpre-

7. Ernst Gellner, *Language and Solitude: Wittgenstein, Malinowski and the Hapsburg Dilemma* (Cambridge: Cambridge University Press, 1998), 57.

tive skills and an occasional bitter desperation, to make sense of it all. He aptly called his late philosophical works "investigations," using the same word detectives used for theirs. Don't think but look, he said, as if renouncing academic philosophy's charisma and systematicity (a tortured task for one who oozed such charismatic intensity). And like Marlowe, he often despaired of the whole enterprise, questing for a childlike ability to see naively, to look at things as they simply are and not as the perps and philosophical spin doctors want us to see them.[8]

8. These thoughts, like many points in this text, owe much to Frank Kelleter.

A very different approach was found in the popularizer Will Durant, who also used techniques of summary in his widely read *The Story of Philosophy* (1926). Unlike the logical positivists, he sidestepped complicated epistemological issues—treating Descartes glancingly in his survey and barely mentioning Leibniz—in order to summarize the "wisdom" of influential thinkers. In his preface to the second edition (1932), Durant defended his "outline" approach against "snobs" as a response to a world in which "human knowledge had become unmanageably vast" and set his work in a long lineage of outlines, starting with Plato's dialogues. His was an "interpretive synthesis," he claimed, for the "busy reader." As Joan Shelley Rubin has remarked, this "outline" approach to culture "promised culture condensed, subdivided, and contained." For rushed readers, there was no reason to get into the subtleties.[63]

Another striking example is the rise of statistical sampling in the 1920s and 1930s. For much of the nineteenth century statistical collection had meant gathering facts. Relatively few efforts were made to synthesize or to represent central tendencies. Threshing out was left to the future. In the late nineteenth century, Francis Galton and Karl Pearson invented techniques for sorting through masses of data, including such statistical staples as "correlation" and "standard deviation." But fact gathering continued to flourish on a massive scale in the early twentieth century despite uncertainty about how to process the accumulated heaps. Statistical research in the twenties and thirties helped propel the discipline in a new direction—one that depended not on a mass of information, but on sampling selected portions of the whole population.

R. A. Fisher's *Statistical Methods for Research Workers* (1925) was the breakthrough book, going through a string of editions in the next two decades. It introduced the idea of random representative sampling. Careful research design could prevent the expense of massive empiricism. A random sample would give a central tendency bounded by a probability, a concept known best through the "margin of error" still tacked on to poll results. On the first page Fisher announces statistics' great contribution to the problem of the age: "the reduction of data." He showed not only how statistics could crunch complex data but how smart experimental design could create efficiencies within the research process.

Work by Fisher and others on population genetics would contribute to the neo-Darwinian synthesis in evolutionary biology of the late 1930s. The synthesis made the population rather than the organism the crucial unit of evolutionary adaptation. This new account of organic evolution was itself a masterpiece of economy in explanation and helped resolve the lack of communication among biologists. Whereas Darwin powered through his vast accumulation of data about mollusks and worms, the statistical tools of the neo-Darwinian synthesis offered biologists a more streamlined mode of analysis.[64]

Statistical method also enabled a new kind of synthesis: quantitatively measured public opinion. It proved its efficacy in 1936 when George Gallup and Elmo Roper, using representative sampling techniques, did a much better job of predicting Roosevelt's election than the *Literary Digest*, which relied on a massive but insufficiently random accumulation of individual opinion.[65] The Gallup poll was a summarizing device of the first order. In the 1930s "public opinion" took on a new quantitative meaning. Instead of being the symbolic precipitate of face-to-face civic deliberation, public opinion was now defined as the aggregate of individual opinion as discovered by sampling. The possibility of tapping public opinion not as a vague mood or atmosphere but as a representative sample was very exciting to social scientists and policy makers. In 1937 the journal *Public Opinion Quarterly* published its first issue. It reveled in the new techniques that allowed for new aggregated understandings. Much more than the plaything of a few social scientists, such polling techniques were quickly adopted by journalists, capitalists, and politicians. Representative sampling became a central technique by which the culture represented itself to itself. Polls were a kind of distillation of the nation—"the pulse of democracy," as Gallup exuberantly put it.[66]

Even so, political scientists and sociologists continued to rely on the part-for-whole logic of single-city studies until regular national polling was in place in the 1950s. Robert and Helen Lynd's *Middletown* (1929) led the way in finding America in miniature (in Muncie, Indiana). During the 1940s a series of famous social-scientific studies were carried out in small towns—Sandusky, Ohio, Decatur, Illinois, Elmira, New York, and "Yankee City" (Newburyport, Massachusetts). Theories of the middle range, as Robert Merton called this approach, seemed to flourish in towns of the middle size.[67] (He himself carried out an important study in Dover, New Jersey.) In 1930s and 1940s social research, synecdoche was a convincing strategy. *The People's Choice* (1944), for instance, was comfortable in representing a national election through a panel of six hundred people polled from every fourth home in Erie County, Ohio. Such studies shared with a Norman Rockwell illustration a belief that the whole could be decently represented through the part.

"Culture" and the Culture of Summary

Perhaps the ultimate example of how the culture of summary became implicated in the production of "truth" was the culture concept itself. "Culture," as understood by the 1930s anthropologists Ruth Benedict and Margaret Mead, their teacher Franz Boas, and their London colleague Bronislaw Malinowski, meant the integrated forms of life of a whole people. The influential late Victorian anthropologist James George Frazer epitomized the old regime they revolted against. His books were like late nineteenth-century museums: chock-full of facts assembled as comparative specimens with little interest in their original embedment in a whole way of life. In his magnum opus, *The Golden Bough*, first published in 1890 as a single volume and swelling to many volumes in subsequent editions, Frazer could skip across the globe in a single paragraph, from the Dayaks of Borneo to the Hottentots of Africa to the "Lapps" and "Eskimos" of the Arctic to East African elephant hunters, only to end up nearly where he started in New Guinea.[68] Through a massive jumble he thought to discern the origins of religion and kingcraft—in general. His Casaubonian project was organized by theme, but not by origin. The original cultural context hardly mattered.

American and British anthropology in the 1920s and 1930s turned sharply away from this magpie universalism. Malinowski set the tone. His book *Argonauts of the Western Pacific* (1922) reoriented the field of anthropology to a new methodological focus on fieldwork carried out in self-contained cultures. Frazer inspired Malinowski to become an anthropologist and wrote the introduction to his *Argonauts of the Western Pacific*, but the book did not try to explain the totality of culture across the globe. Its ambitions were much more focused: to study economic practices in the Trobriand Islands so as to comprehend that culture as "one coherent whole." Ethnography was a crystallizing practice: "the first and basic ideal of ethnographic field-work is to give a clear and firm outline of the social constitution, and disentangle the laws and regularities of all cultural phenomena from the irrelevances." Malinowski defended his use of "mental charts" and "synoptic tables" as techniques for synthesizing "the wide range of facts" gathered by the ethnographer. "Outline" was one of his favorite words, and he used it forty-eight times in *Argonauts.*[69]

Nineteenth-century notions of culture were too diffuse, Ruth Benedict argued in her very influential *Patterns of Culture* (1934). They split culture up into artifacts, rituals, weapons, clothing, and so on. But, she argued, "miscellaneous behavior" naturally tends to fall into patterns. The anthropologist looks for not "a list of unrelated facts" but "a consistent pattern of thought and word," something "integrated." The "quest for culture," she wrote, "is the search for meaning and value."[70] Decontextualized artifacts could never reveal the system of meanings characteristic of a single culture. The culture concept, as historian Warren Susman has argued, worked on a number of levels at once. It was a way to reduce anxiety in a newly "complex" machine civilization. It was a way to teach community and conformity. And it was a way to organize experience. That is, it was a way to make sense of the variegated mass of data that flew at us each day. "Culture" became the basic patterns of a civilization that made sense of what on the surface might look like the randomness of experience. It structured the manifold confusion of the empirical flux. It was a concept usable both by expert and by ordinary citizen.[71]

Sidebar 3.2 John Dewey and the Cultural Politics of Summary

One complaint was that condensation seemed to move the power of judgment away from citizens into the hands of cultural arbiters. What would that do to an informed citizenry?

One writer who directly confronted these issues was the philosopher John Dewey. By the middle of the 1920s, Dewey's thinking on the matter had two different but complementary strains. On one hand, he called for increased public discussion, openness, and communication, traits he associated with the best of scientific investigation. On the other hand, Dewey also thought there had to be periodic moments of affirmation and synthesis. Here he turned to art and culture.

Recent commentators have tended to see Dewey's increased interest in aesthetics as part of a response to criticisms voiced by writers such as Lewis Mumford and Randolph Bourne.[1] While this is true, just as important was the emerging culture of summation. His aesthetic turn of the 1920s and 1930s reflects one attempt to incorporate this wider phenomenon into a more complicated political theory.

Dewey had his own account of the knowledge crisis. To "the average voter to-day," he wrote in 1927, "the tariff question is a complicated medley of infinite detail, schedules of rates specific and ad valorem on countless things, many of which he does not recognize by name, and with respect to which he can form no judgment." A decade later it was no different. The "increase in number and diversity of unrelated facts" now played "pretty continuously upon the average person," he wrote in 1939, leading that person to choose slogans over analysis, "acquiescence rather than critical inquiry."[2]

At times Dewey seemed sharply at odds with the culture of summation. He complained about the "readymade intellectual good" so prominent in contemporary life.[3] The steady and ongoing participation of all citizens through forums of communication was the way to address problems, he declared in *The Public and Its Problems* (1927). For Dewey, practice preceded insight, and citizens were the real experts on social problems, perhaps without always knowing it. He associated civic participation with the scientific method. Science addressed problems by communication, discussion, and the willingness to revise tentative conclusions in the face of new experience. It was time, Dewey thought, to bring those attitudes to bear on the great social and political issues of the day.[4]

Yet a very different side of Dewey during those years brought him to the center of the culture of crystallized essence. Certainly many of his disciples turned toward the popularization of philosophy in the late

1. See Casey Nelson Blake, *Beloved Community* (Chapel Hill: University of North Carolina Press, 1990); Robert Westbrook, *John Dewey and American Democracy* (Ithaca, NY: Cornell University Press, 1991); Alan Ryan, *John Dewey and the High Tide of American Liberalism* (New York: Norton, 1995).

2. John Dewey, *The Public and Its Problems* (New York: Henry Holt, 1927), 132; John Dewey, *Freedom and Culture* (New York: Putnam's, 1939), 46–47.

3. Dewey, *Freedom and Culture*, 46.

4. Also see John Dewey and James Tufts, *Ethics*, rev. ed. (New York: Henry Holt, 1932), 398–404.

1920s and 1930s.[5] Important was Dewey's interest in what he called "consummatory experience." Dewey divided experience into two sorts, instrumental and consummatory. Instrumental experience solved problems; it was practical, concerned with means. Consummatory experience was enjoyed for its own sake. It was about ends. It was a release from the blur of constant doings.[6]

Art was both instrumental and consummatory to Dewey, but the stress was on the latter. Art was "the culminating event of nature as well as the climax of experience." Moreover, it was an aesthetic exemplum of a social totality, "a record and celebration of the life of a civilization," he said in 1934. While there were "transient" and "enduring" dimensions to any social order, art was "the great force" in reconciling the two. Art had the power of consummation and could reveal the essence of a culture.[7] It should not be surprising that Dewey, by the end of the 1930s, was favorably disposed toward the culture concept,[8] for his sense of consummatory experience and art was close to the meaning of "culture," which created order out of the transient flux and made imaginative embodiments of accumulated experience.

Dewey argued that a well-rounded social order needed both instrumental and consummatory poles. He described consummatory experience variously as "integral," tending to "a close, an ending," a point of "equilibrium," as "enjoyment for its own sake." But none of these meant stasis. The moment of equilibrium also initiated a new period of flux where adjustments had to be made. "The time of consummation is also one of beginning anew."[9] Here was a picture of Dewey's democratic theory—discursive, critical thinking alternating with integral, enthusiastic confirmations of the democratic achievement. Yet he also offset this affirmative moment with a firm commitment to communication and discussion.

At points, however, Dewey gave the aesthetic even more to do. At these moments he sounded very much like the mainstream of the culture of summation. In *The Public and Its Problems*, he worried that straight information would not bring an active public into being. A "technical high-brow presentation would appeal only to the technically

---

5. Cotkin, "Middle-Ground Pragmatists."

6. See John Dewey, *Experience and Nature* (Chicago: Open Court, 1925).

7. Ibid., xvi; John Dewey, *Art as Experience* (New York: Henry Holt 1934), 326.

8. Dewey, *Freedom and Culture*.

9. Dewey, *Art as Experience*, 17; also see Dewey, *Experience and Nature*.

high-brow," he wrote, in a reversal of nineteenth-century assumptions about the thick flow of facts. A newspaper that tried to be a "daily edition of a quarterly journal of sociology or political science would undoubtedly possess a limited circulation and a narrow influence." Spreading huge quantities of sophisticated information was not the answer for Dewey. Instead, he turned to artists, who were the "real" purveyors of the news. Art could be the means to pass new messages to a larger public. Experimenting with modes of presentation could teach the public to grasp complicated positions.[10] It is not surprising that Dewey was enthusiastic, for instance, about the spread of murals celebrating the American nation, as sponsored by the Federal Art Project in the 1930s.[11]

Here art was doing more than serving consummatory experience. It was decidedly instrumental as well. And it certainly was a perfect example of the new culture of the aesthetic exemplum. A striking image would not just sit alongside hoards of information—it would take their place. But what would this do to Dewey's goal of reviving democracy? This aesthetic turn might not undermine his democratic project, at least if one was convinced that artistic renditions would accurately summarize the "news." But if one accepts the legitimacy of artistic summary, one must not level elitist charges against museum curators who direct their audience to selected points, shielding them from elaborate information. One has to accept the culture of summation as a legitimate democratic project to accept Dewey's version of it in *The Public and Its Problems*.

Despite constant calls for a rejuvenated democratic public, Dewey slid in a more elitist direction at various points, suggesting that the public could not do everything once expected of it. Replacing elaborate information with art was one example. His last major work, *Freedom and Culture*, gave another. Discussing the culture concept, Dewey wrote that we "are beginning to realize that emotions and imagination are more potent in shaping public sentiment and opinion than information and reason."[12] Yet he did not say how he squared this concession with his hope for a democratic, rational culture.

10. Dewey, *Public and Its Problems*, 183–84.

11. John Dewey, radio address for the NBC Blue Network, broadcast April 25, 1940, quoted in Marlene Park and Gerald E. Markowitz, *Democratic Vistas: Post Offices and Public Art in the New Deal* (Philadelphia: Temple University Press, 1984), v.

12. Dewey, *Freedom and Culture*, 10.

At his best, Dewey thought the culture of summation balanced more instrumental modes. Dialogue and conversation were the means by which a society could critique itself; and points of aesthetic experience were necessary to orient the body politic. But there were also moments— and we stress that they were only moments—when it appeared that Dewey lost faith in the power of average citizens to assimilate knowledge or make rational decisions. At moments like this he veered, however briefly, toward a more thoroughgoing embrace of the new mode. Dewey's dance with happy summary exposes its many underlying tensions.

The concept of "national character" was an important focus for social scientists of the period, especially anthropologists who studied civilian morale during the war, such as Mead, Gregory Bateson—her husband at the time—Benedict, and Geoffrey Gorer, often under the auspices of the Office of War Information.[72] Mead's *And Keep Your Powder Dry* (1942), Benedict's *The Chrysanthemum and the Sword: Patterns of Japanese Culture* (1946), and Gorer's *The American People* (1948) were the leading studies of national character. Written during the war, Benedict's book grew out of strategic studies of civilian morale and cultural life that would end up guiding the occupation of a postwar Japan. Similar works were written during the war on German culture, some by members of the Frankfurt school in exile.[73] Benedict also wrote a now famous study of the Dutch national character without ever setting foot in the Netherlands.[74] She even consulted with Roosevelt on plans for invading Japan and advocated an ongoing postwar role for the emperor. The notion of national character also informed David Riesman's *The Lonely Crowd: A Study of the Changing American Character* (1950), one of the defining works of postwar American sociology.

"National character" very much belonged to the summarizing mood of social thought in the two middle decades of the century. In the first essay that introduced the notion of "national character" into social science, Morris Ginsberg expressly defined this notion as "a summary of the most important traits of any nation."[75] Again the notion of crystallized essence. Again the sense that nothing significant would be lost in framing the discussion this way.

Like "public opinion," the concept of national character aimed to provide a unified portrait of complex collective phenomena. Unlike public opinion, the study of national character, as many noted at the time, lacked a rigorous method, being the potentially shaky application of methods from cultural anthropology to entire nations.[76] Both public opinion and national character were born as empirically researchable concepts in the 1930s and played a key role in the midcentury culture of summary.

By late in the century the concept of national character was as dead as a doornail, while that of public opinion was flourishing. Representative sampling equipped public opinion polling with the ability to reveal internal variance in distribution of opinion, which gave it a pass amid the late-century rejection of synecdoche and celebration of difference (chapter 5). At midcentury national character was a useful concept for soldiers, businessmen abroad, or intellectuals interested in the kind of sweeping analysis Tocqueville and other nineteenth-century writers had pioneered. Decades later it would be seen as intolerably baggy conceptually and a damnable whitewash of internal diversity politically. One of its earliest critics was Ludwig Wittgenstein, who broke off relations with his student Norman Malcolm for a period after Malcolm had breezily used a loose form of the concept. Wittgenstein could not stand the ways such thinking lumped particulars. As was typical for him, Wittgenstein escalated the stakes, seeing nation-sized thinking as potentially responsible for the mayhem of war.[77]

Sidebar 3.3 Vietnamese Impressions

It was just one sentence in the middle of page 260. Actually, just a clause. But there it was: "Facts make little impression on the Annamite mind." What was this all about?

"Annamite," of course, means Vietnamese. The term is still commonly used in French and in 1937, when the sentence was written, was common enough in English as well. The sentence is from *French Indo-China*, written by one Virginia Thompson, PhD.[1] Not everyone liked the book. Herbert Ingram Priestley, in the *American Historical Review*, called it "adequate." Another reviewer complained of loose writing. Still other reviewers found it remarkable, and the book was one of the most widely consulted studies on the subject for the next decade. Thompson,

---

1. Virginia Thompson, *French Indo-China* (New York: Macmillan, 1937), 260.

not a specialist herself, nevertheless summarized all the specialist literature there was on Southeast Asia, drawing especially on French sources.[2]

And she added her own point of view. The inability to grasp fact was but one tiny float in Thompson's parade of prejudice. Vietnamese were trapped by ritual. Their thinking was "confused and imprecise," unable to grasp scientific method. Annamites were cruel and fatalistic, with a "flair for imaginative lying." Their nervous system was "certainly less sensitive than the Occidentals." If Edward Said hadn't invented the study of "orientalism" in the late 1970s, it would have to be created for Ms. Thompson. Her work, popular at the time, is almost a caricature of the genre.[3]

Thompson wasn't any right-wing crank. She hung out in popular front circles in the late thirties and forties, most notably with the Institute for Pacific Relations, which Joseph McCarthy attacked after World War II. Thompson was a bit player in the Cold War dramas but not entirely offstage. In 1952 the McCarran Committee, the Senate committee ferreting out communism in American life, identified her as a "writer for official publications of the Communist Party" and for "pro-Communist press services."[4] No demonstrable Marxist point of view turns up in Thompson's 1937 book. She was a liberal. Her book does indicate, though, how widespread such prejudices about the Vietnamese were at the time.

Whatever the new interest in image in the United States, Thompson's prejudices also highlight the still common belief that information was the special province of the West. We assimilate facts; "they" don't get it. Moreover, the new Western distrust of the fact was *not* about information itself, just about communication. An image might simplify complicated research, but it didn't replace it. Southeast Asia, for Thompson, was an entirely different place: "It is impossible to get precise information from an Annamite."[5]

2. Herbert Ingram Priestley, *American Historical Review* 43, no. 4 (1938): 876–77; John E. Orchard, *Geographical Review* 28 (1938): 515–16.

3. Thompson, *French Indo-China*, 46, 44.

4. Institute of Pacific Relations, *Report of the Committee on the Judiciary, Internal Security Subcommittee: 82nd Congress, July 2, 1952* (Washington, DC: US Government Printing Office, 1952), 158.

5. Thompson, *French Indo-China*, 43.

In all its expressions, the culture of crystallized essence sidestepped information and process. It communicated to the public in a new way, replacing a dense flow of facts with an imaginative summation of the whole. Whether in a museum exhibition, a newspaper article, or a discussion of a culture, it tried to embody a core, not pour on detail. What was to be communicated to the public was the sum, not the parts added up to get the sum. This was not the conspicuous overload of the cabinet of curiosities or the sprawling, contradictory mass of the Enlightenment *Encyclopédie*. It wasn't Greeley's detail-mongering or Langdell's compilations. It was a new strategy of using parts to represent wholes.

The culture of summary was an extremely important element of mid-twentieth-century mass culture. Mass culture was a number of things. It was a set of business institutions—Hollywood, the music industry, the news media. It was an accumulation of consumers. It was a series of representations and genres. By the late 1930s there was a widespread assumption among those working in cultural fields that the nation was a unity. In contrast to the chaotic years around the turn of the century, there was increasing confidence that the whole could be crystallized into an essence. This is what Roy Stryker, head of the Farm Security Administration photo project, meant when he said, "We are introducing America to Americans."

The 1930s was when the phrase "the American way of life" came into wide use. All sorts of things became the "essence" of "America"—folk songs, Frank Capra heroes, Norman Rockwell images, the common man. The celebration of American life was found across the political spectrum. Composer Aaron Copland and novelist John Dos Passos were among many leftist intellectuals who found no incompatibility between radical politics and celebration of the nation. The culture concept was the best expression of a society that responded to complexity by championing synecdoche.

The cult of happy abridgment not only was a style of managing information, it was an element in the creation of national solidarity. The nation had a real grip on minds and hearts, both as representation and as experience. Even those expelled from the life of the nation could couch their struggles for recognition in Americanist terms. Summary was both a truth game and a feeling of fraternity. America the nation was itself a condensation.

It would not last. In locating the essence in the whole the practice of abridgment militated against finding complexity in the pieces of the whole. "Culture" would later be used precisely to point to the experiences of those who had been left out of the happy summary. Since each minority group had a unique culture—a legacy of Boas—national distillations would come to be seen as oppressive. The culture concept would undermine the summarizing work it was created to do. People of goodwill cannot but welcome such developments in many ways, but in the conviction that cracking open national synecdoche is necessarily a victory for the oppressed and for justice, we show that we live on the far side of the culture of summary. The revolt against the welfare state in late twentieth-century American politics and the rise of multiculturalism are parts of the same historical development—the crumbling means of compelling national summary. The collapse of these means is one mark of the distance between the culture of happy summary and our own time.

* 4 *

The Age of the World Picture,
1925–45

The fundamental process of modernity is the conquest of
the world as image.
MARTIN HEIDEGGER (1938)[1]

The camera seems to me . . . the central instrument of our time.
JAMES AGEE (1941)[2]

In 1945, the most compelling images made in America were huge. Larger than life. Wondrous. They glided across movie screens at hundreds of local theaters and paraded through the hugely popular weeklies *Life* and *Look*. Millions looked at these pictures each week. A tank with guns blazing, a bright orange Oldsmobile, a gigantic green 7-Up bottle, starlets and statesmen in action—these images caught the life of the country—sometimes with a maddening superficiality, sometimes with great profundity. Yet they caught it. The country was *in control* of its visual culture.

The story of the next fifty years was of the gradual erosion of that assurance. By the new millennium, the country's images were far more chaotic. There was more play than before, more freedom. But there was also more nervousness and concern. To cultural conservatives by the 1970s, and even to many moderates by the 1990s, the image culture seemed dangerous, even sinister. Internet pornography, movie violence, the erosion of TV censorship, the mind-numbing distraction of video games—it all seemed so crass, so ugly. Starting in the 1970s film theorists, using sophisticated Freudian and Marxist theory, told us how sinister images could be. Technology, style, and the law had all colluded to disturb the midcentury safety. Images had spun out of control. But that is the story not of this chapter, but of the next. This chapter shows how images around 1945 had a summarizing, stabilizing quality parallel to the culture of happy summary.

The Nation in Pictures: Art, Technology, and Law

The single most important purveyor of images in the United States was Hollywood. Through World War II, weekly movie attendance was in the tens of millions. Even in the first few years after the war, although attendance was dipping, movies remained the most compelling images there were. Hits from the late 1930s to the early 1950s, films such as *Stagecoach* (1939), *Casablanca* (1942), *Singin' in the Rain* (1952), *High Noon* (1952), or *Stalag 17* (1953), attested to the importance of Hollywood in producing images for the nation.

Sidebar 4.1 The Size of the Image

The image in the early to middle nineteenth century was huge in other ways. Early in the century, the largest man-made images an American would likely see outside an art museum, theater, or cathedral were posters and broadsheets. These were usually 18 by 24 inches, with images made from woodcuts and words in letterpress. By mid-century, posters 28 by 42 inches became standard, limited by the size of the lithograph stone. Theater impresarios in cities announced shows, and the Civil War gave a boost to the poster medium by using it to recruit soldiers. Barnum produced some of the most widely circulated poster images. The young Henry James loved the posted bills of coming events at Barnum's American Museum; he found them "in their way marvels of attractive composition."[1]

In the late nineteenth century outdoor images got big. Multisheet lithograph posters up to ten feet in size started to be used in the last two decades of the century in cities like New York and Chicago that were swelling with immigrants. In 1891 the industry group Associated Billposters was formed. The group worked to standardize billboard sizes to ensure that the growing array of corporations could develop nationwide advertising campaigns for brands without having to resize their outdoor advertising in each city. By 1912 the industry standard became roughly 8 feet by 19 feet. By the teens, some billboards swelled to 12 by 25, but the

1. Henry James, *A Small Boy and Others* (London: Macmillan, 1913), 164.

1917 Times Square display for Wrigley's Chewing Gum outdid all com-
petitors. It was 250 feet long and 50 feet high, illuminated with 17,000
lights. The high-minded inevitably raged against what they considered
a new form of visual blight.[2]

Movies and billboards were cousins in the art of grandiose display.
The new movie theaters showed moving pictures to a stationary group
of people; billboards showed stationary pictures to a moving group of
people on foot or in vehicles of some kind.[3] One of the earliest forms
of film exhibition was a solitary experience: the kinetoscope, which
let a single viewer look through binocular glasses. Nickelodeon parlors enabled the collective viewing of a projected image, often in rather
cramped urban spaces. The teens saw the emergence of the film palace.
(*The Oxford English Dictionary* dates the term *big screen* to 1914 and
1916.) Screen size was a function of the exhibition space, so some designers decided to build the theater around the screen. Though screen
sizes varied from venue to venue, their dimensions began to mushroom
in the 1920s and 1930s as the modest, working-class nickelodeons and
the short films they screened gave way to feature-length studio movies
and the cavernous, opulent palaces that presented them. Additionally,
majestic prosceniums, architectural detail, and intricate lighting focused attention on the bloated screens in new ways that tended to enhance and exaggerate their actual size (in some cases, thirty feet high).

Screens had come in various dimensions and configurations, but in
the 1930s the aspect ratio of 4:3 solidified—the "Academy ratio," as it
was called. With the use of the close-up, which film director D. W. Griffith had introduced by 1910, spectators could view hands and faces on a
scale that they would see in real life only by being within touching distance. The bigger screen did not necessarily add to viewers' alienation,
but it did add to the perceived intimacy and reality of the viewing experience. Some were alarmed by precisely this immediacy of experience,

2. Catherine Gudis, *Buyways: Billboards, Automobiles, and the American Land-
scape* (London: Routledge, 2004), 80, 109, and passim; Wiley Lee Umphlett, *The
Visual Focus of American Media Culture in the Twentieth Century* (Teaneck, NJ:
Fairleigh Dickinson University Press, 2004), 90; Quentin J. Schultze, "Legislating
Morality: The Progressive Response to American Outdoor Advertising, 1900–1917,"
Journal of Popular Culture 17 (Spring 1984): 37–44.

3. Gudis, *Buyways*, 73.

the simultaneous distance from and closeness to a person you'd never met in the flesh.

The 1930s also saw the fresh popularity of murals, an art form requiring a large, publicly visible canvas. They were devoted to broad social themes, to narratives of the formation of people or industry. In the 1940s, abstract expressionist canvases could be shockingly large. Jackson Pollock's aptly titled *Mural* (1943) was just over eight feet tall and just under twenty feet wide—the size of a billboard. At midcentury, the image was huge.

During the teens, twenties, and thirties, Hollywood learned how to weave countless bits of film together into seemingly seamless stories. By the forties, cameras were mobile and directors and editors had mastered techniques like the "eyeline match," the "180 degree rule," and the "shot/reverse shot" to move action along in scenes. The introduction of incandescent lighting in the twenties helped directors use light to draw viewers' eyes to particular points on the screen or to create mood. Light no longer just lit a set, and shadowy lighting would come to define the entire genre of film noir.[3] An ethos grew in Hollywood, not as strong among European filmmakers, to create smoothly edited "product." (Postwar European art film would explicitly reject these norms.) In 1947 two industry insiders announced the conventional wisdom: "The use of pictorial continuity is the secret of *good* movie making."[4]

The results were dazzling. Although all the techniques had been developed in the teens and early twenties, such as in the work of D. W. Griffith, it took some time for them to become routine practice. In movies like Rudolph Valentino's *Four Horsemen of the Apocalypse* (1921) or Douglas Fairbanks's *The Mark of Zorro* (1920), it is not unusual for a single camera shot to stay put for an entire scene. These movies often feel like stage plays being filmed. Soon, however, a stagey feeling became increasingly uncommon. By the forties, classic Hollywood films like *Casablanca* or *Citizen Kane* fade in and out, their cameras roll along as actors move, and their lighting pulls our eyes to particular figures or objects. Each scene is carefully sutured together, linking establishing shots, close-ups, character reactions, and cuts back and forth between speakers. *Citizen Kane* especially was famous for the deep-focus photography of its cinematographer, Gregg Toland. Within each shot, characters are posed with nearly the same care that Caravaggio used to set subjects in his paintings. There was nothing casual about it. Whether we count *Citizen Kane* as the culmination of classical Hollywood techniques or the opening to something new, it clearly marks cinema's maturity as a modernist art form.

Hollywood's elaborate staging and editing was meant to make the final product seem utterly effortless, to direct attention away from the movie-making process and toward the characters and story. As with precisionist art or refrigerators, the techniques were meant to be hidden. Hollywood held no "operational aesthetic" eager to let ordinary folks see how the magic was done. Directors didn't care that moviegoers didn't know what a "shot/reverse shot" was. They wanted to keep the public staring at the screen, eyes riveted on the unfolding stories. The staging and editing were elaborate devices to keep people fascinated with the images but ignorant of the mechanics, only occasionally revealing "the man behind the curtain" as in *The Wizard of Oz* (1939), a film that in many ways is an allegory of Hollywood.

Hollywood didn't express as much pain as photojournalism did. It leaned more toward fantasy than reality. Yet its images were just as mythic, just as iconic. The stories were fables—of everyman fighting corruption (*Mr. Smith Goes to Washington*), of overcoming class and gender divides (*It Happened One Night*), of confronting the unknown (*The Wizard of Oz*), of learning to stand up for yourself (*The Grapes of Wrath*). The convention of generally uplifting endings limited Hollywood's range but also helped shape the narratives. Movies defined values to the nation at large. Academics, literary people, and journalists of the time commonly claimed that movies had "the power to create the nation's myths and dreams."[5] Never before had Hollywood achieved such a smoothly integrated economic system of production, distribution, and exhibition, all of it to be broken apart by the Paramount Decision of 1948, the Supreme Court ruling that put an end to studio monopolies.

Hollywood also produced a second sort of image—the newsreel. Newsreels were two- to ten-minute short films shown before feature films, and most of them were made in Hollywood. They usually combined short snippets of four or five stories. Rumblings in Europe or Asia might be one story, the latest jitterbug another. Made from the 1910s to the early 1970s, newsreels were most important during the years of the famous "March of Time" reels—from 1935 to 1951. A 1938 commentator thought "it was safe to say that the average citizen acquired most of his news through the medium of pictures."[6] (Later in the century such observations would be complaints about how TV images and sound bites had overwhelmed print journalism.) Newsreels were a sharp contrast to

the copious style of the nineteenth-century newspaper. Sometimes serious, sometimes fun, the newsreels were always wholesome. Alongside
the movies they accompanied, newsreels were an important set of pictures trying to define the life of the nation.

A third defining image was the documentary photograph. The thirties
and forties witnessed the emergence of a new class of magazines devoted to giving the news through photographs. *Life* was the first. Henry
Luce bought *Life*, a very different kind of magazine established in the
1880s, to gain the rights to the name after having decided against other
telling options such as *Dime, Eye, Nuze-Vuze, Candid,* and the *Show-Book
of the World.* He began publishing in November 1936. After a briefly rocky
financial start, *Life* quickly became the most popular magazine in the nation. By the late 1940s it was taking in nearly one-fifth of all the revenue
spent on magazine ads, an enormous share in a crowded field. Shortly
afterward, *Look* was founded by the Iowa publisher Gardner Cowles, and
soon the *Saturday Evening Post* adapted itself to the new genre, though
with more prose than pictures and more illustrations than photographs.
Led by *Life*, these magazines imported the "photo-essay" from its European origins and perfected it for American tastes, stringing one to two
dozen pictures on a single theme together into a story. For the first time
in modern journalism, the pictures were the stars and the prose played
a supporting role.[7]

The secret to the success of *Life* and *Look* compared with older weekly
picture magazines such as the *New York Times Mid-Week Pictorial* was that
they treated pictures not as decoration for text or an unrelated list, but
as the story itself. *Look*, one rung below *Life* on the prestige ladder, casually referred to some of its spreads as "picture-arguments" and boasted
in its promos that it "writes in pictures."

These magazines celebrated the art of looking at pictures and found
ways to educate their readers in this art. *Life* saw itself as a tutor in pictorial appreciation. In its very first issue in 1936 there were photographs
not only of people, places, and things, but of paintings. Almost every
issue had at least one page in color, and Luce was devoted to what he
called "Art." There were stories on surrealism (especially the ubiquitous
self-promoter Salvador Dalí), Picasso, photo-essays on Rembrandt's
paintings, even a photo-essay on Hitler's biography, including a hoax
picture of a very ugly baby Hitler. *Life*'s editors actively commissioned
visual artists to provide images for stories, not only photographers, and
featured American regionalist painters in twenty-nine stories from 1936
to 1942.[8] Soon *Life* would help popularize abstract expressionism, asking
about Jackson Pollock, "Is he the greatest living painter in the United

States?"[9] *Life* presented not only photographs of the world, but images of images. It gave us a picture of the world as a picture, as Martin Heidegger would say.

Photojournalism offered a pedagogy of the eye. *Life*'s rivals also carried features explicitly designed to train readers to look closely, such as *Look*'s "photoquiz" feature. Offering about twenty disconnected two-inch by two-inch photographs over a two-page spread, the photoquiz provided a realist panorama of modern visual culture, ranging from famous cartoon characters and live-action starlets to heavy machinery and birds. They were often, as this list suggests, pictures of other pictures. Often defamiliarizing close-ups tested or teased the eye by removing the contextual Gestalt. Since these quizzes showed items depicted in the magazine, they invited readers not only to appreciate photographic detail but to regard the magazine as a serious object of study. Most of these images were as forgettable as the advertising that surrounded them, but the point was the attitude they embodied: *Look* was not only a title but a command.

Apart from the great weekly magazines, documentary photography was also produced by some government agencies. The New Deal's Farm Security Administration (FSA) hired dozens of photographers to scour the country to, as Jack Delano, an FSA photographer, said, "search for the heart of the American people." Some eighty thousand photos were taken for the FSA from 1935 to 1943. After the project ended, the pictures continued to circulate—and to resonate. Some became phenomenally famous, such as Walker Evans's photos of Alabama sharecroppers or Dorothea Lange's *Migrant Mother.*[10]

Early in the century, photographs by Lewis W. Hine and Jacob Riis portrayed the working-class poor to middle-class audiences. But the documentary photographers of the thirties and forties had their own craft and technology. The photojournalist movement owes its origins in large part to a new sort of camera—the Leica. The Leica was the first small, hand-held camera that could produce high-quality pictures. In the nineteenth century, the bourgeois portrait was a backbone of photography, along with pictures of nature, of the monuments of the world, and of scientific phenomena for research. But given long exposure times and the clumsiness of large cameras, photojournalism was not practical. In the early 1900s Hine, the photographer of poor whites in American slums, factories, mines, and farms, had to lug his box camera around and set it on a tripod. It was big and clumsy—"fifty pounds of cumbersome apparatus"—and Hine often had to pose his subjects.[11] Many of the photos in *Life* or *Look* could never have been taken with older camera technology.

FIGURE 4.1. Dorothea Lange, "Destitute peapickers in California; a 32 year old
mother of seven children. February 1936," also known as *Migrant Mother*.
Library of Congress, Prints and Photographs Division, LC-DIG-fsa-8b29516.

The Leica, on the other hand, was easy to carry and easy to use. It
combined portability and high aesthetic standards. Invented in 1913 by
Oskar Barnack, a German microscope technician who wanted to make a
small 35 mm camera usable by the movie industry for test pictures, the
Leica (from *Leitz ca*mera) was mass produced for the first time in 1925.
The Leica's shutter speed—1/1,000 second by the mid-1930s—was phenomenal for the time, allowing it to catch unposed action. Leitz also

introduced the first telephoto lens in 1933 (200 mm). The "Reporter" model of 1934 held thirty-three feet of film, had a synchronized flash option, and allowed 250 exposures without a reload, producing more material for magazine editors to choose from. It also fed the demand for unposed shots, "related pictures," and candid shooting.[12] (*Snapshot* was originally a term for "a quick or hurried [gun] shot taken without deliberate aim" [*OED*]. Until cameras sped up, the hunting analogy was only a dream.) Every major *Life* photographer through the 1940s except Margaret Bourke-White used a Leica.[13] First conceived as an industrial adjunct to the movie camera, the Leica found its calling in a similarly grand field of picture making—photojournalism.

Western Union first sent a half-tone image by wire in 1921, and the Associated Press's "wirephoto" service was up and running by the mid-1930s. The new ability to transmit photographs over telegraph wires with great clarity, the ancestor of our fax machines, was the final ingredient in the photojournalism of the mid-twentieth century.

Technology might have made photojournalism possible, but its characteristic style was not dictated by the camera. Photojournalism, and documentary photography more widely, conveyed an attitude about the image. Created in Germany, the transplanted photomagazine flourished in the United States and took on a very different character. German pioneers of photojournalism—Dadaists such as John Heartfield and Hannah Höch—were politically on the left and aesthetically in the avant-garde. The photograph, like the social order, was to be scrambled in the service of radical change. Others in Europe, such as the constructivist Alexander Rodchenko or the surrealist Man Ray, took photographs from points of view that would be contortionist in actual life or altered them beyond anything you could see with a naked eye. Such artists never signed the realist contract.

In America, *Life* and *Look* were more socially and aesthetically middle-of-the-road. Their photographers did not emphasize the fragmentation, artificiality, or collage of images. They aimed to "document" or even to "witness" reality. They thought the artistic medium of the camera provided them with a special tie to the real. "Whatever facts a person writes," according to Bourke-White, "have to be colored by his prejudice and bias. With a camera, the shutter opens and closes and the only rays that come in to be registered come directly from the object in front of you."[14] Most American photojournalists mouthed such ideas of the camera's veracity.

But this was only one half of the attitude about the image. The other half was a frank embrace of artfulness. While the Leica could capture swift unposed action cleanly on film, documentary photos could still be as carefully crafted as any Hollywood production. According to Arthur Rothstein, a leading documentary photographer, the picture taker had to be "not only a cameraman but a scenarist, dramatist, and director as well." He could say without irony that a "truly candid photograph" was "carefully planned." Roy Stryker, the influential leader of the FSA documentary photography project, said there were "times when you simply have to pose your model." The key, for Stryker, was how you did it, "honestly" or "dishonestly." "Truth," he said, "is a balance." The image did not have to be natural, it had to look natural. Henry Luce put it more starkly: picture takers should use "fakery in allegiance to the truth."[15]

Mainstream documentary photography, then, was defined not by artlessness so much as by the feel of artlessness. Realism and artfulness had not yet grown estranged in image making as they did when late twentieth-century attitudes hardened. Most important, the image had to be more than just a picture, more than an illustration of an event. It was an axiom of photojournalists that the picture had to capture what the French photographer Henri Cartier-Bresson called "the decisive moment," that instant where formal and psychological elements meshed perfectly. Form and content had to merge to say something important. Wilson Hicks, the executive editor of *Life* in the forties, recalled that the magazine's photographers had to grasp "the camera's extraordinary capacity for recording more than a mere image." Good photojournalists used pictures to express an "essence interpreted."[16]

Images from the 1930s and 1940s were also shaped by the law. Censors finally got firm hold of the movie industry in 1934 after long agitation by various interest groups such as the Catholic Legion of Decency. The Production Code, in effect until the 1960s, seriously limited what could be shown on screen. There could be no undress and only the most chaste contact between the sexes. Even mild profanity was strictly forbidden. Viewers had to fill in the blanks with their imaginations—and of course directors found plenty of ways to tickle the code's boundaries.

World War II only intensified the censorship. The most censored war in US history touched film, newsreels, and magazines. Movie scripts had to be approved by the Office of War Information. Pictures had to be cleared by army censors. Only after long debates about the effects of graphic war imagery on morale did government officials finally approve publication of pictures of dead US soldiers in *Life* in September 1943, with faces not shown and identities withheld. The increasing graphicness was a conscious decision by the Roosevelt administration. From 1942 to 1945, the nation monitored its images as at no other time in its history. "Never have men been so in need of a believable image," wrote one observer in 1942.[17] Censorship was one clear ingredient in the nation-integrating force of images around 1945.

Varieties of Photographic Practice

Mythic images raised a key question: Did these images accurately capture larger truths? Did they actually did summarize "fact"? A museum's summaries were backed by repositories of hidden collections managed by experts, but where was the backing for these pictures? The culture of the mythic or synthesizing image was not without its critics. Some thought the new image culture too sensationalistic, deadening to the spirit, or given to "unreal" fantasy. Photojournalists, moviemakers, and museum curators all had to confront the question whether the new attitude to image presentation was *too* fantastic. How great could the gap between image and information actually be?

The celebrity photography of George Hurrell, perfected in the 1930s, raised these issues in acute form. Hurrell was a master of the Hollywood studio portrait and perhaps the principal inventor of the glamour shot.[18] A would-be painter who briefly studied at the Art Institute of Chicago, his early apprenticeship in commercial photography included work in hand coloring, retouching negatives, and airbrushing. He contracted with *Esquire* in 1936 to deliver a monthly "Hurrell girl" and served as the West Coast photo manager of the magazine in 1941. He was a master of seductive portraits. One critic said Hurrell's favorite pose for his female subjects was "ready to ravish." He worked for studios such as MGM, Warner Brothers, and Columbia, with a brief stint in the army during World War II, where the task of photographing military brass no doubt posed different challenges than shooting stars and starlets in Hollywood.

One secret of his technique was an exquisite and exacting use of lighting, including a boom light he invented, which strove to match the lighting and look of classical Hollywood cinema. Two more secrets were avoiding the thick makeup of the day and fastidiously retouching negatives. All this allowed a smooth, unearthly glow over the skin of the demigods fortunate enough to appear in his portraits. Hurrell turned stars into patterns of perfection in black and white—or in color, as they appeared in *Esquire*. The play of light and shadow on gorgeous faces invited viewers to worship or drool. He shot his subjects against a background of drapes and other cloth, in unmarked interior spaces far removed from everyday life. There were no artifacts identifying time or place. He helped feed Hollywood's voracious appetite for still photography in the 1930s. In 1931, for instance, the studios provided nearly one million free pictures to magazines and newspapers around the world. Portrait shots serviced the film industry's star-making machinery, and still photography remains an important aspect of the movie business.

Hurrell's confectionary style was the flip side of documentary realism. Hurrell, like many of his Hollywood colleagues, pictured a world that wasn't ours, and wasn't real, a world where there were no beings but the beautiful. Walker Evans, Dorothea Lange, and their colleagues pictured a world equally mythic, but one more real than real. Their subjects may not have had immaculate complexions, but they were still "immortal," as Roy Stryker said of *Migrant Mother*. Hurrell's work reminds us that the tensions between authenticity and forgery, grit and glamour, realism and fantasy are inherent in all forms of photography, not just digital.

Another contrast to the documentary realism of the FSA was the work of James VanDerZee (1886–1983), the photographic chronicler of the black bourgeoisie. His photographs, like Hurrell's, improved their subjects by airbrushing and retouching; but the alternative universe they portrayed was one not of glamour, but of Sunday afternoon well-being. He shot the canonical images of Marcus Garvey, and African American politicians, athletes, musicians, and ministers sought him out in the years of the Harlem Renaissance. He opened a photography shop in Harlem in 1912 and was in demand for over two decades. His work went into eclipse about World War II owing to the rise of amateur photography, his no longer fashionable late Victorian pictorial conventions, and economic and demographic changes, but it was rescued from obscurity with an exhibition in 1969 at the Metropolitan Museum of Art in New York.[19]

VanDerZee's images and subjects were always composed and posed, with no pretense of having been caught unawares. His subjects claim no rawness of authenticity but always put their best foot forward. He shot important life events such as graduations, weddings, births, or funerals, and his African American subjects are shown with gravitas and sometimes with sly humor. They were always elegantly dressed, sometimes in clothes he kept in his studio for that purpose, and they faced the camera with confidence, embedded in their material circumstances. Furniture, clothing, flowers, interiors, ornaments, musical instruments—both subject and scene were well appointed. Bad teeth or blemishes were spirited away by retouching.

In *Evening Attire*, the image from 1922 that we include here—"a perfectly wondrous, odd image" as Jacqueline Goldsby puts it—you can see a bit of retouching about the eyes and the lips and VanDerZee's vertical signature and date, almost brazenly in the middle of the image, apparently made with the same brush.[20] There is some ghostly blurriness about the bottom of the elegant young woman's dress, and her feet don't seem to quite line up with conventional anatomy. She almost hovers in the air. Her hat has a double-exposure shadow, as if she moved slightly during the shot. A curious small figurine sits on the table she leans on—chinoiserie, idol, trinket, studio prop, objet d'art?—which mirrors her pose of cradling something in its hands. The overall image is exquisitely composed, with a doubled vertical line motif repeated in the window, the wall hanging, the table legs, and the carpet, in contrast to the rounded contours of her hat, dress, arm, and overall mien. (Indeed, doubling might be one theme of the image, a metaphotographic comment.) VanDerZee used the gelatin silver print to bring out great variety in the intensity and saturation of the monochromatic medium, from the bright light of the window or flowers to the dark spots on the brim of the hat or under the table near her left hip. He may well have used a base paper with a bias toward a warm tone, and perhaps even with a built in yellow-red coloring.[21] The image is full of decorative surfaces, as Jennifer Raab notes—the backdrop, the rug, the beaded dress.[22] It's not too far a stretch to suggest an Old Masters sensibility of abundant well-being in interior spaces, as the studio backdrop depicts a curtained window and a tapestry, perfectly mirroring each other in size and composition, with light pouring through the window.[23]

VanDerZee's work falls in the lineage of nineteenth-century bourgeois portraiture, photography serving as a ceremonial marker of life's turning points, though he denied wider influences or any knowledge of art photography; in a late-life interview he claimed never to have heard of such groundbreaking photographers as Edward Steichen, Alfred Stieglitz, Lewis Hine, or Carl van Vechten. He claimed to be a naïf. His retouching of funerary portraits, sometimes showing an image of the deceased hovering over the mourners, also recalled late Victorian and Edwardian "spirit photography." The almost double exposure evident in *Evening Attire* might echo this spiritualist doubling. Some scholars link this practice to avant-garde photomontage artists of the 1920s. Perhaps. But his alterations of the image were never jarring; they were affirming. Like a Heartfield or a Rodchenko, he pointed to an alternative social order, but unlike them he did so by reassurance rather than by disturbance.[24]

VanDerZee's pictures of dignity amid plenty run counter to another theme in African American iconography, dignity—or misery—amid

FIGURE 4.2. James VanDerZee, *Evening Attire*, 1922. Smithsonian American Art Museum, Washington, DC/Art Resource, New York.

poverty. Diego Rivera, the radical Mexican muralist, thought blacks should be portrayed as downtrodden in order to mobilize revolutionary political sentiment. This was not VanDerZee's view. Critical reception of his work has emphasized that it offered an alternative to other images of African Americans from the time, such as lynching postcards. His work tried to present the best of his world. To treat black people as subjects worthy of the conventions of bourgeois representation could be a radical act. The young woman in evening attire may be slightly double-exposed, but she may have also sensed, as Goldsby reflects, "the illuminations of a 'double life' beyond DuBois-ian double consciousness that [VanDerZee's] Black sitters undoubtedly experienced in their studio sessions. . . . The aspiration, the ambition, of this woman to be seen in and connect with the wider world trembles in the stillness of the Chinese figurine on the table."[25] VanDerZee presented one option of image making—the solid, warm, composed, confident depiction of a whole way of life—in the second quarter of the century. This was not Lange, with her distracted subjects peering off into the distance as if too exhausted to notice the camera, or Hurrell, with his unattainable Venuses and Adonises.

Nor was it Lee Miller, with her aestheticizing of any subject matter, no matter how traumatic. Closely tied to the surrealists (she shot many of their portraits), her work raised more questions about the relation between the image and reality. As an accredited documentary war photographer in the European theater, Lee Miller crossed all kinds of lines. Her surrealist work—a genre normally thought to leave everyday reality for flights of fancy—has a spark of "having happenedness," and her war photography—a genre whose gravity is often thought to make any concern for aesthetics superfluous—is often infused with an uncanny beauty. Her *Bombs Bursting on the Cité d'Aleth* (1944), for instance, is framed through a window with a surrealistic grillwork at the bottom.[26] In the center is a dark form like a misshapen head of cauliflower. From the image alone one would not necessarily realize we are seeing a bomb. The mark of the surrealist, said André Bazin in 1945, is that the distinction between the real and the imaginary begins to disappear. With Miller it was hard to tell which was which. Perhaps she didn't know herself.[27]

Miller was a muse for other artists and photographers—Picasso painted her, and Steichen used her as a model for his photographs for *Vogue*, which published much of her work. Her photography was both about artists and itself art. She claimed that about 1930 she had discovered the technique of solarizing, an effect achieved by exposing the negative to light during developing, which adds a glowing halo to the image. (Man Ray, her mentor and lover, also claimed the discovery for himself.) Such techniques as solarizing altered images within the photographic medium itself, forfeiting any claim to realism. Miller took photos of the invasion of Normandy and visited the concentration camps Buchenwald and Dachau soon after their liberation. Her camera told a kinkier tale than did Bourke-White's canonical photos of the camps. Bourke-White showed groups of dazed survivors slowly hatching their way back into the daylight. Miller showed guards beaten and murdered in vengeance, survivors scrounging in waste dumps, and ovens holding half-charred bodies, as well as the corpses of Nazi suicides frozen in a macabre choreography. In a way her work was squarely in the tradition of surrealist photography, for which the corpse was always the artistic object par excellence.

In one famous photograph, taken by *Life* photographer David Scherman, her companion at the time, she posed nude in Hitler's Munich bathtub between a small classical sculpture of the "Aryan" type Nazis promoted and a photograph of Hitler. On the smudged bathmat before the tub sit her military boots, dirty with the ashes of Dachau. Was this art, documentary, social criticism, or surrealist outrageousness? Was the photograph washing away the grit of death by art, or was it a stunt of "callous clowning"?[28] Just what was the image's responsibility to suffering? Miller's photographs were not the place to look for an answer.

Bombs and Bombshells

The bomb was perhaps the hugest image made in America in 1945. Three airplanes flew to Hiroshima in the dawn's early light of August 6, 1945. One, the *Enola Gay*, carried "Little Boy," the atomic bomb. Another carried scientists and instruments. A third carried cameras, both still and motion picture, though the plane had trouble making the rendezvous with the *Enola Gay*, leaving the mission underdocumented photographically. The picture that was eventually released to the world on August 11 was taken by Sgt. George Caron, the tail gunner of the *Enola Gay*, with a borrowed K-20 camera. The photo is a grainy black-and-white image of a column of cloud, slightly off the vertical, topped by a separate crown-shaped puff. No sign of the instant vaporizing of eighty thousand people appears in the abstraction of this extreme long shot.[29] It was published in the August 20, 1945, issue of *Life*, which covered the explosion in great aerial detail. But the US occupation kept a tight lid on images of the devastation, and when *Life* first published ground-level photographs in 1952, the magazine seemed more interested in the prestige of being the first to do so than in the human consequences of nuclear war.

Excess of joy weeps, and excess of sorrow laughs, said William Blake, and bathos was one way to contain the awful sublimity of the bomb. The mushroom cloud took off in postwar iconography and was a key image in popular culture and advertising of the late 1940s and early 1950s. The visual symbol showed up in comic strips and neon signs, on candy boxes and jazz album covers, in the shapes of hairstyles and cakes, and adorning beauty queens. It also inspired the 1950 hillbilly gospel song "Jesus Hits Like an Atom Bomb," by Lowell Blanchard and the Valley Trio. The

Sidebar 4.2 Weegee

The celebrated tabloid photographer Weegee (Arthur Fellig, 1899–1968) shows how working-class crime imagery stood outside the main drift of the culture of summation. He is probably best known for his freelance work for *PM* and other New York City newspapers from 1936 to 1946. He polished his reputation for psychic ability—Weegee as the telepathic reader of the urban Ouija board—to arrive at a crime or death scene in his 1938 Chevrolet at the perfect moment, but his practices were perfected after years of hard work as a tabloid photographer. Listening in to police radio and taking tips from his network of informants, he was an accomplished ambulance chaser whose prey was astonishing scenes.

A skilled self-promoter who signed photographs "Weegee the Famous," he was a loner among New York photographers. His photographs always stage what it means to look, and they often include an internal spectator. He had a special gift for finding brutally ironic verbal captions inside the frame. In a 1937 photo, he caught a fire hose squirting a jet of water on a burning apartment building. On the building were billboards for "Hygrade all beef Frankfurters" exhorting passersby to "simply add boiling water." Clouds of light billow from the building, blurring water, fire, and smoke against the black night sky. In *On the Spot* (1940), he photographed three cops standing over a well-dressed shooting victim in front of the Spot Bar and Grill. The spot symbol on the bar's sign eerily echoes the pool of blood forming by the victim's head in the gutter. The beautifully balanced play of light against dark ground in both pictures creates a jarring, almost jaunty contrast with the traumatic events they depict.

Weegee's book *Naked City* (1945) made him famous. He styled himself as a hard-boiled figure like the detectives of *Black Mask* magazine. An early adopter of infrared film, he was able to take pictures in the night hours as few photographers had done before. His pictures did not represent the daylight world shared by all; they showed what went on in the murky underworld after sunset.

Weegee's images contain in embryo sinister signs that later critics would see in images everywhere. His was, to say the least, an aesthetic and moral universe very different from *Life*'s. The photojournalistic weeklies of the 1940s had a rich bounty of shocking pictures, of course; it was not all statesmen, starlets, and surrealists. In September 1943 *Life* began to print pictures of dead American soldiers, though no faces or blood were shown. But the viewer's supreme and secure position was never questioned. In *Life* and *Look*, every horrifying picture had a catharsis close at hand.

But Weegee provided comparatively little salve for the viewer's conscience. His camera did not assume a genteel discretion about the facts of life. It embraced an unvarnished fascination with the seamy side of the city and the kinky side of the will to look. *Life* showed a common world, at least a world that everyone was supposed to feel a natural participant in and be licensed to look at. Such ease of spectatorship, the idea that looking at pictures was completely innocent and natural, would be a chief target of image-skeptical thinking later in the century. With Weegee, you never had the assurance that your looking was innocent.

Their First Murder (1941), for instance, depicts the reactions of a motley crew of white children and older women, none of them looking sentimentally innocent and some appearing deranged, distressed, or delighted. (Weegee loved to catch people looking freakish, something he shared with a slightly later American photographer, Diane Arbus, who curated a posthumous exhibition of his work.) The children were leaving their Brooklyn School, PS 143, when a small-time hustler was gunned down in broad daylight. We do not see Peter Mancuso, the murder victim, only the onlookers. (The original spread in *PM* did run a separate photograph of the bloody body, covered with newspapers.) They certainly do not look like angelic virgins of the gaze. They've already seen plenty, and they're eagerly drinking it in; boys in the back crane their necks to get a glimpse over the crowd. The picture shows gawkers at violence, and in its spectacle of spectators it might be a cunning self-reflexive commentary on Weegee's art. In the lower left a child with furrowed brow looks inquiringly at the photographer like the conscience within the frame. Those who see his photos are gawkers too.[1]

But the genteel viewer looking at this photograph is tempted to deny any identification with anyone: "I would never look like that!" in either sense of *look*, as gazing or as appearing. But reflective viewers are reminded at once that they are in fact looking at a twistedly interesting picture. The very act of looking destroys any pretense of a higher righteousness. Weegee hooks us into complicity. He teaches us something about the common urge to look that connects us all, though he might reject the idea that his pictures had any moral mission. Susan Sontag

1. Thanks to Jenny Raab for help on the details of this photograph.

FIGURE 4.3. Weegee, *Their First Murder*, October 8, 1941.
© Weegee/International Center of Photography (13.1997).

could have been thinking of Weegee when she called photography a kind of "soft murder."[2]

Weegee unsettled Henry Luce's call for a culture of pictures that would teach us "to see and take pleasure in seeing." There were pleasures enough to be had in Weegee's photographs, but they were not the innocent pleasures of middle-class access to a world that could be seen and mastered. They taught something more painful, a wicked wisdom acquainted with the night and its imponderabilia. Here was a gallows beauty, a chiaroscuro exploration of depths that *Life* and its counterparts rarely exposed. Weegee shows that not all pictures in the 1940s were designed to summarize the world; some were meant to cast irony on the very idea that looking was smooth and safe or that the world made sense.[3] He offered the rough solidarity of shared perversity, not the genteel distance of safe viewing.

2. Susan Sontag, *On Photography* (New York: Farrar, Straus and Giroux, 1977), 15.

3. Miles Barth, *Weegee's World* (New York: Bulfinch Press, 1997); V. Penelope Pelizzon and Nancy M. West, "'Good Stories' from the Mean Streets: Weegee and Hard-Boiled Autobiography," *Yale Journal of Criticism* 17 (2004): 20–50.

FIGURE 4.4. George Robert Caron, *Mushroom Cloud over Hiroshima*, 1945.

mushroom cloud famously reminded Robert Oppenheimer, director
of the Manhattan Project, of a passage from the *Bhagavad Gita*, but for
most Americans its cultural resonance was less highbrow. The bomb was
treated in postwar popular culture with a spooky lightheartedness, even
banality.[30] As early as 1946, *Fortune*, the third leg in Luce's magazine empire, wanted to counter the "blasé" attitude toward the bomb, the mushroom cloud having become "so familiar a symbol."[31] It seemed the bomb
had vaporized not only two Japanese cities but also public memory and
the ethical horror of impending apocalypse.[32]

On the day that "Fat Man" exploded over Nagasaki, all the major
Hollywood studios began placing calls to the Pentagon's Bureau of Pub-

lic Relations lobbying to be the first studio to dramatize the bombing in film. President Harry Truman personally selected MGM, and his administration oversaw production of the film from start to finish. The eventual docudrama, *The Beginning or the End* (1947), fizzled at the box office but lived on as a cult classic thanks to its campy grappling with something too big to be handled by the Hollywood conventions of the day.[33] (The clever term "stuplimity" might be applied here.)

But it was no surprise that the military invested in image-making technology. Cinema about war and war *as* cinema are well-known themes. In 1947 the US Air Force even started a secret motion picture studio in the hills above Hollywood called Lookout Mountain Laboratories. Many innovative techniques such as 3-D and Cinemascope were tested there before they were used for popular film. The strategy of making the unthinkable as mundane as possible informed a series of civil defense films inviting schoolchildren to "duck and cover." Surviving an atomic blast could be pitched as a lesson in classroom decorum. Even the bomb could be normalized.[34]

Very little explicit information about nuclear fission circulated among the American public during the 1940s. The administration feared security breaches and believed the public could not grasp the complex science involved in the bomb, a sharp contrast to the later urban legend that anyone could find instructions on how to build a bomb on the internet. Instead, the Atomic Energy Commission and the Manhattan Project selectively released photographs of nuclear explosions and bombs— familiar imagery that the public could easily grasp—to publications such as *Life* to promote public awareness of the new nuclear science.

These "press kits" were similar to those released by the public relations arms of Hollywood studios ahead of the release of a film. The images were carefully composed and framed as if the action were unfolding under a proscenium arch. As Scott Kirsch notes in his study of atomic photos, no additional information accompanied the AEC's photo press releases, which were supposed to speak for themselves.[35] Significantly, the atomic photos *Life* published were among the very few photos the magazine used that were not taken by its own photographers. The aestheticized imagery fed to *Life* and other outlets by the military effectively disassociated the technology from death and suffering and helped to produce a mythos that linked the bomb to forces of creative destruction. Whatever else the bomb created—jitters, the cold war, damage and death, the military-academic complex, the internet, or a clear Upper Holocene boundary marker—it certainly created spectacle, a kind of imagery sometimes known as the atomic sublime.

For nuclear testing, cameras were an essential part of the mechanism. Photographic images of bombs provided both popular spectacle and scientific data. Still and motion-picture cameras were the best way to measure the immediate properties, effects, and impact of the blasts. (Computers were developed in part to simulate nuclear explosions: data and visualization techniques typically follow each other.) Early detonations were attended by cavalier observers in shorts and summer wear, protected from the fallout by nothing more than sunglasses and baseball caps. We look at them the way we look at actors brandishing their cigarettes in films of the same era—as revealing an innocence about mortal hazards that we have long since lost. Los Alamos had a special Photographic and Optics Division that designed cameras to document the first nuclear explosion on July 16, 1945. More than fifty still and motion-picture cameras were on hand that day. At the test of the first hydrogen bomb at Bikini Atoll in the Marshall Islands in 1946, cameras of every sort surrounded the site on the ground, and thirty-six aircraft provided a photographic "umbrella" of over 250 airborne movie cameras.[36] Bikini was, among other things, an outdoor film set. Bruce Connor's sublime film *Crossroads* (1976) used archival footage of the blast to make a melancholy, slow meditation on creation and destruction. You cannot watch this film without feeling that the bomb was made to be filmed.

Photography was an essential part of the scientific follow-up to nuclear explosions. But atomic and hydrogen bombs had distinct photographic requirements. The mushroom cloud is visible to the human eye and can be captured by conventional cameras. The hydrogen bomb, however, operates at intensities of light that can cripple eyes and conventional cameras and at speeds that are completely inaccessible to human perception. Ultra-high-speed photography emerged as a twin to the hydrogen bomb. In the H-bomb, firing and timing could not be separated. To make an image of the explosion the camera needed to share the same timing mechanism as the detonation.

The Atomic Energy Commission outsourced this coalescence of optics and ballistics to EG&G (Edgerton, Germeshausen, and Grier), a company founded in 1947. Harold "Doc" Edgerton, an electrical engineering professor at Massachusetts Institute of Technology, was an innovator in high-speed photography. His 1930s photo of a drop of milk bouncing on impact to make a symmetrical little crown showed, as Muybridge had done, something no one had seen before. In contrast to Daguerre's early photograph, which wiped the Paris streets of anything moving, Edgerton's images made the fleeting fluid world solid and lasting. Later, stroboscopic images taken by his collaborator Gjon Mili—of

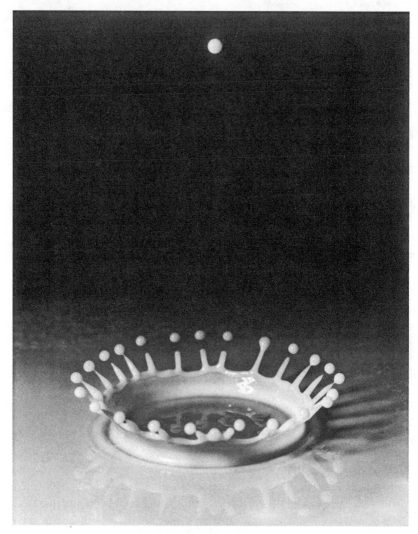

FIGURE 4.5. Harold Edgerton, *Milk Drop Coronet*, 1936.
© 2010 MIT. Courtesy MIT Museum.

drummers, dancers, baseball pitchers, and an actual nude descending a staircase—became popular spreads in *Life* magazine. Some of the movie cameras Mili and Edgerton used shot as many as two thousand frames a second. But EG&G had to operate at much higher speeds than that to make visual records of the early moments of a thermonuclear explosion. The company developed a firing-timing nexus that rendered "the technologies of bombs and cameras virtually interchangeable." Images could be made at two to three microseconds (millionths of a second) precisely because the camera and the detonation mechanism were combined.[37]

The problem had been getting the camera to survive the blast it was documenting. Shock waves, heat, dust, and most insidiously radiation all posed threats to the photographic process. Radiation exposes film (as we know from airport security), and color film was especially susceptible to "fogging" by gamma radiation, so it was not used closer to ground zero than four thousand feet. Edgerton used a "Rapatronic" camera to take images of the very first phases of thermonuclear blasts. These embryonic explosions, captured when barely more than twenty meters in diameter and a few microseconds old, yield uncanny images that look variously like bulbous suns, bloated navel oranges, skulls, big-eyeballed insects or aliens, sea creatures, insect larvae, spacecraft, spores, or even a kohlrabi. They are round weirdnesses reminiscent of Robert Hooke's printer's point discussed in chapter 1. Sometimes the blast images sprout stalactite-like legs. As Jennifer Raab notes, "So strange how these images register as at once vast and as microscopic . . . like mutant dust mites."[38] The fireball is a veritable Rorschach test of postwar horrors.[39] Unlike the much more famous mushroom cloud, the ultra-high-speed fireball can be seen only by way of a device that shares in the timing mechanism of the explosion itself. Fireballs are a kind of flash photography that transcends human ocular and physiological capacities, made possible by the same machinery that makes the bomb possible.[40]

There were other sorts of bombs and bombshells around in 1945. Graham Greene, living in London during the Blitz, found something romantic about air raids: "The nightly routine of sirens, barrage, the probing raider, the unmistakable engine (Where are you? Where are you? Where are you?), the bomb-bursts moving nearer and then moving away, hold one like a love-charm."[41] A popular song from 1940 sung by Una Mae Carlisle blended sexual innuendo and armaments, including the lines "I don't want no infantry / Blitzkrieg Baby, you can't bomb me." Perversely but reliably, *eros* and *thanatos* go together, and the bomb never lacked a romantic or erotic significance.

A new two-piece bathing suit was christened the bikini three days after the atomic blast at Bikini Atoll in July 1946, forever linking sex appeal and megatonnage, "atomic fission and orgasmic pleasure."[42] The name was given by the French designer Louis Réard in an apparent effort to outdo a better-known rival who had designed a swimsuit called the *atome* for its minute size and explosive effect.[43] The bikini's "four triangles of nothing" and nuclear explosions were irresistible metaphorical partners in devastating heat. The term *bombshell* had taken on a sexual meaning in the 1930s, perhaps beginning with the Jean Harlow screwball comedy *Bombshell* (1933), but it acquired a fresh meaning when World War II pilots started to adorn their planes and bombs with sultry pic-

FIGURE 4.6. Harold Edgerton, *Atomic Bomb Explosion*, HEE-NC-52010, 1952.
© 2010 MIT. Courtesy MIT Museum.

tures, such as the pinup of Rita Hayworth that is rumored to have been attached to Little Boy (much to her distress). Other actresses were marketed as blond bombshells. For instance, in September 1945 *Life* magazine introduced actress Linda Christians posing in a two-piece bathing suit as an "Anatomic Bomb." Looking back with eyes trained by feminist sensibilities, we cannot help but see something telling in this pairing of sex and violence, but that is not how it was received at the time.

Another pairing of Venus and Mars was the wartime pinup. While pinups might now be seen to hint of a more salacious future, at the time they had a patriotic feel as a healthy diversion for the boys in uniform, a way to channel (or encourage) heterosexual desire. The pinup genre, though it has older roots, was developed in the 1930s by the airbrush artists George Petty and Alberto Vargas. *Esquire*, a men's magazine with annual circulation of over half a million in this decade, which also employed George Hurrell, was the main outlet for these images, and once the editors realized their popularity, by the 1940s pinups moved from cigarette and soda advertisements to full-pages and double-page spreads of their own. About twenty thousand copies a week of the famous Betty Grable pinup were said to be distributed throughout the war, credited with helping troop morale. The pinup genre was perhaps "the premier vessel of pro-war propaganda." Though later critics would see the pin-up's suppressed affinity with pornography, at the time it was widely received as wholesome, patriotic, and innocent.[44]

The delicacy of obscenity is that calling something dirty can make it so, and there were, of course, dissident voices that did not see the pinup as healthy. The postmaster general, channeling the spirit of Comstock, briefly sought to repeal *Esquire*'s second-class mailing privileges during the war, accusing the magazine of being "obscene, lewd, and lascivious." The particular targets of his wrath were the popular "Varga girls" drawn by Alberto Vargas—full-bodied, leggy, wasp-waisted women clothed in one-piece bathing suits who were posed as if flying. (Vargas's images made women aerodynamic just as pilots made airplanes into symbolic women.) In self-defense, the magazine claimed that the pictures boosted the troops' morale and that pinups were in constant demand. Summoning various witnesses at a two-month hearing called by the postmaster, *Esquire* successfully argued that its sexy images did no harm. One Harvard psychiatrist added that he found the Varga girl "inspiring." And the *New York Times* reported a public opinion poll saying that most Americans regarded the pinups as "good clean pictures, glorifying good figures, and a tribute to American womanhood." Betty Grable's pinup lost no popularity after she married in 1943. Pinups plugged a hole in liberal political theory by showing the troops what they were fighting for.[45] The pinup was safe, her sexuality contained by the urgency of war or the call of motherhood.

The French film theorist and critic André Bazin argued that the pinup girl's success lay in her ability to call up erotic feelings without stepping into salacious or pornographic territory. One of a long line of Europeans looking across the Atlantic to American sexual mores with a baffled or condescending eye, he found the pinup an expression of Protestant censorship, a distillation of sexuality into a kind of vital energy purged of all real erotic danger. The pinup girl, he complained, was "nothing more than chewing gum for the imagination."[46] She kept the soldiers pumped up without offering any erotic authenticity. Bazin anticipated the moral fuzziness that was to envelop the pinup girl in later decades. The pinup was a summarizing picture, something whose center could not hold.

Sidebar 4.3 War Photography

While the grim potential of the new medium of photography was immediately apparent, there are multiple reasons why the facts of war have typically not been portrayed in detail. Technological limitations, the reluctance of political leaders to show violence, the partisanship of journalists, and the queasiness of editors have all, at various times, contributed to softening war coverage. The story is how little anyone wants to see brutal pictures of death.

Despite photography's power to portray graphic destruction, there were still many technological limits on how brutal our portrayal of war violence would be. During the Civil War, photographs could not be printed in newspapers, magazines, or books. Nor were cameras capable of action shots. As a consequence, pen-and-ink drawings remained the most common way citizens at home "saw" the war. There was an important difference between the photos taken and the photos *seen*—how citizens commonly saw war at the time. It is a mistake to confuse our own easy access to images with what people could see in the past. The best way to view Mathew Brady's Civil War pictures was to go to his gallery in New York City. At first, photography was not the most common way to see war.

The technological barriers took a long time to lift. It was only in the late 1930s during the Spanish Civil War that photographers could take action-filled shots, transport them quickly to the other side of the world, and print them in newspapers and magazines. From the Civil War through the First World War, technology limited how graphic war pictures might be.

Yet as one limitation was lifting, another was settling in. The American federal government became increasingly interested in corralling journalists, in shaping the imagery of war, a practice that started during the Spanish-American War, was perfected during World War I, and reached its apogee in World War II and the Korean War. As technological limits were disappearing, the state started to intervene.

The US government, in wartime, rarely formally censored. Curtailing First Amendment rights to stop publication of images happened only during the Second World War. Instead, early in the twentieth century the government developed the means of controlling access to the front. The president's war powers as commander-in-chief became, by World War I, the way to control what pictures might be taken. The characteristic means by which the government has managed the flow of images in warfare during the past hundred years has been finding ways to shape what pictures get taken, not formally censoring content. It was easier to limit access than to control pictures.

This system broke down in Vietnam, but it was re-created during the two wars in Iraq. The various strategies used to manage media—such as "embedding" reporters with the troops—are new only in their particulars. As a general strategy, such practices simply revived the means used from 1898 to 1965—managing the flow of imagery by controlling access to the front. This particular practice, by the way, explains the dual character of contemporary war imagery—less death and maiming is portrayed than was shown during the Vietnam War, but it has a global and electric spread. The Abu Ghraib pictures of American soldiers torturing Iraqi prisoners became known all the world over within days of their release. Less gore, quicker circulation. This was the closest the new millennium got to iconic images.

If technology is one limit and the state another, journalists themselves are the third. First, once the technological limits of portraying death were overcome, editors immediately started using the "breakfast test" for war photography: scenes that might nauseate people at the breakfast table should not be used. Besides this limit, a survey of photographers and journalists from the 1860s to the very recent past suggests that in only one conflict—Vietnam—did considerable distance emerge between military and civilian photographers. Mathew Brady wanted the North to win. He did not think in terms of journalistic "objectivity." The same thing—the basic journalistic support for the military cause—was true during every conflict through Korea. In this regard too the 1990s should be seen as a reversion to an older pattern, one where US journalists, and the images they take, aim to support the troops. This is a story that needs some nuance, because this is a point where Vietnam has left a mark.

About 2000, US elites born from 1945 to 1960 were shaped by the Vietnam crucible. Dick Cheney and George Bush, just as much as Hillary Clinton and John Kerry, all thought about war in relation to Vietnam. (Obama is the first president born after this generation.) We suggest that this is misguided, that a longer look at our war imagery shows that the norm consists in limits on graphic representation, holding back on the portrayal of brutality and suffering, in a hesitancy about criticizing US martial efforts. Vietnam is the exception, not the norm.

Poles of Painting

Photographs were not the only ingredient in mythic midcentury image culture. Take two poles of painting as announced in the title of Clement Greenberg's seminal essay, "Avant-Garde and Kitsch" (1939), one of the high-water statements at midcentury of the gulf between levels of cultural quality: "One and the same civilization produces simultaneously two such different things as a poem by T. S. Eliot and a Tin Pan alley song, or a painting by Braque and a *Saturday Evening Post* cover."[47]

The height of the avant-garde in the 1940s was abstract expressionist painting, and Greenberg was one of its champions. Abstract expressionism had a source in the social realism of 1930s painting and photography, a current that united a Grant Wood and a Dorothea Lange, a Thomas Hart Benton and a Walker Evans, a Diego Rivera and the American Guides. Jackson Pollock began his career as a disciple of Benton, executing regionalist themes. As if on cue according to the cliché, thesis gave birth to antithesis, and Pollock broke with the style in the early 1940s to do his massive formal experiments with action painting. At least that's how the story has long been told by Pollock and other insiders; it is clear in retrospect that Pollock in many ways radicalized and extended the regionalist aesthetic. If there was a break, it was political. Benton believed in art that could move people, New Deal style; Pollock dropped the art as democracy covenant and lived in a world of the bomb, the cold war, and the lone artist.[48]

The focus of abstract expressionism was not a collective tie to the land but individualist creativity. Paint and the action of painting—the medium—were the thing, not some external reality. Pollock's canvases made no effort to depict a social world or objects. Abstract expressionists drew on surrealist ideas of automatic writing and on the psychoanalytic idea that truth appeared in the free associations overflowing from the unconscious. Some works were vaguely figural, such as Willem de Kooning's series of women (which paid tribute to the Freudian id as the source of primal energy), but most renounced any duty to the object. In 1943, the year Pollock painted his famous *Mural*, painter Stuart Davis announced, "From now on the painting must stand on its own legs as pure color-position, solidity, symbols, and textures."[49] In the same vein, Greenberg had praised a "pure" interest in "the medium" of painting itself.

As regionalism is associated with the New Deal, abstract expression is usually associated with the cold war. Abstract expressionism was often billed as the political antipode to Soviet socialist realism and as an inherently antitotalitarian art form. Its formal freedom from politics was thus one of its direct political claims. Indirect CIA funding supported the movement along with jazz as an international export advertising the creativity of American life.[50] A devout anticommunist like Luce celebrated the drips, splatters, and wild brushstrokes of the abstract expressionists as hymns to liberty. *Life* treated the new style as evidence of the vitality and dynamism of the West without sharing *Life*'s realist aesthetic. For Luce, abstract expressionism's freedom from representation was the representation of freedom.

Greenberg left no doubt about the identity of his prime nominee for the category of kitsch: Norman Rockwell, who had provided over three hundred *Saturday Evening Post* covers from 1916 to 1963. His spot on the cultural map is well shown by his having illustrated the annual Boy Scouts of America calendar for over fifty years.[51] Rockwell's homey vignettes can seem corny and sentimental, even cloying, dreaming of America the way it never was, though he had a genius for providing the telling detail in everyday dramas and his artistry has recently been reevaluated upward. As put by the *New Yorker*'s art critic, Peter Schjeldahl, who has led that reevaluation over the past two decades together with the renegade critic Dave Hickey, "the art of Norman Rockwell keeps getting better."[52] It turns out that de Kooning was one of Rockwell's admirers and even found abstract expressionist techniques in his painting. The passing years have shown how much onetime opposites held in common.

Rockwell called himself an illustrator, not an artist. Once asked if there was anything he still wanted to accomplish, he replied: "Yes—to do a good painting!"[53] Rockwell lacked pretensions to grandeur, setting him apart from more self-regarding colleagues. He was a commercial artist who did not claim to be driven by the id or by manic inspiration. He did study in Paris in the 1930s and kept up with innovations in cubism and surrealism, but his two abstract *Saturday Evening Post* covers failed miserably. Though he was born and raised in New York City, his themes were the quiet dramas of boyhood, kinship, nation, and small-town life. His genre scenes depicted the quiet tangles of democratic culture, funny or touching, with a whimsical, idyllic, and uplifting eye—if there was sadness it was pleasantly sad, and if there were problems they were humorous, as he put it. He had no interest in landscape: people were always his theme.

Rockwell was the illustrator of national solidarity, of the culture that produced the New Deal and introduced America to Americans. "I showed the America I knew and observed to others who might not have noticed," he said. His mode was one of summary, of miniature standing for magnitude. Probably Rockwell's most famous images are his paintings of the four freedoms as articulated by FDR. Before the internet and television, his pictures enjoyed massive circulation. Statisticians in 1945 suggested that his Boy Scouts of America calendars got 1.6 billion views every single day (a number to die for on YouTube). The Office of War Information ordered 2.5 million posters of *The Four Freedoms* for war-bond drives, and there was a traveling exhibition of the works as well. Rockwell created the iconic 1943 image of an androgynous *Rosie the Riveter*, though it is less well remembered than—and often confused with—J. Howard Miller's *We Can Do It*, a 1942 image of a woman flexing her biceps. Viewers found in Rockwell's ordinary folk a certain national solidarity.

Critics like Greenberg thought Rockwell's work hopelessly middlebrow, but no one at the time complained about his strategy of using a few white people to stand for the nation as a whole. Style was the dominant complaint. His work was admired by African American leaders and artists such as Romare Bearden, and in the 1960s the NAACP commissioned him to produce what proved to be a very popular illustration of three slain civil rights workers. As a liberal, he was glad to support the movement.[54] No one at midcentury saw Rockwell's pictures as a celebration of whitebread culture or an oppressive effacement of national differences; such sensitivity came later.[55] Neither did anyone see his work as canny with hidden sexual knowingness; that also came later.[56] The reception of Rockwell is an index of the changing climate of how Americans looked at and thought about images between midcentury and late century.

Philosophy and the Image

Leading thinkers at midcentury underscored the new status of images as reality-defining. In a lecture given in 1938, Martin Heidegger argued that the unique thing about the modern world was its status as a picture. In calling the era "the age of the world-picture," Heidegger did not claim the moderns had invented a metaphysical understanding of the "world" as a totality. Every age had that. It was that we took the world *as* a picture. "World picture, when understood essentially, does not mean a picture of the world but the world conceived and grasped as a picture." He did not make clear what concrete pictures he had in mind, nor did he understand pictures in the ordinary sense, but the point was that the world lost some reality when it came to be treated as something to be represented for and by humans, a momentous shift that he traced to the philosophy of Descartes. Airplanes and radio played a role by destroying distances and bringing foreign worlds into our everyday life; doubtless he would have thought something similar about *Life* and *Look*.[57]

Ludwig Wittgenstein was also obsessed with pictures, in a very different way. His *Philosophical Investigations* (1951), written intermittently with excruciating labor during the 1930s and 1940s and one of the two or three most influential philosophical works of the century, treated pictures, along with logic, words, and actions, as a main way we knew and engaged with the world. Whereas Heidegger saw the world turning into a representation, Wittgenstein was more interested in the cognitive puzzles posed by diagrams and pictures, the funny ways these little devices offered apertures onto states of affairs. One of the most famous remarks of the book was a self-criticism. In his earlier philosophy, Wittgenstein explained, he had been captivated by a picture: "Ein Bild hielt uns gefangen," an image held us captive.[58] He was certainly not the only person in his time to be snagged in this way.

American philosopher Susanne Langer's *Philosophy in a New Key* (1942) drew on the neo-Kantian Ernst Cassirer's philosophy of symbolic forms.[59] This book studied the languages and symbolic forms of art, especially the visual arts and music. Langer noted the "incredible wealth of detail and information" of the photograph compared with verbal descriptions. But these details were contingent and unique. Images lacked a syntax or grammar, a set of general rules by which one patch of light related to another one. The meanings held in images were radically contextual and self-contained. They did not easily survive translation to other mediums; a picture might well be worth a thousand words, but those words would never exhaust the picture. Photographs were not reducible to general rules of meaning, giving them a unique referential oomph. "The correspondence between a word-picture and a visible object can never be as close as that between the object and its photograph." Given the choice, you would never use a verbal description or identification documents in a police lineup if you could use a photograph.[60] Though she found photographs unruly in their excess of meaning and undisciplined compared with the syntactical structures of discourse, they nonetheless had a privileged tie to the real world. Photographs could crystallize objects in a way no other medium could.

Perhaps the greatest midcentury thinker claiming the reality-binding power of the image was French film theorist André Bazin. Cofounder of the immensely influential journal *Cahiers du cinéma*, he argued in a now canonic 1945 essay, "Ontology of the Photographic Image," that the camera was nothing less than part of reality itself.[61] Bazin provided a deep

philosophical context for dominant midcentury popular aesthetics—
documentary photography, continuity editing, and zero-degree style.

Bazin called himself a realist. In this he contrasts with the first generation of film theorists, who were more interested in cinema's ability
to make new forms of illusion than its ability to imitate nature. But
what he meant by realism was subtle. For one thing, cinema was not
simply a machine for making visual duplicates of things. Its mechanism of copying was not only drawing resemblances but also casting
molds and taking impressions of footprints. He understood photography as having a physical tie to the world, not just making pictures of it.
(To use the terms favored in later film theory, the photograph had an
indexical and not only an iconic relation to what exists.) For another
thing, he took from Catholic thought the notion that reality has the
character of a sign. Realism need not be a brute aping of what appears
but can be an attunement to spiritual truths. A true realism would include what does not appear at first or at all, since not all reality is visible.
Finally, the artistic urge to copy was primordial both in human history
(he traced his famous notion of a "mummy complex" to ancient Egypt)
and in human psychology (life's need to wrest what it can from death
and time). Humans had an "appetite for illusion," and cinema helped
satisfy that appetite in historically unprecedented ways.

Bazin saw realism and artifice as partners rather than opponents.
They had always been key dimensions of the visual arts. "The great artists, of course, have always been able to combine the two tendencies . . .
holding reality at their command and molding it at will into the fabric
of their art." But photography changed everything. It was the most decisive break in the history of the plastic arts. "For the first time, between
the originating object and its reproduction intervenes only the instru-
mentality of a nonliving agent. For the first time an image of the world
is formed automatically, without the creative intervention of man."
The inhuman quality of the camera as a recording device allied it more
closely to nature than to artifice. Bazin, who had an avid interest in ge-
ology, botany, and evolutionary biology, saw film as a vehicle for the self-
expression of nature. (Emerson had entertained similar ideas.) Photography was the only art that profited from human absence. Its mechanical
or "objective" nature gave it a "quality of credibility" unique among the
arts. For Bazin there was a real presence on the other side of the image.

Bazin wasn't in the least naive about the human choices embedded
in both the art and the technology of photography; he did not believe
the photograph was some kind of instant readout of things. A favorite example was the shroud of Turin, an image that would be endowed

with more power than the most beautiful picture of Jesus. A photograph is both an image of and a point of contact with the universe. "Photography does not create eternity, as art does, it embalms time." In contrast to paintings, photographs harbored an "irrational power," the power to "bear away our faith." In some deep way, the photographic image shared the being of the object pictured. "The photographic image is the object itself, the object freed from the conditions of time and space that govern it." This is why Bazin thought photography worthy of the most weighty of all philosophical terms, *ontology*.[62]

Bazin's view of the image as deeply attuned with the material and immaterial order of things was in good company around 1945. (EG&G's cameras prove this connection in a different way.) This does not mean he completely approved of everything about Hollywood, photojournalism, or the image culture of his time; as we have seen with the pinup, he definitely did not. Hollywood's standardizing into obligatory forms often wasted the magical potential of the cinema to teach us how to see. But at a very sophisticated level, he articulated a leading attitude toward pictures at midcentury. The image combined artifice and reality. It had the power to compel our credence and suspend our skepticism. It could catch small moments in time like bugs in amber and could also be molded by artistry. The image was not a sickness or an oppression, it was an opening onto being. Thanks to his brilliance Bazin would endure, but on a broad cultural level views like his would lose their power.

It might seem strange to end a chapter on images in America around 1945 with a discussion of mostly European philosophers, but they were all responding to experiences they associated with the picture-happy culture of the United States, and they all thought of images as more than mirrors or replicas: they were symptoms, lures, or shards of matter. In 1945 the image was huge in every way, and it churned with explosive stuff—the bomb, death camps, film noir, the allure or homeyness of pinups. Everything that would break loose in the coming decades was there—violence, sex, and death, the glitter of fantasy, and the stab of real pain. There were plenty of disturbing things to see at midcentury. Looking backward, it is hard to miss the shadows and malignancy that would later become the keynote of intellectual argument about images. But images were contained and kept relatively safe—even wholesome— by law, the state, the film industry, the anticommunist nationalism of Luce, and by thinkers who understood them as portals to reality. The powers brewing in the image were still relatively dormant. The age's images were not yet campy or sinister. Images might have been harboring strange powers, but that is not how people talked about them.

Within a few decades the stability and safety of the image would crumble as a mainstream cultural position. This chapter ends with a culture on the verge of a great disillusionment, before pictures lost their cachet as holders of social solidarity. We might wonder, Were people in 1945 naive? Perhaps they were still shell-shocked or numb or dazzled and barely knew what had hit them.

Or perhaps they knew something we've forgotten.

* 5 *

Delirious Images,
1975–2000

In nineteenth-century America, diverse intellectuals believed the thick flow of facts would enhance democratic citizenship. Reformers later in the century sought not to stop the flood of information, but to channel and organize it for the use of many. Both were a sharp contrast to the second quarter of the twentieth century, which left the flood of facts to experts who prepared summaries and synecdoches to distill and display what they thought mattered to the public. The mid-twentieth-century culture of crystallized essence depended on the belief that knowledge might be successfully represented in an image, that there was nobility and beauty in an essence. Detail was clutter to be avoided. Since there was so much to track in a complicated world, reducing fact to essence was how we kept things in order. In the early and middle twentieth century, cultural arbiters hoped to fruitfully contain information in a variety of ways, including by outline culture and by mythic images. Confidence in the trope of synecdoche was part of a mass-culture system that celebrated national solidarity and unity.

At the turn of the millennium this culture, like the welfare state that incubated it, was in disrepair. Especially since the 1970s, practically all of its assumptions were seriously questioned. Or it might be better to say they were overrun. Images, we feared, could not be stabilized in the way we once thought. Successful summary ceased to claim credence because new technology and practices created images that were more fragmented or spectacular, because images seemed less able to bear the load of knowledge, and because synecdoche as a means of visual presentation increasingly came under fire. A culture of cynicism arose against happy summaries and pictures of central tendency. The image culture—the dominant character and quantity of images circulating through the society—changed sharply. That is the story of this chapter; promiscuous knowledge is the story of the next.

Fade-out

During the 1950s and 1960s the system of mythic images crystallizing a national mass culture slowly crumbled. The first sign was shrinking movie attendance. In 1948, eighty million people in the United States attended the movies each week. In 1949 it was sixty-five million, and by 1953, forty-five million. By 1960, according to US Census Bureau estimates, it was forty million.[1] A decline in revenue accompanied this drop. In 1946 the industry pulled in $1.7 billion, the top box-office take (in adjusted dollars) of the twentieth century. By 1962 box office receipts were only $900 million. In those same years production costs rose, putting the pinch on the industry.[2] The Paramount Decision of 1948, which broke up vertical integration in Hollywood, forcing the studios to sell off their movie theaters, also forced a reorientation. No longer was the "culture industry" quite the monolith that German critical theorists Max Horkheimer and Theodor Adorno, for instance, had viewed with alarm during their sojourn in Los Angeles in the 1940s.

Although the decline started before the explosion of television, the competition of the new medium after 1950 intensified the pressure on Hollywood. TV sets were in about one million American homes in 1949 but in ten million by 1952. Within a few years they were ubiquitous, contributing to the decline in movie attendance and the disappearance of the movie newsreel. TV news provided the same images more immediately. Newsreels now seemed old-fashioned, and by 1960 they played no important role in the distribution of the news, though they would limp along awhile longer.

TV, moreover, produced a new sort of image. At first TV pictures were grainy, without the clarity and high resolution of movie images. Even when the quality improved later in the decade, television remained different. The larger-than-life image of the big screen was gone. TV images could not overwhelm you or draw you in to their magic the way movies did. Television did its work differently, by allowing viewers to watch in a comfortable, private setting. You could stretch out on the couch, lounge on the floor, talk during the show, even watch in your underwear. TV's attraction was not its images, but the comfort and privacy of the home viewing environment. It was "radio with pictures."

Other changes in the visual culture were under way at the same time. A stream of darker images about American life began to surface outside the grimy world of tabloid newspapers. The vogue of film noir was one sign. Films like *Mildred Pierce* (1945) or *Out of the Past* (1947) explored murder, female duplicity, and the general hardness of urban life. Such themes were portrayed as the norm rather than the exception and were not leavened by happy endings. The visual style of noir helped build the mood. Interiors tended to be dark and grim. Characters often found themselves enveloped in shadows or swirling clouds of cigarette smoke, contributing to the pervasive sense of unease and claustrophobia. Bleak and shadowy streetscapes painted a menacing picture of the modern city. Noir used a black-and-white palette at the moment when Hollywood was going color.

The same darkness turned up in the increasing creepiness of Alfred Hitchcock's films through the fifties and early sixties—*Rear Window* (1954), *Vertigo* (1958), *Psycho* (1960), *The Birds* (1963). Similarly, Robert Frank's important book of photos, *The Americans* (1958), displayed a very different United States than had the great photojournalism of the thirties and forties. It offered a panoramic view of the nation, but its sociological sensibility was like that of a Tocqueville on downers. Jack Kerouac's introduction gave it added literary prestige. The American flag, the symbol of national unity, was glorified in Rosenthal's Iwo Jima image but treated sardonically by Frank's camera. His harsh light and grainy textures created a bleaker mood than the Depression-era pictures of Dorothea Lange. Frank shot his pictures without respect for the traditional rules of composition. Skylines were askew, faces obscured by shadows, smoke, and American flags, subjects "halved" or "T-boned" by more prominent objects in the foreground such as trees—and very few people smile. Although Lange portrayed poverty, there was also a dignity to her subjects. They were holding up under adversity. Frank's late 1950s camera was less forgiving. The bleakness was not offset. The morose quietness in his pictures does not honor or romanticize his subjects, perhaps in the end because it's not clear that the people were the main focus in Frank's photos as they were in Lange's.[3]

The censorship that had kept the system running was also breaking down. The legal regime that had propped up the 1940s image culture came under attack shortly after the war ended. By December 1953 it was possible for *Playboy*, which saw itself as a racier update of *Esquire*, to publish without recrimination. The now-famous nude pictures of Marilyn Monroe appeared in that first issue. In the first few days after publication Hugh Hefner, the magazine's founder, kept waiting for the police to pull the magazine from the newsstands, but they never turned up.

In 1952 the US Supreme Court overturned a 1915 decision, *Mutual v.*

Industrial Commission, that had declared film "a business pure and simple" and thus consigned to a low First Amendment standing. The new decision, *Burstyn v. Wilson,* which concerned a Fellini short charged with violating New York State's statute against "sacrilegious" films, admitted cinema to the status of potentially protected speech.

But the Court alone did not immediately end censorship. In 1934 the Motion Picture Association of America (MPAA), Hollywood's trade organization, had established the Production Code Administration (PCA) to review—and censor—scripts and images. The 1952 ruling did not eliminate the PCA but did give directors new courage to fight it. In the next few years, various moviemakers locked horns with the PCA: Otto Preminger for his light sex farce *The Moon Is Blue* (1953) and his grim portrayal of heroin addiction *The Man with the Golden Arm* (1955); László Benedek for his tale of roaming motorcycle hoodlums *The Wild One* (1953); and Elia Kazan for *Baby Doll* (1956), his nasty southern gothic of adolescent female sexuality and slobbering men in tow. Censors were on the defensive, but they weren't dead. Kazan had to negotiate scene changes in *Baby Doll* just as he had five years earlier for *A Streetcar Named Desire.* Through the fifties and early sixties, such negotiations continued. The movie industry was not willing to make a full-on challenge. In the 1950s and the early 1960s, new frontiers were portrayed on film, but there were still limits to what could be shown.[4]

The same was true of other visual media. Few in the magazine business wanted to challenge conventions. *Life, Look,* and the *Saturday Evening Post* all fixed limits on what they portrayed. Television was the most conservative of all the popular media. In the 1950s, shows like *The Adventures of Superman, Father Knows Best,* and *Gunsmoke* portrayed a strong, self-confident, and benign United States of America. Nuclear families were intact. Leaders cared about the public good. "For truth, justice, and the American way" was how Superman was introduced each week during the show's run from 1952 to 1958. Even into the next decade, family fare like *Bewitched* or *The Dick Van Dyke Show* was the norm. *The Beverly Hillbillies* and *Bonanza* remained among the most popular shows on television. From October 1967 to April 1968, the most-watched television shows in the country were *The Andy Griffith Show, The Lucy Show, Gomer Pyle, USMC,* and *Gunsmoke,* all far, far removed from any counterculture influence.[5] Despite the occasional "daring" show in the late sixties, TV was a very conservative medium.

Still, the fade-out of the old system continued. Despite a renewed idealism among early 1960s photojournalists, particularly around the civil rights movement, the long-term trend was against striking print pictures. With a few notable exceptions, the 1960s saw the last set of iconic images that ruled the nation—Martin Luther King speaking at the March on Washington, Muhammad Ali roaring over a fallen Sonny Liston, the dying Robert F. Kennedy awash in a halo of light, the napalmed girl in Vietnam. Television news and shifting patterns of advertising revenue would soon kill the great photo-based magazines. The *Saturday Evening Post* died in February 1969, *Look* in October 1971. *Life* hung on until December 1972, when it too folded. The old photojournalism, with the centrality of the photo-essay and iconic picture, was dead.

The old censorship system, the movie Production Code, staggered along into the midsixties when it too died, battered by European art cinema, the rise of campus film societies, neighborhood movie houses, a better-defined youth demographic, and a looser, countercultural mood.[6] Changing legal norms also contributed, as a string of Supreme Court decisions in the 1950s and 1960s liberalized obscenity law.[7] Shots of female frontal nudity started to appear in movies like *The Pawnbroker* (1965), *Blow-Up* (1966), and *Five Easy Pieces* (1970).

In the end it was *Blow-Up*, a British movie directed by an Italian, that struck one of the final blows. Michelangelo Antonioni's film broke all the old rules. Released in December 1966, *Blow-Up* was the story of a hip fashion photographer in Swinging London who accidentally took pictures of a murder in a park. Since there was nudity in the film, the producers worried about the censors. After a bout of hand-wringing, MGM decided to simply ignore the censors and release the film in the United States through a subsidiary company without any rating—in blatant disregard of an agreement by MPAA members not to distribute a film without a seal of approval from the Production Code. The film did well, and there were no repercussions. The old censorship system was dead.[8]

Blow-Up marked the end of an era in another way. In the film, Thomas, the photographer, took pictures of what he thought was an illicit tryst in a park. When the woman in the pictures tracks him down and demands the roll of film, he gives her a placebo roll and, his curiosity sparked about what could be so interesting, develops the pictures. In the background he sees a hand clasping a gun and a dead body in the bushes. He returns to the park and finds the body. In a kind of psychotic frenzy, Thomas goes back to his darkroom and gradually blows up his photos in larger and larger versions to find proof of the crime. Yet the more he blows up the image, the more abstract and unreadable it becomes. If he can only zoom in a bit more, he thinks, he'll discover the truth. But the more manically he explodes the detail, the more the evidence begins to resemble one of the abstract paintings produced by his neighbor

Bill. In the end the image dissolves into mere blotches that—like those in Bill's paintings—generate more questions than answers, more confusion than certainty.

In its characterization of the camera's failure to secure truth and its role in Thomas's psychotic break, the film abandons an older faith in photography as a trace of reality. It suggests that vision—both mechanized and natural—is always essentially ambiguous, and that if we continue trying to chase down truth exclusively with cameras, we'll always come up just as short (and perhaps as mad) as the film's antihero. It overturned the view floated by Edgar Allan Poe and other pioneering commentators that the photographic image was "infinitely more accurate" than painting and a kind of archive whose every layer could be combed for microscopic truth. Since the invention of the daguerreotype, it had been an incessantly invoked truism that the camera helped us see more clearly. It was a window on the world, revealing evidence of what wasn't immediately visible to the naked eye. *Blow-Up*, however, suggested that the camera was not necessarily an honest witness of things. The failure of zooming in to reveal anything but blotches anticipated digital pixelation. In a few years the idea that the camera captured reality would be increasingly suspect. (More recent refinements in digital image making— in 2016, for instance, Hasselblad released a hundred-megapixel camera capable of astonishing levels of resolution—have brought the rhetoric of absolute fidelity back with a vengeance.)[9]

The New Regime

In the 1970s and 1980s a new, far more varied image culture took shape. There were fewer icons. Nothing defined the country the way the great midcentury photojournalism had. Movies didn't code national myths with the same confidence. In the forties, movies, newsreels, and the news magazines were generally marketed to the great mass of adult Americans. In the 1970s and 1980s, niche marketing to segments of the population took over. Corporate culture in practically every industry started to appeal to precisely delineated audience slices rather than to the whole nation. The rise of cable television was one expression of this splintering of the public. There were channels for kids, teenagers, adults, and seniors, for men, for women, for African Americans, Hispanics, country music fans, news junkies, sports nuts, old movie buffs, and more. There were now fewer images that everyone saw. The total number of images in circulation was way up, but the number viewed in common was way down.[10]

Sidebar 5.1 The Lonely Crowd or the Daily Me?

In the 1970s and 1980s, cable TV and VCRs vastly multiplied the quantity of images we could choose to view. The middle class had a candy store. Advertisers realized they could stop wasting money on diffuse audiences and aim for demographic sweet spots. And channel capacity kept getting bigger and cheaper. The result was a less common image and information culture in which it was easy to avoid concerns that were of interest to everyone. We might all dial in on some catastrophic occasion like 9/11, but otherwise we worked, lived, and watched in our market segments. Some lamented the breakdown of the nation, the fragmentation of America.[1]

The internet took things even further than cable TV. One book stood for many in greeting the new millennium's promise of information utopia skeptically. Law professor and establishment liberal Cass Sunstein's *Republic.com* (2001) argued that the internet was bad for American democracy in organizing information into waterproof ideological compartments: "New technologies, emphatically including the internet, are dramatically increasing people's ability to hear echoes of their own voices and to wall themselves off from others."[2] Sunstein was worried that personalizing information would deliver us only the news we were interested in. The old-fashioned labors of going from one place to another on public transportation or rifling the pages of a newspaper were small rites of grace in which democratically relevant interaction could occur. Against the grain of internet triumphalism, Sunstein opposed disintermediation and praised the apparent inefficiencies of intermediaries like editors.

Though he may have had no conscious thought of it, Sunstein, who was then at the University of Chicago, echoed a view held by earlier Chicago sociologists such as Robert Park, Herbert Blumer, and Louis Wirth: that democracy means public circulation among strangers. Surprising, unplanned encounters would open up our insulated worlds. There was a serendipity to public milling around and spontaneous interaction, of

1. Joseph Turow, *Breaking Up America* (Chicago: University of Chicago Press, 1997); Robert B. Reich, "Secession of the Successful," *New York Times Magazine,* January 20, 1991.

2. Cass R. Sunstein, *Republic.com* (Princeton, NJ: Princeton University Press, 2001), 16.

bumping into new people and ideas. And Sunstein celebrated the newspaper as the informational analogue to such social boundary crossing.

Yet he reversed classic Chicago sociology's excitement about how communication media eliminate the limits of geography. A hundred years earlier, Progressive Era sociologists thought the turn from place-based communities to interest-based collectives spelled the onset of a new democratic order, the "great community." Sunstein thought just the opposite: place offers a beneficial friction, not just a transaction cost but a transaction benefit. We needed common media that not only spanned space but also integrated it.

Sunstein's thesis that the internet brings a novel separation of ideological worlds suffered from the problem that people have been managing to filter information for a long time without fancy technologies. That people do value surprises and that the internet can bring new ideas were facts Sunstein conceded or at least more explicitly emphasized in the second edition of the book.[3] Even if he did miss some nuances, Sunstein anticipated the online phenomena we now recognize as echo chambers and filter bubbles. He was absolutely right to see a rich menu of deliberatively usable discourse as a democratic requirement, but he sidestepped an older and thornier problem: citizens' ordinary barriers to interest and information. Preaching to the choir is an old habit. Selective exposure, reception, and perception were all identified in communication research starting in the 1940s. Each political party, Paul Lazarsfeld noted in 1944, had its own medium: radio for the Democrats, newspapers for the Republicans. The informed citizen who sampled all sources, he and his colleagues concluded, was a figment of the imagination.[4]

Republic.com praised general interest media. Sunstein singled out television news as the privileged agent of agenda setting, making the rather over-the-top claim that network news can create "something like a speaker's corner beyond anything ever imagined in Hyde Park" (36). He worried about social fragmentation—not the atomization that was worried about at midcentury but rather faction in Madison's sense—groups

3. Cass R. Sunstein, *Republic.com 2.0* (Princeton, NJ: Princeton University Press, 2007), 12.

4. Paul F. Lazarsfeld, Bernard Berelson, and Hazel Gaudet, *The People's Choice: How the Voter Makes Up His Mind in a Presidential Campaign* (New York: Columbia University Press, 1944); for a more recent version, see Lee Drutman, "Ballot Pox," *Chronicle Review*, October 23, 2016, www.chronicle.com/article/Ballot-Pox/238131.

riding ideological hobbyhorses. In *The Lonely Crowd* (1950), the University of Chicago's David Riesman discerned a shift in national character—from inner-directed to other-directed—that sounds uncannily like the same shift more recent theorists worry about. Riesman thought we were lonely because we were looking to each other for direction in neo-Tocquevillean conformity, like a flock of birds or a school of fish, having no guide but the behavior of our immediate neighbors.

Here's the odd thing: Sunstein loves what his Chicago predecessors feared. Concerning things imagined in Hyde Park—Chicago, not London—he extols what his Chicago ancestors watched with trepidation: masses of people all attending to a common media stimulus. Sunstein sees in mass society the Founding Fathers' program of republican representation. What was once the bulwark against mass society, the small group, Sunstein sees as the incubator of the old bugaboo "faction." In the 1950s it was considered dangerous to have huge anonymous audiences all attending to the same media; in the early millennium, Sunstein praises the vanishing mass media as agencies of a common culture. When broadcast media prevailed, the main fear was the loss of individuality in a lonely crowd; when niche media prevailed, the fear was the narcissism of the "daily me."[5] Theory repeats itself: as tragedy and farce, as hope and despair.

5. See also Elihu Katz, "And Deliver Us from Segmentation," *Annals of the American Academy of Political and Social Science* 546 (1996): 22-33. For a more recent discussion of a similar inversion, see Fred Turner, "Machine Politics: The Rise of the Internet and a New Age of Authoritarianism," *Atlantic Monthly*, January 2019, https://harpers.org/archive/2019/01/machine-politics-facebook-political-polarization/.

The country increasingly did not look at the same pictures. Apart from the rare blockbuster movie, people tended to watch different things. Magazines were now addressed to increasingly fine gradations of age and interest groups. During these same years, the number of people going to the movies continued to shrink. Hollywood ceased to define the cultural center of the nation. No image really did. To be sure, certain images could still capture national or global attention—Bill Clinton denying he had "sexual relations with that woman," the *Challenger* space shuttle exploding, or the TV vigil of 9/11—but day to day, the country's viewing habits were increasingly fragmented. "Media events" that riveted the nation had become more intermittent and often more bleak.[11]

Pictures multiplied. There were more of them, more types of them, and more machines to watch them on. Video games, cable TV, the internet, and home video cameras all became popular in the twenty years after 1975. Compared with a historical baseline just one or two decades earlier, the nation now more than ever seemed to be drowning in pictures. British scholar Raymond Williams arrived in the United States for a sabbatical in 1973 and was astonished to find on television an "irresponsible flow of images and feelings" strikingly different from what he was used to seeing on British public service television.[12] Williams saw just the opening salvo of the onslaught. The box itself proliferated: by the late 1950s the average American home had one television set, but by the late 1990s the norm was about 2.4 sets per household, and today it approaches 3. In the late 1990s, 65 percent of teenagers had television sets in their bedrooms.[13] In the 1950s, TV sets outside the home were generally found only in the local tavern. In the eighties and nineties they spread to sports bars, hotel lobbies, casual restaurants, doctors' waiting rooms, airports, and elevators. New channels surfaced for capturing audiences in special places—the Airport Network, the Food Court Entertainment Network, Channel One in the public schools. By 1993, over twenty-eight million people watched television outside their homes each week.[14]

In our moment of ubiquitous images on hand-held devices, when the television set has lost its monopoly on video programming, the dispersion of screens into public spaces may not seem impressive, but it was a significant step in the trend that Williams called "mobile privatization." The picture itself got smaller, diminishing the power of the image. The "small screen" started with TV in the fifties and sixties. Then, in the late seventies and after, videotape and then DVD allowed people to watch films on television. This changed cinematic scale and also the experience. Motion pictures could now be watched with the same casualness as a TV show and with the same peril of interruption by ordinary life. Consuming movies was less a special event—set off in a distinct ritual space with the expectation of quiet, sustained attention—than it had been at midcentury. By the new millennium, teens were learning to download whole movies on their desktop computers, making the images even smaller than TV. A few years later they were watching video clips on their cell phones. In the 1940s Hollywood had been larger than life. Since 2000, the world of moving images is a mixed one, with many images smaller than life and many more splashed onto the huge displays of jumbotrons and wide-screen TVs.[15]

One place to see the diminished role of the image was in *People* magazine, the Time-Life Corporation's replacement for *Life*. *People* was first published in 1974, just over a year after *Life* had folded. Almost immediately, the weekly became one of the top-selling magazines in the nation, just as *Life* had been in the 1940s and 1950s, though with a smaller circulation. In the age of television, no general interest magazine could attain the cultural centrality of *Life*, with its circulation in 1950 of 5.3 million and much higher pass-along rate. *People* reached 1.9 million in 1976, its third year of operation.[16]

The differences between the two were instructive. The shift in names caught something important—from trying to record modern life to chatting with celebrities. *People* had no ambition to paint an ideal of middle-class America or to serve as the show book of the world.[17] The difference in pictures was just as telling. Most obvious was the shift in scale: *People* shrank from *Life*'s large format (10½ by 14) to a standard magazine size (8½ by 11). There were actually more pictures in a typical issue of *People* than in *Life*. Yet where *Life* struggled to make the image open out to something large and important, *People*'s photos were smaller and generally inconsequential. Two sorts of shots dominated the new magazine—the home snapshot and the paparazzi shot. One tried to reproduce what families did with their home cameras—genial images of friends and kin in comfortable surroundings, skiing, in restaurants, sprawled in well-appointed living rooms, getting a haircut. The other sort provided voyeuristic glimpses into the lives of political personalities, professional athletes, and garden-variety celebrities. These pictures differed from the "ambush" shots that would later become standard in celebrity journalism. At first *People*'s subjects were poised and clearly performing for the photographer, never caught off guard. But in the end both styles were ephemeral. Unlike its Time-Life forerunner, *People* did not produce memorable pictures. It didn't try to. *People*'s cascade of photos was just so much passing eye candy.

Even when the pictures were not physically smaller, the new image culture was faster-paced, more frenetic. While 1940s films—"moving pictures"—were meant to flow smoothly, the new image culture was less coherent, jumpier. Increasingly the motion itself—rather than any story or myth—was what fascinated.

There was an explosion in special effects. Spectacle, of course, has always been a part of the movies: the burning of Atlanta in *Gone with the Wind* (1939), the splendor of the Emerald City in *The Wizard of Oz* (1939), even the mammoth orientalist sets of D. W. Griffith's *Intolerance* (1916). Yet beginning with the first James Bond movie, *Dr. No* (1962), the poetically slow-motion deaths in *Bonnie and Clyde* (1967) or the ballet-like massacre in *The Wild Bunch* (1968), and the cavernous portrayal of outer space in *2001: A Space Odyssey* (1968), Hollywood spent more time (and vast sums of money) finding new ways to create stunning images of violence, mayhem, and the fantastic.

In the seventies the creeping trend grew to a gallop. The mayhem of the popular disaster movies (the *Airport* series from 1970 to 1979 or *The Towering Inferno* in 1974) were done without any new special effects, yet they had great explosions. Two 1977 films, *Star Wars* and *Close Encounters of the Third Kind*, combined new and elaborate uses of older techniques like optical compositing and model building with innovative early computer animation to make all sorts of action in outer space seem possible. And while these were widely considered turning points in the history of special effects, there were other less well-known innovations. Viewers of the first *Godfather* (1972) film watched the murder of Sonny Corleone (James Caan) in grisly detail, thanks both to slow-motion photography and to the perfection of a small squib put under fake skin that simulated with great realism the effect of flesh and blood bursting as a bullet struck. By the end of the decade, special effects artists were nearly as important as actors.[18] The first Academy Award for makeup, an essential part of grisly effects, was given in 1981.

In the 1990s came the digital revolution. George Lucas's company, Industrial Light and Magic, became a hub for the new technology, although many others were also involved. In movies like *Terminator 2* (1991), *Jurassic Park* (1993), and *Forrest Gump* (1994), digital moviemaking matured. Whole characters were now created digitally. Digital backdrops were commonplace. Historical figures were dropped into scenes in which they interacted with fictional characters. There were flashy new techniques like morphing, the seamless transformation of one shape into another (an important part of *Terminator 2*). It is hard for us to realize just how strange and radical such techniques were at the time.

Perhaps most important was the digital editing of film. Once film content could be shifted to a computer, edited there, and then put back on film, all without loss of quality, there was practically no end to what stunning things moviemakers could portray. Digital technology meant editing within the frame, not only between frames. The awesome tilting of the *Titanic* in James Cameron's 1997 epic is a perfect example. The hundreds of bodies sliding down the deck into the ocean were digital inventions. What this all meant for fidelity to the real world was a question many asked.

By the nineties, new technological possibilities were changing popular moviemaking. Some critics have overemphasized how much computer technology changed the product. Violence and spectacle have been a key to megapopularity since the 1970s. The increasing global reach of Hollywood played a part as well—action dramas are widely thought to travel across international borders better than humor or romance, perhaps because car chases and fistfights demand little background knowledge about culture, history, or language. Still, by the nineties, stunning explosions and digital aliens, freaks, or dinosaurs were disproportionately part of the nation's most popular films.[19]

The very "wowness" of the effects, moreover, often replaced character development. Spectacle overwhelmed story. Unlike the classic Hollywood cinema that meshed national myths with seamless editing, for these movies the story *was* the special effects. Film scholar Scott Bukatman termed flicks like *Dick Tracy* (1990) or *Jurassic Park* (1993) "theme park" films. On amusement park rides we care about the thrills, not the story. These new movies were the same. Hostile critics complained of "rootless, textureless images," of lousy plots and one-dimensional characters. Most of the independent film movement in the eighties and early nineties was devoted to bucking mainstream Hollywood by making smaller movies with interesting characters and no extravagant effects (another sort of niche marketing). But mainstream moviegoers, most importantly young males, loved the new movies. Big, flashy, jumping pictures—computerized dinosaurs galloping toward us, chiseled tough guys impossibly leaping clear of fantastic explosions, martial arts heroes and heroines running up trees—these were now among the most popular images on the screen.[20]

The new flashiness invaded television as well. Early television, like midcentury cinema, rarely called attention to its "made" quality. It preferred what has been called a "zero-degree" or invisible style. In the 1970s and 1980s, however, electronic nonlinear editing machines, new fast film stock, and the ability to warp, move, and bend images in editing rooms opened new possibilities. In the 1980s, television production started to shift away from the zero-degree aesthetic. The cool brio of a show like *Miami Vice* used the new technology to create images that called attention to their very stylishness, showing its affinity with the new genre of music video. Other shows, like the popular *Hill Street Blues* and later *NYPD Blue*, adopted an exaggerated cinema verité style. These jumpy images made with hand-held cameras and a rolled focus had the paradoxical effect of seeming very naturalistic and at the same time so unusual that viewers clearly saw them as artfully constructed for a TV show.[21] Their producer, Steven Bochco, famously declared that the aim was to "make it messy." "Rather than the 'window on the world' concept that was so important in the early years of television," one observer noted, "contemporary televisuality flaunts 'videographic art-objects' of the world."[22]

The new special effects changed the television viewing experience at all levels. Even ads and promotions were part of it. In the 1960s NBC's logo was its famous peacock—a single picture, unmoving, on the screen for a few seconds to identify the network. Its rainbow color was the most visually compelling thing about it. In the late seventies, however, such logos started to move. Now in network promos, ads of all kinds, and news and sporting events, images, graphics, and logos floated, jumped, bent backward, and sailed on and off the screen. Viewers often didn't realize all that had changed, how much of their television experience—prime time, news, ads, network promos, sports—was different than before, how much of their attention was now being grabbed by jumping pictures and graphics. Insiders, however, knew what was going on. By the early 1980s, many veteran newsmen were indignant. One observed that "bells ring, pictures flip and tumble, and everybody seems to be shouting at me. . . . The news is bad enough without added jingle and flash."[23]

Videotape was remarkably important for the new visual culture. It made possible the music video, the political sound bite, and pornography production. Images in these genres differed sharply from the seamless editing of classic Hollywood cinema or the synthetic drive of classic photojournalism. Videotape dates from the 1950s, but its editing was physical, like film. At first it was principally used for taped shows rather than live news. In the late sixties and early seventies, the size of the tape became more manageable, the costs shrank, and the general ease of use improved dramatically. In 1974 the first commercial computerized videotape editing machine was put on the market. The first live video feed for television news was the 1974 Symbionese Liberation Army shootout in Los Angeles. All coverage of the war in Vietnam came via cans of film flown back to the United States, but video would soon change all that: soon immediate live feeds were the norm in news coverage. One commentator proposed that television graphics be divided into two eras, with 1975 as the meridian: BC (before computer) and AD (aided design).[24]

At the same time, relatively lightweight video cameras became available for news outlets. Now reporting "live from the scene" was possible, thanks to the link between video and satellites. News could take on a less edited, more cinema verité style thanks to what insiders called ENG—electronic news gathering. Local television news underwent a sea change in the 1970s from a staid and money-draining enterprise to a visually jazzy and profitable one. (Unlike network programming, local stations collected all the advertising fees during local newscasts.) Leading the way were so-called news doctors such as Frank Magid Associates, who used a mix of social science research about neural attention patterns and seat-of-the-pants tinkering to prescribe fixes for local news programs. Some recommendations were structural—more segments, shorter stories, new marketing taglines ("Action News" instead of "Ralph Renick reports"), the introduction of packaged health or consumer features. Others were cosmetic—better haircuts, between-stories banter or "happy talk" among the announcers, more stories about puppies or children. News doctors even gave advice on how to hold a pencil during newscasts. Fancier weather graphics, Doppler radar, and helicopters followed.[25]

When video replaced film in early 1970s television production, the potential for rapid juxtaposition of images rose exponentially. Video editors in New York and Los Angeles began thinking of the virtuosity of quick cutting.[26] The ease of electronic editing left ample time for experimenting even in the daily news shows. News came to have the same motion, the same artfulness that had appeared in ads and sports a decade earlier. Once computerized video editing machines came on the market in the mid-1970s, news editors could readily rearrange image and sound. Editing film (as opposed to videotape) had required cutting and splicing the actual film, a time-consuming, clumsy process unsuited to the daily deadline pressures of the evening news. The new equipment allowed images to be edited with the press of a button. Moreover, unlike splicing film, which could not be readily undone, digital editing could soon be reversed with just another click of the mouse.

The result was increasingly slick meshing of image and sound, with far more editing cuts and montage than before and far less uninterrupted talk. The sound bite grew from the new ease with which words from one tape could now be correlated with the picture from another. News production crews grew far more self-conscious about blending pithy sayings with dazzling images. In 1968 the average uninterrupted time a politician spoke on network news was about forty seconds; twenty years later it was just nine seconds. Politicians altered their speechmaking to develop the one catchy "sound bite" that would make the news, like a synecdoche where the part had lost any connection to a whole. The new style changed the way reporters worked as well. One executive producer for CBS news observed that, because of the new pacing, "the correspondent is not allowed to talk more than twelve or fifteen seconds before there is some intermediate sound." An NBC reporter observed that he was now "making little movies," directing camera crews, writing script to illustrate images, and spending a lot less time searching out information.[27]

The decreasing cost and increasing mobility enabled a proliferation of new images. The O. J. Simpson car chase (1994) and the beating of Rodney King by the Los Angeles police (1991)—rare (and unhappy) media events that captivated the whole nation—were seen only because of the videotape revolution of the 1970s and 1980s.[28] Thanks to satellites, the entire world could watch live reports on CNN about where Scud missiles were landing in Israel during the Persian Gulf War of 1991. The potential audience included, of course, the Iraqi military personnel who had launched the missiles. CNN was inadvertently supplying the Iraqis with invaluable reconnaissance intelligence. The line between objective detachment and battlefield engagement had eroded. Some commentators wondered if anyone was in charge of these images: Where had the editor gone, the person traditionally responsible for deciding what is made public?[29]

One of the most striking new visual genres of the late twentieth century directly attacked Hollywood's continuity editing. The music video premiered in August 1981 during MTV's first broadcast moments. Within a few years the video network was a huge success, mirroring the growth of cable in general at that time. From the beginning, music videos simply ignored continuity editing. Each video generally mixed three sorts of shots with apparent randomness: musicians performing, a surreal dreamlike fantasy motif or two, and good-looking women to look at. Individual shots were extremely short, with an editing cut at least every two or three seconds. Scenes shifted abruptly. Jump cuts were de rigueur. Perspective changed with similar abruptness. Unlike classic Hollywood cinema, music videos were not sutured together to appear as if one shot "naturally" led to another. Quite the contrary—discontinuity was the goal. The narrative link between music and video was often exceedingly loose. It was the rare video that created defined narratives with beginnings, middles, and ends. Instead, video makers created moods. Surrealism was an important visual forebear.[30]

The visuals often *contradicted* the music, as in Olivia Newton-John's "[Let's Get] Physical" or Bruce Springsteen's "Glory Days." "Physical" was released for radio play in 1981 and was instantly controversial owing to its suggestive lyrics ("I took you to an intimate restaurant / Then to a suggestive movie / There's nothin' left to talk about, / Unless it's hori-zontally"). KSL-AM in Salt Lake City banned it outright, and KFMY-FM in Provo, Utah, pulled it after receiving complaints. When it was released as a Grammy-winning video in 1983, the visuals showed Newton-John leading a workout session of overweight men, trying to sculpt them into beefcakes. Whereas the song is sexy and seductive, the video is comedic. But those upset by the song's radio play would probably not have liked the video any better if they had understood it, given its now obvious gay coding: the beefcakes who emerge from Newton-John's training regimen are more interested in each other than in her.

Likewise, *Glory Days* provides two vignettes of losers buffeted by aging and by gender roles, but the video dampens Springsteen's social criti-cism. The lyrics leave a washed-up baseball player boring his friend with presumably drunken talk of high school triumphs, but the video por-trays the same character embarking on the newer glories of fatherhood and traditional family life. The video rescues the fading stars in the end, whereas the lyrics had left them to wallow. Not all music videos, of course, shoehorned downbeat or leering songs into visually happy endings, and many were content simply to improvise a passing visual hookup for the music. The point was the disconnect between sound and image.

Other techniques developed in the latter half of the 1980s, like skip framing and morphing, further contributed to the frantic mutation of images. Advertisers joined pop artists and journalists in becoming "image scavengers," grabbing images that littered the cultural landscape well before this became easy to do online. With such visual thrills simul-taneously tantalizing and taunting us, was there room for the consum-matory forms of art that Dewey thought would summarize our experi-ence?[31]

New technology made these new images possible, but they were not determined by the technology any more than the Leica determined the myth-making ambition of 1930s and 1940s photojournalism. The new images were part of a new style, a new aesthetic. "Special effects were no longer just a way of producing difficult or impossible shots—they were becoming the star of the show, and audiences wanted to see more."[32] Un-like the zero-degree style of earlier television, by the 1990s many news-room directors were committed to "*showing off* their proficiency at *pic-ture making.*"[33]

Slick editing, fantastic special effects, cinema verité, and direct at-tacks on continuity editing all contradicted the effortless feel of the midcentury popular visual culture. But one last innovation did as much as anything else to increase the discontinuity and jumpiness of the new image culture. Between the mideighties and the midnineties, the number of households with television remote controls jumped from 29 percent to 90 percent. This device altered viewing habits dramatically. New slang terms such as *grazing, zapping, zipping,* and *surfing* described characteristic uses of the remote, such as running quickly through all channels, following multiple programs simultaneously, muting the sound, and avoiding commercials. Research, in case you needed any convincing, showed that men wanted to control the remotes and flipped channels far more frequently than women. The result, for the men with the gadgets and the women who loved them (or just put up with them), was one more way that images quickly jumped about without care for the continuity between them.[34]

In the new visual culture images were not intensely watched but glanced at casually. Grasping the difference between *Life* and *People* makes this point: there were more pictures, but none were iconic. So many of our images had become random and fleeting that we looked less carefully. The new visual culture was a culture of distraction, of visual Muzak. It grabbed our eyes without focusing our minds.

The dispersion of the image was not without precedent. Many of the same developments happened earlier in auditory culture. Records in the 1910s and jukeboxes in the 1930s foreshadowed the personal selection of video material on VCRs in the late 1970s. Elevator music foreshadowed ambient television. Transistor radios and personal stereos foreshadowed the mobile viewing enabled by cell phones and laptop computers. By about 1960 sound was washing over us everywhere, and images were soon to follow.

In his famous 1936 essay "The Work of Art in the Age of Mechanical Reproduction," Walter Benjamin argued that in the modern industrial world we looked at movies distractedly. Benjamin—who was thinking of avant-garde Soviet film with its heavy use of montage—had it entirely wrong on this point, at least regarding the visual culture of the United States. At the very moment he was writing, Hollywood cinematographers had perfected the narrative, editing, and lighting techniques that drew the audience's eyes to the screen and kept them staring raptly. Beautiful sets, beautiful stars, and a story nicely packaged with a beginning, middle, and end were all designed not to distract us but to hold our attention. All of this, moreover, was consumed in dark, quiet theaters, sometimes vast movie palaces, with gazing silently at the screen the norm. Psychologists of the day contrasted the intensity of viewing movies with the distractedness of casual listening to the radio at home.

Classic Hollywood movies wanted to draw us into their worlds and make us consecrate our time to a concentrated experience. They were part of ongoing efforts by industrialists, psychologists, artists, and moralists to make us pay attention. Richard Wagner's total work of art set in darkened theaters was one progenitor.[35]

But if Benjamin was wrong in 1936, by the turn of the millennium he was correct, which has helped his posthumous fame. Increasingly, we viewed our images distractedly. We glanced at televisions in sports bars and elevators or at the airport. In our homes, we watched and chatted at the same time. When we watched a music video, the disjointed images caught the eye as the ear found the music. While some early critics thought television demanded more attention, others saw it differently. The movie critic Pauline Kael spoke for many when she claimed that TV viewing, with "all its breaks and cuts, and the inattention, except for action" was contributing to the "destruction of the narrative sense."[36] Apart from occasional "must-see TV" shows, absorptive viewing around 2000 was no longer the norm. The spread of moving images to all sorts of public venues, the manic pace of digital editing, and the quick flip of the remote control and click of the computer mouse had made such distracted viewing commonplace. One grand exception was the video game, where intense concentration made virtuosos. But apart from that, there was far more skipping and far less gawking at images. (The rise of binge-watching of high-quality television has brought back absorptive viewing, but such focus is still a relative island amid a vast sea of distraction.)

The Vanishing Censor

The new sense of disorder in the visual culture of the 1970s was bolstered by the continuing erosion of censorship. Images that would have been illegal a generation before—most notably of people having sex—were now so easily accessible that a time traveler from the past would have been astounded. The inability to contain such images contributed mightily to the widespread sense of images out of control.

In response to the collapse of the old system of film censorship by the mid-1960s, the Motion Picture Association of America developed a voluntary system of ratings. It was a strategic move to self-regulate than risk the uncertainty of external governance. Between the late sixties and the mideighties the MPAA started with the categories of G (no restrictions), M (parental guidance suggested), R (no one under sixteen unless accompanied by a parent), and X (no one under sixteen) and evolved through a number of other categories such as PG, PG-13, and NC-17. Unlike the old Production Code, in the new regime movies weren't censored, they were rated. One result was that sex scenes started appearing in movies like *Last Tango in Paris* (1972) and *Don't Look Back* (1973), the former portraying anal sex. Over the next few decades, more taboos slowly peeled away. In the early 1990s, Hollywood for the first time portrayed glimpses of the genitalia of both men (*The Sheltering Sky* [1990]) and women (*Basic Instinct* [1992]).[37]

Mainstream Hollywood, however, looked tame compared with its nastier cousin, the porn industry. The popularity of soft-core pornography like Russ Meyer's *Vixen* (1968) or Just Jaeckin's *Emmanuelle* series (1974–77) was one thing. In 1971, though, hard-core pornography, showing real intercourse and oral sex, became readily available to large audiences in film theaters. Between June 1972 and June 1973 the "big three"—*Deep Throat, Behind the Green Door*, and *The Devil in Miss Jones*, all produced in 1971 and 1972—earned more in theaters than almost every mainstream movie.[38]

Some measure of the changes since the early 1970s can be had by trying to imagine pornography being shown in movie theaters today. Beginning in the late seventies, the porn industry put itself on a firmer footing by shifting, like television news, from film to videotape. The porn industry's discreetly but widely marketed tapes meant that viewers could play them on their VCRs. They no longer had to venture to some seedy downtown theater and watch along with strangers. No one had a good handle on just who was watching pornography, but that was exactly the point. Porn had become a private indulgence. By 1985 it was credibly estimated that sixty-five million X-rated videotapes were played in American homes each year.[39]

Magazines addressed to male voyeurism underwent a parallel shift. In 1969 *Playboy* found itself challenged in the United States by a rawer *Penthouse* magazine (first published in Britain in 1965). *Penthouse* reached the height of its popularity in the 1970s and 1980s. In August 1971 it showed female genitalia for the first time. *Playboy* followed suit five months later.[40] In 1980s *Penthouse* found itself gradually outflanked by Larry Flint's even rawer magazine, *Hustler*. In response, *Penthouse* in the late 1990s added pictures of penises, oral sex, and close-ups of penises entering vaginas. *Playboy*, meanwhile, seemed hopelessly passé.[41] Things had changed a lot since the pinup.

A variety of factors contributed to the new obscenity. Technology was one. Videotape, as we mentioned above, changed the porn industry. The regulatory environment also mattered. HBO and Cinemax, with their doses of nudity and sex, became commercially viable only when the Federal Communications Commission opened the door to the cable industry in 1972.[42] Similarly, the Supreme Court simply gave more space to sexual images in the general culture than it had in the past. In *Miller v. California* (1973), the landmark case on obscenity, the Court upheld the idea that obscenity was not entitled to constitutional protection, but it defined obscenity in such an exacting way that it did little to stem the flow of porn. Commercial pressures were a third force propelling the new explicitness. Men's magazines were under pressure to keep up with each other and not to lose audience to the porn movie trade.

Television held on longer and never went nearly as far as other media, but by the 1990s the older codes were reeling there as well. Television in the 1950s had adopted the same production code used by the film industry. While there were some tangles with censors in the 1960s, controversy really accelerated in the early 1970s. Beginning with *All in the Family* (first aired in January 1971) and its spin-off *Maude* (fall 1972), prime-time TV was willing to tackle new, controversial ground. "During the season that began last week," *Time* magazine breathlessly reported in 1972, "programmers will actually be competing with each other to trace the largest number of touchy—and heretofore forbidden—ethnic, sexual and psychological themes. Religious quirks, wife swapping, child abuse, venereal disease—all the old taboos will be toppling."[43] A few years later the new thematic explicitness was joined by new visuals. "Jiggle" or "T&A" shows like *Charlie's Angels* added a dollop of adolescent titillation to prime-time lineups. From 1950 to 1970, the main pressure groups trying to alter TV content were liberals who pushed for more black faces and integrated programs as well as less violence. At the end of the 1960s, feminists joined this liberal push, looking for better portrayals of women. In the next decade, however, conservatives took over as the dominant critics of TV. New organizations, mostly led by Christian ministers, organized to complain about the "new era" of TV: "reckless hedonism and hostility toward morals, religion, marriage, free enterprise, family, and country."[44]

This expansion of the possible had limits. TV images were not nearly as explicit as movies or magazines. Still, the 1970s shift created controversy and was one factor in the turn of evangelical Christians to conservative politics in the late seventies. Certainly the new license in mainstream visual culture was one piece of what mobilized them for Ronald Reagan in 1980. It also was part of their wholesale move into the medium as both televangelists and hosts. In the 1950s, mainline Protestant churches had flirted with television as a medium of religious outreach and education. After some consideration they largely abandoned television, thinking it both ineffective in persuasion and unworthy as a vehicle for the gospel and leaving it wide open for appropriation by a less genteel, more aggressive brand of Christian broadcaster such as Jerry Falwell, Jim and Tammy Faye Bakker, Pat Robertson, and Patrick Buchanan.[45]

But one paradox of the last decades of the century is that though conservatives were able to win an increasing number of elections, they were not able to change the overall visual culture. They could add more niches to the new mix, but that's all. Ronald Reagan's 1980 victory did not turn TV back to the 1950s. Instead, during the 1980s, images were appearing in mass media that would have been unthinkable just a few years before. The channels outside the standard cable package could feature nudity, simulated sex, and foul language. With cable stations winning more viewers, the networks responded in kind. In 1992 the popular comedy *Seinfeld* ran an episode about a contest among friends to see who could resist masturbating the longest. The next year the Reverend Donald Wildmon of the American Family Association denounced the popular police drama *NYPD Blue* as "soft-core porn" for its signature shots of unclad rear ends and occasional short sex scenes (with breasts and genitalia tastefully obscured). In 1994, *Roseanne* aired a lesbian kiss. (This was one of several in the 1990s, most of them probably ploys to spike ratings during sweeps weeks.) All this appeared on network television in prime time. (In the lobby of the Rockefeller Center, NBC happily sold T-shirts commemorating the *Seinfeld* episode.) By 2003 *TV Guide* was asking, "How much freedom is too much?"[46] The idea of an evening "family viewing hour" safe from risqué material—briefly mandated by the FCC from 1975 to 1977—collapsed under the networks' struggle to prevent the audience from switching to cable.

Far outweighing the erosion of "decency" on TV in the 1990s was the emergence of internet pornography. With the explosion of the World Wide Web from 1992 to 1996, literally millions of images of every conceivable kind of porn were now entering computers in homes, schools, and public libraries. Kids had enormously easy access. With both parents commonly working, after school was becoming prime time for porn viewing! Congress tried twice to regulate internet porn in the 1990s, hoping to force filters onto school and public library computers to block this material. The Communications Decency Act of 1996, though vigorously supported by Congress and the Clinton administration, was struck down by the Supreme Court in 1997 for its overly broad definition of "indecency" and its infringement of free speech rights of both parents and minors. The more narrowly focused Child Online Protection Act of 1998 was struck down by federal courts within months of being proposed. Both acts would have blocked websites with information about birth control or abortion, and even sites preaching abstinence. In the late 1990s the new images were easily available in millions of homes and in your local public library. The Children's Internet Protection Act of 2000, which was found constitutional in 2004, finally put a lid on things by forcing schools and libraries that took federal funds to maintain filters against obscenity, including child pornography. Still, it was the young people who were most savvy with the technical know-how to subvert such efforts.

Changing Attitudes

By the year 2000, American visual culture differed fundamentally from that of 1945. It seemed more chaotic, more out of control, more full of delirious images. Visual culture seemed less a force of integration than of fragmentation. And while there were always crosscurrents to complicate the story, there were important changes in the way the image—the very nature of the image—was perceived.

Visual culture now seemed disruptive. Since the middle of the nineteenth century, photographs were broadly thought to stop time, to interrupt and thereby even bring order to the flow of experience. A photo captured forever the fleeting moment. Even the new "moving pictures" of the twentieth century did not dramatically change that mainstream perception. Especially once the censorship system was in place, Hollywood movies tended to reinforce myth. Publicity stills embalmed moments to dream of. But in the closing decades of the century, as we have seen, production methods, new technologies, and changing attitudes made the visual culture less soothing, far jerkier. Pictures were increasingly spoken of as upsetting the larger society instead of stabilizing it.

New practices contributed to a waning faith in the documentary power of the image. Playing off popular conspiracy theories that the moon landing was a hoax, the 1978 film *Capricorn One* portrayed a failed mission to Mars that NASA had staged in a film studio. As early as 1982 *National Geographic*, long respected for its photojournalism, found itself embroiled in controversy when it was revealed that it had digitally squeezed the pyramids at Giza together to make a more attractive cover picture. In August 1989 *TV Guide* depicted Oprah Winfrey on top of a pile of money, wearing a revealing dress. Having recently lost sixty-seven pounds on a diet, she's shown with an improbably svelte physique—

which turned out to belong to the actress Ann-Margret. The cover picture was nowhere identified as a composite. Oprah's spokeswoman said that Oprah would never have agreed to such a risqué dress or so vulgar a pose. In response to the criticism, *TV Guide*'s editor told the artist responsible for the image "not to do it again."

That year, 1989, the *Wall Street Journal* estimated that a full 10 percent of color pictures published in the United States had been digitally doctored,[47] well before "photoshopping" was a household word. This was Luce's fakery—but without allegiance to the truth.

"The computer image," one theorist flatly stated, "is forgery incarnate."[48] To be sure, trick films showing the camera's magical powers are as old as cinema, and there is a long predigital tradition of photo manipulation, as we saw in sidebar 2.3 on airbrushing.[49] But photographic trickery had been generally understood as manipulating some harvest of reality, not as creating pure fantasy. Now crowds, explosions, and complete characters were conjured up in computers with no connection to an original. Artfully meshed with film, these digital inventions were inserted into movie scenes where reality and invention could mix promiscuously. Digital photographs, at the same time, increasingly smoothed edges, removed blemishes, and made pictures look better while also raising questions about their "realness." The editors of the *Whole Earth Review* proclaimed in 1985 that digital manipulation meant "the end of photography as evidence of anything."[50]

By the end of the 1960s, intellectuals started attacking the notion of realism. In 1968 the French literary critic Roland Barthes wrote an influential essay suggesting that there was no such thing as "realism." Instead, there were "reality effects," assorted techniques that successfully created the illusion that the artifice was real. Claims to a fullness of reference—like those present in photojournalism or in myth-making Hollywood—were, he bluntly stated, "regressive." Instead, he advocated hollowing out texts so as to challenge the very idea of representation. Translated into English, this essay proved to be a seminal contribution to contemporary discussion of visual culture. It is one landmark in a turn against intellectuals' long-held position that both photography and the movies had some intrinsic bias toward realism, thanks to the traces of the real world inevitably captured on a film negative. This connection to "the real," moreover, was something to be celebrated, not condemned.[51] Barthes's antirealism fit a moment when countless American academics were writing about "the social construction of reality." Nor was this the position of academics only. By the early nineties, variations on the

FIGURE 5.1. Oprah Winfrey on *TV Guide*, August 1989.

theme could easily be found in the *New York Times* and other mainstream media outlets.[52]

New thinking in the 1970s provided a much more nefarious understanding of images in general and cinema specifically, making strange bedfellows with another leading voice against the unsettling new image culture—evangelicals. The widely influential British journal *Screen* offered a rather dark view of cinema as an agency of "subject formation." Using a hip, heady, and forbidding mixture of Marxist and psychoanalytic ideas, *Screen* could make going to the movies sound pernicious. The cinema (a term it preferred to the humbler "movies" or "film" to emphasis its status as an apparatus of power) both revealed and colluded with the psychological structure of bourgeois society. Spectators sat in a fantastical position of mastery vis-à-vis the image, thus gratifying a primeval narcissistic urge to see the ego projected as a totality, as in a mirror. "Renaissance perspective" (a bad thing) flattered viewers into thinking themselves masters of the universe. The ego was fortified by the fantasy of a complete image projected on the screen. Like families, schools, labor unions, and churches, the cinema trained ("constituted") people as compliant subjects of a patriarchal capitalist order. Absorption in a movie was tacit assent to that order and training in it. Viewers at times could sound almost pathological in 1970s film theory—scopophiliacs, alienated, repressed, obsessed. Though roundly criticized in the following two decades by reception-oriented film scholars for its sense of no exit and its antipopulist slant, *Screen* theory was one version of 1970s suspicion about images, precisely because of their potency.

One of the most influential essays in the history of film theory, Laura Mulvey's "Visual Pleasure and Narrative Cinema," directly attacked the idea that watching a movie should be fun or absorbing. First published in *Screen* in 1975, the essay called for the "destruction of pleasure as a radical weapon." "Narrative cinema" meant Hollywood, and visual pleasure implied the objectification of women. The camerawork of classical Hollywood, she argued, assumed a male point of view. Films were designed to put spectators in the masculine position of desiring the woman and identifying with the man. Whatever pleasure audiences took in movies came at the expense of others. Men had the easy road of fantasy, but women's pleasure could only be masochistic. (And both men and women were figured as heterosexual.) Smoothness was domination. Her essay became the canonical exposé of a sexism so rooted in Hollywood that it showed up in the deep structure of film itself.[53] No one could watch a movie the same way after reading it—for many it produced a complete and instant conversion to a new way of seeing. (Filmmakers and video

makers, having read Mulvey in film school, started to toy with the sexist gazing conventions in following years.) It was one mark of a shift
from the mainstream confidence in fun at the movies that was common
around 1945 and the notion that something like a pinup could be healthy
and innocent. "Wholesome" was a word few 1970s film theorists would
care to use for movies.

Screen, of course, was by no means the main voice of opposition to
the image culture of the 1970s. That came from the right of the political
spectrum. Yet suspicions about pictures were sprouting all over. In the
1980s there was a coalition against pornography between some Christians and some feminists. In the early nineties, the crassness of music
videos and video games became fodder for skirmishes in what were
called the "culture wars," a series of clashes between cultural conservatives and cultural liberals about the shape and future of American art
and entertainment. By the mid-1990s, public opposition to the visual
culture was no longer coming overwhelmingly from the Right, as it had
been in the late seventies.

Especially in its postmodern version, this new turn in intellectual life
rejected the earlier idea that the image captured a denser reality. Central to postmodern aesthetics was a distrust of realism understood as
everyday experience or common sense. Postmodern film and architecture have little ballast of stored experience to balance the flights of fantasy. This made postmodernism thrilling; it also did nothing to solve
the political disaffection and other forms of alienation that people felt.
What a postmodernist like Frank Gehry achieved in architecture was the
same thing that turned ordinary people away from politics: a discon-
nection from everyday experience.[54] Instead, images lived a life of their
own. According to literary critic Fredric Jameson, we were witnessing
"the transformation of reality into images." Historian Martin Jay noted
that postmodernism combined deep skepticism about the image with
awe about its power. Postmodernism, he claimed, was paradoxically
both "the hypertrophy of the visual" and "its denigration."[55]

The summarizing power of mythic images was part of their unreality.
Rather than referencing anything outside, they were reinterpreted as
pointing only to other images. The media politics of a Ronald Reagan,
in which movies he had seen became "realities" that he remembered ex-
periencing, was widely commented on.[56] But the late twentieth century
was gripped by a much larger image politics, where spin doctors and
media consultants were weighty players, all hoping to change political
momentum by attaching favored policy to dramatic images. Critics complained that Bill Clinton's Bosnia policy was captive to images seen on

TV news. The debate about the revival of orphanages at the end of 1994 was framed by two fictive images of the institution—Dickens's *Oliver Twist* and Spencer Tracy in *Boys Town*. Members of the Clinton White House glibly dismissed orphanage talk with a reference to the former. Newt Gingrich rather tendentiously introduced a showing of the latter on Ted Turner's cable network.[57] Theorists like Jean Baudrillard, who argued that we maneuvered our way through a fun house of simulacra in which reality was in the service of spectacle, might have overstated our condition, but it didn't sound bad as an understanding of the O. J. Simpson extravaganza. There was much in the media environment that gave such ideas a surface plausibility.

One measure of the new antirealism was the academic reevaluation of the iconic documentary images of the 1930s and 1940s. By the 1980s, researchers were chipping away at the mythic status of Farm Security Administration photographs. Since authenticity and truthful representation were questionable propositions, these images were no longer timeless documents or testimonies to historic nobility in suffering. The evidence of negatives on deposit in the Library of Congress showed that FSA photographers such as Walker Evans and Dorothea Lange consciously sought particular aesthetic effects. Lange's *Migrant Mother*, it was discovered, was not a transcendent image captured in a single moment but rather the sixth in a series of poses. Moreover, Lange chose not to depict all the mother's children, presumably to appeal to middle-class sensibilities about proper family size. The historical digging was not motivated by an effort to understand the art as much as to expose the artificiality. Where once artistry had been openly embraced as part of the documentary genre, now it was suspect for its manipulation. Here is Jay's combined hypertrophy and denigration of the image.

This was just part of a wholesale debunking of iconic images in the 1980s. Joe Rosenthal's flag raising at Iwo Jima was shown to be a reenactment of the actual flag raising, which took place earlier on the day he took the photograph; Robert Capa's man falling in Spain, it turns out, fell again and again before the camera until Capa got the shot he wanted. Two women and nearly a dozen men have plausible claims to have been to be the nurse and sailor in Alfred Eisenstaedt's photograph of the kiss in Time Square on VJ Day[58] Such historical miniscandals were part of a mood that had little faith in the testimonial power of pictures. Artifice crowded out the facts; reality, as Barthes said, was an effect. Artist Sherrie Levine's photographs of Walker Evans's photographs, which she exhibited without comment in a show in 1980, presented documentary truth as ironic appropriation. All these were examples of the crumbling faith in the power of synecdoche.

Topping off the fall from grace, in 1978 an Associated Press reporter revealed that the migrant mother's name was Florence Owens Thompson. She was not an "immortal," as Roy Stryker had called her, but a particular person living in a mobile home in Modesto, California, who complained bitterly about not having benefited in the least from having her likeness embalmed in the famous photograph. (She was also of Cherokee descent rather than a poor white, as is often thought.) Immortal icons could be ordinary humans.[59] What was once understood as documentary truth about the plight of real people was being reread as calculated aesthetic and political craft or as exploitation. Summary was not a form of nation building but a scab picked off a wound.

Another example of shifting attitudes among intellectuals toward iconic images of the earlier century was Donna Haraway's critical reading of the African Hall at the American Museum of Natural History, whose dioramas were a stunning example of the art of visual synthesis in the 1930s. Her article "Teddy Bear Patriarchy," first published in 1985, focused on Carl Akeley, the man the hall is named for. She saw the hall as a "visual technology" for producing gender, race, and class identities. Like Mulvey, she attacked "the aesthetic ideology of realism." The presentational strategy of summary, she argued, papered over a complex network of power relations: "Behind every mounted animal, bronze sculpture, or photograph lies a profusion of objects and social interactions." Realism concealed a partisan point of view: "What is so painfully constructed appears effortlessly, spontaneously found, discovered, simply there if one will only look." But such artlessness was a kind of trick. The killing and mounting of animals served Haraway as an apt symbol for visual cultural summary: "Taxidermy fulfills the fatal desire to represent, to be whole." Synecdoche was no longer democratic, it was murderous. In Haraway's reading, Akeley preyed on African animals, his ghostwriter wife, and black servants alike to fortify his uncertain masculinity. He even designed a camera that, as he boasted in a quotation Haraway provides as incriminating evidence, "you can aim . . . with about the same ease that you can point a pistol." Looking at museum exhibits had rarely sounded so iniquitous.[60]

Of course there were countercurrents against the suspicion of images late in the century. The Rodney King trial was one wake-up call. In March 1991 a bystander had made a video recording of Los Angeles police who pulled King, a black motorist, over for a routine stop, then savagely beat him. The lawyers for the defense in the policemen's trial argued that the tape showed King was actually the aggressor, and they played the video for the jurors frame by frame rather than as normally viewed, construing his defensive gestures as aggressive. As some scholars more or less penitently admitted at the time, it was as if the defense team had read film theory and taken to heart the lesson that videotape's truth content was malleable and socially constructed.[61] The defense's deconstruction of the video persuaded the all-white jury, but not the thousands who rioted when the officers were acquitted or the millions who looked on in sympathetic horror and outrage. Perhaps there was, after all, some hard kernel of fact in photography—its relation to pain and to bodies.

In the 1990s film scholars intensified their interest in the "indexicality" of the image—the notion that images can be traces of events—as a founding question of their field. At the precise historical moment when the digital was triumphing in both amateur and professional image making, scholars began looking anew for lost traces of truth in the image, for what Walter Benjamin had called "a tiny spark of contingency."[62] The turn back to the index was a small boat on a great sea of image skepticism. Bazin's interest in the photographic image as a relic was freshly appreciated, as was Barthes's notion of the "punctum," a little pinprick of truth or "having-happenedness" that arrests a viewer of a photograph.[63]

Attitudes toward the new looseness of images were of course more widely varied. Elsewhere in the culture, in the 1980s and 1990s there was increased respect for the notion that visuality was related to learning. Not just simplification, but actual learning. There was a huge growth of interest in visual intelligence among cognitive psychologists. This echo of Marshall McLuhan contrasts with early twentieth-century behaviorists who dismissed the image. Gingrich's Toffleresque futurism was quite optimistic about the democratizing of information that the new computer graphics might bring. The development of graphic user interfaces in personal computers and the Windows operating system made pictures into everyday work tools. Everyone at a personal computer with a mouse had the power to edit and control what was on the screen just as much as any TV viewer with a remote. Gone were fixed and monumental images or a screen held aloof at an untouchable distance.

Changes in image production helped spawn an intellectual interest in images that went far beyond theory. Images continued to sneak into places where print once reigned supreme, a trend that might be read as part of a gnawing sense among the late twentieth-century bourgeoisie that they should not miss out on the age of images. The *American His-*

torical Review began using pictures in 1979, the *Journal of American History* in 1986. Both started gingerly, but pictures have since become a regular part of each issue. Both began to review films in the 1980s. University classrooms started to become "smart," wired for pictures, sound, and the internet. Microsoft's PowerPoint, developed in the 1980s, was standard in many university classrooms by early in the new millennium. Despite widespread complaints by students and teachers alike about its deadening effects, PowerPoint made educators an offer they couldn't refuse—a single package for integrating text, image, word, and sound.[64] Advances in printing in the 1990s made six-color images much less difficult to produce, giving one of the last bastions of the culture of thick fact—the textbook—visually busy and occasionally even inviting designs. Some textbooks looked like "television in print"—a label that had been applied to *USA Today* in the early 1980s. Langdell's cluttered casebook was dead as a textbook format, at least at the undergraduate level.

The graphics of *USA Today* as well as the jazzing up of more staid publications—the *New York Times* went color in 1997—hint at a fusion of the visual and the factual.

By the turn of the millennium, image jitters were pervasive in the culture. The widespread support for efforts to keep internet porn away from kids was one sign. Nervous discussions about how hard it was to raise a child, and how the mass media did not help, were another. Recent polls showed solid support for the idea that mass media imagery had gotten out of control. When the singer Janet Jackson briefly bared her breast at in the 2004 Super bowl half-time show, there was national outrage, although it was hard to tell where the authentic outrage ended and the hall-of-mirrors media circus began, since certainly more people saw the "wardrobe malfunction" on postmortem replays than the fleeting glimpse offered by the live broadcast.[65] It was a meta-outrage about something hardly visible; Baudrillard could have scripted it.

The widespread concern did not lead to any dramatic cultural rollback. The inability to craft law able to satisfy even a fairly conservative Supreme Court was one reason. The suspicion that government censorship was not a good thing no matter what was another. The quiet and private enjoyment of porn by many adults was still a third. Finally, the sheer dazzle of the music video, internet, Hollywood explosions, TV flash, and video games was also undeniable. Their energy was enormous, their creativity inescapable. They could be wildly entertaining, whatever their flaws. American media, with all their vulgarity and crassness, were loved by millions.

The Failure of Visual Summary

In 1993 *Time* magazine put on its cover a computer-generated image that portrayed a composite of different ethnicities in a single female face. Less ambitious in its aim at a universal synthesis than the *Pioneer* plaque, the picture sought to represent only one nation, not all humanity. Each racial and ethnic group was given a percentage in the final composite that matched its expected population share in the United States in the year 2050. *Time*'s editors were excited by the portrait—the "new face of America." But this image was roundly attacked by the cultural studies Left. The picture was too white; it smoothed over the real ethnicities that would continue to exist; its happy blending effaced the real conflicts of race and ethnicity by perpetuating the old dream of regenerative miscegenation; it used a woman to represent the nation, as usual, and made use of traditional norms of youth and beauty.[66]

Multicultural activists on the left fought the claim that summarizing images were sufficient to capture the real "differences" within American society. Low-resolution gestures toward larger totalities were widely considered oppressive. In one typical example, in 1997 law students at the University of Virginia protested the rehanging of eight oil portraits of the former deans of the law school, all of them white men. Formerly hung in a relatively obscure spot in the library, the paintings were moved to a more prominent spot in a new corridor after the school underwent a major renovation. Some students dubbed the gallery Dead White Male Hall. One student asked a key question about the pictures: "Where are the representations of minorities and women?"[67] The dean defended the lineup as a group the entire community could be proud of and agreed to hang portraits of the first woman and first African American to graduate from the school, as well as a photograph of the current, much more diverse student body.[68] The old logic of summary by representatives did not hold. For many people this shift was a kind of relief from and resistance to a culture—with images only the tip of the iceberg—designed to reinforce the legitimacy of white people and men.

In 1997 the Franklin Delano Roosevelt memorial was the subject of a national debate. The main statue of Roosevelt portrayed him seated, wearing a voluminous cape that obscures his lower body, with his beloved Scottish terrier Fala at his feet. The question was how to depict his disability—as he had lived (cloaked) or as some wanted him remembered (out). The memorial already featured one of only two extant photographs showing him in a wheelchair as well as a granite inscription explaining that after 1921 he could not walk without aid.[69] The

FALL 1993 $3.50

SPECIAL ISSUE
TIME

Take a good look
at this woman.
She was created by
a computer from a
mix of several
races. What you see
is a remarkable
preview of...

THE NEW FACE OF AMERICA
How Immigrants Are Shaping the World's First Multicultural Society

FIGURE 5.2. "The New Face of America," *Time*, November 18, 1993.

question was not the availability of information—the site had plenty of documentation about his polio and resulting limitations to his mobility. The question was what the iconic image could and could not contain. Many called for an additional statue of FDR in a wheelchair.

The debate split the public in two. On the same page of the *New York Times*, disability activists represented both sides of the question. Showing the wheelchair, some argued, would tarnish Roosevelt's triumph over a society that oppressed the disabled; others argued that it was the nondisabled who really needed to see the wheelchair.[70] On the whole, activists strongly supported the additional statue, as did presidents

Sidebar 5.2 An Image for Aliens

In 1972 astronomer Carl Sagan, working with his second wife, artist Linda Salzman Sagan, and his colleague, astronomer Frank Drake, designed a plaque for the space exploration probes *Pioneer 10* and *Pioneer 11*. It was supposed to be a greeting from the human race to extraterrestrial intelligences, a kind of cosmic message in a bottle. Hedging their bets about what kind of message would best reach unknown minds, they used a variety of representational media. (Later efforts would include a vinyl LP of selected sounds.)[1] Along with an abstract, quasi-mathematical figure that provided the celestial location of Earth in what Sagan exuberantly called "the only language we share with the recipients: Science," the plaque provided an image of a naked man with his right arm raised to the square in greeting while a naked woman at his side looks vaguely in his direction. If ever there was an attempt at a summarizing image, this was it. The sender: humanity as a whole. The receiver: unknown. The message: hello. Though the team recognized from the beginning many obstacles to what was always an implausible project of universal translation, the plaque was supposed to be a generic image accessible to any intelligent creature who found it.

It was instantly controversial. The plaque instantly and miserably failed to convey a single clear message to earthlings, let alone to alien "interceptor societies." The great visual theorist E. H. Gombrich pointed out at the time that "our 'scientifically educated' fellow creatures in space might be forgiven if they saw the figures as wire constructs with loose bits and pieces hovering in between." The image was packed with presuppositions. And as to our fellow creatures on Earth, he noted that the man's gesture would not even be understood as a greeting by Chinese and Indians.[2]

Instead, the plaque became what Sagan later ruefully called "a cosmic Rorschach test." One leading complaint was the nudity. Letters to the editor wondered why NASA wanted to "spread this filth even beyond our own solar system." The man's genitals were depicted, but not the

1. See Luke Stacks, "Planetary Consciousness and the Voyager Golden Record," Seminar Paper, Department of Communication Studies, University of Iowa, Spring 2007.

2. E. H. Gombrich, "The Visual Image," *Scientific American* 227 (September 1972): 92.

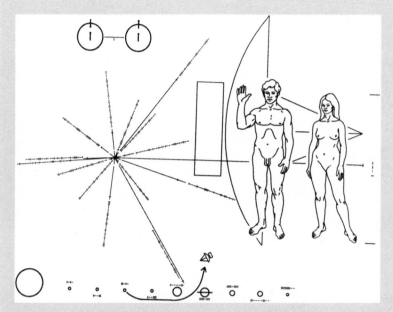

FIGURE 5.3. Illustration on Pioneer Plaque, 1972.
Courtesy NASA on The Commons, image #: 72-H-192.

woman's, as if following the norms of Greek sculpture. This distortion
was criticized by feminists and *Playboy* alike. Sagan said he had considered adding a small vertical line to her pubic area but did not want to
risk further alienating NASA. Even interstellar acts of communication
could not escape earthly compunctions. For an alien trying to figure out
human beings, perhaps the most telling thing to understand about the
picture would be why one small line could stir up so much trouble. This
absence took liberties in depicting human anatomy, but it accurately
represented long-standing taboos in human culture. If the aliens were
interested in figuring out our species, they would be very well served
by understanding why a convention representing the origin of every
human being was so contentious.

Other critics complained that the female was too passive. Her stance
is slightly off balance, as if she were executing a toe sweep, while the
man stands centered and erect. He waves, but she looks sideways to the
man instead of joining in the greeting. Is she asking him for permission,
admiring his leadership, or lightly mocking him? As is always the case
with images, it is impossible to distill its meaning without remainder,

but the picture is clearly charged with some sort of gender ideology. Why was her body off center? Why wasn't she waving as well?

Others complained about the racism of the image. Why were the couple Caucasian when whites formed only a small minority of the human species? The image added to the criticism common among African Americans that NASA was a white project more concerned with unknown alien intelligences than with real black people.[3] Sagan says in self-defense that the image was supposed to be "panracial." He regretted that the man had lost the "short 'Afro' haircut" of the original design and that the woman's hair, because it is shown only in outline, could appear to be blond. (It is in any case straight hair.) Despite the vaguely almond-shaped eyes and flattened noses of the final version, few critics could find nonwhite features in this Adam and Eve.[4]

So much for the effort to make an image that would encompass the essence of humanity. As the team admitted from the outset, "the message inadvertently contains anthropocentric content."[5] Today the image looks much less than universal or timeless; it looks like a transmission from the distant planet of the 1970s. No one, naked or clothed, would look quite like that today. It is a document of a 1970s vision of liberal multiculturalism. Perhaps the biggest period giveaway was the hairstyles. Today we'd have as much trouble automatically recognizing the meaning of the image as we would finding a record player to play the gold-plated copper LPs they sent in the later *Voyager* probes. (The choice of an acoustic medium for the later message to aliens may have been based on the *Pioneer* experience: sounds tend to be less controversial than pictures.)

The range of attacks foreshadowed things to come. The right side of the cultural-political spectrum brought traditional worries about indecency, and the left brought newer suspicions about how representations do an indignity to race and gender. Such were the armies gathering against the image in the late twentieth century.

3. Lynn Spigel, *Welcome to the Dream House* (Durham, NC: Duke University Press, 2001), 141–85.

4. All quotations in this sidebar are taken from Carl Sagan, *The Cosmic Connection: An Extraterrestrial Perspective* (New York: Doubleday, 1973), 18–33. John Durham Peters remembers his mother complaining thus.

5. Carl Sagan, Linda Salzman Sagan, and Frank Drake, "A Message from Earth," *Science* 175 (February 25, 1972): 881–84, at 881.

Ford, Carter, Reagan, and Clinton, all against the general drift of public opinion. Even among Roosevelt's twenty-five grandchildren opinion was split. Another statue was eventually added by the entrance to
the memorial site, portraying FDR in a wheeled chair that he used. A
single statue could no longer encompass the full complexities of FDR;
the front stage could no longer imply the backstage in a happy abridgment. No one trusted a single image to tell the whole story. Squabbles
among elites showed that the culture of monumental summary was
under duress. As the coalition of Ford, Carter, Reagan, and Clinton suggests, it was not only the political Left that had problems with cultural
summary.

Hardly a soul, however, objected that FDR's signature cigarette holder
had been left out of the new image.[71] Activists argued that we needed a
new FDR statue to be true to how things really were, but on the topic of
tobacco, "history" was no match for current opinion.

In January 2002 the New York City Fire Department (FDNY) decided to build a statue outside its Brooklyn headquarters memorializing the three firefighters who raised the flag on a heap of rubble near
the destroyed Twin Towers on September 11, 2001. The photo, taken by
Thomas Franklin, a New Jersey photographer, evoked memories of the
flag raising at Iwo Jima and quickly became one of the most circulated
images of the attack. It was another effort to have a dramatic picture tell
a more complicated story. The photograph won numerous awards and
traveled widely throughout the culture in late 2001 and early 2002—in
newspapers, magazines, encyclopedias, websites, coffee mugs, T-shirts,
and decals—and was reenacted at the 2002 Super Bowl.[72]

Yet the FDNY's proposed statue fell into controversy almost at once.
The mockup for the sculpture used professional models, one of them
white, one black, and one Hispanic. The faces and figures of the three
white firemen in the original photo were not going to be used. Fire Department officials defended the design as representing all firefighters:
"Ultimately, a decision was made to honor no one in particular but
everyone who made the supreme sacrifice," said an FDNY spokesman.

The gamble that one image could include everyone lost. A wave of
critical response ensued. The firefighters in the photograph hired a law-
yer, arguing that the proposed statue violated history, a charge that
opponents of the statue of FDR in a wheelchair had also made. (Again,
the past was subject to the demands of the present: no one was so concerned for historical accuracy as to complain that one of the firemen
had lost a sizable paunch in the revisionist sculpture.) The Firefighters
Union condemned the proposed statue as "'political correctness' run

amok."[73] Another fireman complained, "You wouldn't change Iwo Jima, so why would you change that?"[74] (Ironically, he invoked an iconic image with an equally charged relation to an original event.) Defenders of the proposed monument praised its inclusiveness. Others, following the old point that if you want to change the image you should change the reality, noted that the photograph might have stood a better chance of being ethnically diverse in the first place had the FDNY been less restrictively white in its hiring practices. Officials at the New York Fire Department eventually dropped the plan, and the donor pulled out.

A 2002 effort to commemorate heroism 1945-style utterly failed. There were profound ambiguities at the heart of the debate that reached back to concerns about realism in painting and photographic accuracy as discussed in chapters 1 and 2. A painting of a tulip, a photograph of a cloud, or an X-ray of a skull often provides too much detail. The profusion of particulars can work against the desire to represent a type or essence, one reason anatomy textbooks are often illustrated by hand.[75] In the 9/11 case, the subject of the memorial was profoundly unclear. The confusion doomed the project: Did the image represent the specific act at a single moment of three men raising a flag as captured by a photographer or the much less picturable fact that 343 firefighters had died on September 11? No single image could bear the full story. No one seems to have argued that a little drama of triumph could be the part that stood for the whole.

In a kind of ironic conclusion, the image did finally appear in a public memorial in March 2002: on a commemorative forty-five-cent postage stamp. The resolution on the tiny picture was too poor to make out the ethnicity of the faces in any detail, but the paunch, at least, was restored. Perhaps postage stamps were the last refuge of the iconic image in the early millennium—miniatures that are canceled after a single use.

The moral authority of synecdoche had completely broken down by the 1990s. The notion of a single image encapsulating a larger social totality was met with utter disbelief. Nothing is more anathema to a culture that celebrates diversity than the idea that a Norman Rockwell picture of four white boys playing by a creek represents the "essence of American youth." The notion that a white rural family at the Thanksgiving table could stand for "America" became similarly questionable. Rockwell's 1943 image dramatizing Roosevelt's promise of "Freedom from Want" was attacked in its time for its hopelessly mainstream rendering. But standing in for the whole of the nation? That wasn't a problem in the 1940s. Rockwell's work is a perfect example of the midcentury culture of summary. Whereas our more knowing eyes are tempted to see

FIGURE 5.4. "Heroes of 2001" stamp, issued June 7, 2002.
Smithsonian Institution, National Postal Museum.
© United States Postal Service. All rights reserved.

his pictures as celebrations of whiteness or patriarchy, critics of the time complained not about the exclusions of his subject matter but about the undemanding sweetness of his style. A few tokens could stand in for the whole. In social representations around 2000, however, the part could no longer bear the whole. What we see today as a whitewash results from a revolution in attitudes toward the image. In our more jaded moment, Rockwell's apparent innocence is read as a lure to be deconstructed and a warning about the perils of looking.

In intellectual life, the collapse of the notion of a "national character," one dimension of the culture concept, reflects the same shift. Around

2000 such a concept had become laughable in a scholarly forum. This uneasiness about synecdoche itself contributes to the instability of images. Representation must always be selective. Some of the fights over image representation in the 1990s (Should AIDS-prevention posters on San Francisco buses feature white males or a different combination? How does one visualize the university community in promotional brochures? What mix of representations of minorities of all kinds should we have on television and in film?) reflect the tensions inherent in the all-inclusive approach to the image. There were no "solutions" to such issues. There was only constant flux and debate. No frames could manage the flow.[76] FDR with wheelchair or cigarette? The firefighters who raised the flag or the firefighters who died? Consensus was impossible.

Though those on the right were the most prominent critics of the proposed firefighters memorial, it is striking to see how a search for inclusive images in the 1990s ingratiated itself into those conservative circles that preached hostility to the new idioms of diversity and continued to pay lip service to a synecdochic approach to representation. A figure like Newt Gingrich sought out women and African Americans for his staff, especially those who might find themselves in front of a TV camera. Something "looked" wrong in being represented by a phalanx of white men in suits, even though such images could still be found. Conservatives wanted such "symbols" as Clarence Thomas. George W. Bush appointed blacks, Hispanics, and women who shared his ideology, disappointing the pious expectation that diversity per se brings a more liberal outlook. I once talked with a conservative Republican banker from suburban Chicago who told me how embarrassed he was by not having people of color shown on the bank's cartoon invitation to its Christmas party. It was not that he was particularly sensitive; it was that he wanted to "look right" to his employees.

White faces can no longer summarize the whole of America, but faces of color often do. In any promotional picture today—for a product, university, or company—it is virtually guaranteed that there will be at least one person of color, and probably more. Nothing but white faces, Rockwell style, would simply look wrong as a picture of an American collective. Former Speaker of the House Paul Ryan (R-WI) got in trouble in July 2016 when he posted a selfie with dozens of White House interns behind him—all of them Republicans and all, apparently, white.[77] But a group picture consisting of nothing but faces of color would not seem strange and might even seem festive or celebratory. Indeed, Lin-Manuel Miranda's rap musical *Hamilton* (2015), featuring a cast composed exclusively of actors of color, has been the most feted American musical in

Sidebar 5.3 The Selfie

In November 2013, Oxford Dictionaries announced *selfie* as the word of the year. Their research showed that its use had increased by 17,000 percent within the previous year! How they could possibly be so precise in such a nebulous realm as speech is a cause for wonder, but even lexicographers are in the big data business today. The word's Australian origin, with the *-ie* ending (as in *barbie* for *barbecue*), they noted, softened what might otherwise seem a rather egocentric act.[1]

Indeed, the boom in digital self-portraits uploaded to social media sites called forth a wave of popular consternation. Not only had smartphones destroyed the ability to talk face-to-face, went the lament, but their built-in cameras had produced a generation of narcissists. Other critics went with the old standbys of voyeurism and exhibitionism. Psychotherapists jumped in, opining about body image and depression. Disneyland and Beijing's Forbidden City outlawed selfie sticks to spare both the guests and the exhibits. Some Muslim clerics, concerned about the conduct of a recent generation of hajjis, have suggested that taking selfies at Mecca goes against the principles of Islam.

In fact, the practice is much more nuanced. The selfie is also about sociability and is governed by primordial codes of nonverbal communication. This point is made by Paul Frosh, who points to the "gestural economy of affection" built into selfies. The framing and field of vision of every selfie are defined anthropometrically. The genre is invitational, the arm beckoning as if reaching out to both the viewer and the camera. The viewer gets to participate in the intimate moment of seeing someone pose for a picture. The distance from the person in the frame to the camera is the companionable reach of an arm. Each image documents the act of inviting others to see us as we see ourselves and suggests the "phatic communion" of staying in touch. It is one of many digital genres that puts living bodies into motion, ranging from Nintendo's Wii to porn.[2]

The selfie is highly self-referential: director and actor are one. For

---

1. "Word of the Year 2013," English: Oxford Living Dictionaries, http://blog.oxforddictionaries.com/press-releases/oxford-dictionaries-word-of-the-year-2013/.

2. Paul Frosh, "The Gestural Image: The Selfie, Photography Theory, and Kinesthetic Sociability," *International Journal of Communication* 9 (2015): 1607–28, at 1622.

most of the history of photography, taking a picture typically meant not being in it (unless you had special gear such as a tripod and a timer or manipulated the image). But in selfies the outstretched arm points to the device. The camera and the hand that holds it form a vanishing point *behind* the image. Selfies belong in the lineage of mirrors rather than painting. With selfies we look into other people's mirrors and see what they see.

Selfies require sensorimotor coordination, and dexterity is taken to an extreme in the "selfie Olympics," a ragtag mock event staged in 2014 and 2018 in which contestants outdo each other with contortionist antics that hover in the register between absurdist self-mockery, frat-boy pranks, and classical play with mirrors, as in Velázquez's 1656 painting *Las Meninas*. Some images play with the vanishing point behind the camera, building in mirrors and echoes in Escher-like labyrinths behind the gymnastics.[3] Something about the selfie courts physical extremity. One British tourist in 2014 was fined three thousand euros for snapping a selfie of himself running with the bulls in the annual festival of San Fermín in Pamplona, Spain.[4] From 2011 to 2017, over 250 people died in the act of taking a selfie. (India led the world in selfie fatalities.)[5] Selfies are more dangerous than shark attacks, to invoke a widely circulated statistic. Many theorists have noted a deep link between photography and death, but rarely so concretely!

The selfie tries to redeem digital life from the charge of fakery and loneliness. The counterpart to the universal self-absorbed slouch of communion with a smartphone, the selfie is a celebration of being in the moment—and with a presentable posture. It is also a locative medium that includes a notable landmark as a backdrop. The selfie claims to be the dialectical opposite of digital self-immersion: selfies point to people and places outside social media. The selfie implies pilgrimage. It reintroduces a quantum of "being there." It marks both a self and a place.

3. Jakob Schiller, "The 10 Best Photos from the Selfie Olympics," *Wired*, January 10, 2014, https://www.wired.com/2014/01/the-10-best-photos-from-the-selfie-olympics/.

4. Alex Dunham, "Risky Business: Man Snaps Bull Run Selfie," *Local*, July 11, 2014, http://www.thelocal.es/20140711/is-this-the-most-dangerous-selfie-ever; accessed July 19, 2016.

5. Allyson Chiu, "More Than 250 People Worldwide Have Died Taking Selfies, Study Finds," *Washington Post*, October 3, 2018.

FIGURE 5.5. Photo by rawpixel on Unsplash.

It says, I am here. As Lilie Chouliaraki points out, it is both an existential genre (*I am* here) and a locative one (I am *here*). Because it announces the fact of being alive, it is an essential genre for migrants, who can use it to broadcast and celebrate their survival. The selfie can be a moral practice.[6]

Many selfies, of course, are group selfies—also known as "ussies" or "groupies." The occasion gives people an excuse to squeeze in cozily together: the frame of the selfie, like a virtual photo booth, invites a legal cuddle, an opportunity for sideways bodily contact. In the summer of 2016 Chicago's O'Hare Airport was plastered with large photo displays showing off its multicultural team of workers in food service, baggage, and security. Each image was a group selfie—one arm reaching out, the team packed closely together side by side, rubbing shoulders or elbows. Why didn't O'Hare commission more traditional portraits? Because the selfie means *unrehearsed* and *fresh*—though who knows how long that aura will last. The people you appear with in selfies are supposed to be the people you choose to share your life with. These are not colleagues but companions—or so the genre says.

One of the key spinoffs of the genre is not just an ussie, but images of people taking an ussie. This genre's claim to spontaneous fun and

6. Lilie Chouliaraki, "Symbolic Bordering: The Self-Representation of Migrants and Refugees in Digital News," *Popular Communication: The International Journal of Media and Culture* 15, no. 2 (2017): 78–94.

authentic togetherness makes it almost irresistible for public relations purposes. Figure 5.5 is a free online image showing cheerful, cool multicultural young people doing the thing that denotes togetherness these days. The next time you see an image of people posing for a group selfie, notice how it wants to shout freedom and fun off the grid. Here, it says, finally we have belonging. That such images will be uploaded again into digital circulation is a weary truth worthy of a cultural grump like Theodor Adorno.

decades. A few have groused about its casting call, but schoolchildren of all ethnicities can now sing vast portions of the play and talk excitedly about the American founders. "Visually, at least," as Robert Hariman and John Lucaites note, "we are all multiculturalists now."[78] Diversity has become at least an aesthetic imperative.

By about 2000 all political persuasions had become suspicious of synecdoche. Critics on the left attacked the composite "new American" on the cover of *Time* and lineups of dead white European men in university course syllabi, while critics on the right attacked the revisionist firefighters memorial and critics from both sides attacked the single FDR statue. In all cases the critics complained about historical inaccuracy, not noticing the ways they played history slant as well. The culture of happy abridgment was a thing of the past. Condensation had become a precarious truth game.

In a moment when the channels of communication were furiously multiplying and people were increasingly able to serve as their own media producers or curators to ever smaller audiences—perhaps most often to themselves—the big fights were about the central space of representation. The portraits in the University of Virginia law school would likely have sparked no controversy had they been left in an obscure corner of the library. It was their elevation to a new central space that seemed a comment on the nature of the whole institution. In the same way, no one denied that that the FDR memorial should be rich with information and images about his disability. No one called for a historical cover-up. It was common knowledge that one of the most powerful men of the century could not walk without aid for well over the last two decades of his life. But everyone had become a communications expert, worrying about what message pictures would send to *other* people. As general interest media content became rarer—restricted to disasters like

9/11 or occasional media events such as the Olympics—the fights over general representation, and the scarce resource of central public space, got more and more bitter. A single iconic image needed asterisks and footnotes. The image's power to condense and compress was taken as a dangerous monopoly. It was no longer a benign synthesis accommodating many subtexts, but rather an imperious form of erasure. To ensure plurality, the image needed to broken up—not one FDR statue, but two. Everybody wanted a piece of the central space, but nobody found it good enough—a nice recipe for general unhappiness.

The critique of summary could feel like a rather bleak commentary on the capacities of one's fellow citizens and an assault on the democratic faith that people could figure things out for themselves if the facts were freely available. Since you couldn't trust others to get the background, you had to fight so that the image everyone would see would include the message you wanted it to convey. The critique of summary was also, in its way, an effort to punish the image for what it does well: wordlessly dramatize totalities. In a time when images ran riot, no one trusted a single image to tell the whole story. We distrusted images deeply and depended on them desperately.

From the beginning, democracy has always turned on the question of representation. Representation could mean condensation, as when we talk about representatives in Congress, who presumably stand in for the unique views of their constituencies. It could also mean the inclusion of all varieties, as when we talk about a representative sample that aims to sample with equal odds of capturing the full range within a population. Representation could be both elitist and populist, unifying and scattering, clarifying and obscuring. The late twentieth-century revolt against the idea of condensation aroused all the old tensions.

Communism failed, Milan Kundera wrote in 1990, because ideology was defeated by the facts. Eastern Europeans stopped believing that the proletariat would grow poorer and poorer in the capitalist West but better and better off under state socialism. Reality, Kundera claimed, proved stronger than ideology. But Kundera was not so glib as to claim that "reality" ruled in the West. Rather, we were at the sufferance of what he called "imagology," the play of images that coursed through our minds and mass media. While reality proved to be stronger than ideology, images turned out to be stronger than reality.[79] Not a bad epitaph for the midcentury culture of condensing representation.

The question remained whether the image could no longer hold the facts or the facts themselves had grown too hairy to be contained. The breaking up of the image was a symptom of many other kinds of fragmentation; it is the cultural expression of a much bigger set of shifts in the infrastructure of the common life. These changes can be characterized in many ways—as, for instance, the secession of the successful, the shift from industrial to finance capitalism, or the dismantling of the welfare state. Our point is not to criticize those who fought for a well-deserved spot in the psychic real estate of public life. The culture of summary obviously preferred some identities over others, just as the American welfare state was designed, to put it bluntly, to help white men. Justice and democracy require an ongoing accounting of forgotten faces. Our point is that since the 1970s nobody has figured out how to build the new framework to hold the nation or the globe together. At one point in the century, intellectuals, artists, curators, librarians, and politicians sought to do so by means of summarizing institutions, images, and information. In the 1970s and onward most abandoned the project, some with glee, some with world-weariness. Only now are we starting to get clear about how steep a price we have paid in abandoning that effort.

Promiscuous Knowledge,
1975–2000

The claims for the digital age are many. It is the fulfillment of the Enlightenment. It is the hypertrophy of modernity. It will bring on a new world of individual fulfillment and bounty. It creates a new divide between the information rich and poor. Paper will become obsolete, and crusty bureaucracies will crumble. It unleashes creativity. It opens up new outlets for propaganda. It is mind numbing.

We add our own claim to the list: the digital age is the age of promiscuous knowledge. One of the most important trends of recent decades has been the blending and blurring of the line separating popular knowledge from expert knowledge. It's not that the line has been erased; it's that the line is constantly challenged. Professional knowledge is increasingly confronted by popular sensibilities, but without the goal of eliminating knowledge elites. Nor is promiscuous knowledge simply marked by popular or commonsense resistance to formal knowledge, something that has existed perennially. Promiscuous knowledge is the ongoing negotiation between elite knowledge producers and those outside the formal system or with no formal accreditation. It is the simultaneous reliance on and suspicion of expertise.

Some years ago the influential anthropologist Clifford Geertz wrote an essay called "Blurred Genres." Formerly separate academic disciplines were merging, borrowing, and trading with each other, Geertz argued. Social scientists were adopting literary techniques, presenting their research in forms that sounded like crime novels or travelogues, and historians were turning into retrospective cultural anthropologists.[1] Geertz's elegant essay touched on shifts going on at the time in some parts of the humanities and social sciences. But what the essay was just a bit too early to catch was the blurring of the line between the formal disciplines and popular knowledge. That was just moving into a new phase. It has since evolved into one important strain of intellectual life in late twentieth-century America and the new millennium.

Promiscuous knowledge emerged with distrust of the professional project and a decline in the prestige of experts. Promiscuous knowledge is, quite literally, the unholy blend of the profane and the professional, the outsider and the expert. It is marked by professionals' inability to maintain the "purity" of knowledge production amid its continued necessity. From its first rumblings in the early 1970s, it turned into one of the more important trends of the past few decades. Knowledge did not lose its containers altogether, but they increasingly eroded. Grand narratives may have collapsed, but plenty of people chugged along producing bench science. The prophets of postmodern meltdown or all-is-well techno-utopia were both wrong. The persistence of knowledge claims amid widespread cynicism was the story. Promiscuous knowledge was a renewal of the thick flow of facts without the faith in either democracy or progress.[2]

The Attack on Expertise in the 1970s:
Medicine, Law, the University

The 1970s have to be seen as the hinge in the rise of promiscuous knowledge. There were cultural reasons for this blurring of formal and informal knowledge that reach well beyond digital technology. Professionals lost respect in the early 1970s. Between 1967 and 1974, the repute of every sliver of the upper middle class fell, with the exception of the press, buoyed by the Watergate heroism. Lawyers, politicians, professors, military leaders, doctors—all suffered declining popularity. (The press would sink similarly in the next few years.) The cynicism of the era touched the reputations of all the professionals running major institutions.

Watergate's revelation that the central government could be rotten set the tone. The claims made for the ability of a managerial class to produce a rational, planned future frayed significantly. Economists were among the first to fall. The stagflation of the seventies dented the dreams of a nicely "fine-tuned" economy, and the faltering of Keynesian economics helped support the return of market thinking during the 1970s, growing virulent in the time of Thatcher and Reagan. Economic chaos undermined the presumption that professionals could effectively manage modernity. The popularity of the books of Ivan Illich signaled a new skepticism about the medical and educational professions. His writings were one more challenge to modernity's claim to be able to manage the future rationally. He was part of a much bigger wave of radical critique by people such as Herbert Marcuse, Norman O. Brown, Angela Davis, Shulamith Firestone, and Susan Brownmiller.

Much more important than the ruminations of intellectuals, however, was the work of activists. It was there that the challenges to formal knowledge burst out in the first years of the 1970s. Feminists, gay rights activists, African American activists, Native American activists, environmental activists, psychiatric patients—all emerged, with the support of investigative journalism, to challenge the authority of knowledge professionals. The 1970s are often treated as the moment when reform impulses in American life dissipated, but this explosion of activism tells a different story. The 1970s should be seen neither as a point of flagging liberal energies nor as a simple follow-on to the sixties but as a moment of more basic political restructuring, one that put the production of knowledge at the heart of politics.[3]

Medicine was a chief target. In May 1970, sessions at the American Psychiatric Association (APA) convention were disrupted for the first time by activists attacking psychiatrists who defined homosexuality as a mental illness. Speakers were shouted down. Explanations were laughed at. Epithets like "torturer," "vicious," and "motherfucker" were tossed at the psychiatrists. Activists demanded to respond to offending papers, turning at least one panel into chaos. Another psychiatrist was met with the shout, "Where did you take your residency, Auschwitz?"

At the heart of the anger was that the APA's *Diagnostic and Statistical Manual of Psychiatric Disorders* (the *DSM*), the most important diagnostic handbook in the nation and the world, included homosexuality. Up to the early 1970s, in other words, the APA officially declared that homosexuals were mentally ill. In the next few years activists continue to intrude on psychiatric gatherings, trying to force the profession to confront its prejudice. Never without a few supporters within the profession, the activists pulled others to their side in those years. In May 1973 the APA voted to take homosexuality off the list of mental disorders.[4]

The deinstitutionalization movement—advocating that those in mental institutions would be better off if released to live on their own—challenged medical authority in a similar way. Scattered intellectuals had expressed hostility to prevailing psychiatric practice during the 1960s. Antipsychiatrists like R. D. Laing and Thomas Szasz, writers like Ken Kesey and Sylvia Plath, and social theorists like Michel Foucault and Erving Goffman all produced critical work attacking psychiatric practice in the early 1960s. But it was not until the end of the decade and the early seventies that the animus against psychiatry moved from intellectual inquiry to political activism. In 1967, California passed the Lanterman-Petris-Short Act, creating the first state mental health system influenced by the antipsychiatry movement. In 1968 the New York chapter of the American Civil Liberties Union began a campaign to protect the rights of mentally ill patients. In the Paris uprising of May 1968, the student radicals made it a first point of business to occupy the office of Dr. Jean Delay, the coinventor of the psychiatric drug chlorpromazine.[5] In the early seventies, former patients began their own political organizing against forced treatment. In 1972 lawyers working to change the system filed a case that would lead to their first major success, overturning Wisconsin's civil commitment law. This was just one of hundreds of suits brought in the early and middle seventies against forced commitment or for the right to refuse treatment. By the end of the 1970s, the practice of psychiatry had changed significantly, not because of the internal evolution of the discipline, but owing to political pressures brought by outside activists—both former patients and civil liberties lawyers.[6]

A final blow to the legitimacy of psychiatry came in the study "On Being Sane in Insane Places," published in *Science* in 1973 and cited repeatedly in following decades. David Rosenhan, a Stanford psychologist, recruited "pseudopatients" to go to West Coast psychiatric hospitals, where they complained of a single flimsy symptom—"hearing voices" that said such things as "empty," "hollow," and "thud." All the actors (including himself) except one were admitted and diagnosed with schizophrenia. Once taken on as patients, the plants stopped feigning any symptoms and behaved normally, except for incessant note taking (which doctors and nurses chalked up to their illness). The pseudopatients were hospitalized for stays ranging from seven to fifty-two days before being released with diagnoses such as "schizophrenia in remission." (One wonders how Rosenhan compensated the plants for this massive inconvenience.) The great irony was that the supposedly sane psychiatrists couldn't tell that the actors were normal, but their fellow patients invariably knew. Mental institutions were seen as producing the madness they were supposed to be treating, and the mad were shown to be more discerning than the doctors. The overall conclusion that psychiatry was in cahoots with the illness stuck, even though the study's results demonstrated something more limited: that doctors, like the rest of us, can be duped.[7] The experiment was widely taken as a dagger in the heart of psychiatric authority.

Another group that had long-standing problems with officially sanctioned knowledge was African Americans. In the 1860s Frederick Douglass lectured about the racist social science of the day. W. E. B. Du Bois's opposition to white portrayals of Reconstruction is now well known—at least inside the tribe of professional historians. In the late sixties, distrust of white social science was not uncommon in African American communities. In the last two decades of the century a persistent rumor circulated in these communities that the epidemics of crack cocaine and AIDS were intentionally concocted by the CIA or other putative agents of race warfare. Of all the outsider suspicions of official knowledge, African Americans' distrust has perhaps the deepest roots.

The summer of 1972 brought a huge boost to the suspicion. Anger bubbled up over a long-term research project at Tuskegee Institute in Alabama, a project supposed to search for treatments and cures for syphilis. On July 25, 1972, the Associated Press sent a story over the wires reporting the grim fact that for decades African American men with syphilis had been in the cohort but were not treated so that they would serve as a control group for others who did receive treatment. About six hundred men suffered this way. Health professionals involved had known for decades that lack of treatment for syphilis condemned patients to a slow, painful death and produced such symptoms as blindness. In the name of "science," however, the control group continued untreated. The Rockefeller Foundation had been funding this research since 1929, and the US Public Health Service since 1932.

Scattered concerns had been raised within professional circles about the Tuskegee study since the mid-1960s. They were not acted on, however, and stayed internal to the review process. In 1972, though, when the story hit the national press, the outrage was public and immense. The disgust over the easy disposal of African Americans' lives reached well beyond the African American community. Senator William Proxmire called it "a moral and ethical nightmare," and Senator Teddy Kennedy termed it "outrageous and intolerable." Government officials who managed the program at first tried to make excuses, but pressure from the news media continued. In August the Department of Health, Education, and Welfare had appointed a group to review the study. By the spring of 1973 the project was dead.[8]

A good number of African Americans were not surprised at the abuse of black bodies in the name of science. What was new in 1972 was white support of their outrage and the decision of editors at the mainstream media not to ignore the subject. There was significant support for the proposition that the Tuskegee study could not be tolerated and that the scientific establishment had not monitored itself appropriately.

A final attack on medical authority was the feminist critique of medicine, especially obstetrics and gynecology, in the women's health movement of the 1970s. The best seller *Our Bodies, Ourselves* was first published in 1971 and has taken on canonic status in multiple editions since. The book attacked the medical establishment for treating pregnancy like an illness and preferring impersonal technologies to nurturing relationships. The book defended the relevance of women's experience against masculinist medical authority. Medicine was complicit in an overall social system that denied women access to knowledge of their bodies and saddled them with the burdens that followed such ignorance.

The courtroom was another place where the purity of scientific authority was under pressure. To be sure, the courtroom was always a site of promiscuous knowledge, especially in practices of evidence and witnessing, which have always blended popular and elite modes. (The ancient art of rhetoric emerged partly from this nexus.) The paradox of expert witnessing is that juries are supposed to sort out wrangles among the learned. But the reason experts are needed is that the jury is not qualified to decide on certain technical matters.[9] This makes the jury a prime site for the collision of expert and lay knowledge.

Up until the early 1970s, the basic standard regarding expert testimony in US courts went back to a 1923 decision, *Frye v. United States*, which dictated that only expertise generally accepted by the scientific community was acceptable in the courtroom. This case overturned the confusion about expert witnesses that had been common in the late nineteenth century, mingling quacks and specialists without clear criteria. *Frye* marked a turning point establishing the authority of expertise, the reliance on expert knowledge to adequately manage the modern world.

As faith in knowledge elites and professional authority dimmed in general, however, so did respect for that opinion. It was challenged several times during 1967–74. Then, in 1975 the new Federal Rules of Evidence proclaimed a new standard. Now expert testimony only had to be "relevant" and "reliable." No longer did testimony have to relate itself to an accepted canon. Instead, experts could introduce unorthodox opinions. By the 1990s the neoconservative Manhattan Institute orchestrated a well-funded campaign to fight the intrusion of "junk science" into courtrooms.[10]

The movement of activists into certain pockets of the university is another part of the story of the 1970s. The revival of Frankfurt school Marxism, including a wave of new translations around 1970 and, later, the import of British cultural studies and the rise of Foucaultian cultural analysis, are examples of analyses showing that truth was not necessarily trapped in the claws of the ruling class. Truth games were now played on a wider field. These theories paralleled the *success* of the outsider challenges to formal knowledge. While the slipperiness of elites' command of what counts as truth was not always recognized in more traditional versions of Marxist theory, cases such as the campaign to remove homosexuality from the DSM taught activists that specific interventions into knowledge communities could alter social practice and conceptions. Even if there was a dominant establishment, there was space for successful strategic incursions. Post-Marxist theorists such as Stuart Hall and Chantal Mouffe started to celebrate popular knowledge in the 1970s and 1980s, in tune with the new confidence in bottom-up agitation.

The arrival of feminist scholars was probably the most prominent and successful change on the academic landscape of the 1970s. Feminist radicalism might have fallen apart between 1971 and 1974, as Alice Echols has nicely shown,[11] but on the heels of this collapse came the emergence of women's history, women's studies programs, Title IX sports reform, and sexual harassment law—all products of the 1970s, all depending on research and the production of knowledge.

Foucault also saw knowledge as deeply tied to the war of positions in society, but at least up to the mid-1970s, he insisted on the ultimate contingency of any cognitive order. In the opening to *The Order of Things* (1970; French original *Les mots et les choses*, 1966), he famously discussed a supposed Chinese encyclopedia that divided the animal kingdom into such absurd categories as animals "that have just broken the flower vase." Few readers noticed that he was referring to an essay by Jorge Luis Borges on the wild empiricism of the seventeenth century.[12] Foucault was tweaking those who thought rational planning could order the world; John Wilkins, the hero of Borges's story, was trying to find a system of nomenclature that would bring order to knowledge. Thinkers of the 1960s and the 1660s were worried and fascinated by the leakiness of conceptual schemes. Foucault's tales of scientific disciplines as instruments of power fed the antiexpert mood. But the attacks of the early 1970s were not about destroying the professional class. Rather, they instituted the coupling of perpetual research and chronic distrust.

All this activism fed on the antiestablishment outrage of the 1960s. Yet it was also a sign of something new. Knowledge professionals could be challenged from the outside; their authority was not sacrosanct. Truth did not emerge from the internal development of professional discourse, as modernization theorists suggested. Peer review was not the only arbiter of validity. Truth was political and could be challenged politically. Just a decade earlier, Thomas Kuhn's famous *Structure of Scientific Revo-*

Sidebar 6.1 Bell and Lyotard on the Knowledge Society in the 1970s

A new wave of discussion about the knowledge revolution began in the 1960s. Authors like Fritz Machlup, Karl Popper, and Derek de Solla Price explored the ways that the crush of information was restructuring society and the production of knowledge was defining economic performance.[1] Here the information revolution was not simply envisioned as a necessary part of industrial civilization; it was pictured as a driving force.

At first this literature was very optimistic, replete with praise for the beauties of the social planning of research. In the 1970s more skeptical voices emerged. Two names in particular stand out. Harvard sociologist Daniel Bell began thinking about what he called the "knowledge society" in the late 1950s. In 1973 he published his massive summation, *The Coming of Post-industrial Society.* Six years later French philosopher Jean-François Lyotard published one of the most famous essays of the late twentieth century, *The Postmodern Condition.* Both highlighted the role of the computer in altering the knowledge landscape. Yet both also began to understand knowledge and information as out of control, unable to bring enlightenment or social peace. Both moved toward a postmanagerial sense of knowledge. Lyotard the anarchist celebrated it; Bell the cultural conservative hated it.

Despite obvious and sharp differences, their similarities were striking, especially compared with the perspectives of the 1940s. Both embraced new and more complicated attitudes toward the place of knowledge and information in the social order and took distance from the Enlightenment dream of a world guided by knowledge for the betterment of humanity. Both rejected the dream of a healthy planned society. For Bell it was a failure to be bemoaned; for Lyotard it was a prospect to be avoided. Nevertheless, both came to believe in a fundamental antagonism between knowledge and the social order, quite unlike earlier knowledge visionaries such as Vannevar Bush or J. D. Bernal.

1. Fritz Machlup, *The Production and Distribution of Knowledge in the United States* (Princeton, NJ: Princeton University Press, 1962); Karl Popper, *Objective Knowledge: An Evolutionary Approach* (New York: Oxford University Press, 1972); Derek de Solla Price, *Big Science, Little Science* (New York: Columbia University Press, 1963).

Take Bell. In the 1970s he found himself very far from 1940s ideas about the rational planning of information. For him knowledge was not the dutiful servant of industrial civilization. It had become the engine of the economy. "The major source of structural change in society," he wrote, "is the change in the character of knowledge."[2] But he had a specific understanding of knowledge. *The Coming of Post-industrial Society* had very little to say about data. It was theoretical knowledge that was crucial; information was relatively inconsequential. By theoretical knowledge, Bell meant the generalizations produced by formal research. Powerful formal models and mathematical equations were the heart of almost all fields, from genetics to microeconomics, from accounting to information theory. Such knowledge extended managerial capacity, scientific reach, technological prowess, and economic productivity. Its importance could not be underestimated: "In effect, theoretical knowledge increasingly becomes the strategic resource, the axial principle, of a society."[3]

If Bell believed in managerialism, he was certainly no technocrat. Indeed, he spent nearly a hundred pages arguing against technocracy. There was, he claimed, a fundamental divide between scientists and politicians. The former were driven by evidence and technical rationality, the latter by values and interests. Never would knowledge and politics go hand in glove.

If science for Bell was in constant conflict with politics, it also collided with basic cultural values. Bell believed, in the aftermath of the 1960s, that egalitarianism and the lust for self-fulfillment were epidemic in American life. These strains pushed Bell to neoconservatism in the mid- and late seventies (he withdrew from those circles in the early 1980s). Everyone, Bell sniffed, now claimed all sorts of rights. There was a new sense of entitlement in the air. People felt free to "do their own thing." Philosophers like John Rawls fed such sentiments. Gurus like Herbert Marcuse and Norman O. Brown preached them directly. These antinomian and anti-institutional values conflicted sharply with the patient, sober rationality needed to produce the knowledge for a post-industrial society. Bell's knowledge society was in constant conflict with politics and broad-based self-centeredness.

2. Daniel Bell, *The Coming of Post-industrial Society: A Venture in Social Forecasting* (New York: Basic Books, 1973), 389, 44.

3. Bell, *Post-industrial Society*, 26.

In the few years after the publication of *The Coming of Post-industrial Society*, Bell grew more disenchanted with the drift of American life. The tensions between the culture of self-fulfillment and the knowledge-based economy became the binding theme of his next book, *The Cultural Contradictions of Capitalism* (1976). The second half of the 1970s saw Bell at his most explicitly neoconservative. It was at this point that he wrote another take on the knowledge society. "Teletext and Technology: New Networks of Knowledge and Information in Postindustrial Society" (1977) contained far more pointed comments on computers than the 1973 book.[4] In *The Coming of Post-industrial Society*, he criticized other writers for overemphasizing their importance. He felt computerization was an enabler, contributing to the capacity for better modeling; it was at best a "bridge" between "the body of formal theory and the large data bases of recent years." For Bell, the models themselves—the theoretical knowledge—were what mattered. They were the backbone of postindustrial life.[5]

But in 1977 Bell argued that the miniaturization of electronics, and the computer in particular, was central to an ongoing media revolution. Among other things this was creating a tidal wave of information, information that could be sent immediately around the world. Bell's examples, which sound rather quaint now, included United Press International's new online system, where stories could be filed from anyplace on the globe, edited in New York, then downloaded anywhere; or the 800 banks and 250 corporations, "from Hong Kong to Europe and across the United States," that were now "plugged into a computerized monitoring service on the floating exchange rate." Bell was impressed by the phenomenal amounts of data computers could generate. During "any manned space flight," Bell noted, "there is data transmission of the rate of 52 kilobits per second, the equivalent of an *Encyclopaedia Britannica* every minute." (This rate, though enormous, is dwarfed by current speeds.) Since this explosion of information was going to continue, he thought, we had to find ways "to organize this torrential flood of Babel."[6]

4. Daniel Bell, "Teletext and Technocracy: New Networks of Knowledge and Information in Postindustrial Society" (1977), in *The Winding Passage: Essays and Sociological Journeys, 1960–1980* (New York: Basic Books, 1980), 34–65.

5. Ibid., 38, 28.

6. Ibid., 39–40, 61, 57.

Yet Bell was not so sure it could all be organized. He was convinced that older notions of the unity of science, of the coherent encyclopedia, or of the library that contained "all the world's recorded knowledge" were now obsolete. It was time to give up the ghost: "The attempts to discipline human knowledge and create a vast and unified edifice . . . were bound to fail. The efforts to formalize knowledge or construct 'artificial' languages have proved inadequate."[7] His vaunted "theoretic knowledge" was being choked by the waves of information now pouring between our computers.

Science could not regulate the flow; the only hope was human management. But this was exactly where Bell was becoming more sour in the 1970s. Cultural values were running up against successful management. The communication and information revolution opened the nation to the "volatility of emotions, accentuation of demagoguery, and the possibility of plebiscitary democracy." He summed up: "The reduction of distance, clearly, has introduced a great potential for instability into political systems."[8]

Six years after Bell's mammoth *Coming of Post-industrial Society*, and two years after "Teletext and Technology," Lyotard published his pathbreaking book *The Postmodern Condition*. Lyotard, like Bell in 1977, saw computerization as the jumping-off point for recent social change. Though postmodernism is often associated with image politics, it is useful to note that the book was subtitled *A Report on Knowledge*. The very character of knowledge was changing—and not for the better. The biggest change was what Lyotard called "the mercantilization of knowledge." Knowledge had a monetary value. Corporations could hoard huge banks of data, something already weakening governments' capacity to rule. "Increasingly, "Lyotard wrote, "the central question is who will have access to the information."[9]

Yet Lyotard thought something else was going on at the same time. Faith in metanarratives was breaking down. Postmodernity implied a loss of faith both in historical progress and in the sense that knowledge

7. Ibid., 58, 59.

8. Ibid., 61.

9. Jean-François Lyotard, *The Postmodern Condition: A Report on Knowledge*, trans. Geoff Bennington and Brian Massumi (Minneapolis: University of Minnesota Press, 1983) (originally published 1979), 14.

would set us free. The postmodern condition was paradoxical: distrustful of science but utterly dependent on it.[10]

Lyotard did suggest ways to navigate. Since the faith in a scientific metanarrative had collapsed, he thought, there was now "a multiplication in methods of argumentation and a rising complexity in the process of establishing truth."[11] The pragmatics of knowledge were infinitely more complicated than when we simply trusted science. Now we had multiple language games: we could tell stories, recite statistics, or polemicize. There was no single ground for establishing truth.

To oppose the increasing mercantilization of knowledge, Lyotard suggested "postmodern science," which tried to create disorder, raise problems, challenge truths. The best language games were agonistic, and the best science was "the antimodel of a stable system." "Consensus," he argued, "has become an outmoded and suspect value."[12] Truth was now to be defined as pragmatics, useful according to context; science should be devoted to puncturing settled truths rather than finding them, creating dissensus rather than consensus.

In the end, Lyotard thought, computerization could become the "dream instrument for controlling and regulating the market system." In that case "it would inevitably involve terror." But it could also aid activists by "supplying them with information they usually lack for making knowledgeable decisions." In the final paragraph of the book he laid down his last prescription, one that was, in his own words, "quite simple: give the public free access to the memory and data banks."[13]

Like Bell, Lyotard saw the world in conflict. Neither thinker was a systems theorist, technocrat, or functionalist. For Bell the conflict was tragic, reflecting the sorry but inevitable tensions between culture and technology. Lyotard, on the other hand, loved conflict. It was a sign of a free society. The *absence* of conflict was the real danger. Lyotard saw consensus as nothing less than totalitarian.

Bell, even in the mid-1970s, was trapped by the politics of the 1960s. For him scientific rationality was arrayed against hippie antinomianism.

---

10. Lyotard, like a number of postmodern writers, wavered between seeing the postmodern as resulting from a new historical situation or from an epistemological breakthrough. In *The Postmodern Condition*, Lyotard emphasized the former.

11. Ibid., 41.

12. Ibid., 64, 66.

13. Ibid., 67.

Lyotard intuited the new sort of activism emerging in the 1970s, when environmentalists, feminists, and human rights activists, to name just three, began producing alternative bodies of knowledge. Research was marshaled by all sides, not just by scientists trying to rationalize society. Information could puncture consensus as much as solve problems. Political actors used all sorts of language games as it pragmatically suited them. Postmodernism did not mean hostility to science, Lyotard argued, and the nostalgia for the premodern was pretty much over. Postmodernism meant multiple language games in agonistic contests.

Both thinkers believed that not only did the explosion of information subvert the claim that knowledge would order society, it also undermined the sense that knowledge could be rationally ordered. For Bell the dream of knowledge setting us free was drowned in the flood of information. Bell's lost faith in an encyclopedia was Lyotard's hope for a fresh outbreak of combative sciences of all kinds.

lutions (1962) had presented an utterly serene and self-contained picture of how science worked. In Kuhn's account, scientists directed their own disciplines; the only politics were internal. Knowledge followed the technical discussions of experts. Research "paradigms" (this word owes its popularity to Kuhn) were challenged by mounting anomalies of evidence, not by pressure from the outside. The events of the early 1970s suggested something else, a pattern of science where the popular, or the outsider, or the political—pick your term—intruded at key moments on professional autonomy.

Moreover, these challenges were more than opposition to formal knowledge or the authority of experts. Such opposition is widely found among the disenfranchised throughout history. But these protests were *successful* challenges to professional knowledge. What is crucial is not that gay activists protested the diagnostics of the APA. What matters is that they entered the professional ranks and pressured change in what knowledge was actually considered to be.

While such attacks on elite knowledge had their origins in 1960s sensibilities, they lacked—in practice if not always in ideology—the more utopian, romantic dimension of the 1960s. These were not projects devoted to toppling the psychiatric profession or ending scientific research. They were practical reforms that activists wanted to see happen. While someone like Ivan Illich dreamed of "de-schooling society" or undermining the "medical nemesis," the goals of gay, deinstitutional-izing, African American, and feminist activists were more pointed. They wanted categories changed, experiments stopped, patients heard. This scaling down of romantic postures gave promiscuous knowledge a link with the more sober positivist past. But it was a link with a difference, since it reflected the tarnished reputation of the knowledge class.

One last context for understanding the changing authority of experts in the 1970s was the rising tide of information. Earlier in the century thinkers like Walter Lippmann had called for more data for the use of political observers in think tanks. Now policy makers faced a new mana-gerial task: learning how to digest massive amounts of data rather than choke on them. The growth of big government had made Washington, DC, for instance, into a town awash in reports, newsletters, indexes, hearings, and other printed words and numbers. Legislators and policy makers needed help navigating it all. Institutions had to find ways to respond. David Ricci has argued that Washington think tanks exploded in number and prominence in the early 1970s to help various ideological factions in Congress sort out the avalanche of information now coming at them. And Ricci shows how certain of the think tanks, notably the conservative Heritage Foundation, quickly developed sophisticated pub-lic relations arms. They learned to play the information game and the image game at the same time.[13]

The same is true of human rights activism. Amnesty International was founded in London in 1961 and started off precariously. Inter-nal bickering almost brought the initiative to an end in 1967, and its US office nearly folded in 1970 because of financial problems. But in the years 1970 to 1976, its dues-paying members grew from six thou-sand to thirty-five thousand, it consolidated full-time staffers, and in 1977 the organization won the Nobel Peace Prize. Central to Amnesty's success was massive and reliable fact-finding. Its bylaws summarized the strategy: "Information is the core of the work of the movement." But another side to Amnesty's success was its mastery of the new lin-gua franca of images. Amnesty mobilized celebrities, invented a catchy slogan ("torture is a curable disease"), designed a memorable logo, dis-tributed T-shirts, and aggressively sought visibility for its cause. Am-nesty no less than the right-wing Heritage Foundation learned to deal in masses of information and images that mobilized attention. In the era of power-knowledge, all sides were playing the game.[14]

Libraries in the 1970s were on the front lines of dealing with mounds of information. Among librarians there was the sense that information stores had become so outrageously huge that a macro-order was simply

irrelevant. Instead of discovering some late twentieth-century equivalent of the Dewey decimal system, energy was invested in finding ways
to allow individuals and organizations to access information as they
needed it. The World Wide Web, which completely dispenses with any
overall intellectual order, is the most recent example of this program.
The development of LexisNexis in the 1970s and 1980s was an earlier
version. The shift in how most American librarians viewed their job was
one more.

The massive computerization of the library since the mid-1970s centered on "information retrieval." The Defense Department in the 1950s,
for example, funded research for online bibliographical retrieval systems. They were installed experimentally in a few major libraries during
the 1960s, although as late as 1968 most librarians remained skeptical of
major changes in library management. Over the next decade, however,
libraries began automating in significant numbers. A commercial market emerged in that decade to install online systems in libraries.[15]

By the end of the 1970s, librarians were routinely discussing these
changes in terms of a shift to an "information society." Schools of library
science started to use the term *information* in their titles in the 1980s. In
their descriptions of the new library, the distance from earlier ideas was
evident. "Information replaces culture in our civilisation" was how two
librarians put it in 1977. We were seeing the birth of what another library
scholar termed LOTFs, libraries of the future that would serve as networks for scholarly "information" instead of as storehouses for books.
Such LOTFs might not even have a single location or affiliation with a
single library. The trend toward the library as an information center for
a diversity of personal uses instead of a book collection for concentrated
study has continued since. The Google books project, based not on books
in a physical building but rather on the supposed "cloud" of online storage, continues the trend.[16]

Late-Century Knowledge Fights

If the 1970s saw the rise of promiscuous knowledge, the 1980s and 1990s
saw it shift into high gear. One of the most striking knowledge fights in
the last two decades of the twentieth century was about AIDS research.
Very shortly after the disease first surfaced in the early 1980s, bitter disputes broke out over how research should take place and what treatments should be authorized. Perhaps the best-known activist group was
ACT-UP (AIDS Coalition to Unleash Power), loosely organized sets of
radical gay and lesbian activists devoted to pushing the research estab-

lishment and the federal government. The first ACT-UP chapters formed in 1987. Two issues in particular were important: getting the Food and Drug Administration (FDA) to approve the AZT "cocktail" for HIV-positive women and men, and loosening the norm of strict adherence to blind clinical trials. The research norms were firmly in place before the late eighties and were important pillars of standard medical practice. AIDS activists wanted them overthrown.

What made ACT-UP so striking was its combination of effective street theater and solid insider knowledge of the issues involved. The group could embarrass the FDA one day and sit down to negotiate the next. By 1988 that ACT-UP activists *were* sitting down with government officials was itself part of the story. They effectively joined the players deciding how AIDS research would be conducted. What had been a process ruled by the internal autonomy of scientists became a version of what one scholar has called "impure science."[17]

To be sure, medical research always had a certain level of "impurity," just as juries always mingled popular and elite knowledge. Medicine and the law are sciences of practice and judgment, not of lawlike generalization. You get a legal or medical "opinion," not a proven fact. Medical knowledge has always been promiscuous in the sense that diagnosis must rely partly on self-reports by patients given in nontechnical language. And medical research is inherently practical because of its reliance on clinical trials whose risks are so great that their small sample sizes almost invariably compromise strict experimental design. (The Tuskegee debacle was a glaring example of the abuse of clinical trials.) On the other hand, desperate patients can agitate to take part in medical experiments even at great risk.

The authority of both law and medicine saw a new level of attack in the last decades of the century. Another regulatory battle emerged in the 1990s. In 1992 David Kessler, head of the FDA, decided to ban silicone breast implants. Marcia Angell, the physician-editor of the *New England Journal of Medicine* at the time, was appalled. There was, she argued, not one solid piece of epidemiological evidence that implants caused tissue disease. Angell might have been appalled that the FDA had banned silicone breast implants, but she was just as concerned that, because of the new standards of evidence—quite lax by her reckoning—the courts were handing out gigantic awards to women with implants. The problem, in Angell's mind, was that there was no valid scientific evidence. The whole chain of events was a sign of the rejection of scientific authority.[18]

By the early 1990s Congress joined the trend of distrusting professional knowledge communities. In 1992, thanks to the efforts of Senator

Tom Harkin of Iowa, the National Institutes of Health created the Office of Alternative Medicine. Right from the start there was controversy about how antiestablishment the office would actually become—stories of support for the use of shark cartilage to treat cancer, mental healing at a distance, and "biofield therapeutics" made most scientists cringe.

Distrust of established knowledge communities was no monopoly of the Left. When the pushing and shoving started, conservatives could be just as insistent that professional communities were not effective arbiters of truth. AIDS activists, for example, were not alone in rejecting the scientific mainstream in the late 1980s. They were joined by renegade scientists like Berkeley virologist Peter Duesberg, who was by no stretch a man of the Left. He both provided some of the key research and arguments for the activists *and* denied that HIV caused AIDS, arguing instead that it was a result of behavioral choices, especially illicit drug use. Though he was at first hailed as a hero by activists for his willingness to take on the scientific consensus about AIDS, the welcome soon cooled as he let slip comments about how gay lifestyles, "criminal just a few decades earlier," had caused the disease. He also blamed AZT for causing the disease. In a 1996 book he argued that the AIDS virus was a rhetorical creation, a new name for a host of old maladies, providing ammunition for AIDS deniers around the world. As with the Rodney King video, progressives recoiled from the implications of a thoroughgoing social constructionism. The idea that a virus was "invented" lost its appeal when people were dying. AIDS, "this monstrous tidal wave of death," as activist Larry Kramer called it, was clearly some kind of brutally real fact.[19]

Equally intriguing is that conservative policy activists interested in deregulation joined in to condemn mainstream science. Intellectuals at the Heritage Foundation and the *Wall Street Journal*'s editorial page regularly expressed opinions on specific policy issues very close to those of ACT-UP activists. (In chapter 5 we saw a similar alignment in the 1970s as evangelicals and critical film theorists alike attacked the power of images.) A 1990 article in the Heritage Foundation's journal, *Policy Review*, proved to be one of the best-known attacks on the FDA and establishment research, expressing opinions that, until that moment, had been kept from gatekeeper medical journals like the *Journal of the American Medical Association* or *Science*. The *Village Voice*, a New York City left weekly very sympathetic to ACT-UP, summed it up this way in 1988: "Bad science makes for strange bedfellows."[20]

Another site for knowledge fights was the museum. In the 1990s a string of controversies erupted around museum exhibitions. There had been plenty of debates about museums over the twentieth century, but these were new in their intensity, focus, and public resonance. Earlier debates, in broad strokes, were about which objects were included; 1990s debates were about which subjects were excluded. Once indecency (nudes) or incomprehensibility (abstract expressionism) riled the public; now the key issue was representation of marginalized groups. One backdrop was the massive redefinition of museums since the 1960s. Museum administrators were turning from endowments to merchandising as the main source of financial support, thus opening themselves up to the populist forces of the market. Museums had become a leisure activity, and their status as bastions of impartial research had eroded.[21] Margaret Mead's claim that museum leaders first asked "Is this true?" rather than "Will this make a hit?" no longer held.

In the museum battles of the 1990s a string of exhibitions were attacked by outsiders, almost all with a populist rhetoric, all arrayed against the professionals trying to mount the exhibition. The first major museum battle of the late twentieth century happened in 1989–90 in Toronto, a cosmopolitan city filled with immigrants from around the globe. In an exhibition called *Into the Heart of Africa* in the Royal Ontario Museum, curators exhibited items collected in Africa by Protestant missionaries and the Canadian military from 1875 to 1925, including letters and other documents these people had written about African peoples and artifacts. These texts came from a different time and sensibility and were frankly racist to contemporary ears. For curators and academics versed in debates about imperialism, representation, and historicity, the exhibition was simultaneously a critique of imperialism, a celebration of African art, and a metadiscussion within museum studies. Their insider knowledge provided them with the distancing and contextualizing frames to navigate the blatant racism of the display. For a public less familiar with historiographical norms of letting the documents speak for themselves, the exhibition portrayed Africans as passive, voiceless objects whose lives were depicted through the prejudiced writings of colonizing white people. The curators, despite their protests to the contrary, had failed to design the exhibition to be intelligible to outsiders. For a broader audience, its edifying mission was unfocused. Like the single Roosevelt statue, it left too much implicit. A caption was most definitely needed.

Representation of African peoples was controversial in US museums as well. After well-orchestrated criticism during the 1980s from members of the local community about its exhibitions on Africa, in 1993 the Smithsonian Institution began a collaborative effort consisting of a team of scholars inside and outside the Smithsonian and African immigrants in the Washington, DC, area. The scholars wanted more detail and internal variety, while the public seemed to prefer exhibitions providing a single narrative thread. African Americans wanted to emphasize coverage of urban Africa, lest an image of a backward or primitive Africa be perpetuated. In the face of so many demands, the Museum decided to provide an ever-changing series of exhibits.[22] Conflicts of interest across professional and popular lines defied a stable summary. By the 1990s, the earlier strategy of dividing museums into detailed research collections for the specialist and appealing exhibits for the public had collapsed. Everybody felt qualified to dictate what was displayed.

Populist attacks on the museum again came not only from the Left. Conservatives led some museum fights of the early nineties. One notorious campaign attacked a 1990 exhibition at the Cincinnati Contemporary Arts Center of Robert Mapplethorpe photographs that included homoerotic and sadomasochistic themes. "Just look at the pictures!" (as if they spoke for themselves) announced Senator Jesse Helms, a chief critic of Mapplethorpe and his funding by the National Endowment for the Arts. As the pictures traveled beyond the museum, they lost their framing context.

Another was the attack on the proposed *Enola Gay* exhibition at the Smithsonian, a wake-up call to the historical profession.[23] In 1994, part of the fuselage of the bomber that dropped the bomb on Hiroshima was to be exhibited in the Air and Space Museum, commemorating the fiftieth anniversary of the bombing. Veterans groups and their allies lobbied to shut down the exhibition, which they found offensive and unpatriotic in its sustained treatment of the suffering of Japanese victims. And yet the exhibition was based on the best work of professional historians. It became clear that solid research—information—did not necessarily establish a realm of truth but instead gave rise to complaints about the arrogance of experts. Ironically, since the 1970s historians themselves have, in other contexts, been prominent among those who have helped teach the public to distrust expertise, to see information as biased by interpretation and shaped by its source.

The *Enola Gay* affair provides a prominent example of how conservative forces can attack liberal knowledge producers and how outsiders can pressure knowledge communities. Professional historians found themselves attacked by the American Legion. The new Speaker of the House at the time, Newt Gingrich, said the protest against the exhibition amounted to "most Americans" saying "that they are sick and tired of being told by some cultural elite that they ought to be ashamed of their country."[24] In vain did historians argue that the facts were on their side. At exactly the same time that Marcia Angell was arguing about evidence and breast implants, historians were defending their own reading of the evidence about the dropping of the atomic bomb. Like Angell, the historians believed they should be deferred to. Both thought the outsiders were uninformed. Both lost. In the end, despite the concerted efforts of the community of professional historians, the Smithsonian regents canceled the exhibition. Just as in AIDS research a couple of years before, the consensus of the relevant professional community was set aside. Outsider activists intruded on the autonomy of the professions. It was another example of promiscuous knowledge. Knowledge had become a site of extreme contention even while it claimed less and less.

The *Enola Gay* controversy also points to something more subtle: there were battles within professions as well. It was no longer the hoary humanist complaining about soulless scientism, it was now Paul Feyerabend, the extravagantly anarchistic philosopher of science. It was not some Protestant minister fighting the truth claims of Charles Darwin, it was Bruno Latour questioning the truth claims of Louis Pasteur. Within my own field of history, there was a sustained debate in the 1980s and 1990s about its mission. The gap between the generalist mission of historians as teachers and the specialist mission of historians as scholars was widening, the *Journal of American History* lamented in 1986.

Perhaps even more significant but less conspicuous was the new policy announced in the same issue: the journal would no longer check the accuracy of all footnotes. Instead they would be spot-checked, shifting the burden of scholarly evidence to the individual historian. The loosening grip of centrally managed quality control devolved responsibility to the individual scholar. No longer was historical truth monitored centrally by the profession's flagship publication; it was outsourced to scholars working on their own.[25] Such is one tiny episode in a massive cultural shift in which individuals have to fend for themselves, unmoored from overseeing institutions.

Another worry internal to the professions was increasing doubt about the effectiveness of peer review in scientific publications. The essence of professionalism was always self-regulation, with standards set by peers rather than the public. Peer review was long the gold standard for certifying professional knowledge in scholarly and scientific journals. But in medicine and other professions, the guarantees were off. One problem was fairly allocating credit for authorship; another was biased citations toward research done in one's own field and one's own language and by prestigious authors and universities, rather than hewing to strictly scientific criteria of relevance; a third was the tendency to underreport nonconfirming findings; a fourth was the potential bias following lavish funding of research by large pharmaceutical companies. In consequence, some critics worried, the edifice of medical knowledge was dangerously flimsy.[26] Other fields shared similar worries. But the publishing machine never stopped. It just moved along without the old assurance that professional self-regulation would produce more and more truth.[27]

By focusing on the blurring line between professional and popular knowledge, we have linked a string of phenomena often treated separately. From ACT-UP to changing laws about expert witnesses to the *Enola Gay* controversy, we see the intrusion of outsider sensibilities into the province of formal learning. Promiscuous knowledge is not solely "owned" or practiced by either end of the political spectrum. It is available to all sides. When political forces are threatened by some knowledge claim, they now have the option of mobilizing in opposition, of injecting themselves into the process. That both Left and Right will use this tactic is itself a good sign that this knowledge regime now reigns. What we are facing is the lack of credibility of knowledge producers, the ridicule of their ethos.

Yet these fights do not happen everywhere. All kinds of science and research continue without public controversy. For these battles to erupt, two other conditions are necessary. First, controversies erupt only when either activists, policy makers, or the larger public can be convinced that an issue truly matters. Whatever I say on nineteenth-century cultural history in an academic journal will be ignored, since it doesn't seem to matter that much. Second, controversies most often emerge at the point where knowledge leaves the expert community in contexts such as medical research, courts of law, or museums. These are the sites where controversy erupts with the public, but where that professionally created knowledge leaves the tribe and heads out into a larger world. At that point, skepticism breaks out about knowledge creators, be they conservative medical researchers or liberal or radical humanities professors. (And of course the classroom is another arena of promiscuous knowledge.)

We have not treated these fights as "culture wars." Such a label assumes that they are a battle of the Left and the Right. This mistakes the particular fights—which often *are* some form of Left versus Right—for the larger cultural pattern. They are about a much more pervasive distrust of formal knowledge. Such distrust has a distinguished history in the United States. Since the 1970s, however, it has taken a new form. Experts remain in place. Their research continues to be supported at taxpayer expense. But at key places, outsiders assault and enter into

the public representation of truth. These are not the same old political squabbles; they fit a larger context of postmodern paranoia. They
are symptoms of the collapse of faith in the division of elite and lay
knowledge.

Digital Promiscuity and the Erosion of Ethos

A new cult of information arose in the late twentieth century. There
were a range of signs: popular culture phenomena like the game Trivial
Pursuit, first marketed in 1983, or *USA Today*'s coining *factoid*; the turn
of libraries to the "information sciences"; the burst of sociological commentary on "the information age"; and the emergence of new forms of
data research, culminating in "big data" of all kinds. It was a return to a
moment that emphasized the thick flow of fact.

Whereas the culture of happy summary had shored up the authority
of professionals, the return to a thicker culture of fact in the 1990s unsettled it.[28] Without experts to soften the blow, people butted up against
masses of information more abruptly. Cultural summary became suspect
in part because experts made the summaries. New bundles and channels
of information allowed do-it-yourself knowledge production. Internet
chat rooms let patients discuss their treatments outside the presence of
doctors; day trading allowed people to invest in the stock market without the advice of a broker; blogs bypassed editorial control in allowing
anyone to publish. These are all examples of disintermediation—cutting
out the middleman.[29]

Since the 1950s "information" has had two very different meanings.
The first refers to the technical breakthroughs of information theory.
Information is understood here in the rather arcane terms of entropy
or uncertainty reduction, as the nonsubstance that nonhuman technologies such as telephones and computers traffic in. It is quite distinct
from the second, more ordinary usage: facts useful for navigating the
world. The "information age" in this reckoning refers to the growing
availability of all sorts of facts and clusters of fact in exponentially increasing data storehouses around the world.

If the culture we described in chapters 3 and 4 banked on summaries,
there was a vital late twentieth-century sense that images and information swirled madly around us, independent of each other, each successfully manipulated by those in touch with their particular powers.
In the age of Reagan, many worried, images could overshadow information.[30] Infomercials, docudramas, and the slippage of the mainstream
press into tabloid techniques suggested a new relation between fact and

Sidebar 6.2 Desk Set

Walter Lang's 1957 film *Desk Set* is a bridge to the information age.[1] It pits Spencer Tracy as an MIT-trained "methods engineer" against Katharine Hepburn as the director of the reference and research section of the "Federal Broadcasting Network" (clearly modeled on NBC) and adds a feminist spin to the history of computing by showing the rivalry between female labor and machine labor. Tracy has been called in to install a new computer in the reference department. This is a female space where Hepburn and three other women use pencil and paper, desks, filing cabinets, maps, a large reference library, and their own formidable knowledge of the system to answer queries by telephone. These queries for information range widely and presumably arise in the network's news and production departments. The women are essentially reference librarians, a 1950s version of Google, and are examples of the long history when women served as "computers."[2] The building has an underground communication exchange among the women via word of mouth and telephone, and when the four fear they are about to be fired, they vow, "We'll open our own network." In one sense that is what they already have—a network of knowledge and practice pitted against the new information machines introduced by Tracy.

A would-be PhD who couldn't afford graduate school, Hepburn's character has a formidable intellect (despite a few jarring moments of compensatory ditziness). She possesses remarkable numerical skills, does the accounting for her commitment-phobic boyfriend, which gets him promoted to vice president, and does sums in her head. "You calculate rapidly," Tracy says to her early in their relationship, in a way he manages to make sound almost romantic. She customarily converts words into numbers, and she completely outmatches Tracy on his personality inventory, a series of brainteasers that she solves instantly.

But she is a computer with a difference. One of his questions is, "What is the first thing you notice about a person?" We are set up to think the answer should be eyes, nose, or shoes, but she replies, "Whether they

1. See the nice treatment in Nathan L. Ensmenger, *The Computer Boys Take Over: Computers, Programmers, and the Politics of Technical Expertise* (Cambridge, MA: MIT Press, 2010), 137–40.

2. See Jennifer S. Light, "When Computers Were Women," *Technology and Culture* 40 (July 1999): 455–83.

are male or female." When he offers her a palindrome (Napoleon's supposed "able was I ere I saw Elba"), she gives one right back (Adam's supposed "Madam, I'm Adam"). His palindrome concerns a great man defeated; hers concerns the opening to a fruitful male-female partnership. And when he asks if she always converts words into numbers and vice versa, she replies, as if offering a form of counterintelligence to the computer, "I associate many things with many things." Gender difference is flagged repeatedly in their conversations, as it is in the movie as a whole. *Desk Set* both celebrates an associative feminine style of intelligence and perpetuates a stereotypical gendered division of labor.

When Tracy's character—played with slovenly charm rather than nerdishness—first comes into the reference department and starts measuring distances, the women get the idea that they are going to be replaced with a computer or an "electronic brain." Tracy has been sworn to secrecy by the network's president, so the women—in the typical paranoia of office politics—spin all kinds of worrisome scenarios about what will happen next. The story comes together in a happy ending after some plot twists and confusions, with Tracy explaining that the computer was never intended to replace anyone but only to "free up more time for research." The movie is essentially a love letter to computerization. IBM actively cooperated in the production, as the opening credits loudly attest, and the film serves as a kind of sales pitch for the advent of the business computer. *Desk Set* has none of the technological jitters of contemporary films such as *Forbidden Planet* (1956) or *Invasion of the Body Snatchers* (1958) or the television series *The Twilight Zone*. It provided balm for late 1950s technophobe worries.

The computer itself is a mammoth device that fills an entire room and emits space-age noises (rather like Robbie the Robot in *Forbidden Planet*) when she is upset. Named EMERAC, sometimes "Emily EMERAC," the computer is indisputably female. As in Alan Turing's monumental essay "Computing Machinery and Intelligence" (1950), the question of gender is never far away from AI. Hepburn is concerned that Tracy loves only the computer and can never love her. Hepburn and EMERAC are always compared: Tracy tells Hepburn that she and EMERAC are both "very sensitive" and "single-minded." The film sets them up as rivals in both knowledge and love. In their first conversation, Tracy ventures the classic nerdish dream of the end of sexual reproduction, saying it wouldn't surprise him if "they stopped making people" altogether. Hepburn looks at him as if she can't tell if this is a bit of boy-ish nihilism or a complete lack of sexual interest.

Hepburn has knowledge, if not quite carnal, certainly embodied, while the computer needs to be "fed" with "information" and is busy "digesting everything." (The new computer cannot tolerate the dust of the old reference volumes.) Through a series of comic errors, the computer proves able to spout "available statistics" at great speed, though "the human element" and "wrong classification" keep it prone to error. There is no threat of people being replaced here (the worry of *Invasion of the Body Snatchers*). The coup de grâce of reassurance comes when the computer mediates Tracy's marriage proposal to Hepburn. When EMERAC says they should not get married, Tracy suavely says that computers make mistakes and sweeps Hepburn off her feet. At some point Hepburn vigorously pats the machine, saying "good girl." The big scary beast of automation has been domesticated.

Desk Set played on the anxieties raised by a rising generation of computer scientists. The machines only spit out information. The men bear technical knowledge, both about the corporate planning and about the design of computers. The women are in between, the great human providers of information but also the grounded knowers, in whatever sense, that computers cannot replace. Information is on its way, but it's only a supplement and will free us from drudgery. In this the film is close to the 1950s dream of the end of work through abundance.

image, one where image is primary, not summarizing information but making it irrelevant. But insiders in the academic, social service, corporate, and political worlds continued to face an avalanche of information that none would ever control or conquer. Information remains a teeming, wild resource with no firm boundaries, a roiling and ever-expanding mass that those with the right skills can tap for instrumental purposes. In both public life and the work of institutions, no one in the late twentieth century believed in the idea of the image or anything else as a crystallized essence.

Broadly speaking, the new information flows had two very different uses. One use was for countless individual projects of personal empowerment. I can get any music I want through amazon.com even though there is no local store with a good selection in Iowa City. I can plan my vacation or follow my retirement portfolio online. Data collection, however, also served a new managerialism. University deans now have at their fingertips databases showing how many students have enrolled in my classes over the past five years, and educational decisions are based on this information. Online academic searches give deans power to second-guess decisions made by departmental committees. Doctors find their suggestions overturned by HMO reps using risk-analysis data. Instead of bolstering professional autonomy, the mid-twentieth-century goal, the new accounting procedures lead to management of professionals, and not simply by professionals.

Digital culture embodies these unholy concoctions, the disinclination to sort the "pure" from the impure, popular from professional, activist from objective. There is no better example than the emergence of the powerful search engines in the mid-1990s. In sharp contrast to the Dewey Decimal System of the 1870s, which was explicitly designed to neatly categorize different ranks of "knowledge," a Google or Yahoo! search resulted in a potpourri of authoritative and popular knowledge— of truth and fantasy, trivia and substance, sobriety and sensationalism. To click on Google's "I'm feeling lucky" button was to pull the lever on the information slot machine; anything could happen. (Now you often land on a Wikipedia page.) We were back in the universe of a thick register of information. No doubt about it.

Beyond that, however, the differences from the later nineteenth century could not be more striking. First, the search parameter is set by a bit of information (the keyword entry) instead of an elaborate tree of knowledge. Second, search engines, as noted, produce a salad of the serious and crackpot, the true and false, instead of trying to build a firewall between the official and the whimsical. Third, the results come out of a culture—Silicon Valley—more enamored of entrepreneurs than professionals and often downright hostile to established knowledge hierarchies. A few years after he created the Dewey Decimal System, Melvil Dewey formed the American Library Association. The founders of Yahoo! and Google went in the opposite direction, abandoning the core commitments of the university for a wilder world where risk trumps routine, even though Google, with its "campus" and offbeat culture of creativity, models its culture on that of an elite university.[31] Silicon Valley's material conditions have always favored antiauthoritarian attitudes about knowledge. (Several high-tech gurus have been fascinated with Ayn Rand's philosophy at some point in their thinking, including Stewart Brand, Peter Thiel, Jimmy Wales, Craig Newmark, and Jeff Bezos.) Such people built institutions to open up professional enclosures; Dewey built one to close the gates. Dewey had a vast architectonic plan for organizing knowledge; Google hoovers up the digital crumbs left behind by millions of searchers and keeps its precious ever-updated map of the internet to itself.

Digital culture encourages declining respect for the ethos of the professional knowledge creator. In his *Rhetoric*, Aristotle famously argued that there were three sources of persuasion—*ethos*, *logos*, and *pathos*. Distrust of professionals has meant not so much the abandonment of logos as the suspicion of ethos. Arguing ex cathedra, by authority, will always happen, but it became less persuasive. Less trust was given to someone simply because they "were" an expert. But we have not eliminated the knowledge creators, just devalued them—the culture still pays homage to claims of rationality (*logos*). Such claims blend freely with emotional appeals designed to move us to a point of view—the *pathos* of the world of advertising. These trends, all markers of promiscuous knowledge, are reflected and encouraged in digital culture.

Bred out of the hothouse mix of 1960s critical culture with 1970s bows to felt necessity, the unholy mix of popular and professional easily incorporated itself into digital culture. The distrust of authority tugged at many of the digital innovators and spilled into the democratic communalist style of chat rooms and search engines. The *Whole Earth Catalog*, a text first published in 1968 by Stewart Brand, was a promiscuous mix of self-help, technofuturism, and revolutionary dream. It was a harbinger of things to come. By the 1971 issue it had swelled to 448 pages. Many of the items were contributed by readers, foreshadowing the "user-generated content" of the internet. It was, precisely, a *catalog* of miscellaneous items ready to be put to use by readers, not a streamlined synthesis. This copious, do-it-yourself spirit, as Fred Turner has shown so well, lives on in the ideology, practice, and personnel of cyberculture.[32] Making light of the claim that knowledge professionals have some special access to truth is the ideology of *Wired*. Internet porn in the public library was another example of digital distrust of authority, this time of parents. The information age, we would argue, is marked by the strong distrust of ethos. As with the entire web, it has decreased our ability to judge the reputation of the speaker.

By the 1990s, chat groups emerged on nearly every topic, radically increasing the ability to pass around information but at the same time eliminating all control over participants. Even moderated lists patrolled more for civility than for expertise: Who knew if the people making certain claims actually had the foggiest idea what they were talking about? I had been on several chat rooms relating to professional interests for about a year but quit basically because there wasn't enough content control. Even people who did know what they were talking about often just blurted out the last thing to come into their heads.

Lack of filtering is a general problem with the web. The ongoing crisis of journalism is not just a question of getting people to pay for news online—good news is expensive to produce—but a question of justifying the authority to sort out legitimate knowledge. On social media platforms news releases from trusted institutions and snarky comments about them nestle side by side. The very same channel brings you the official and the unfiltered without hierarchical arrangement. The internet lowered barriers to entry for publishing. In the blogosphere, anyone could be a journalist, but few if any were editors, gatekeepers who organized and prioritized what is important for a larger public. The leveling of the information cosmos made it harder to sort out what to believe. This flattening of access to public space could be both empowering and confusing. Search engines and news aggregators would step into the vacuum left by this "disappearance of the editor."[33]

Some notoriously fallacious entries on wikipedia.com have made the problem more prominent. Sometimes they are subtle: one of us once read on Wikipedia that "George W. Bush is alleged to be the 43rd President of the United States." A phrase as innocuous as "alleged to be" flew below the radar for a while before one of Wikipedia's volunteer army of editors corrected it. Other times such fallacious entries are vicious, as in the case of John Seigenthaler, a distinguished American journalist, whose Wikipedia page suggested, with no basis in fact, that he had been a suspect in the assassinations of John F. and Robert Kennedy. It turned out a hoaxer had altered the page, which went undetected for months in the summer of 2005 before it was finally corrected. It is no surprise that a string of sites have turned up to teach people to assess other sites. I have found huge amounts of misinformation through web searches (which I generally enjoy!). But as a source of information the web has none of the authenticating practices we have seen for making knowledge secure—printing protocols, replication by colleagues, scientific reputation, academic certification, peer review, and so on.

The real menace of rampant online opinion came home to me when my mother produced sheets of messages she had printed out from a chat room devoted to her congenital heart condition. There were wildly differing opinions, all stated as gospel truth. Serious decisions about her health were at stake, bringing the issue far closer to me. It was no longer some flamer going on about the latest interpretation of John Dewey. It was—and this is not too dramatic a way to put it—my mother's life.

Sidebar 6.3 Google and the Dream of a Universal Library

In the late 1970s Bell and Lyotard despaired of any higher ordering of knowledge. By 2000 the dream of a universal library had come roaring back. Google had much to do with this shift.

Historically the project of a universal library was imperial, pursued by the emperors in Egypt, Babylon, China, and Hellenistic Greece, among other places. No ancient city-state in Greece or even the Roman republic created a public library, and it was the Ptolemaic rulers of Egypt, heirs of Alexander the Great, who built the library at Alexandria. A library limited to a single nation could never claim to be universal. Google, as many have noted, certainly is imperial in its ambitions. Its domain is the World Wide Web, and algorithms are its means of governance and control. There still remain pockets of resistance, most notably in European countries with strong data-protection laws and in China, and much of the web remains off-limits to Google spiders, such as the vast password-protected gardens of Facebook and Apple or the dark web.

The mathematical organization of knowledge is an old dream. Among his other activities, Leibniz was a royal librarian who tried to implement the Renaissance ideal of a universal library. The problem with such a library is the catalog. If everything is in the library, what finding aids are there? A universal library faces the vertigo of infinity, since the catalog's description of its contents is potentially inexhaustible and infinite.[1] Calculus, by introducing the notion of an infinitesimal, provides an answer to the thorny problem of how to calculate a function that is infinitely subdividable.

The most famous imaginative vision of a universal library is Jorge Luis Borges's story "The Library of Babel." It concerns an exhaustive library consisting of every possible combination of the letters of the alphabet. Somewhere in its huge repertoire—the library would be almost infinitely greater than the known universe—there was the catalog of the library, but the catalog would also have to exist in an all but infinity of spurious versions. Naturally enough, Borges's story exists in multiple versions: "The Total Library" (1939), "The Library of Babel" (1941), and the late "Prologue to the Library of Babel."[2]

1. Siegert, *Passage des Digitalen*, 156–90.

2. William Goldbloom Bloch, *The Unimaginable Mathematics of Borges' Library of Babel* (New York: Oxford University Press, 2008).

Borges is one of the patron saints of Google. The dream is of a total record of the literature of the human race. Of course it will never succeed, but the dream is itself noteworthy. Google's corporate mission is "to organize the world's information and make it universally accessible and useful." (Note that the term is information, not knowledge.) What Google's algorithms and servers can do with the confused warehouse of the web is truly remarkable, but the last thing Google offers is ultimate organization of knowledge, let alone truth. Instead it dribbles out search results one at a time, serving the varied life projects of its users. Since it has a unique access to the aggregate of billions of searches daily, Google potentially has enormous power to discern (and manipulate) the collective desires of the species. It can tell where the flu is breaking out and when "users" are pregnant. It is probably much more compendious in its knowledge of personal preferences than Facebook. Its accumulated data is the treasure-house of the twenty-first century. Part of that treasure is access to the online universe; part of it lies in the data it mines about people's searches in that universe.

But Google's wealth and power come without any synthetic ambition, at least any that is open to public inspection. This is not to say Google isn't ambitious: any company that wants to "solve death" certainly is! The point is that Google lacks any synthetic vision of the organization of knowledge. Google absolutely thrives in the messy disorder of the internet, its tangle of hyperlinks, and is happy to profit from the flotsam of "clickstreams" and search terms. It takes the manure of our data trails and turns it into online gold. It is a service that sorts what we need but never frames the whole. Google likes to evoke the old idea of divine omniscience—Sergey Brin, the company's cofounder, once compared the perfect search engine to the "mind of God"—but this is a funny kind of divinity that traffics indifferently in news, maps, weather, and porn. Google offers a single portal to a churning mass of confusion. It is the new face of promiscuous knowledge.

Truth in Our Time

The erosion of professional authority without the collapse of the professions has created promiscuous knowledge, the blurring of formal and informal knowledge, of authoritative and popular learning. New technology did not create this situation, it just fed into it. The inability of professionals to maintain boundaries is not new, but it is newly impor-

tant in our time and harks back to the empirical sprawl of the seventeenth century. We have always had promiscuous knowledge. Courts,
clinics, newspapers, and laboratories have never segregated the true
from the popular as successfully as their ideology suggested.

The seventeenth and eighteenth centuries felt the pressure of wild
fact. The nineteenth century hungered for it, then sought to organize
it. The early twentieth century trusted its experts and artists to distill
it. Around the turn of the millennium, we learned to live without the
hope of reason, progress, or the growth of knowledge, but that did not
mean everything had collapsed. Thin and thick culture coexist side by
side. In this respect Bruno Latour's contention that "we have never been
modern" is certainly correct. At the dawn of the modern era, new ide-
ologies of experimentation mingled with ancient belief in monsters.
Newton's physics coexisted with alchemy in the same minds. The drift
of an entire generation of research in the history of science has been to
claim that the seventeenth-century scientific "revolution" had actually
not split the old and the new, that there was not the clarity that existed
later about what science was. In High Enlightenment salons, mesmerist
frauds mingled with the era's leading scientists. In Victorian America,
cultural critics routinely bemoaned the inability of science to segregate
itself from entrepreneurial culture, a culture at best with insufficient
rigor about the truth, at worst populated by eager gawkers waiting to see
the fake mermaids in Barnum's New York "museum." Boundaries have
never been completely secure.

What, then, is new for us? Attitude. What has developed in recent
generations is a *relatively* relaxed acceptance of the phenomenon. Academics developed theories of popular participation in the construction
of museum displays. The courts toyed with granting popular knowledge
evidentiary weight along with formal science. Conservatives applauded
outsider challenges to left-oriented museum exhibitions. Progressives
approved of ACT-UP's entry into the halls of science. The Senate funded
research on "alternative" health care. With each example, the autonomy
of professional judgment diminished while professional practice per-
sisted. The results produced by the great search engines of the 1990s—
Yahoo! and Google—only codified larger cultural presumptions about
copious knowledge available to all, but without the promise of progress
or order.

Not only have we never been modern, we will never *be* modern. Promiscuous knowledge seems to be here for good, or at least for the fore-
seeable future. This might very well be the nub of what is new about
all this: we cannot imagine a "beyond." There is no dream of a "purer"

future. Right and Left chafe when outsiders come after one dear to them, but no one challenges the new practices across the board. Activist pressure is now a form of democracy. Unlike the past, nothing is envisioned beyond the mix of the popular and professional, political actor and credentialed expert. This *is* the contemporary organization of knowledge. It is our condition.

In the past it was very different. There was confidence in the future. "Truth reveals itself," wrote Spinoza, and in this he spoke for his age. Similarly, from about the 1860s to the 1960s, there was great faith inside expert communities that modern professionalism would secure better and more accurate knowledge. Dissenters existed, of course. Friedrich Nietzsche compared *Homo sapiens*—the "clever animal" who "invented knowledge"—to a self-important mosquito flying through the air.[34] But they were few. Just as in the seventeenth century, new institutions were supposed to create truths that could be secure.

Our age is also quite different from the midcentury culture of happy summary and mythic pictures. We have powerful machines able to generate a plethora of information and spirit it around the globe. The computer did not exist in the 1930s; it was at best a gleam in the eyes of visionaries. Nor did the infrastructure exist to carry the digital pulses that stand for money, music, pictures, and words. Despite the global reach of the web, we should not lose sight of the disaggregating tendencies of digital information culture. The late twentieth century did not invent the community study as a microcosm of the nation, the GNP, or national public opinion polling. It invented "difference," niche marketing, and forms of data collection that put us into smaller and smaller groups. Our residences are sorted by nine-digit zip codes, our online searches are tracked by cookies, and our shopping is recorded by entries in MCIF systems (Marketing Consumer Information Files). What I buy at the supermarket is entered into a database that is combined with other information about me, then sold to marketers who send me coupons and reorganize the layout of the store to maximize sales. Instead of looking for aggregate information about the society, this is the collection of large quantities of information on particular people. Data has become the new currency of money and power.

Perhaps most important, however, is the loosening connection of "fact" to "knowledge." Whether it is the latest stock quotes, the most recent reports of human rights abuses around the world, or the route maps and hotel reservations needed to plan your summer vacation—information is bundles of practical information, used for personal life projects that come to the fore. While "knowledge" obviously still matters, "information flows" are most prominent. What is at stake is the drift from knowledge, understood as disciplined generalizations about the social and natural world accepted by authority, to information, the massing of facts on particular topics by dispersed groups.

Obviously the results of cyberculture are not adequately described as the latest manifestation of technological rationality, as the apotheosis of the Enlightenment, or as the ringing triumph of modernity, for good or ill. Such evaluations look selectively at the age and miss the dialectic going on all around us. Digital culture has weakened our established sorting mechanisms while offering a few of its own. The information age is a strange mix of the hyperrational and the popular. The continued prominence of expertise has to be set next to the distrust of expertise. Knowledge is increasingly marked by blends with the idiosyncratic. Expert classifications jostle with "folksonomies" on the web.

And this populist hubbub only provides Facebook, Amazon, Google, and Apple with the raw materials they need to make money and wield power, thanks to their expert data analysts. Such high priests of computer code are definitely experts in having specialized knowledge, and though they can sometimes think of themselves as the stewards of humanity, they are different from earlier visions of expertise. In the latter half of the twentieth century the discourse on the production and use of knowledge gradually drifted away from the high modern faith in rational planning. This was bound up with the move from knowledge to information. Without the faith in coherent knowledge, depending on our dispositions we either pursued our own agendas, searched for meaning, tried to keep our balance, or looked to the state for protection. In the rhetoric of the enthusiasts, faith in technology replaced the disciplined search for knowledge as the social glue.

The information age traveled in the wake of the Enlightenment, certainly, but in a nuanced way. The encyclopedia was largely gone, as was its twentieth-century replacement—the social organization of knowledge production. The closest the new millennium got was the peer-produced online encyclopedia Wikipedia, which is full of useful stuff and the occasional outrageous howler (par for the course in the previous history of encyclopedias). This was Kant's program split down the middle. The political and ethical value of personal autonomy remained, but with no promise of universal principles for understanding. The information age reflects an ambivalence about the Enlightenment, rejecting its dream of social harmony through knowledge but leaving intact the belief in personal autonomy and salvation through technology.

In the end, the world is an abundant, strange place, and all our efforts to arrange facts and draw pictures of them will fail. But they will fail in different ways in different times. It is the abandonment of the search for ultimate containers for truth that is the peculiar mark of our age. The most prominent spokespeople for the metanarrative of liberation through knowledge are in exile (NSA whistle-blower Edward Snowden), harassed (filmmaker Laura Poitras), or dead (information activist Aaron Swartz). Grand narratives about knowledge as a historical force generally remain piecemeal or sound tinny to our ears, though occasionally they arise from the promotional cultures of Silicon Valley. Many people go about their lives unterrified at the lack of a center for knowledge. Others dream of salvation in insurrection, planetary seed banks, machine learning, geoengineering, or religious revival. Apart from a few hard-core true believers, no one looks for salvation to the professional growth of knowledge.

Bureaucracy, as Max Weber knew, was the price moderns paid for order. To make order in knowledge, moderns built classification systems, popular strategies of display, crystallized essences, classes of experts, and much more. For the past several decades, many have chipped away at those structures. The structures are leaky but still afloat, and they don't look ready to sink anytime soon. Much good has come from making expert knowledge accountable to public pressure and opening it to vernacular input. Indeed, activists of various sorts have all but repurposed the old metanarrative of liberation through knowledge, though on a more modest scale.

But the more virulent forms of that story should give us pause. Both postmodernists and technolibertarians liked to suggest that the information age left stodgy rules and procedures behind for the open frontier of risk and creativity. We could all become the authors of our own encyclopedias. Such a view has an uncanny doppelgänger in the long-simmering populist distrust of expertise and contempt for institutions that erupted so openly onto the world stage with the United Kingdom's Brexit vote in 2015 and the United States' presidential election of 2016. In the light of recent efforts "to deconstruct the administrative state," as conservative operative Steve Bannon put it, we might want to cultivate a renewed appreciation for the way bureaucratic systems correct, however imperfectly, the abuses of everyday life.[35] Knowledge's containers stabilize the world, putting bounds and limits to things that might otherwise run out of control. Infrastructures are not glamorous, but they anchor our existence.

Of course, no container of the world is ever fully adequate. Leaks point to a universe larger than we can grasp. Any understanding of the world that is too well ordered is probably not true to the world. There are more things in the world than order. Truth is precisely what keeps breaking our best ideas and dearest prejudices. But too much smashing of the vessels leaves all of us vulnerable, especially the weak. That order can be both stifling and precious is perhaps an oddly consoling thought as we sit on edge, waiting to see what will happen next.

Postscript

The Promiscuous Knowledge of Ken Cmiel

Unpacking His Library

Nathaniel Hawthorne's *The Scarlet Letter* opens in a Salem customs house, surrounded by papers alive with the stirrings of the dead whose stories wait to be told. I sit in a room containing dozens of books once owned by Kenneth Cmiel, and the basement of the house where I write holds many hundreds more. My task here is to explain how a portion of the preceding pages came into my possession.

After Ken died, I soon inherited much of his enormous book collection. Apparently he had once told his wife, Anne Duggan, that if anything happened to him I should get his books. He once said something like that to me as well, but I shrugged it off and assured him he would live a long life. Ken was always nervous about his health, a topic he avoided, and the precedent of early deaths among the men in his family, but no one was ready for this. After he died Anne didn't want the books, nor did Willa, Cordelia, or Noah, their three children. Ken was a great book collector, so inheriting his library seemed an enormous windfall. Some of the books went to the University of Iowa Center for Human Rights and some to others of his friends. His library was a treasury of his particular tastes and curiosities: American music, the history of political thought, cultural history, social theory, visual culture, and too many other interests and quirky little specimens to mention. There was little that didn't swim into his ken at some point or another. I never did a full count, but a quick and dirty *Durchmusterung* (catalog) of his books in my basement, multiplied by two or three to account for the books that were given away, suggests he owned several thousand.

The books were shelved in several rooms in the Cmiel home on East Bloomington Street, Iowa City, and my son Daniel and I spread them out on the living room floor there and sorted them into piles to keep or give away, the latter going to the Iowa City Public Library's resale store and the former to the many shelves in the basement of our house in Iowa City, a place beneath where the living are wont to assemble. Daniel and I also sorted books left behind in Ken's large campus office. I felt almost like a vulture perched among so much bibliographic wealth, dividing the spoils and doing rapid triage about what had once entered and formed Ken's completely unusual mind. But if I was sure there was no possible future that a book and I could cohabit, I gave it away, hoping it would cross paths with someone else whose life would make space for it. It would be nice if when buying a book you could also buy the time to read it, said Arthur Schopenhauer.[1] Every new book is a utopian lien, a dream of future time, an investment in possible worlds, and Ken invested richly in futures that never came. With the books, I inherited those futures, however untransferable.

Libraries are places of commerce between souls and bodies, between the alive and the once alive. While working on this book I often thought about philosopher-critic Walter Benjamin's charming 1928 lecture "Unpacking My Library." In it he portrays himself as standing jubilantly by an open crate of books freshly arrived after sitting in storage for two years. Memories spill forth right and left as Benjamin, who supported himself on and off as a collector and seller of rare books, sorts through the treasures as happily as a child on Christmas morning.

Benjamin begins by noting that organizing one's books is an adventure in remembrance. Memories reside, he suggests, not in a book's typographical content but rather in an individual copy's idiosyncratic journey through time and space. What would not even register on an e-reader is the most important thing for a personal library—bindings, dust jackets, scuff marks, scribbles, slips of paper left between pages, stains on the pages of a cookbook, the family tree written in a Bible, and all the contingent material details in individual copies.[2] For the collector, accident is essence, since accidents distinguish one copy from another and make books a haven of memory against the universal dissipation of too many copies. Each book can serve its owner as what Benjamin calls a "magic encyclopedia," storing up histories available to nobody else. A library is a mnemonic device—collection implies recollection—and a thermodynamic system whose delicate order is maintained by the mind of the collector.

The library as a theater of memory dissolves when its owner dies; entropy is unleashed. This was Benjamin's key point. The hieroglyphic marks in the books are decipherable to only one person; to anyone else its little islands of order remain unnavigable. This was the crucial difference between Benjamin and me: he was unpacking his own library and so had ready access to the "little spirits" (*Geisterchen*) dwelling jointly in his books and his memory, whereas in unpacking Ken's books I had access only to the bodies of the books, not to the souls that once dwelt in them. The books were there, but only occasionally did I glimpse the vapor trails of meaning left behind. It seemed that the little spirits that inhabit books, whether genies or demons, had fled into their paper hideouts or vanished altogether. Little makes the bridge between subject and object so stark as a library.

Why did I think I could find Ken's memories in his books? Most of what happened to me yesterday or even a minute ago is already gone without a trace: Why should we think we could ever retrieve the memories of someone who is dead? A close friend of mine recently wrote that his aging mother "is disappearing mentally. I can find her sometimes, but less and less these days. Watching memories and concepts fade is scary, because it reminds me that this is not an all-or nothing proposition. There is never a secure foundation of total memory—just the patchwork quilt we're suspended in, and these patches wear unevenly until we start to fall through the holes. It feels vertiginous to me, watching her try to paper over these holes and failing over and over."[3]

Indeed, we all paper over the holes and fall into them anyway. Occasionally the little spirits in Ken's library would rise up, not yet fully into their Sleeping Beauty phase, as if they didn't want to disappear yet. They especially liked taking form between the books' pages as a kind of patchy archive of Ken's life and times. I kept finding new slips of paper and inserts years later, as if they were breeding at night. His books seemed to be pulling practical jokes so subtle I usually didn't even notice. They were like the squirrelly inhabitants of George Berkeley's idealistic universe, off duty and free to play when God stops perceiving them. Old documents do have a tendency to reappear after a long incubation in no-man's-land. Aristotle's *Constitution of Athens* showed up in 1879; the first Dead Sea scrolls were found in 1946; a photograph of Lincoln's body lying in state surfaced only in 1952, the same year as Evita Perón's death and embalming;[4] a Beethoven manuscript popped up in 2005. Previously unknown "first folios" of Shakespeare's plays showed up in both 2014 and 2016, centuries after their first publication in 1623. How does the past manage to keep bringing forth so many new old things?[5]

Papers stashed absently between the pages of Ken's books were a local example of the fertility of the historical record. I recently found a letter inviting Ken to give a lecture at the Department of Communication Studies at Northwestern University in November 1995, where he talked about Rush Limbaugh, Jacques Derrida, and the ACLU—a trio only Ken could have put together (he saw them as united by "the gamble of reform-minded cynicism"). The letter is stuffed inside an envelope from Routledge publishers; on the back Ken had penciled some complicated calculations, likely for a mortgage on the new, roomier house he and Anne bought on Bloomington Street, a house that came with 1970s avocado carpet and an intermittently nudist neighbor.

I found printed emails from colleagues inquiring gently about the status of manuscripts under deadline, a blank deposit slip at the now defunct Iowa State Bank, and a bill for a doctor visit to treat an ear infection. A reading list for a graduate student's comprehensive exams (on "Concepts of Culture in American Thought") was wedged in Ian Hacking's *The Social Construction of What?* Sometimes the documents provided ironic commentaries on their holders, such as a Michelin guide to restaurants inside Anthony Grafton's book on the Renaissance genius Leon Battista Alberti (culinary connoisseurship within intellectual connoisseurship), or a monthly mortgage statement in Nikolas Rose's *Powers of Freedom* (1999), a book about how neoliberal capitalism had redistributed financial responsibility (among other forms).

In Ken's copy of Hannah Arendt's *Life of the Mind*, I found the white and canary copies of a receipt for the lunch he had on June 6, 1997, at the Airliner, a beloved pub and burger joint on the main drag between the campus and downtown Iowa City, about a block from his campus office in Schaeffer Hall. (The only other item was a bookmark from the legendary Seminary Co-op Bookstore at the University of Chicago, where he must have bought the book.) The receipts show he had a cheeseburger (medium rare) with swiss cheese, fries, water, a Coke, and coffee. The bill came to $8.75, and he gave a tip of $1.50 to the waitress, Christy, who drew a smiley face next to her handwritten note of "Thanksalot." His signature is clear on the canary copy, not on the white. It was a late lunch when school was out, his credit card being swiped at 2:07 pm, probably on a hot June day, guessing from the abundant fluid intake. Ken's pencil marks in the book show that he barely made it through part of the introduction, at least in this copy, and perhaps he made those marks in the Airliner.

Kenneth J. Cmiel, *The Life of the Mind*, a cheeseburger with fries, water, and caffeinated drinks on a hot June day in Iowa: here we have a singular event in the history of the universe. It happened only once, it will never happen again, and I hold the sole documentary evidence of it. What is my responsibility to history? The problem of preservation is made worse because the receipts bear his signature, which can be a prize for a historical sleuth. There are avid collector's markets for the signatures of famous people such as the signers of the Declaration of Independence.[6] Once Ken's scrawled signature, a relatively legible "Kenneth Cmiel," could be found in many places—on checks, letters of recommendation, credit card receipts. (It was the only time except for publishing that he or anyone else used "Kenneth," although he liked the full version of his name.)[7] His signature was an active force that made the world go round. He once sat at the switchboard of campus and family, but now the waters have closed up over the hole he left behind, and his signature has lost all potency except as an artifact.

Signatures, by the way, do harbor strange powers: Ken and Anne arranged for a bank loan to cover college tuition for one of their children, and for some last-minute reason Anne did not make the signing that day and Ken ended up as the sole signatory. When he died the bank generously forgave the loan. His signature was once worth tens of thousands of dollars. As the days go by, there will be fewer and fewer instances in circulation of this magical token, once so warm and capable of leaving tips, admitting graduate students, securing scholarships, or getting things done.

Evidence of another unique cosmic alignment is found inside his copy of Lisa Jardine's elegant study of Renaissance material culture, *Worldly Goods* (1996), in the form of a multilingual parking pass to Euro Disney near Paris, dated June 21, 1998, issued by the Hotel Santa Fe, a five-minute drive from the park. This perky document, decorated in a now faded red-and-green pattern that signifies "Mexican" in the international lingua franca of design, offers parking instructions in six languages and was placed on a page where Jardine is discussing an Ottoman sultan's negotiations with an Italian lord for the services of an architect and a painter. Somehow both the book and the parking pass concerned international exchanges of worldly goods. This juxtaposition of highbrow and popular, eternal and ephemeral, is classic Ken. He was an ambassador between Lisa Jardine and Euro Disney just as much as a Venetian agent once was between the Ottoman sultan and the potentates of the Italian peninsula.

Sometimes I found early paper premonitions of this book squatting in his books. Jonathan Crary's *Suspensions of Perception* held two receipts for deposits Ken made to the University of Iowa Community Credit Union on May 24, 2000. One of them had been pressed into service as notes for this book: "Fact. Knowledge and Image. Emily Dickinson. Alain Locke. (1) Movement of Promiscuous Mixing. (2) Increasing fear of in-

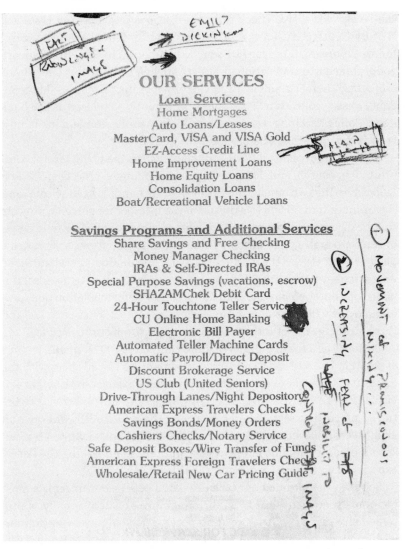

Scribblings on bank receipt, found in book belonging to Kenneth Cmiel.

ability to control the image." Exactly what those resonant arrows meant is lost forever; Dickinson ended up in the version I finished, Locke not so much.

Probably the most common insert in his books is the receipt for the book's purchase or a bookmark from Prairie Lights, Iowa City's legendary independent bookstore, which Ken ardently supported. Other items include an occasional three-by-five card; four small unused envelopes; a coffee-stained napkin with afternoon jottings, no longer intelligible;

the receipt for a $150 check from the *Dictionary of American History*; a History Department form reserving a room for a final exam; a receipt for an express mail package he sent to his mother in Florida in January 2000, parked in a translation of Robert Michels's classic 1915 book *Political Parties*. There is a single blank slip of paper inside Maurice Merleau-Ponty's essay collection *Signes* (1960), apparently as unused as the book itself. Coffee, teaching, service to the history profession and his family, French thought—not a bad roundup of Ken's activities.

There is an occasional head-scratcher such as the blank receipt form printed in Dutch and French in Alberto Manguel's *Reading Pictures* (2000) bearing two cursive notes not in Ken's hand: "priceline.com" and "lastminute.com." (Here was the use of the internet for personal projects that he discussed in chapter 6.) Did some helpful hotel clerk in Brussels or Antwerp grab a piece of scrap paper to jot down options to find Ken a place to stay? He was the master of just-in-time production, whatever he was doing—writing, teaching, traveling—so he may have been scrambling for a hotel, elegant book in hand, somewhere in Belgium one summer; no one will ever know. Anne doesn't remember, I have no clue, and this knowledge is lost forever. Some facts are simply irretrievable.

Besides the Prairie Lights bookmark in James J. O'Donnell's *Avatars of the Word* I also found a top secret document—a folded sheet with the Iowa City High School softball team's system of signals, both verbal and visual (2 = FAKE BUNT AND STEAL; NOSE = SLAP BUNT; I trust I've betrayed no current secrets here). Ken, ever the multitasker, was once an avid baseball player and must have hauled this book along to an afterschool practice or game of one of his children, again mixing the family experience with some reading on the side.

So far I've mentioned only the unrelated papers, but by far the most common specimens in his books are yellow (or occasionally white) folded sheets covered with reading notes, scrawled mostly in capitals, gathering quotations and material. These sheets form a loose-leaf version of the notes he wrote on the pages of his books (see fig. 0.1 in the preface). And not only *his* books—I also kept finding his unmistakable penciled marginalia in books belonging to the University of Iowa libraries! Ken read, as he would say, "a ton," with irrepressible sympathy for almost any position or point of view, and finding his scratchings in the borders of texts that have passed through his hands has sometimes helped me guess at what he might have said in this book. He was an uncommonly absorbent annotator. His scribbles seem chiefly designed to help him quickly recall bits he might want to use or quote later. He was not argumentatively inclined in his notes; he flagged themes, summarizing and highlighting, rarely pushing back against the text or making snarky comments. (He saved those for conversation.) His reading notes were at best chits for his memory palace, marks of his efforts to absorb alien thoughts.

It is rare to find evidence in any volume he owned of cover-to-cover reading—his pencil strokes show up intermittently like clouds in an otherwise clear sky. He liked to quote Samuel Johnson that no one but a fool ever read a book cover to cover, but judging from his library, he actually did so in several cases, such as Arendt's *The Human Condition*, and I can show you all the markings in his copy. But mostly he read like a hungry omnivore, skipping, skimming, and picking out the snack that suited his appetite at the moment. It's not unusual to find a hundred pages without a scratch followed by a sudden outbreak of five intensely annotated pages.

In Slavoj Žižek's *The Plague of Fantasies* (1997), for instance, there are a few pencil scribbles in chapter 1 on the veils of fantasy and chapter 4 on cyberspace. Ken drew lines for emphasis, with a bit of doodling flourish; he was interested in Žižek's thoughts on how blind spots seem to be a necessary condition of seeing and in Lacan's idea that human faking is actually the faking of faking. Only twice does Ken write anything. Inside the back cover stands his fractured German version of one of Freud's dicta that later psychoanalysts have admired for its pre-Socratic density:

Wo id war
Zoll ich verden[8]

[Where it was
I should become]

(Turning *es* into *id* is a nice move!) On page 32 we get his extended gloss on one of Žižek's points: "Desire happens when drive is caught by law; fantasy is narrative of this loss since it expresses [not fully legible] the emergence of law. So fantasy is the screen btn [between] desire and drive. Fantasy provides a rationale for the inherent deadlock of desire. A point witnessing the emergence of the block or 'jouissance.'"

Ken's pencil marks in his books—he rarely used a pen—included vertical lines in the margins, straight and wavy underscores beneath the lines, parentheses around important sentences, and sometimes a double underscore when things got exciting. Ken marked the following line from *Avatars of the Word* with double vertical stripes in the margin, an underline beneath the first clause, and double lines beneath "fluid

Notation by Kenneth Cmiel in Žižek, *The Plague of Fantasies*.

place": "But the world is a fluid place, and it does not always treat kindly those who would freeze it, or part of it, in place."[9] In the following two sentences (about the 1990s internet) the first one merited a wavy underline and the second a double underscore: "There is no organized cataloging, there is no commitment to preservation, there is no support system to help you find the difficult or missing resource. Finally, there is no filter."[10] He was finding evidence of promiscuous knowledge in a version of the internet that hardly exists anymore.

Writing This Book

At first I thought what a gift it was to suddenly inherit so many books, though lugging them from his house and office to my basement gave a premonition of their freight. Ken left no provision in his will for a literary executor and probably gave no thought to what would become of his writings. He was not much of a planner for the long haul. A couple of months before he died he told me he rejected the ethic of living as though you might die tomorrow. He thought it selfish and irresponsible.

Ken and I often discussed this book. He worked steadily on it until about 2002, though "steadily" is probably not quite the right word, given Ken's mode of production: he certainly read, talked, and thought about it steadily, but his written notes were rare. Generalizing from my own work habits, I had expected to find detailed notes on his computer about this book and many other things, but the files and jottings were few. (As I noted in the preface, they can be viewed at https://doi.org/10.17077 /ocj3-36ob.)

I soon realized what I should have already known: that Ken did much of his most creative work in the air, talking with colleagues and students, friends and family. He certainly wrote a lot, but writing was an occasional, sometimes tortured interlude between the rounds of reading, talking, family life, and service. He didn't develop his thoughts on the keyboard, but he would prepare for writing by reading widely, taking notes, and carrying on conversations in places ranging from the university library to the local Donutland; you never knew where he'd turn up. Finally, in a brilliant last-minute burst of caffeinated hair pulling and harrowing physical labor and inspiration, he would bring forth a written text to meet the pressure of a deadline (sometimes long past due) or a nagging, long-suffering colleague. (This book, over a decade in process, honors Ken's memory in its agonized postponement.) His last updates on it came in early 2004, when he got swept up in the administrative leadership of the University of Iowa Center for Human Rights, after having served as chair of the Department of History from 2000 to 2003, and when his writing plans turned to the history of human rights and war photography. We never talked of working together on the book, and he never mentioned wanting me to work with him on it.

I can no longer remember how I decided to take on the project; it was likely in a fit of absent-mindedness. I'll let others figure out the ratio of debt to mourning that went into this book. Big projects seem simple and fun at the beginning. It's easy to commit to an apparently noble cause without having the slightest inkling of the consequences (the story of many a dissertation and many a marriage). Perhaps I thought working on "the Ken book" would provide a pleasant distraction during my service as chair of the Department of Communication Studies at the University of Iowa from 2008 to 2011, when I would otherwise be preoccupied by course schedules and a never-ending flow of email, disgruntled parents, and collegial woes. Indeed, my volunteering to serve as chair was probably in part homage to Ken's example of noble and rather self-punishing university service. I somehow kidded myself that the book would require few painful decisions and smoothly unfold a ready-made agenda of interesting wormholes to explore. The latter was certainly true about the sidebars—at times I thought of turning the book into nothing but a string of sidebars—and there were some spots where Ken's prose had left room for my own cadenzas, but the main chapters were often excruciating. Years into the writing it became clear that I could work on it forever.

Speaker for the Dead

One problem was finding the right voice. At first my plan was to disappear into the background and channel Ken's voice transparently, in a quite literal effort at ghostwriting. I wanted to achieve that condition of interchangeability of longtime partners described by Charles Dickens in *A Christmas Carol*, a book whose combination of gallows humor and generous sentimentality Ken loved: "Sometimes people new to the business called Scrooge Scrooge, and sometimes Marley, but he answered to both names. It was all the same to him." In the first version I wrote, every time the word *I* appeared in the text it was supposed to belong to Ken, even if I had written the sentence. It took me several years to see that it was a failed experiment. Despite my efforts at ventriloquism, I couldn't keep my lips from moving. Our styles are different enough, to say nothing of our outlooks, that I couldn't have fooled anyone.

The plan was to offer life support to the dead, effacing myself in a kind of joyous enabling. Indeed, most of history's creative work has been done without authorial glory. The most central creative work in the human drama, childbirth and child rearing, has been almost completely unsung. The same is true for the labors of cooks, farmers, singers, poets, and makers of all kinds. Authorship is just a brief blip on the historical screen of human creation. The will to serve is a genuine human motivation. An assistant in Rembrandt's workshop could work on a painting signed by the master and take honor in that. A serious basketball player would rather make a great pass than a great shot. Amid all the uproar in recent theory about ravenous affect, someone has forgotten the sheer joy of service, the pleasure of marching as a foot soldier in a cause you feel sure is just. People not only seek command, they seek the relief of disappearing into something greater. The data-mining industries pile up cash by exploiting the human will to share. The nations have always wanted to have kings to obey. It's an open question whether the tendency to self-assertion or to submission is more dangerous to the general welfare.

Speaking for the dead, in any case, can take many forms. Plato never wrote for himself but always in the persona of his teacher Socrates, providing posterity with a voice the hemlock had silenced and whose relation to his own thinking remains disputed. Confucius spent his scholarly energies editing the Chinese classics, not recording his own doctrine, which he taught orally; those who came after wrote it down. Plato at least claimed authorship of his philosophical dialogues and never pretended to be offering a faithful account of the teachings of Socrates, who is often more an interrogator than an expositor, but many other ancient texts, both East and West, are pseudepigraphic—attributed to an earlier eminence by an anonymous writer—sometimes centuries after the fact. The Homeric hymns were written not by Homer (the paradigmatic case of a mystery author) but in Alexandria many centuries later.[11] Despite traditional ascriptions of biblical books to authors such as Moses, David, Solomon, or Daniel, we have little idea who wrote the most important book in the Western world except for the epistles of Paul. Even there, several New Testament letters attributed to him were written by people either close to him (the "deutero-Pauline" epistles) or imitatively declaring what they thought he should have said ("pseudo-Pauline"). Ptolemy's astronomical works contain data added by Byzantine scholars centuries after he wrote. Before modern Europe invented authorship, copyright, and intellectual property about three centuries ago, such entanglements were routine. And those inventions only made for new entanglements.

Sometimes I considered serving as a scrupulous posthumous editor for Ken's work. Many books owe their legacy to the self-sacrificing labor of collaborators, archivists, and editors. Friedrich Engels saw Marx's unfinished *Capital* through but ignored many of the master's early manuscripts, published only in the 1930s, when they sparkled with relevance they could not have had in Engels's time. Students of Aristotle, G. W. F. Hegel, Ferdinand de Saussure, George Herbert Mead, Ludwig Wittgenstein, and many others have immortalized the otherwise unwritten teachings of their masters with contestable degrees of fidelity. (Those who lectured in the presence of tape recorders, such as Harvey Sacks and Saul Kripke, perhaps leave more reliable renditions.) Samuel Johnson had Boswell, and Johann Wolfgang von Goethe had Eckermann. Ken stocked a large collection of books on and by Isaiah Berlin, a man known for both his sparkling conversation and his lack of writing *Sitzfleisch*, whose intellectual afterlife is being preserved by the devoted editorial labor of Henry Hardy.

Posthumous editors can find themselves in a moral pickle. Franz Kafka asked his friend Max Brod to burn his manuscripts; Brod edited and published them instead. Like the rapper Tupac Shakur, Kafka was much more prolific after death. Ernest Hemingway, Ralph Ellison, and David Foster Wallace, among others, had novels published after their deaths thanks to editorial magic and toil. The Genevan linguist Ferdinand de Saussure, who suffered from a decades-long writer's block, was immortalized in the *Cours de linguistique générale*, a text produced by his students Charles Bally and Albert Sechehaye, neither of whom was present at any of the original three lecture series the volume is based on. This means that the poststructuralist fans of Saussure who celebrated the "death of the author" were inspired by a text not written by an author they celebrated.

Cases like these spark puzzlement, and occasional controversy, because they reveal an uncomfortable fact that life's normal illusion of an endless supply of tomorrows can obscure—that works are always collaborations and incomplete. (Is David Foster Wallace's sprawling *Infinite Jest*, published during his lifetime, a more complete book than his posthumous *Pale King*?) Editing anyone's work, one's own or someone else's, requires great care, sometimes to the point of tedium; despite the best intentions, works always turn out to be something other than what you intended.

With enough attention lavished on it, any piece of paper can be legion with meaning. Bohumil Hrabal, the great Czech novelist, jokingly drew his philosophy of life from a slip he got from a dry cleaner: "Some stains can be removed only by the destruction of the material itself." Søren Kierkegaard's doodlings have been the subject of philosophical analysis.[12] If revelations lurk in the oddments of papers, should we keep everything? Thankfully, authors toss most of what they write. (The editors of the chaotic papers of Charles Sanders Peirce are following the philosopher's principles in deciding how to treat the thorniest archival problems, such as what to toss.) In Foucault's famous words, "the author is the principle of thrift in the proliferation of meaning."[13]

Perhaps awareness of the heir's responsibility in making or breaking posthumous fame added to the burden. Sociological studies of artistic renown have shown that several ingredients are necessary to prevent a body of work from sinking into oblivion. The heirs must take charge of the corpus and protect it, since posthumous value turns on the work's finite quantity. Because the dispersal of an estate is generally bad for a legacy, a critical mass of the work must be kept together, and this labor is often done by widows or other heirs. (Aha, you note! Finally a female presence after several pages dominated by male worthies! There may well be something to the feminist suspicion that writing and preserving a legacy of documents constitute a kind of reproduction envy.)[14] The legacy must have a stable toehold in a cultural institution such as a museum or library. Critical or scholarly writing about the work aids its spread through networks of reputation and appreciation. Sociologists of art have no sentimentality about inherent quality; they believe that a work's survival depends on how well the networks are built and put in place.[15]

In questions of legacy the pressure of minute choices is great. Those critics who complained that social constructionism was a lazy or licentious philosophy had no idea! The notion that reality is constructed should make us fear and tremble, not kick back and watch the world pass by. Emerson was right: "If any one imagine that this law is lax, let him keep its commandment one day."[16]

The living produce traces freely and easily, but the dead do so only with great effort. The words of the dead belong to a different order of being. They suddenly become rare and precious. Ken would give me drafts of his essays marked with self-deprecating comments like "for the birdcage," but when I consult his papers in the Special Collections room at the University of Iowa library, I can't even remove an item to make a photocopy. I must work with a pencil and a laptop lest ink besmear holy papers that once he would have recycled. Editing the living is one thing; editing the dead is quite another.

Hannah Arendt, who was probably, with Isaiah Berlin, the author Ken read (and read about) most avidly, benefited from editorial coworkers after she arrived in the United States in 1941 as a stateless refugee from Europe. Her collaborators ranged from magazine and book editors to friends, all of whom helped straighten out her quirky English by placing the adverbs in the right places, supplying the proper prepositions, and putting idioms back into their ironclad forms. Mary McCarthy—her close friend, pool partner, and literary executor—in particular took part in "a collaboration and an exchange" with Arendt on several major writings.

Things changed after Arendt's sudden death from a heart attack in

1975. In editing Arendt's last and unfinished book, *The Life of the Mind*, McCarthy felt at times as if she were "a sort of mind-reader or medium. With eyes closed, I am talking to a quite lively ghost. She has haunted me, given pause to my pencil, caused erasures and re-erasures." Here McCarthy calls up the language of spiritualism, the nineteenth-century movement that sought to communicate with the spirits of the dead. "I am aware that she is dead but I am simultaneously aware of her as a distinct presence in this room, listening to my words as I write, possibly assenting with her musing nod, possibly stifling a yawn." McCarthy's description captures my experience precisely. Ken has no doubt also often yawned during my work. It was something he would do. He'd let you know if he was bored.

McCarthy found herself in a bind, puzzled after death by a process that had been so fluid in life. Collaboratively editing a deceased author turned out to be very different from implicitly coauthoring with a living one. Where McCarthy once would have not hesitated to take "trigger" out of the living Arendt's draft and replace it with "set in motion," she now worried about imposing her own quirky style preferences.[17] In the obituary economics of modern historicism, documents undergo a sea change after the author dies. They become finite, rare, and fixed—a *corpus*, to use the chillingly precise word. Death severs the delicate balance of oral and literate production and guarantees the value and ontology of the opus. So do institutions like archives. The author can no longer recant or revise earlier work. There is a fierce taboo on posthumous tampering, as if reverence for the corpse spilled into legal-editorial policies. Upon death, words suddenly change from gaseous and fluid states to one that is too too solid.

Edits that would have been done in person with a raise of Ken's eyebrow or a smirk burned up lots of second-guessing on my part. Of the complex range of emotional tints in facts, he wrote: "To hear some day that the Chicago Cubs have won a World Series (a claim with a Prester John-like ring to it) would be a fact not neutral and flat but one reigning joy down on the long suffering." Here Ken lifts a curtain on his Chicago soul, celebrating the hapless delight in infinite deferral entailed by being a Cubs fan before they finally won the World Series in 2016. Should I leave "reigning," a contribution to the language, since a World Series victory would in fact enable a reign of joy, or change it (as I did in the end) to the sound-alike "raining," which is what he surely meant? The living Ken would have approved the change without a second thought, but the dead impose different obligations than the living.

Ken was among other things a scholar of the history of style, with an

acute lived sense for form and music, and this also made it difficult to retain some closeness to his voice. He once told me he might have majored
in music if he'd been able to sing. On those rare occasions when he had
to indicate a melody, he would do so with a stylish Sinatraesque growl;
in light of singers like Tom Waits, I'm not sure we might not have missed
out on one of the better croakers of our era. Ken's preferred music was
light and uplifting, and he was a fan of Josquin des Prez, Aretha Franklin,
and Burt Bacharach among others. Style was almost an ethical matter
for him. I once forwarded him an essay by an author I thought he'd like,
and he replied, demurring, "it doesn't sing for me."

And Ken loved to chop prose. In chapter 3 of *Democratic Eloquence*,
his first book, which was about the struggles over political style in the
nineteenth-century United States, he shows in detail how Lincoln "cut
the flab" from a draft of his first inaugural address written by William
Seward. Seward wrote "We are not, we must not be, aliens or enemies,
but fellow-countrymen and brethren." Lincoln changed it to "We are not
enemies, but friends. We must not be enemies."[18] The quest of the ages—
expressed in sublime minimalism!

Inevitably I made several cuts, most of them routine removal of repetition. Some made me think twice. Regarding early MTV, Ken wrote that
one of the dominant ingredients of its images was "good looking women
for men to look at." I chopped out the "for men." His was a critical but
compassionate take on the slovenly male gaze, but I wanted to honor
the common cultural studies finding that MTV was actively scrambling
who was looking at whom. Here was another case of gender pruning:
describing a new level of graphicness in pornographic magazines Ken
wrote that "men's penises" started to be shown. I dropped the "men's,"
thinking it superfluous (though one never knows).[19]

Of mid-1990s efforts to police decency on the internet he wrote: "Unfortunately, these filters also blocked sites with information about birth
control, abortion, and even sites devoted to preaching abstinence." It
was not clear what judgment he was making about this politically in-
compatible mess of issues, so I changed *unfortunately* to *yet*. His essay
"Drowning in Pictures" formed the backbone of chapters 4 and 5 and
ended with this line: "American media, with all their vulgarity and crassness, was loved by millions." Saying "media are" is a professional shibbo-
leth in media studies, in part to remind us that each medium has its own
grammar, so I changed it to "American media, with all their vulgarity
and crassness, were loved by millions," leaving both the passive voice
and Ken's sense for the ways people vote with their feet on popular taste.

Each edit I made is of course disputable in a way it never would have

been could Ken and I have talked it out; the written record is cruel in fixing thoughts in their larval and pupal stages, indeed as one can see by
consulting on the University of Iowa website the raw materials he left
behind. (On the other hand, libraries are full of dynamically evolving
matter.) Explaining my choices here only makes them look less legitimate, as always happens when you try to justify yourself. Now that you
see the options, *unfortunately* actually looks like a good Ken term, span-
ning but also reconciling very different political positions on three hot-
button issues about sex and public life.

I wondered at times if I should use the more liberal natural sciences
model of authorship. You can get your name on a scientific publication
by being the department chair, running the lab, writing the grant, directing the fieldwork, or servicing the computer. Coauthors on science articles can belly up to the bar like would-be heirs at a rich man's
funeral in a nineteenth-century novel. The comic cosmologist George
Gamow placed the name of physicist Hans Bethe (pronounced beta) on
a groundbreaking article so the authorship would read Alpher, Bethe,
Gamow even though Bethe hadn't written it. (The joke messed up credit
ever after.) My father, a medical researcher who always worked in teams,
had a more stringent than average rule for determining authorship:
anyone listed should be able to explain the whole article, though he admitted that the exotic biostatistics or the technicalities behind the as-
says of atmospheric chemistry sometimes escaped him. I doubt I can
live up to the standard of explaining everything here—at several points
I am playing at "kittlybenders," as Thoreau called it—seeing how far I
can walk on thin ice. I can explain what Ken meant, but I'm not sure I
always agree or grasp the implications. Disagreeing with someone who
can't answer back is a completely unfair contest. At its most uncomfortable spots, I feared that the book states what I don't believe in a way Ken
wouldn't have said it.

I learned valuable lessons from Ken's style. Some once fashionable
scholars have lampooned the historian's supposed dream of narrating
the past "as it really was"—a dream few practicing historians ever pro-
fess—but trying to write in Ken's mode taught me tricks of pleasant eva-
siveness. Historiography for Ken was not only the fixation of detail, it
was also the sketching of atmosphere. Ken liked the art of vagueness.
He avoided overspecification. He starts a paragraph in chapter 6, "Some
years ago ... Clifford Geertz wrote an essay called 'Blurred Genres.'" Such
a relaxed and casual statement! Ken doesn't provide the date (1979, if
you're asking), and he lets "some" be elastic enough to stretch back in
time. I was briefly tempted to do the math and specify the time differ-

ence, but that would doom the statement to almost instant expiration. His "some years" was elegant in its refusal to tie things down.

I also learned the quiet joy of the past tense. The general stylistic advice I give to students is to use past tense for events and present tense for texts. Thus Shakespeare *wrote Hamlet*, but Hamlet *wonders* whether to be or not to be. Here the present tense marks the text's eternal present. But there is an intermediate zone that can't quite be sorted into either events or texts. Intellectual historians can use the past tense to explain what someone thought, as implied quotation marks, and Ken was a master of this.[20] The past tense points not necessarily to what really happened, but to a curiously counterfactual world of suppositions and assumptions. "For Bazin, the camera partook of the same being as its object." Here the past tense is a kind of subjunctive or indirect discourse, and indeed in English grammar the past tense and the subjunctive are often next-door neighbors ("If I were a rich man . . ."). The past is actually less pinned down than the present; it is a storehouse of possibility, not the realm of fixity. The historian's art consists in pulling ever new things out the past. You can even talk about the present in the past tense, giving it a sense of culmination or story: "In the 2016 US presidential election, few candidates except Bernie Sanders had genuine popular appeal." (By the time you read this sentence, of course, it really is past tense.)

The Problem of Lag

What is interpretive fidelity? I had difficulty deciding what faithfulness to Ken's vision meant. A biblical scholar once quipped, "Translations are so much more enjoyable than originals, because they contain many things that the originals leave out."[21] Without a doubt "all that is solid melts into air" is a huge improvement on Karl Marx's original "alles Ständische und Stehende verdampft." We might naively ask, If Homer were alive today, how would he compose the *Iliad*? Or if Mozart had the resources of the modern symphony orchestra, what would he sound like? But if Homer were alive today he wouldn't be Homer, and if Mozart worried about accuracy to the past instead of making the best sound possible he wouldn't be Mozart. Fidelity implies metamorphosis and adaptation. The gap between past and present is productive; fidelity depends on this gap. Absolute fidelity to the past would be nothing but the thing itself, and we'd find ourselves erased by the time machine.

I grappled with the untranslatability of the historical context in which Ken imagined this book. The recent past, as Benjamin liked to say, is often more inaccessible than the distant past. Many of Ken's claims about the information age no longer hold up. In the changing world of academic fashion, 1999 and 2004 are already generations ago, and in the computer universe they are positively antediluvian. Much has changed since Ken wrote about drowning in pictures or the helter-skelter of the internet. Every word has an ecological tie to its historical moment, and every word has a relation, however slight, to every other word. The presence of iPhones, Donald Trump, CTE, the Zika virus, and Syrian refugees exerted some remote pressure, however slight, on every sentence written in 2016. The same words written by Cervantes in the seventeenth century and by a French poet in the twentieth century, to use Jorge Luis Borges's famous example, do not mean the same thing.[22] Words that Ken wrote in 2002 might still be bubbly had they had been bottled and published in 2004. We forgive dead authors for not knowing what they could not have known and often treasure them precisely for speaking to us so freshly. Dead artists or authors cannot be hip to what's happening now, and for this we thank them passionately.

But if what Ken wrote in 2002 was published straight today (rather than as, say, a document of what he was thinking in 2002), it would be flat as day-old root beer. He wrote of "our moment" and the lessons "we" had learned from the bursting of the dot.com bubble in 2000. He liked using the new millennium as a narrative crux. He began one of his drafts, "This is the age of information. The internet, World Wide Web, databases circling the globe. Information saturates us. Yet this is also the age of the image. MTV, the Nike swoosh, iconic sports heroes, the collapse of literature." The words *this* and *us* stand like bare ruined choirs. Obsolescence sometimes comes on fast; we call this wind and weather history. "Information age" sounds stale and was probably already well past its sell-by date when Ken was using it. He treated Yahoo! as an amazing search engine—a fact that reliably gets laughs when I repeat it today—and was fascinated with Yahoo! news, an early aggregation service that allowed you to jump from newspaper to newspaper around the globe. Nobody would use Yahoo!, MTV, or the World Wide Web as the chief examples of images and information today; we might talk about ISIS videos, NSA surveillance, trolls, corporate data mining, or bitcoin—much of which will be irrelevant tomorrow.

Aging in people and in books comes on without being announced. Some people turn gray and wrinkled before their time, others hold their youth late into life. It's profoundly unfair! The same is true for scholarly topics. Neighborhoods are slowly abandoned, the action moves to other parts of town. (As Ken once quipped, "Nothing ever dies out in twentieth-century intellectual life—it just gets its own journal.")[23] The

world no longer comes into focus so clearly. What was once so urgent becomes historical. Your jokes get moldy, and the cultural references you
know resonate with fewer and fewer people. My very funny jokes about
Saddam Hussein and the election of 2000 are now museum pieces.

Metanonfiction: Editing the Book

I obviously also gave up on being a scrupulous editor of this book. I could
hardly remember all the edits I had done on his original documents
since I started working on them in 2006 or 2007, trying to fill in some of
the more obvious blanks. The more I worked the more tangled it got. At
this point I don't know exactly which words I've added and which were
his, and a philologically precise comparison of Ken's words and mine
would be laborious and interest no one. My wife, Marsha Paulsen Peters,
once suggested that every word Ken wrote be put in a different font or
italicized, kind of like the way museums reconstruct classical sculptures
using plaster of a different color for the parts added later. But Ken's jottings on this book were not on the order of classical sculpture, nor was
my method one of source-critical historicism. At some point in early
2016 I finally faced the prospect of completely abandoning the book. The
thought that I could drop it liberated me to finish it. Consider this book's
existence a tribute to the unwillingness to abandon sunk costs.

Fortunately our time is richly stocked with books about the impossibility of writing books, so there were many models of "going meta,"
as my late friend and editor Doug Mitchell encouraged.[24] And there is
much reflection about the place of the book in the digital era. Indeed,
much of recent American literature is an extended generic experiment
with whatever things books might be in a digital world.[25] I enjoyed Geoff
Dyer's *Out of Sheer Rage* (1997), for instance, a confessional memoir about
the book he can't write about D. H. Lawrence. It's written in the piled-on,
self-undermining, interminably ironic and repetitious sentences Lawrence favored. Dyer manages to go on for pages about not being able to
write. Particularly entertaining are Dyer's interminably comic delibera-
tions about whether to take the bulky *Complete Poems of D. H. Lawrence*
on a trip to a Greek island, because it's always the book you don't have
that you need, while you never need the book you bring along, the way
carrying an umbrella fends off rain.

Weirdly enough, you actually learn a lot about Lawrence from Dyer.
He finds Lawrence's secondary writings, memorabilia, photos, and jot-
tings more interesting than the novels, which he never bothers to read.
Given the choice between a photograph and a six-hundred-page novel,

who wouldn't go with the photo? I may have spent more time pondering Ken's receipts for cheeseburgers than rereading his books and essays. Are our collective brains wilting under the digital sun, losing the cardio to run book-length distances, as the clichés would tell us? This was, of course, the question Ken sought to answer (and it's pretty clear that distraction, as Augustine and Montaigne would remind us, has always been part of what it means to be a curious animal).

Another book about an impossible book is my colleague Judith Pascoe's *The Sarah Siddons Audio Files*, a brilliant investigation of a quixotic quest: to discover what Siddons, the most acclaimed British actress of the Romantic era, whose voice regularly sent audiences into fits of hysterical emotion, actually sounded like. Pascoe shows that a rich archive of acoustic clues remains for the ingenious investigator, even long before sound recording existed. She embraces the impossibility of her quest, using techniques from metafiction without slighting the scholarship, and creates a delightful and funny treatment of her subject.

But neither of these models quite fits the Ken book. Dyer never gets around to writing the book about Lawrence, but here I did try to complete the history Ken started. Pascoe is a master of her subject, in complete command of the scholarship about Siddons and British Romantic theater. I'm not an expert on the history of visual culture or information management. Pascoe tried to hear a distant sound that had left no records, but I was trying to give life to a voice that had not yet spoken on many topics. The Ken book turned the old task of hermeneutics upside down. Instead of reading a text in conditions of historical and cultural displacement, I had to write, not read, the alien text. Call me Pierre Menard.

Dialectic of Reverence

There was at least one model of memorializing I never considered: that of Alfred, Lord Tennyson, whose *In Memoriam A. H. H.* (1849) was the Victorian era's most characteristic poem. Dazed by the sudden death at age twenty-two of his best friend Arthur Henry Hallam, a fellow poet and Cambridge apostle who was engaged to marry his sister, Tennyson spent sixteen years writing the long poem as an exercise in grief and mourning. It resonated far and wide across the culture of the time, and even Queen Victoria found comfort in it after her beloved Prince Albert died in 1861 (she mourned him by setting out his shaving kit daily till her death four decades later). Eventually Tennyson pulled out of the abyss and went on to lead an official life as poet laureate—those Victorians had unparalleled stamina for grieving. I could not sustain such depth of feeling. I mourn my poverty in mourning, though I love Tennyson's poem and have read it several times. Such histrionics just would not be fitting for Ken. He had little patience for romantic melancholia or sustained lugubriousness. Reverential awe for the loss of a platonic soul mate was not the right register. Ken would think Tennyson was, to borrow Emerson's line, "spinning his thread too fine."[26]

Indeed, the temptation to be reverential about Ken's words and jottings was tempered by the memory of how ruthless he could be in any cleanup operation. He would toss almost everything. One Saturday morning, having been informed by the managers of a journal I was guest-editing that they had severely overestimated the page budget for the special issue and we had to somehow go from 250 pages to 150, Ken sat down with me at the computer and hacked away at his brilliant sixty-page essay as decisively and mercilessly as he would clean up an office or bedroom.[27] He certainly never treated his own writing as a treasure. You didn't want to ask him to help you tidy up. Once when they were moving Ken innocently threw away a sweater belonging to a friend of a friend who had showed up to help pack and load. He saw it lying around (maybe it was a warm day) and tossed it in the last-minute commotion of liquidating random objects.

Ken seemed completely unburdened by a sentimental attachment to old papers or objects, perhaps unusually for a historian. The earth was full enough. He didn't clutch at what he had. Despite his love of buying books, he would have been happy to strip this book, and much else, to a resonant, Zen-like zero. Why then was I so haunted by his clingy leavings? The things he threw away stuck to me like burs. The irony did not escape me that I was feeling angst about the papers of a man who had never succeeded in keeping his papers in order but always attended to more urgent people and things.

The Spiritualist Option

One often-tried way to augment writings is to invite the author to compose them from the beyond. Posthumous coauthoring "mediums" have abounded since the late nineteenth century. Through living intermediaries, such authors as Shakespeare, Benjamin Franklin, Oscar Wilde, Leo Tolstoy, Percy Shelley, and Henry and William James have all been prolific dictators from the other side. Secretaries often stepped forward to take dictation from authors they had worked for, whose productivity was hampered by the inconvenience of being dead. Mediumship was one path for women left behind to leverage their position as authors.[28]

In a recursive twist, psychical researchers and spiritualists who had been eager to communicate with the dead when they were alive turned out to be especially talkative once they too reached the other side. W. T. Stead, for instance, a British journalist, reformer, and spiritualist who died on the *Titanic*, continued to dictate to the same secretaries (including his daughter) who had recorded his words in life. Richard Hodgson, William James's friend and fellow psychical researcher, regularly spoke through Leonora Piper, a medium James had observed (or enabled) for almost twenty-five years. Hodgson would sometimes plead, through Mrs. Piper, for his posthumous authenticity, saying, "I am not rubbish!" James was never fully persuaded that it was really Hodgson's spirit poking through, and even if it was, James found the communications mixed with interference, Piper's dramatic flair being the ample main ingredient.

Spiritualists rarely succeeded in finding a clear channel to the dead. Even though they helped create the ideal of communication as mind-to-mind contact, their practical results were always noisy and fragmentary. Frederic W. H. Myers, another psychical researcher, a friend of James who coined the term *telepathy*, dictated an entire book called *The Road to Immortality* (1932) three decades after he "died" in 1901. He posthumously told Geraldine Cummins, the Irish secretary-author to whom he dictated the book: "The medium is not a medium, she is an *interpreter*."[29] This admirable statement of two core principles of media theory—that media are always both biased and gendered—could be carved into granite, but it is well established in psychical research that the dead are lousy communicators. They sink to the level of their mortal mouthpieces. They sound like aphasia patients finding their way back to language, sometimes repeating a word or string of words, often defying the rules of syntax. The dead may speak, but they do not speak like the living. The often unstated corollary is that living minds are much more interesting than their revenants.

This is certainly true of William James's own posthumous performances. His spirit too could not remain silent from the beyond. Alas, however much his themes are still in play, he sounds at best like a thoughtful uncle dispensing timeless advice rather than a slightly tortured genius trying to figure out a pluralistic universe. If we go by what Jane Roberts, an American poet and psychic, produced on tuning into the James channel (the TV metaphor comes from "Seth," her intermediary with the spiritual world), James suffered a severe decline after death. His invention, zip, and wild genius are all gone. His work as a writer and thinker depended precisely on his ability to dance around the questions no mortal can know; by speaking from the other side, James's most urgent questions are ipso facto already answered before he says anything. The riddle of the soul's survival of bodily death is solved by the very fact of his speaking: What room does that leave for sallies into the possible?

And what would an author be without a body? Spirits without bodies, taught the latter-day prophet Joseph Smith, are in bondage, thus reversing the standard view in Western thought that the body is the prison of the soul.[30] Judging from the results of spiritualism, the spirits of the dead are boring, at least when they speak to us: they have no looming crisis to solve, no cycle of bodily needs to attend to, no headlines to read or deadlines to heed, no decisions to make, no people to welcome or ignore, no horizon of dying. Finitude concentrates the mind. A postmortal spirit would be deprived of the many powers that come from mortal embodiment, including the looming inevitability of death: How could we communicate with a being suffering from such framelessness? Nothing sharpens the style like the prospect of dying.

Ken, of course, did not rule out anything, even postmortal contact. In the introduction to this book he wrote, "'There are more things in heaven and earth, Horatio, than are dreamt of in your philosophy.' Hamlet's famous advice, remember, came on the heels of seeing a ghost." And William James was one of his heroes. In Ken's or James's spirit, I cannot rule out ripples in the fabric of space-time or declare it impossible that Ken's shade could visit me and dictate the book. If he did show up to visit, I'm sure he'd tell me to drop the whole thing. If. If he were here, I wouldn't have to finish the job because he would. He's not here and has thereby forfeited his right to direct. So I lurched ahead.

The spiritualist option was as closed a door for me as it was for Mary McCarthy. The dream of communicating with the dead in some kind of face-to-face or mind-to-mind encounter was both an intellectual and a religious nonstarter. The dead, it seems, sign a nondisclosure agreement on passing over.[31] For a certain kind of religious believer, spiritualism is a hunt in the wrong place for a sign that is already there. For a materialist, it is folly to think the dead would behave like the living or that they would behave at all. For a media theorist, it is silly to fall for dreams of immediacy. I agree with Florian Sprenger: "Theories of immediacy are instructions on how to be powerless."[32] (And efforts at spiritualist communion always teach us just how deep the layers of mediation go.) A pincer movement of several converging armies to which I belong squashes the spiritualist ambition of meeting minds in the same way that both the Judeo-Christian and the Greco-Roman traditions warn us off from looking for faces or animal shapes in the clouds.

The materialist or rationalist objection to spiritualist contact is obvious, but the religious one is equally well grounded. The parable of Lazarus and the rich man in Luke 16 founds one tradition of thinking about communication with the dead in the Western world. In life, the rich man lives sumptuously, and the poor beggar Lazarus lies at his gate, looking longingly from afar at the delicacies the rich man eats while dogs lick the beggar's sores. Both die, and in the next life the tables are turned. The rich man, roasting in hell, begs Father Abraham to let Lazarus reach across the chasm and touch his tongue with just a single drop of water— in the next world distant desire has gotten even more elemental, shifting from a feast to a drop of water. When Father Abraham denies his request, the rich man asks for Lazarus to return from the dead to warn his five brothers to repent so they won't suffer the same fate. Abraham again says no. Let them listen to Moses and the prophets: if they won't listen to them, neither would they receive one back from from the dead. They've already had a message from the dead; they didn't just recognize it.

Father Abraham claims the equivalence of a scriptural text and someone returning from the grave. Moses and the prophets, of course, are two of the three key parts of the Hebrew Bible. A revenant from the other side might be a sign and a wonder, but no more wondrous than the sunrise, and we all know how quickly such marvels get folded into the day's norms and averages. The living live in a world of the living, and even a revenant must conform to this hermetically sealed world. It's not that the dead cannot return, as if there were some law against fraternizing. It's that a dead person among the living wouldn't be dead anymore but would suffer an instant decrescendo into mundanity and become just one more person in our midst, like the other New Testament Lazarus sloughing off his mummy wrap. Sifting through Ken's remnants and recalling our many conversations was by Father Abraham's standards not that different from talking to him. Both involved efforts to understand someone who couldn't talk back. But in another way, making sense of the dead Ken was infinitely more laborious. Our digital technologies may often be designed to confuse presence and text, but there is something radically different about the two modes. Presence matters because it can take place only among the living. Talking to Ken was light and fun; working on the book was often heavy and burdensome. I doubt the parable's equivalence of text and presence, just as I doubt the efforts of platforms like Facebook to pretend that what they offer is sociability. A live mind takes a different shape than text does. Death is the line of demarcation between copresent and mediated communication.

Ken was always a compelling physical presence. He had an animated physique, thin hair that had a will of its own and often looked as if it was channeling a slight excess of voltage, and an expressive face capable of great zaniness in telling stories. A talented baseball player in his youth, he was always light on his feet whatever his weight and full of restless energy. He could lounge on the floor with one ankle on the other knee, making himself into a triangular pretzel, a position he claimed to find comfortable. (I believe his daughters may have inherited this contortionist gift.) He walked with a high-speed, slightly bowlegged shuffle, looking restlessly from side to side, sometimes going comically bug-eyed when he spotted or thought of something amusing. He ate with gusto, and sometimes when talking to him on the phone you could hear him chomping away while typing on his computer, with sounds of the television and the kids in the background. You can't tell me the world is not greatly diminished without his presence. I don't believe a discarnate Ken would be quite him, so in writing this book I have not resorted to such exotic means of conjuring his spirit.

The (Dreaded) Casaubon Option

Nineteenth-century novels were helpful guides in understanding the psychic toll of inheritance, none more so than George Eliot's great *Middlemarch*, a book Ken loved, even if he hadn't read all of it. In a rash, almost life-wrecking burst of idealism, Dorothea, the novel's heroine, marries a much older man, the decrepit scholar Edward Casaubon. She has the delusion that assisting him on what she imagines is his great research project would give her life a transcendent purpose. Dorothea soon realizes her husband's work is absolutely hopeless. She foresees being trapped by the duty to complete his manuscript and fears consignment to "a virtual tomb, where there was the apparatus of a ghastly labor producing what would never see the light."

Casaubon, you see, was trying to write *A Key to All Mythologies* without having the slightest clue about the new science of comparative philology that had arisen in Germany, consigning his project, based on an uncritical mishmash of biblical and classical sources, to irrelevance. At one point the book's narrator, who delightfully combines both an omniscient point of view and a judgmental, even gossipy attitude about the book's characters, wickedly observes him retreating to his study "to chew a cud of erudite mistake." Casaubon's lack of empirical rigor made him "as free from interruption as a plan for threading the stars together"—a comment that could apply to many other forms of research! If Casaubon died, Dorothea feared, he would leave behind "mixed heaps of material" for her to sift. She "pictured to herself the days, and months, and years which she must spend in sorting what might be called shattered mummies." As she sums it up, "There was a deep difference between that devotion to the living, and that indefinite promise of devotion to the dead."[33]

Dorothea dodged guardianship of the accumulated scraps of a lifetime of misdirected learning. We never do learn exactly what happened to Casaubon's papers after he died, but we do know Dorothea did not spend her life as Casaubon's faithful editor like Henry Hardy to Isaiah Berlin. Ken, of course, was no Casaubon; no one could diagnose a learned fool as swiftly as he could, probably in the effort not to become one himself, and memory suggests he may have compared a not-to-be-disclosed colleague or two to Casaubon at some point. (Ken was wonderfully inventive in the art of low-grade insults: *chowder head, chub boy, slime bucket.* This was part of his interest in sizing up character.)

As a brilliant technician of the novel genre, George Eliot well understood the critical role scraps of paper could play as turning points of plot. (Misplaced or ill-sent letters have served as narrative turning points from Euripides and Shakespeare to Thomas Hardy and Ian McEwan.) In *Middlemarch* she repeatedly shows the small turns of fate brought on by pieces of paper. A servant refuses to obey the deathbed command of a rich man to burn one of his two wills, though she knows doing so might benefit her. (Here is another case of the folly of asking someone else to burn documents.) The man quickly dies, and all the money ends up going to a frog-faced stranger, a son nobody had noticed before except for some observant servants, exercising the epistemological privilege of the dominated. Had she burned the document as ordered, many lives would have been different—and not necessarily better.

Eliot again: "As the stone which has been kicked by generations of clowns may come by curious little links of effect under the eyes of a scholar, through whose labours it may at last fix the date of invasions and unlock religions, so a bit of ink and paper which has long been an innocent wrapping or stop-gap may at last be laid open under the one pair of eyes which have knowledge enough to turn it into the opening of a catastrophe."[34] Anything recorded has the potential to tilt the world. DNA from a humanoid thigh bone can suddenly revolutionize past epochs. Historians know the richness of the slightest fragment. Oh, for a stool sample from a Roman emperor or a ceramic pot smeared with remnants of an Aztec peasant's meal! What was I supposed to do with Ken's effects, harboring so many potential treasures?

Ken certainly left behind a lot of innocent wrappings and stop-gaps, but I have yet to find the telltale piece of evidence that establishes the missing link. There is no happy summary, no synecdoche of his project. His books sprawl in my house as in a Victorian museum *before* the specimens have been ordered into rows in the glass display cases. I've searched the pages of his abandoned book collection for the key to knowledge, but all I've found are small summaries that are as digestible, metabolized, and gone as the cheeseburger he ate on June 6, 1997.

Mind and Brain

A brain is a physical organ, but mind takes many shapes, sizes, and forms. You can find mind in the feedback loops of an ecosystem, in rows of cornstalks, or in the sounds of music. New York City, says a friend of mine, is mind exteriorized. Ken's books and papers were remnants of his mind, dripping a "nectarous humor," as John Milton in *Paradise Lost* said of celestial spirits. Such a precarious stewardship I had! His finished mortality weighed against my own unfinished version of the same. Books are designed for mortals, but they are also too much for mortals. Their value is weighed by all the other books we choose not to read. (Opportunity cost is literature's secret logic.) A character in a recent novel remarks, "Maybe that's the reason we fill the world with books. So many lost lives. And yet books are so inadequate. If they weren't, why would we write so many?"[35] And yet the shortness of life, though limiting what you can read or whom you can know, also guarantees meaningfulness. How hard it might be to fill our days with meaning if we knew they would last forever and we'd pay no price for squandering them.

It's hard to say where the pressure has come from while I was writing this book. I'd done everything within my resources to soothe the spirits of the dead, being baptized on Ken's behalf, with Anne's permission, in the Nauvoo Temple of the Church of Jesus Christ of Latter-day Saints, a sacred building they had toured during its open house in the summer of 2002. I did the ritual available to me for offering service to the dead, and it was satisfying. Joseph Smith, who designed that temple and a religious system that allows the living to vicariously reach out the dead, anticipated a messianic kind of book that would inscribe—not only inscribe, but bind forever—the entire human family. He offered a vision of a nonhaunted book as an antidote to the gothic curse of documents out of control that weighed on his contemporaries such as Hawthorne, Marx, Melville, and Tocqueville. And the ceremonies he left behind were supposed to be one-and-done, easy to put behind you, a sealing that neutralizes the historical record's zombie-like refusal to stay in place. His vision of the redemption of the dead through paperwork sought to relieve their grip on the living.[36] Paperwork has always been "a battle against entropy."[37] In the Nauvoo Temple the past is truly subjunctive.

But stilling the dead is a difficult art, because you want them to rest in peace without killing them a second time. I had to find a way to still the chattering of the paper around me and let the grave lie undisturbed. Sometimes, buried amid the project, a bright idea would pop into my head about the perfect person to give me advice. But then, as if emerging from a dream, I'd remember that that person's absence is the reason I have the question in the first place. (Our dreams make a moral claim against the injustice of the universe.) Writing this book raised problems Ken knew well—an excess of interests, ambitions, and projects dreamed or promised, an eagerness to serve, a shortage of time, several linear feet of interesting paper, and an aging library I could never hope to fully digest. It's one local version of promiscuous knowledge.

I'm still not sure why Ken's books chose me as their host. Saint Paul taught that guilt leads to grace, but as much religious experience makes clear, the converse is just as true. The gift was an obligation. In their dumb, unread physical bulk, his books defied any effort at Buddhist detachment. In its very form and mode of presentation, Ken wanted *Promiscuous Knowledge* to synthesize copious amounts of information into crystallized essences. He wanted it to be a light book, a quick sketch, digestible in a single read, a series of illuminations, not a weighty work of scholarship. According to a long paragraph quoted in the preface, he wanted "each project [to have] fewer and fewer facts, until, like the well-known cat, all that's left is the grin." He had both an overly sardonic take on his own achievements and a Zen-like notion of a book that would vanish into nothingness. The best way to leave nothing but the grin would be to not write the book!

Mourning can be perversely arbitrary. The traumatic suddenness of his death surely had something to do with it. His dying was an extraordinary rendition, a phase transition from a light to a heavy state. The cruelty of a tumor in such a rare brain! How can a human boil down to this thing, a brain? How could one organ contain a universe? Though Kurt Gödel might seem rather mad for locating mathematical intuition in the pineal gland, he raised a larger question we might not otherwise face: How can intelligence sit in any biological organ at all? Is it any crazier to locate the soul in a pineal gland than in a brain?[38]

After spending most of two days at the hospital in early February 2006, in doleful sociability with a crowd of Ken's family and friends coming and going, all of us engaged in a fruitless but determined vigil, I went with a compassionate friend to see Ken's body for the last time on the morning of the day he was officially declared dead, Saturday February 4, 2006. I couldn't stay in the room long. I bid him farewell, my eyes darting toward and away from the grayish presence, wired and kept alive for potential organ donation. His face seemed flattened. He looked like an archetype, a sphinx, not like Ken. He looked dead. I got out of the room quickly.

The gothic presence of his books in my house has been a constant background hum since that day. They were a gain that marked a loss. I have to face the brutal fact: Ken's books too were bodies whose brains were dead. Completing this book was an effort to achieve a resurrection that only a god could perform. It is assuredly not the book Ken would have written, but it is something: I wanted to make sure more was left than the grin.

Acknowledgments

Ken Cmiel had a great talent for friendship, and though I liked to consider him my best friend, I had the sense that many people felt that way. Some of these people, David Depew, Tom Lutz, Mark Sidel, and Peter Simonson, aided materially and morally in my finishing this book. Without the labors of Alexis Bushnell, who served as Ken's research assistant at the University of Iowa Center for Human Rights and organized his papers and computer files after his death, none of this would have been possible. Daniel Peters assisted materially in sorting, transporting, and shelving Ken's library. Marsha Paulsen Peters supported the hours I spent and offered sage advice, especially on the many occasions when I felt like abandoning the project, as did Benjamin Peters.

Douglas C. Mitchell at the University of Chicago Press knew just how to shepherd my manuscripts, and the two reviewers he invited, Peter Simonson and Fred Turner, shaped this book in both magnitude and miniature. My thanks to all three, two of them good friends of Ken's, and also to Kyle Adam Wagner at the Press. On the occasion of Doug's retirement, I presented this book to him for his *Festschrift*—though every book he has ever edited belongs in that most massive virtual volume! Doug edited all four of my books, and his passing makes this book doubly a work of mourning. The book both mourns and celebrates two great Chicagoans.

Other readers who offered helpful advice on drafts include Benjamin Peters on chapter 1 and throughout, Nick Yablon on chapter 2, and Chad Vollrath on chapters 1 through 4. Doctoral students in my fall 2014 seminar offered many useful suggestions, especially about chapter 4. For help and advice on specific points I thank Mark Andrejevic, Dudley Andrew, Marisa Bass, Mark Carnes, Lilie Chouliaraki, Noam Elcott, Sorin Gog,

Margarida Medeiros, David Paul Nord, Judith Pascoe, Jennifer Raab, Chitra Ramalingam, Ignacio Redondo, Stefan Schöberlein, Janne Seppänen, Greg Siegel, Johanna Sumiala, Christina Vagt, Sarah Wasserman, and Chang-Min Yu. David McCartney of the University of Iowa Special Collections Library has actively supported this project and the archiving of Ken's papers, and Mark F. Anderson helped prepare an archive of his original documents. Kembrew McLeod offered key tips on overall shape, as did Benjamin Peters. Alice Bennett offered superb copyediting. Colleagues at the Digital Cultures Research Lab at Leuphana University of Lüneburg, Germany, gave helpful suggestions at a crucial moment in January 2016. So did Frank Kelleter and Alexander Starre during my stay at the John F. Kennedy Institute for North American Studies at the Freie Universität Berlin in summer 2016. Frank read a complete draft and made more crucial and essential suggestions than I can count; he has made a mighty difference in how the book turned out. Amanda Lagerkvist provided a wonderful eleventh-hour appreciation of the whole text. If only I could have followed up on all the leads offered by these friends.

I gratefully acknowledge the Frederick W. Hilles Publication Fund at Yale for supporting the publication of this book.

Many research assistants helped on this project. Scotti Myhre served as an Iowa Center for Research by Undergraduates (ICRU) research assistant in 2008–9 during her senior year at the University of Iowa. She made sure the sentences made sense and could find absolutely any fact in this digital world of promiscuous knowledge. Samantha Cooper, as an ICRU fellow in 2011–12, helped fill in many holes. After the book had lain fallow for more than two years, I took up the work again in 2013–14 in the hospitable conditions of the Helsinki Collegium for Advanced Studies, with research assistance from Jani Ahtiainen. Finally, as an ICRU fellow in 2016–17, Morgan Jones made smart structural observations and offered detailed pointers as well; her eagle-eyed editing has saved me from many errors, and she did so once more in the summer and fall of 2018 when she stepped in again with her sharp editorial gifts. She will have a great career in publishing.

Gina Giotta served as a research assistant at a key moment of the book's development, thanks to support from Jay Semel, former associate vice president for research at the University of Iowa. Gina's singular gift at finding historical gems and presenting them in lovely turns of phrase has greatly improved the text and supplied it with a thick flow of fact. Specifically, she wrote three sidebars in chapter 2 and drafted parts on Baedeker's Greece, daguerreotypy and photography, *Reader's Di-*

gest, movie palaces, Robert Frank, MTV, *Blow-Up*, Peter Duesberg, and the Toronto museum controversy. And then, again at the last minute, she stepped in to help with images before passing the baton to Morgan Jones. In tracking down the images and permission to use them, Gina and Morgan turned up a great many fascinating facts about just how weirdly images and their proprietors behave. It could have made another sidebar! Antic collectors, dusty attics, absurdist laws, and greedy estates—but some stories best remain untold.

Anne Duggan has been very supportive of this book from the beginning, and I dedicate it to the best legacy of Kenneth Cmiel: Willa, Cordelia, and Noah Cmiel.

Notes

Preface

1. See Kenneth Cmiel, "The Swirl of Image and Sound: On the Latest Version of Antirealism," in *The Arts of Democracy: Art, Public Culture, and the State*, ed. Casey Nelson Blake (Philadelphia: University of Pennsylvania Press, 2007), 233–52.

2. Vladimir Nabokov, *Pale Fire* (1962; repr., New York: Vintage, 1989), 29.

3. Kenneth Cmiel, "Drowning in Pictures," in *The Columbia History of Post–World War II America*, ed. Mark C. Carnes (New York: Columbia University Press, 2007), 36–54.

4. François Ewald's work on the welfare state was important for him.

5. Frank Kelleter, in a stellar critique of the manuscript, found chapter 5's "dominant tone" to be that of "cheap jeremiad," and Fred Turner said chapters 5 and 6 both went off the rails in missing the story of the rise of computation. I have sympathies with both criticisms, but to answer them fully would be to write a different book.

6. See, for instance, "The Swirl of Image and Sound" or Kenneth Cmiel, "The Politics of Civility," in *The Sixties: From Memory to History*, ed. David Farber (Chapel Hill: University of North Carolina Press, 1994), 263–90.

7. For Ken in rare apocalyptic high dudgeon, see his "The Fate of the Nation and the Withering of the State," *American Literary History* 8 (Spring 1996): 184–202, at 200.

Introduction

1. Lila Guterman, "Learning to Swim in the Rising Tide of Scientific Data," *Chronicle of Higher Education*, June 29, 2001, https://www.chronicle.com/article /Learning-to-Swim-in-the-Rising/11827. A more recent installment concerns students rather than scholars: Alison J. Head and John Wihbey, "At Sea in a Deluge of Data," *Chronicle of Higher Education*, July 7, 2014.

2. David Shenk, *Data Smog: Surviving the Information Glut* (New York: Harper-Collins, 1997).

3. Bruno Latour, *Pandora's Hope: Essays on the Reality of Science Studies* (Cambridge, MA: Harvard University Press, 1999), 39.

4. See the discussion thread at info.org.il/english/books_on_the_floor.html, accessed April 21, 2016.

5. Louis Bertrand Castel, the Jesuit philosopher, quoted in Peter Dear, *Discipline and Experience* (Chicago: University of Chicago Press, 1995), 18.

6. E. L. Youmans, *The Culture Demanded by Modern Life* (New York: Appleton, 1867), 27.

7. John Dewey, *Freedom and Culture* (New York: G. P. Putnam's Sons, 1939), 46–47.

8. Regarding another nineteenth-century author: "A single photograph of Dickens is sufficient to accommodate thirty years and ten thousand pages of work." Geoff Dyer, *Out of Sheer Rage: Wrestling with D. H. Lawrence* (New York: Picador, 1997), 36.

9. Julia Glum, "Millennials Selfies: Young Adults Will Take More Than 25,000 Pictures of Themselves during Their Lifetimes: Report," *International Business Times*, September 22, 2015, http://www.ibtimes.com/millennials-selfies-young -adults-will-take-more-25000-pictures-themselves-during-2108417.

10. The rarely spotted writer Thomas Pynchon is the exception that proves the rule.

11. See, for instance, Camille Paglia and Neil Postman, "She Wants Her TV! He Wants His Book!" *Harper's*, March 1991, 44–59, and Mitchell Stephens, *The Rise of the Image, the Fall of the Word* (New York: Oxford University Press, 1998), a book that correctly predicted YouTube.

12. Language lifted from Kenneth Cmiel, "Seeing and Believing," *Culturefront* (Summer 1999): 88–90 (review of Steven Conn, *Museums and American Intellectual Life, 1876–1926* [Chicago: University of Chicago Press, 1998]).

13. Mark Mueller, "Full text of President Obama's speech at Rutgers commencement," nj.com. Last modified May 15, 2016. http://www.nj.com/news/index.ssf /2016/05/full_text_of_president_obamas_speech_at_rutgers_co.html.

14. See also Kenneth Cmiel, "After Objectivity: What Comes Next in History?" *American Literary History* 2, no. 1 (1990): 170–81.

15. In addition to works cited throughout, see Lorraine Daston, "The Glass Flowers," in *Things That Talk: Object Lessons from Art and Science* (New York: Zone, 2004), 223–54; Daston, "Cloud Physiognomy," *Representations* 135 (Summer 2016): 45–71, and Lorraine Daston and Peter Galison, *Objectivity* (New York: Zone, 2007).

Chapter One

1. Friedrich Nietzsche, *The Will to Power*, trans. Walter Kaufmann and R. J. Hollingdale (New York: Vintage Books, 1967), 301.

2. Howard Caygill, ed., *A Kant Dictionary* (Oxford: Blackwell, 1995), s.v. "fact."

3. The Cubs did, in fact, win the World Series in 2016, ten years after Ken Cmiel died.

4. See Kenneth Cmiel, *Democratic Eloquence: The Fight over Popular Speech in Nineteenth-Century America* (New York: Morrow, 1990).

5. The critique of social constructionism here and the comments in this para-

graph on the nature of "facts" owe much to Ian Hacking's *The Social Construction of What?* (Cambridge, MA: Harvard University Press, 1999). For specific comments on what Hacking calls "elevator words" (and we here call "pointer words"), see 21–24.

6. Paul Feyerabend, *Against Method*, 3rd ed., (London: Verso, 1993), 11, 22.

7. For Feyerabend's picture of Galileo, see *Against Method*, passim; but for a more ambiguous picture of Galileo, see Umberto Eco, *Kant and the Platypus* (New York: Harcourt, Brace, 1997), 359–60.

8. Fredric Jameson, *Signatures of the Visible* (London: Routledge, 1990), 1. The whole sentence reads: "The visible is *essentially* pornographic, which is to say that it has its end in rapt, mindless fascination; thinking about its attributes becomes an adjunct to that, if it is unwilling to betray its object." Jameson associates "pornography" with the obsessive and not necessarily with the sexual. Note, too, that he sees images as somehow pulling us away from critical thought.

9. Alberto Manguel gets it much better than Jameson in his beautiful *Reading Pictures* (New York: Knopf, 2000). Images, for Manguel, can be stories, absences, riddles, nightmares, violence, philosophy, and more.

10. Jean-Luc Godard, *Son + Image, 1974–1991* (New York: Museum of Modern Art, 1992), 171.

11. Lorraine Daston, "Marvelous Facts and Miraculous Evidence in Early Modern Europe," *Critical Inquiry* 18 (Fall 1991): 93.

12. John Durham Peters, "Information: Notes toward a Critical History," *Journal of Communication Inquiry* 12, no. 2 (1988): 9–23.

13. Richard Panek, *Seeing and Believing: How the Telescope Opened Our Eyes and Minds to the Heavens* (New York: Viking, 1998), 55.

14. Guy DeBrock, "Aristotle Wittgenstein, *Alias* Isaac Newton between Fact and Substance," in *Newton's Scientific and Philosophical Legacy*, ed. P. B. Scheurer and Guy DeBrock (Dordrecht: Kluwer, 1988), 355–77.

15. Lorraine Daston, "The Cold Light of Facts and the Facts of Cold Light: Luminescence and the Transformation of the Scientific Fact, 1600–1750," in *Signs of Early Modern France II: 17th Century and Beyond*, ed. David Rubin (Charlottesville, NC: Rockwood Press 1997): 17–44, at 21.

16. Raymond Chandler, *The Big Sleep* (New York: Vintage Books, 1992), 169.

17. Barbara Shapiro, *A Culture of Fact: England, 1550–1720* (Ithaca, NY: Cornell University Press, 2000).

18. Morris S. Arnold, "Law and Fact in the Medieval Jury Trial: Out of Sight, Out of Mind," *American Journal of Legal History* 18 (1974): 267–80; Jerome G. Lee, "The Law-Fact Distinction: From Trial by Ordeal to Trial by Jury," *AIPLA Quarterly Journal* 12 (1984): 288–94.

19. Thomas Hobbes, "Of the Severall Subjects of Knowledge," in *Leviathan* (1651). See also Steven Shapin and Simon Schaffer, *Leviathan and the Air-Pump: Hobbes, Boyle, and the Experimental Life* (Princeton, NJ: Princeton University Press, 1985), 101.

20. On the distinction between facts and evidence, see Daston, "Marvelous Facts," 93; on the general meaning of fact as something done, see Shapiro, *Culture of Fact*, 9–11.

21. Catherine Gallagher, "Matters of Fact," *Yale Journal of Law and the Humanities* 14 (Summer 2002): 441–47.

22. Peter Dear, *Discipline and Experience: The Mathematical Way in the Scientific Revolution* (Chicago: University of Chicago Press, 1995), at 125.

23. See Debra Hawhee, *Rhetoric in Tooth and Claw: Animals, Language, Sensation* (Chicago: University of Chicago Press, 2017), chap. 6, for a helpful discussion of the trope of *accumulatio* in the Renaissance.

24. Ann M. Blair, *Too Much to Know* (New Haven, CT: Yale University Press, 2010), 6.

25. Bernhard Siegert, *Passage des Digitalen: Zeichenpraktiken der neuzeitlichen Wissenschaften, 1500–1900* (Berlin: Brinkmann und Bose, 2003), 65–120.

26. Steven Shapin, *The Scientific Revolution* (Chicago: University of Chicago Press, 1996), 2.

27. Edward S. Golub, *The Limits of Medicine: How Science Shapes Our Hope for the Cure* (Chicago: University of Chicago Press, 1997), 50–51.

28. Lorraine Daston and Katharine Park, *Wonders and the Order of Nature, 1150–1750* (New York: Zone Books, 1998), chap. 6.

29. Catherine Wilson, *The Invisible World: Early Modern Philosophy and the Invention of the Microscope* (Princeton, NJ: Princeton University Press, 1995), 180; Hans Blumenberg, *Die Lesbarkeit der Welt* (Frankfurt: Suhrkamp, 1981), 68.

30. Siegert, *Passage des Digitalen*, 124 ff.

31. Robert Hooke, "Preface," in *Micrographia, or Some Physiological Descriptions of Minute Bodies Made by Magnifying Glasses with Observations and Inquiries Thereupon* (1665; repr., New York: Dover, 1961), d4.

32. Bacon, *Novum Organum*; quoted in Daston, "Marvelous Facts," 111.

33. Daston, "Marvelous Facts," 124.

34. Lorraine Daston, "The Moral Economy of Science," *Osiris* 10 (1995): 3–24, at 16.

35. Thomas Sprat, *The History of the Royal Society of London for the Improving of Natural Knowledge* (London: J. Martyn, 1667), 469. Original spelling retained.

36. Shapin, *Scientific Revolution*, 150.

37. Daston and Park, *Wonders and the Order of Nature*, 297.

38. Hubert Damisch, *Théorie du nuage: Pour une histoire de la peinture* (Paris: Seuil, 1972), 51–52 for Leonardo quotation, 180 for Erasmus.

39. Horst Bredekamp and Claudia Wedepohl, *Warburg, Cassirer, und Einstein im Gespräch: Kepler als Schlüssel der Moderne* (Berlin: Wagenbach, 2015).

40. See the classic source, David C. Lindberg, *Theories of Vision from al-Kindi to Kepler* (Chicago: University of Chicago Press, 1976), esp. 178–208.

41. Laura J. Snyder, *Eye of the Beholder: Johannes Vermeer, Antoni van Leeuwenhoek, and the Reinvention of Seeing* (New York: Norton, 2015), 140.

42. Lindberg, *Theories of Vision*, 202.

43. René Descartes, *La dioptrique* (1637) 1, https://fr.wikisource.org/wiki/La _Dioptrique.

44. Snyder, *Eye of the Beholder*, 140–42 and passim.

45. Friedrich Kittler, *Grammophon Film Typewriter* (Berlin: Brinkmann und Bose, 1986), 117.

46. Hooke, "Preface," in *Micrographia*.

47. Joseph Vogl, "Becoming-Media: Galileo's Telescope," *Grey Room* 29 (Fall 2007): 15–25.

48. Svetlana Alpers, *The Art of Describing: Dutch Art in the Seventeenth Century* (Chicago: University of Chicago Press, 1983), 18–22, 33–35, and passim.

49. Godfrey Vesey, "Foreword: A History of 'Ideas,'" in *Idealism Past and Present*, ed. Godfrey Vesey (Cambridge: Cambridge University Press, 1982), 1–18.

50. Emanuele Coccia, *Sensible Life: A Micro-ontology of the Image*, trans. Scott Alan Stuart (New York: Fordham University Press, 2016).

51. Adrian Johns, *The Nature of the Book: Print and Knowledge in the Making* (Chicago: University of Chicago Press, 1998), 20–25 and passim.

52. Dear, *Discipline and Experience*, 162. The critic was the Jesuit astronomer Clavius.

53. Snyder, *Eye of the Beholder*, 121–22.

54. Hooke, "Preface," in *Micrographia*, a3, a4.

55. Johns, *Nature of the Book*, 430–31.

56. Hooke, *Micrographia*, 3.

57. Golub, *Limits of Medicine*, 52. For Leeuwenhoek's letters, see https://www .dbnl.org/tekst/leeu027alle00_01/.

58. Wilson, *Invisible World*, 132.

59. Snyder, *Eye of the Beholder*, 247, 277 ff., 313–14, and passim.

60. For a detailed and rather vinegary review see Philip Steadman, review of *Eye of the Beholder: Johannes Vermeer, Antoni van Leeuwenhoek, and the Reinvention of Seeing*, by Laura J. Synder. Amazon.com, March 19, 2015. https://www.amazon.com /gp/customer-reviews/R22326DX82NKS5/ref=cm_cr_getr_d_rvw_ttl?ie=UTF8& ASIN=B00L3KQ30M.

61. Alpers, *Art of Describing*.

62. G. W. F. Hegel, *Vorlesungen über die Ästhetik*, section III, 3, c, www.textlog.de /5792.html.

63. Joseph Leo Koerner, *The Reformation of the Image* (Chicago: University of Chicago Press, 2004); on iconoclasm as a gesture, see Bruno Latour, *Pandora's Hope* (Cambridge, MA: Harvard University Press, 1999), chap. 9.

64. Francis Bacon, *Novum Organum* (1620), book 2:xxxix.

65. Friedrich Kittler, *Optical Media*, trans. Anthony Enns (Cambridge: Polity Press, 2010).

66. Bacon, *Novum Organum*, 1:x, quoted in Wilson, *Invisible World*, 41.

67. "L'imagination se lassera plutôt de concevoir que la nature de fournir." Blaise Pascal, *Pensées de Pascal*, ed. Ernst Havet (Paris: Dezobry et E. Magdeleine, 1852), 2.

68. Daston, "Moral Economy," 16.

69. Shapin and Schaffer, *Leviathan and the Air-Pump*, 25.

70. Hans Blumenberg, *The Genesis of the Copernican World*, trans. Robert M. Wallace (Cambridge, MA: MIT Press, 1987), 617.

71. Steven Shapin, *A Social History of Truth: Civility and Science in Seventeenth-Century England* (Chicago: University of Chicago Press, 1994).

72. Peter Lipton, "The Epistemology of Testimony," *History and Philosophy of Science* 29, no. 1 (1998): 1–31.

73. Johns, *Nature of the Book*, 468.

74. For a nuancing of the "gentlemanly thesis," see Shapiro, *Culture of Fact*, 139–43.

75. This was the argument of C. S. Peirce as well as of Robert K. Merton.

76. Shapin and Schaffer, *Leviathan and the Air-Pump*, 60–65.

77. The creation of "epistemic credit" among printers is crucial for Johns, *Nature of the Book*.

78. Miguel de Cervantes, *Don Quijote de la Mancha* (Madrid: Real Academia Española, 2004), 3–5.

79. Shapin and Schaffer, *Leviathan and the Air-Pump*, 66.

80. Benedict de Spinoza, *On the Improvement of the Understanding; The Ethics; Correspondence* (New York: Dover, 1955), 23, 25.

81. Gottfried Wilhelm von Leibniz, "A Vindication of God's Justice Reconciled with His Other Perfections and All His Actions," in *"Monadology" and Other Philosophical Essays*, trans. Paul Schrecker and Anne Martin Schrecker (Indianapolis: Bobbs-Merrill, 1965), sections 57, 143.

82. Shapin, *Scientific Revolution*, 109–10.

83. Steven Nadler, *Spinoza: A Life* (Cambridge: Cambridge University Press, 1999), 226.

84. Snyder, *Eye of the Beholder*, 288–89.

85. Frances A. Yates, *The Art of Memory* (1966; repr., London: Pimlico, 1994), 365–73.

86. Siegert, *Passage des Digitalen*, 156 ff.

87. By spirits as diverse as Carl Hempel and Bertolt Brecht.

88. Daston, "Moral Economy," 16.

89. Lorraine Daston, "Cloud Physiognomy," *Representations* 135 (Summer 2016): 45–71, at 48.

90. Denis Diderot, "Encyclopédie," in *Encyclopédie, ou Dictionnaire raisonné des sciences, des arts et des métiers*, 5:640A; https://artflsrv03.uchicago.edu/philologic4/encyclopedie1117/navigate/5/2355/.

91. *Enlightenment: Discovering the World in the Eighteenth Century*, ed. Kim Sloan with Andrew Burnett (London: British Museum, 2003).

Chapter Two

1. Susan Strasser, *Waste and Want: A Social History of Trash* (New York: Holt, 1999), 20 and passim.

2. On signatures see Josh Lauer, "Traces of the Real: Autographomania and the Cult of the Signers in Nineteenth-Century America," *Text and Performance Quarterly* 27, no. 2 (2007): 143–63.

3. Natalie Zemon Davis, "Printing and the People," in *Society and Culture in Early Modern France* (Stanford, CA: Stanford University Press, 1975), 189–226.

4. Alexis de Tocqueville, "Of Individualism in Democratic Countries," in *Democracy in America*, vol. 2, trans. Henry Reeve (New York: Knopf, 1965).

5. James Beniger, *The Control Revolution: Technological and Economic Origins of the Information Society* (Cambridge, MA: Harvard University Press, 1986); Richard

Brown, *Knowledge Is Power: The Diffusion of Information in Early America* (New York: Oxford University Press, 1991); Alfred Chandler and James Cortada, eds., *A Nation Transformed by Information* (New York: Oxford University Press, 2000); Richard John, *Spreading the News: The American Postal System from Franklin to Morse* (Cambridge, MA: Harvard University Press, 1998); Daniel Headrick, *When Information Came of Age: Technologies of Knowledge in the Age of Reason and Revolution* (New York: Oxford University Press, 2000).

6. Allan R. Pred, *Urban Growth and the Circulation of Information: The United States System of Cities, 1790–1840* (Cambridge, MA: Harvard University Press, 1973), 80, 162, 21; Paul C. Gutjahr, *An American Bible: A History of the Good Book in the United States, 1777–1880* (Stanford, CA: Stanford University Press, 1999), 187–88.

7. Walt Whitman, *Democratic Vistas, and Other Papers* (London: Walter Scott, 1888), 58.

8. Charles Dickens, *Hard Times* (London: Bradbury and Evans, 1854), chap. 2.

9. Neil Harris, *Humbug: The Life and Art of P. T. Barnum* (New York: Little, Brown, 1973), 74.

10. Ibid.

11. Steven Conn, *Museums and American Intellectual Life, 1876–1926* (Chicago: University of Chicago Press, 1998), 8.

12. *New York Tribune*, 1861, in research folders of Kenneth Cmiel, no longer recoverable.

13. Harris, *Humbug*, 64.

14. Henry James, *A Small Boy and Others* (London: Macmillan, 1913), 171, 163, 171. See Kristin Boudreau, "The Greatest Philosophy on Earth: William James's Lowell Lectures and the Idiom of Showmanship," *William James Studies* 2 (2007), http://williamjamesstudies.org/the-greatest-philosophy-on-earth-william-jamess-lowell-lectures-and-the-idiom-of-showmanship/. Boudreau nicely emphasizes the similarities in boosterish rhetoric, but there is also a clear play with fraud and credulity in both.

15. Bingham's textbooks on grammar and speech had circulations estimated at over 100,000 in the first half of the nineteenth century. See Kenneth Cmiel, *Democratic Eloquence* (New York: Morrow, 1990), 45–46, 75–76.

16. Horace Greeley, "The Relations of Learning to Labor: A Commencement Address" (1844), in *Hints towards Reforms in Lectures, Addresses, and Other Writings* (New York: Harper and Brothers, 1850), 113.

17. Horace Greeley, *Art and Industry as Represented in the Exhibition at the Crystal Palace* (New York: Redfield, 1853), 80–81.

18. See Stefanie Markovits, *The Victorian Verse-Novel: Aspiring to Life* (New York: Oxford University Press, 2017).

19. Edward Mendelson, "Baedeker's Universe," *Yale Review* 74 (April 1985): 386–403.

20. Karl Baedeker, *Baedeker's Greece* (Leipzig: Karl Baedeker, 1894), 104.

21. Quoted in Mendelson, "Baedeker's Universe," 187–88.

22. Greeley, *Art and Industry*, 90; John C. Burnham, *How Superstition Won and Science Lost: Popularizing Science and Health in the United States* (New Brunswick, NJ: Rutgers University Press, 1987); Daniel Goldstein, "'Yours for Science': The Smith-

sonian Institution's Correspondents and the Shape of Scientific Community in Nineteenth-Century America," *Isis* 85, no. 4 (1994): 573–99.

23. E. L. Youmans, *The Culture Demanded by Modern Life* (New York: Appleton, 1867), 11.

24. Emerson, "Nature," in *Selected Writings of Emerson*, ed. Donald McQuade (New York: Modern Library, 1981), 16, 19, 41.

25. Entry of December 16, 1837, in *The Selected Journals of Henry David Thoreau*, ed. Carl Bode (New York: New American Library, 1980), 24.

26. William Whewell, *Philosophy of the Inductive Sciences*, 2nd ed. (London: John W. Parker, 1847), xi.

27. Charles Darwin, *The Autobiography of Charles Darwin, 1809–1822: With Original Omissions Restored*, ed. Nora Barlow (London: Collins, 1958), 139.

28. Ian Hacking, "Biopower and the Avalanche of Printed Numbers," *Humanities and Society* 5 (1982): 279–95.

29. Ian Hacking, *The Taming of Chance* (Cambridge: Cambridge University Press, 1990), chaps. 8 and 9.

30. William James, *Pragmatism*, lecture 1, https://www.gutenberg.org/files/5116/5116-h/5116-h.htm.

31. Lady Elizabeth Eastlake, "Photography," *London Quarterly Review* 101 (April 1857): 442–68.

32. Sir John Robison, "Notes on Daguerre's Photography," *Edinburgh New Philosophical Journal* 27 (1839): 169–71.

33. E. A. Poe, "The Daguerreotype" (1840), in *Classic Essays on Photography*, ed. Alan Trachtenberg (New Haven, CT: Leete's Island Books, 1980), 37–38.

34. Kodak's advertisements, and the toothy grins that filled them, are also responsible for a notable shift in public perceptions of photography. See Christina Kotchemidova, "Why We Say 'Cheese': Producing the Smile in Snapshot Photography," *Critical Studies in Media Communication* 22 (March 2005): 2–25.

35. See Sean Ross Meehan, "Emerson's Photographic Thinking," *Arizona Quarterly* 62 (Summer 2006): 27–58.

36. Oliver Wendell Holmes, "The Stereoscope and the Stereograph," *Atlantic Monthly* 3 (June 1859): 738–48, at 739, 744, 745.

37. See *Mathew Brady and His World: Produced by Time-Life Books from the Meserve Collection* (Boston: Little, Brown, 1977), 44.

38. Holmes, "Stereoscope," 748.

39. Kenneth Cmiel, "Seeing War at a Distance: Photography from Antietam to Abu Ghraib," University of Iowa Presidential Lecture, February 2005.

40. Friedrich Kittler, "Like a Drunken Town Musician," trans. Jocelyn Holland, *MLN* 118 (April 2003): 637–52.

41. Rebecca Solnit, *Motion Studies: Time, Space, and Eadweard Muybridge* (London: Bloomsbury, 2003), 77–83, 179–98. I thank Chitra Ramalingam for detailed help on Muybridge and for this image in particular.

42. Jimena Canales, *Tenth of a Second: A History* (Chicago: University of Chicago Press, 2010), chap. 5.

43. Daston and Galison, *Objectivity*, 77.

44. Eastlake, "Photography," 442.

45. T. S. Arthur, "American Characteristics: No. V.—The Daguerreotypist," *Godey's Lady's Book* 38 (May 1849): 352–55.

46. Holmes, "Stereoscope," 747–48.

47. Reese V. Jenkins, "Technology and the Market: George Eastman and the Origins of Mass Amateur Photography," *Technology and Culture* 16 (January 1975): 1–19. One who did worry was William Wordsworth in his 1849 sonnet, "Illustrated Books and Newspapers."

48. Robert E. Mensel, "'Kodakers Lying in Wait': Amateur Photography and the Right of Privacy in New York, 1885–1915," *American Quarterly* 43 (March 1991): 24–45.

49. Samuel D. Warren and Louis D. Brandeis, "The Right to Privacy," *Harvard Law Review* 4 (1890): 193–220, at 195.

50. Leo Tolstoy, *War and Peace*, trans. Rosemary Edmonds (London: Penguin, 1978), 1429. For an ironic comment, see Mitchell Stephens, *The Rise of the Image, the Fall of the Word* (New York: Oxford University Press, 1998), 35.

51. John Herschel, *A Preliminary Discourse on the Study of Natural Philosophy* (1830), quoted in Carol Armstrong, *Scenes in a Library: Reading the Photograph in the Book, 1843–1875* (Cambridge, MA: MIT Press, 1998), 120.

52. Edward Livingston Youmans, *The Culture Demanded by Modern Life* (New York: Appleton, 1897), 27.

53. Ibid.

54. Harris, *Humbug*, and James W. Cook, *The Arts of Deception: Playing with Fraud in the Age of Barnum* (Cambridge, MA: Harvard University Press, 2001).

55. Thomas Hill, *Geometry and Faith: A Fragmentary Supplement to the Ninth Bridgewater Treatise*, revised and enlarged edition (New York: Putnam's, 1874), 50.

56. James A. Garfield, "The American Census," *Journal of Social Science* 2 (1870): 32, 34.

57. Adrian Johns, *Piracy: The Intellectual Property Wars from Gutenberg to Gates* (Chicago: University of Chicago Press, 2009), 291–94.

58. E. L. Youmans, "Purpose and Plan of Our Enterprise," *Popular Science Monthly* 1 (May 1872): 113–15; "Loose and Accurate Knowledge," *Popular Science Monthly* 1 (June 1872): 238–39. These two articles are also the source in the following two paragraphs of text.

59. Youmans, *Culture Demanded by Modern Life*, 47.

60. [Melvil Dewey], *A Classification and Subject Index for Cataloguing and Arranging the Books and Pamphlets of a Library* (Amherst, MA, 1876); Melvil Dewey, "Arrangement on the Shelves," *Library Journal* 4 (March/May 1879): 117–20, 191–94.

61. Janice Radway, *A Feeling for Books: The Book-of-the-Month Club, Literary Taste, and Middle-Class Desire* (Chapel Hill: University of North Carolina Press, 1999), 135–37.

62. Dewey, *Classification and Subject Index*, 4.

63. Whitman, *Democratic Vistas* (1871).

64. Robert B. Downs, "The Growth of Research Collections," *Library Trends* 25 (July 1976): 55.

65. Quotation from Bloomsbury Academic intern handbook; thanks to Morgan L. Jones.

66. "Accommodations for the Library," speech Delivered by the Hon. D. W. Voorhees of Indiana in the Senate of the United States, March 31, 1879, *Congressional Record* 10 (1879): 3001–4, at 3001.

67. Nick Yablon, *Remembrance of Things Present: The Invention of the Time Capsule* (Chicago: University of Chicago Press, 2019).

68. Robert Wiebe, *The Search for Order* (New York: Hill and Wang, 1967), 40, and Kenneth Cmiel, "Destiny and Amnesia: The Vision of Modernity in Robert Wiebe's *The Search for Order*," *Reviews in American History* 21 (June 1993): 352–68.

69. For more on Godkin, see Kenneth Cmiel, "Whitman the Democrat," in *A Historical Guide to Walt Whitman*, ed. David S. Reynolds (New York: Oxford University Press, 2000), 205–33.

70. Charles Eliot Norton, "A Definition of the Fine Arts," *Forum* 7 (March 1889): 30–40, at 35, 36, 39.

71. Walter Kendrick, *The Secret Museum: Pornography in Modern Culture* (New York: Viking, 1987), 136.

72. Anthony Comstock, *Morals versus Art* (New York: J. S. Ogilvie, 1888), 11, 9.

73. Lester Frank Ward, *Dynamic Sociology* (New York: Appleton, 1883), 1:96, 2. See also the book's chapter 14 on education, which Ward first drafted in 1873.

74. "A Word about Museums," *Nation* (July 1865): 113–14.

75. Conn, *Museums and American Intellectual Life*. See also Miles Orvell, *The Real Thing* (Chapel Hill: University of North Carolina Press, 1990). Some of the language in this and the following two paragraphs is lifted from Kenneth Cmiel, "Seeing and Believing," *Culturefront*, Summer 1999, 88–90.

76. Frederic A. Lucas, *The Story of Museum Groups*, Leaflet Series no. 53 (New York: American Museum of Natural History, 1921), 5.

Chapter Three

1. Georg Simmel, *The Philosophy of Money*, trans. Tom Bottomore and David Frisby (London: Routledge and Kegan Paul, 1978), 448–52.

2. The federal government started collecting a national employment rate by monthly samples in 1940. See Alexander Keyssar, "Appendix B. About the Numbers: Unemployment Statistics before the Great Depression," in *Out of Work: The First Century of Unemployment in Massachusetts* (Cambridge: Cambridge University Press, 1986), 342.

3. Lewis Mumford, *Technics and Civilization* (New York: Harcourt Brace, 1934), 316. This idea is anticipated by Freud's notion of a stimulus shield.

4. "The Public Interest in Science," *Modern Medicine* 2 (1920): 710.

5. Burnham, *How Superstition Won and Science Lost*, 62.

6. Root cited in Wilfred Rumble Jr., *American Legal Realism: Skepticism, Reform, and the Judicial Process* (Ithaca, NY: Cornell University Press, 1968), 156.

7. Herbert Brucker, *The Changing American Newspaper* (New York: Columbia University Press, 1937), 11–12; for background on the rise of interpretive journalism, see Michael Schudson, *Discovering the News: A Social History of American Newspapers* (New York: Basic Books, 1978), 144–51.

8. John Drewry, "A Picture-Language Magazine," *Magazine World* 1 (November 1945): 19.

9. *The 1930 American Scrapbook* (New York: Forum Press, 1930), foreword.

10. Daniel Boorstin, *The Image* (1961; repr., New York: Atheneum, 1972), 135; Samuel Schreiner, *The Condensed World of the* Reader's Digest (New York: Stein and Day, 1977), 49; John Bainbridge in 1946, quoted in Schreiner, *Condensed World*, 56.

11. Jackson Lears, *Fables of Abundance: A Cultural History of Advertising in America* (New York: Basic Books, 1994), 203–18; Roland Marchand, *Advertising the American Dream: Making Way for Modernity, 1920–1940* (Berkeley: University of California Press, 1985), 115.

12. Willa Sibert Cather, "The Novel Démeublé," *New Republic* 30 (April 22, 1922): 5–6. Thanks to Alexander Starre for this reference.

13. "The Contributors' Club," *Atlantic Monthly*, July 1922, 133.

14. Merle Colby, "Presenting America to All Americans," *Publishers Weekly*, May 3, 1941, 1830.

15. Ted Striphas, *The Late Age of Print: Every Book Culture from Consumerism to Control* (New York: Columbia University Press, 2009), 26–31.

16. Neil Harris, "Iconography and Intellectual History: The Halftone Effect," in *Cultural Excursions: Marketing Appetites and Cultural Tastes in Modern America* (Chicago: University of Chicago Press, 1990), 304–17.

17. Frank Gilbreth, *Motion Study* (1911), 99–100, quoted in Sharon Corwin, "Picturing Efficiency: Precision, Scientific Management, and the Effacement of Labor," *Representations*, no. 84 (Autumn 2003): 141.

18. Archer Wilde, *Sounds and Signs: A Criticism of the Alphabet* (London: Constable, 1914), 9.

19. Jan Tschichold, *The New Typography*, trans. Ruari McLean (1928; repr., Berkeley: University of California Press, 1995), 66.

20. L. C. Everard, "Museums and Exhibitions," in *Encyclopedia of the Social Sciences*, vol. 11, ed. E. R. A. Seligman (New York: Macmillan, 1933), 138–42, at 139.

21. Richard F. Bach quoted in "Beauty, Utility, and Museums," *Journal of Home Economics* 20 (March 1928): 182–83.

22. John Cotton Dana, "How Museums Came to Be So Deadly Dull," *Library Journal*, May 15, 1921, 45–46; Forest H. Cooke, "Culture and Fatigue: Some Reflections on Museums," *Century Magazine* 3 (January 1926): 291–96; Dana, "The Functions of a Museum," *Library Journal*, June 15, 1921, 538–40; Dana, "First Steps toward Museum Founding," *Library Journal*, September 1, 1921, 697–99; Dana, "The Literature of Museum Management," *Library Journal*, October 15, 1921, 839–42; Louise Connolly, "The Museum Idea at Pinnacle," *Library Journal*, January 22, 1922, 23–24; Dana, "Pictures in Place of Objects," *Library Journal*, September 1, 1922, 705–8.

23. Mumford, *Technics and Civilization*, 447.

24. D. Graham Burnett, *The Sounding of the Whale: Cetaceans and Science in the Twentieth Century* (Chicago: University of Chicago Press, 2012), 305.

25. Donna Haraway, *Primate Visions: Gender, Race, and Nature in the World of Modern Science* (New York: Routledge, 1989), 223 ff. See also Marshall McLuhan, *Understanding Media: The Extensions of Man* (New York: McGraw-Hill, 1964).

26. Franz Boas, "The Occurrence of Similar Inventions in Areas Widely Apart," *Science* 9 (May 1887): 485–86.

27. Franz Boas, "Reply to Powell," *Science* 9 (May 1887): 614; Boas, *The Shaping of American Anthropology, 1883–1911: A Franz Boas Reader* (New York: Basic Books, 1974), 61–67.

28. Ernst Gellner, *Language and Solitude: Wittgenstein, Malinowski and the Hapsburg Dilemma* (Cambridge: Cambridge University Press, 1998).

29. By the late twentieth century, the AMNH was estimated to display only 1 to 2 percent of its total holdings. Douglas J. Preston, *Dinosaurs in the Attic: An Excursion into the American Museum of Natural History* (New York: St. Martin's Press, 1986), xi.

30. "A Selective Art Museum," *Nation* 82 (May 24, 1906): 422–23.

31. See Ira Jacknis, "Franz Boas and Exhibits: On the Limitations of the Museum Method in Anthropology," in *Objects and Others: Essays on Museums and Museum Culture*, ed. George W. Stocking (Madison: University of Wisconsin Press, 1985), 75–111.

32. Frederic A. Lucas, *The Story of Museum Groups*, Leaflet Series no. 53 (New York: American Museum of Natural History, 1921).

33. Preston, *Dinosaurs in the Attic*, chap. 7.

34. The diorama was presented by J. Watson Webb and A. C. Gilbert, the background was painted by Francis Lee Jaques, and the bears were mounted by Ralph C. Morrill. Thanks to Michael Anderson and Erin Gredell for help with this image.

35. John Rowley, *Taxidermy and Museum Exhibition* (New York: Appleton, 1925), 313.

36. Rowley, *Taxidermy and Museum Exhibition*, 300, 313.

37. "Museum Changes in Tune with Age: Natural History Institution Stresses the Study of Living Things in Environments," *New York Times*, December 18, 1951, 24.

38. Alfred H. Barr Jr., quoted in Brian Wallis, "A Forum, Not a Temple: Notes on the Return of Iconography to the Museum," *American Literary History* 9 (Fall 1997): 617–18; Margaret Mead, "Museums in the Emergency," *Natural History* 9 (1941): 67. On communication as a counter to propaganda in the 1940s, see Kenneth Cmiel, "On Cynicism, Evil, and the Discovery of Communication in the 1940s," *Journal of Communication* 46, no. 3 (1996): 88–107. On Mead within the larger project of building democratic forms of culture, see Fred Turner, *The Democratic Surround: Multimedia and American Liberalism from World War II to the Psychedelic Sixties* (Chicago: University of Chicago Press, 2013), 74–76 and passim.

39. Cooke, "Culture and Fatigue."

40. Ibid., 295; Lee Simonson, "Skyscrapers for Art Museums," *American Mercury* 10 (August 1927): 401–4. For a more detailed discussion, see Neil Harris, "Museums, Merchandising, and Popular Taste: The Struggle for Influence," in *Cultural Excursions: Marketing Appetites and Cultural Tastes in Modern America* (Chicago: University of Chicago Press, 1990), 56–81.

41. Christoph Grunenberg, "The Modern Art Museum," in *Contemporary Cultures of Display*, ed. Emma Baker (New Haven, CT: Yale University Press, 1999), 27; Ruth Bernard Yeazell, *Picture Titles: How and Why Western Paintings Acquired Their Names* (Princeton, NJ: Princeton University Press, 2015), 19–20, 144–46.

42. Charles C. Perkins, "American Art Museums," *North American Review*, no. 228 (July 1870): 14.

43. Amos Stote, "The Everlasting *Saturday Evening Post*," *Magazine World* (October 1946): 6–8; Neil Harris, "Color and Media: Some Comparisons and Speculations," in Harris, *Cultural Excursions*, 336.

44. Rowley, *Taxidermy and Museum Exhibition*, 300, 301.

45. Arthur S. Eddington, *The Expanding Universe* (New York: Macmillan, 1933), 179.

46. Corwin, "Picturing Efficiency," 156, 154.

47. W. F. Ogburn, "Recent Social Trends," in *Library Trends*, ed. L. R. Wilson (Chicago: University of Chicago Press, 1937), 2.

48. See Gabriel Zaid, *Los demasiados libros* (Mexico City: Delbolsillo, 2010), 9–11.

49. J. D. Bernal, "Information Service as an Essential in the Progress of Science," in *Report of the 20th Conference of Aslib* (London: Aslib, 1945), 20; Vannevar Bush, *Science: The Endless Frontier* (Washington, DC: US Government Printing Office, 1945), 1; for FDR, see his letter of November 17, 1944, in *Science: The Endless Frontier*, vii–viii.

50. S. C. Bradford, *Documentation* (London: Crosby, Lockwood, 1948), 106; Vannevar Bush, "As We May Think," *Atlantic Monthly* 176 (1945): 101–2.

51. W. C. Berwick Sayers, *The Revision of the Stock of a Public Library* (London: Grafton, 1929).

52. Fremont Rider, *The Scholar and the Future of the Research Library* (New York: Hadham Press, 1944), 13–14.

53. Warren Weaver, "Recent Contributions to the Mathematical Theory of Communication," reprinted in *The Mathematical Theory of Communication*, ed. Claude E. Shannon and Warren Weaver (Urbana: University of Illinois Press, 1964), 3–28, at 8.

54. R. D. Jameson, "The Scholar and His Library," *Saturday Review of Literature* 20 (August 1939): 10.

55. Bush, *Science*.

56. Robert Lynd, *Knowledge for What? The Place of Social Science in American Culture* (Princeton, NJ: Princeton University Press, 1939), 213.

57. J. D. Bernal, *The Social Function of Science* (London: George Routledge, 1939).

58. Bush, "As We May Think," 108; Bernal, *Social Function of Science*, 306–7.

59. Lynd, *Knowledge for What?*, 124–26.

60. For a brilliant recent history of microfilm see Matts Lindström, *Drömmar om den minsta: Microfilm, Överflöd och Brist, 1900–1970* (Lund: Mediehistoriskt Arkiv, 2017). English summary on 289–92.

61. Otto Neurath, "Museums of the Future," *Survey Graphic* 22 (September 1933): 458–63; Ellen Lupton, "Reading Isotype," in *Design Discourse: History/Theory/Criticism*, ed. Victor Margolin (Chicago: University of Chicago Press, 1989), 147.

62. On arguments about communication in the 1920s, see John Durham Peters, *Speaking into the Air A History of the Idea of Communication* (Chicago: University of Chicago Press, 1999), chap. 1.

63. Will Durant, *The Story of Philosophy*, new rev. ed. (New York: Garden City, 1932), v–xiii; Joan Shelley Rubin, *The Making of Middlebrow Culture* (Chapel Hill:

University of North Carolina Press, 1992), 99, 237, 244. Also see George Cotkin, "Middle-Ground Pragmatists: The Popularization of Philosophy in American Culture," *Journal of the History of Ideas* 55 (April 1994): 283–302, and Janice Radway, *A Feeling for Books: The Book-of-the-Month Club, Literary Taste, and Middle-Class Desire* (Chapel Hill: University of North Carolina Press, 1999).

64. John P. Jackson and David J. Depew, *Darwinism, Democracy, and Race: American Anthropology and Evolutionary Biology in the Twentieth Century* (New York: Routledge, 2017).

65. See Peverill Squire, "Why the 1936 *Literary Digest* Poll Failed," *Public Opinion Quarterly* 52 (1988): 125–33.

66. See Jean M. Converse, *Survey Research in the United States: Roots and Emergence, 1890–1960* (Berkeley: University of California Press, 1987); Robert Brett Westbrook, "Politics as Consumption: Managing the Modern American Election," in *The Culture of Consumption: Critical Essays in American History, 1880–1980*, ed. Richard Wightman Fox and T. J. Jackson Lears (New York: Pantheon, 1983), 145–73; and George Gallup and Saul Forbes Rae, *The Pulse of Democracy: The Public-Opinion Poll and How It Works* (New York: Simon and Schuster, 1940).

67. This quip owes to the late Steve Chaffee.

68. James George Frazer, *The Golden Bough*, 2nd ed., 3 vols. (London: Macmillan, 1900), 1:28–30.

69. Bronislaw Malinowski, *Argonauts of the Western Pacific: An Account of Native Enterprise and Adventure in the Archipelago of Melanesia New Guinea* (1922; repr., New York: E. P. Dutton, 1953), 11, 10–11, 13–17. The online version of this text at www .archive.orgwww.archive.org yields forty-eight hits for the word *outline*.

70. Ruth Benedict, *Patterns of Culture* (New York: Houghton Mifflin, 1934), 46, 48.

71. The relevant essays are in Warren Susman, *Culture as History: The Transformation of American Society in the Twentieth Century* (New York: Pantheon Books, 1984).

72. Federico Neiburg and Marcio Goldman, "Anthropology and Politics in Studies of National Character," trans. Peter Gow, *Cultural Anthropology* 13 (February 1998): 56–81.

73. Barry Kätz, "The Criticism of Arms: The Frankfurt School Goes to War," *Journal of Modern History* 59 (1987): 439–78.

74. Rob van Ginkel, "Typically Dutch . . . Ruth Benedict on the National Character of Netherlanders," *Netherlands Journal of Social Science* 28 (1992): 50–71.

75. Morris Ginsberg, "National Character and National Sentiments," in *Psychology and Modern Problems*, ed. James Hadfield (London: University of London Press, 1935).

76. See, for instance, G. Gordon Brown, review of Geoffrey Gorer, *The American People, Annals of the American Academy* 259 (September 1948): 155–56, and K. L. Little, "Methodology in the Study of Adult Personality and 'National Character,'" *American Anthropologist* 52 (1950): 279–82.

77. Ray Monk, *Ludwig Wittgenstein: The Duty of Genius* (New York: Penguin, 1990), 424.

Chapter Four

1. "Der Grundvorgang der Neuzeit ist die Eroberung der Welt als Bild." Martin Heidegger, "Die Zeit des Weltbildes," in *Holzwege* (1938; repr., Frankfurt: Klostermann, 1972), 94.

2. James Agee and Walker Evans, *Let Us Now Praise Famous Men* (1941; repr., New York: Ballantine, 1976), 11.

3. On incandescent lighting and the increasing sophistication about lighting on movie sets, see "Art of Lighting Film Sets," *New York Times*, February 22, 1925; "Art-Director Explains Intricate Task of Side-Lighting of Settings," *New York Times*, August 15, 1926; and "New Lighting for Movies," *New York Times*, February 12, 1928.

4. Arthur L. Gaskill and David A. Englander, *Pictorial Continuity: How to Shoot a Movie Story* (New York: Duell, Sloan and Pearce, 1947), 146.

5. Robert Sklar, *Movie-Made America: A Cultural History of American Movies*, rev. ed. (New York: Vintage Books, 1994), 195.

6. Raymond Fielding, *The American Newsreel, 1911–1967* (Norman: University of Oklahoma Press, 1972); Vicki Goldberg, *Margaret Bourke-White: A Biography* (Reading, MA: Addison-Wesley, 1987), 173.

7. Erika Doss, "Introduction, Looking at *Life*: Rethinking America's Favorite Magazine, 1936–1972," in *Looking at Life Magazine*, ed. Erika Doss (Washington DC: Smithsonian Institution Press, 2001), 3. This is the best discussion of *Life*; see particularly the essays by Doss, Terry Smith, and James Baughman.

8. Erika Doss, *Benton, Pollock, and the Politics of Modernism: From Regionalism to Abstract Expressionism* (Chicago: University of Chicago Press, 1990), 174–75 and passim.

9. *Life*, August 8, 1949.

10. For the Delano and Stryker quotes, see "Masters of Photography" web page, http://www.mastersofphotography.com/Directory/fsa/fsa_background.html http://www.mastersofphotography.com/Directory/fsa/fsa_background.html; accessed July 18, 2003.

11. "The Perils of Photography," *Nation* 85, no. 2193 (1907): 28–29.

12. James Baughman, *Henry R. Luce and the Rise of the American News Media* (Baltimore: Johns Hopkins University Press, 2001), 85.

13. Anthony Lane, "Candid Camera: The Cult of Leica," *New Yorker*, September 24, 2007.

14. Goldberg, *Margaret Bourke-White*, 193.

15. Edwin Rothstein, "Direction in the Picture Story," in *The Encyclopedia of Photography*, ed. Willard Morgan, 20 vols. (New York: National Educational Alliance, 1949), 4:1356–57; Roy Stryker, "Documentary Photography," in *Encyclopedia of Photography*, 4:1372; Luce is quoted in Richard Whelan, *Robert Capa: A Biography* (New York: Knopf, 1985), 119.

16. Wilson Hicks, *Words and Pictures* (1952; repr., New York: Arno Press, 1973), 85, 33.

17. Gregory Black, *Hollywood Censored: Morality Codes, Catholics, and the Movies* (Cambridge: Cambridge University Press, 1994); George Roeder Jr., *The Censored War: American Visual Experience during World War II* (New Haven, CT: Yale Univer-

sity Press, 1995); Alfred Busselle Jr., "The Future of Education in Museums," *Education*, December 1942, 226–28.

18. Mark A. Vieira, *Hurrell's Hollywood Portraits* (New York: Harry N. Abrams, 1997), 6.

19. See Kobena Mercer, *James VanDerZee* (New York: Phaidon Press, 2003).

20. Jacqueline Goldsby, personal communication, November 26, 2018.

21. Thanks to Paul Messier for technical details on VanDerZee's possible process.

22. Jennifer Raab, personal communication, November 27, 2018.

23. Many Yale colleagues helped on this image: Melissa Barton, Jacqueline Goldsby, Paul Messier, Kobena Mercer, Jennifer Raab, Chitra Ramalingam, and Pooja Sen: thanks to them all.

24. The book accompanying the 1969 exhibition is *The World of James Van Der-Zee: A Visual Record of Black Americans*, ed. Reginald McGhee (New York: Grover Press, 1969); his denial is found on vii. See also Deborah Willis-Braithwaite, *VanDerZee: Photographer, 1886–1983* (New York: Harry N. Abrams, 1993). These two collections differ in the writing of his name. Wikipedia gives Van Der Zee.

25. Jacqueline Goldsby, personal communication, November 27, 2018.

26. This photo is called *U.S. Bombs Exploding on the Fortress of St. Mâlo, France*, in *Lee Miller: An Exhibition of Photographs, 1929–1945* (Los Angeles: CIAF, 1991), 67.

27. André Bazin, "The Ontology of the Photographic Image," trans. Hugh Gray, *Film Quarterly* 13 (Summer 1960): 4–9, at 9.

28. Richard Calvocoressi, *Lee Miller: Portraits from a Life* (London: Thames and Hudson, 2002); Judith Thurman, "The Roving Eye: Lee Miller, Artist and Muse," *New Yorker*, January 21, 2008, 61–67; the phrase "callous clowning" is Thurman's (67).

29. John Faber, *Great News Photos and the Stories Behind Them* (New York: Dover, 1978), 94–95.

30. A. Constandina Titus, "The Mushroom Cloud as Kitsch," in *Atomic Culture: How We Learned to Stop Worrying and Love the Bomb*, ed. Scott C. Zeman and Michael A. Amundson (Boulder: University Press of Colorado, 2004), 101–23. Titus now serves as a member of Congress (D-NV).

31. "Bikini: With Documentary Photographs, Abstract Paintings, and Meteorological Charts Ralston Howard Here Depicts the New Scale of Destruction," *Fortune*, December 1946, 156–61.

32. Kyo Maclear, *Beclouded Visions: Hiroshima-Nagasaki and the Art of Witness* (Albany: SUNY, 1999), 37.

33. Joyce Evans, *Celluloid Mushroom Clouds: Hollywood and the Atom Bomb* (Boulder, CO: Westview Press, 1998).

34. See Paul Schmitt, "Weathering the Bomb, Weathering the Climate," Seminar Paper, University of Iowa, Fall 2016, and Ned O'Gorman and Kevin Hamilton, *Lookout America! The Secret Hollywood Studio at the Heart of the Cold War* (Hanover, NH: Dartmouth College Press, 2019).

35. Scott Kirsch, "Watching the Bombs Go Off: Photography, Nuclear Landscapes, and Spectator Democracy," *Antipode* 29, no. 3 (1997): 227–55.

36. "Eyes on Bikini," *Popular Mechanics* 86 (July 1946): 79.

37. Ned O'Gorman and Kevin Hamilton, "EG&G and the Deep Media of Timing, Firing, and Exposing," *Journal of War and Cultural Studies* 9, no. 2 (2016): 182–201, at 193.

38. Personal communication, November 5, 2018.

39. Peter Kuran, *How to Photograph an Atomic Bomb* (Santa Clarita, CA: VCE, 2006). An online image search for "Rapatronic fireball" will show many of these images.

40. See O'Gorman and Hamilton, "EG&G and the Deep Media."

41. Lara Feigel, *The Love-Charm of Bombs: Restless Lives in the Second World War* (London: Bloomsbury, 2013), 24.

42. Paul Boyer, "The United States, 1941–1963: A Historical Overview," in *Vital Forms: American Art and Design in the Atomic Age*, ed. Brooks Kamin Rapaport and Kevin L. Stayton (New York: Harry N. Abrams, 2001), 56.

43. Patrick Alac, "The Birth of the Bikini," in *Bikini Story* (New York: Parkstone International, 2012), 31.

44. Despina Kakoudaki, "Pinup: The American Secret Weapon in World War II," in *Porn Studies*, ed. Linda Williams (Durham, NC: Duke University Press, 2004), 335–69, at 347.

45. "Scientist Backs Artist: At Postal Hearing He Denies Esquire Cartoons Are 'Lewd,'" *New York Times*, October 21, 1943, 29; "The Esquire Case," *New York Times*, January 2, 1944, E2; Robert B. Westbrook, "'I Want a Girl Just Like the Girl That Married Harry James': American Women and the Problem of Political Obligation in World War II," *American Quarterly* 42, no. 4 (1990): 587–614.

46. André Bazin, "The Entomology of the Pin-up Girl," in *What Is Cinema?*, vol. 2, ed. Hugh Gray (Oakland: University of California Press, 1972), 158–62, at 161.

47. Clement Greenberg, "Avant-Garde and Kitsch," *Partisan Review*, Fall 1939, 34.

48. Doss, *Benton, Pollock, and the Politics of Modernism*, 331.

49. Michael Judge, "A Pollock Saved from the Flood," *Wall Street Journal Online*, July 30, 2008.

50. Frances Stonor Saunders, *The Cultural Cold War: The CIA and the World of Arts and Letters* (New York: New Press, 2000).

51. Carolyn Kitch, *The Girl on the Magazine Cover: The Origins of Visual Stereotypes in the American Mass Media* (Chapel Hill: University of North Carolina Press, 2001), 154.

52. Peter Schjeldahl, "Reading the Mind of Norman Rockwell's Undecided Voter," November 5, 2016, www.newyorker.com/culture/cultural-comment/reading-the-mind-of-norman-rockwells-undecided-voter.

53. James W. Manns, *Aesthetics* (London: M. E. Sharpe, 1997), 56.

54. *Jet*, July 29, 1965, 31.

55. Rockwell's images have inspired a number of remixes with more diverse casts. See, for instance, Laura M. Holson, "Reimagining Norman Rockwell's America," *New York Times*, November 8, 2018, and Abigail Tucker, "A 21st-Century Reimagining of Norman Rockwell's *Four Freedoms*," *Smithsonian Magazine*, March 2018.

56. Richard Halpern, *Norman Rockwell: The Underside of Innocence* (Chicago: University of Chicago Press, 2006), ix.

57. Martin Heidegger, "The Age of the World Picture," in *The Question concerning Technology and Other Essays*, trans. William Lovitt (New York: Harper and Row, 1977), 115–54.

58. Ludwig Wittgenstein, *Philosophical Investigations*, trans. G. E. Anscombe (Oxford: Basil Blackwell, 1953), sec. 115.

59. On Heidegger in the context of neo-Kantianism, see Hans Ruin, "Technology as Destiny in Cassirer and Heidegger: Continuing the Davos Debate," in *Ernst Cassirer on Form and Technology*, ed. Aud Sissel Hoel and Ingvild Folkvord (London: Palgrave Macmillan, 2012), 113–38.

60. Susanne K. Langer, *Philosophy in a New Key: A Study in the Symbolism of Reason, Rite, and Art*, 3rd ed. (Cambridge, MA: Harvard University Press, 2009), 94–95.

61. Bazin, "Ontology of the Photographic Image."

62. Bazin, "Ontology of the Photographic Image." On Bazin, see Dudley Andrew, *The Major Film Theories* (New York: Oxford University Press, 1975), 134–78, and Dudley Andrew, *André Bazin* (New York: Columbia University Press, 1990).

Chapter Five

1. Peter Lev, *Transforming the Screen, 1950–1959* (Berkeley: University of California Press, 2003), 7–9.

2. Gerald Mast, *A Short History of the Movies*, 5th ed., rev. Bruce Kawin (New York: Macmillan, 1992), 275.

3. For a jubilee appreciation, see Anthony Lane, "Road Show: The journey of Robert Frank's 'The Americans,'" *New Yorker*, September 14, 2009, 84–91.

4. Jon Lewis, *Hollywood v. Hard Core: How the Struggle over Censorship Saved the Modern Film Industry* (New York: New York University Press, 2000).

5. See the website "TV Ratings," http://www.fiftiesweb.com/tv-ratings-60s.htm#67–68; accessed July 2003.

6. Douglas Gomery, *Shared Pleasures: A History of Movie Presentation in the United States* (Madison: University of Wisconsin Press, 1992), 180–93.

7. Kenneth Cmiel, "Politics of Civility," in *The Sixties: From Memory to History*, ed. David Farber (Chapel Hill: University of North Carolina Press, 1994), 263–90.

8. Lewis, *Hollywood v. Hard Core*, 146–48; Jacob Septimus, "The MPAA Ratings System: A Regime of Private Censorship and Cultural Manipulation," *Columbia-VLA Journal of Law and the Arts* 21 (Fall 1996): 69–93.

9. See for instance, Raffi Khatchadourian, "The Long View: Edward Burtynsky's Quest to Photograph a Changing Planet," *New Yorker*, December 19–26, 2016, 80–95 (intermittent pagination), esp. 90.

10. On the rise of niche marketing, see Joseph Turow, *Breaking Up America: Advertisers and the New Media World* (Chicago: University of Chicago Press, 1998); Lizabeth Cohen, *A Consumer's Republic: The Politics of Mass Consumption in Postwar America* (New York: Knopf, 2003), 292–344.

11. See Elihu Katz and Tamar Liebes, "'No More Peace!': How Disaster, Terror, and War Have Upstaged Media Events," *International Journal of Communication* 1 (2007): 157–66.

12. Raymond Williams, *Television: Technology and Cultural Form* (New York: Schocken, 1974), 92.

13. Todd Gitlin, *Media Unlimited: How the Torrent of Images and Sound Overwhelms Our Lives* (New York: Metropolitan Books, 2001), 17–18.

14. "Morning Report: Where They're Watching," *Los Angeles Times*, March 11, 1993; Frazier Moore, "From Schools to Truck Stops: 'Place-Based' Media Flourish," *TV Guide*, March 1993, 7. Also see Anna McCarthy, *Ambient Television: Visual Culture and Public Space* (Durham, NC: Duke University Press, 2001).

15. On transformations in screen cultures, see Francesco Casetti, *The Lumière Galaxy* (New York: Columbia University Press, 2015).

16. Figures from *Magazine Circulation and Rate Trends, 1940–1959* (New York: Association of National Advertisers, 1960), 12, and *Magazine Circulation and Rate Trends, 1946–1976* (New York: Association of National Advertisers, 1978), 14.

17. Erika Doss, "Introduction: Looking at *Life*: Rethinking America's Favorite Magazine, 1936–1972," in *Looking at Life Magazine* (Washington, DC: Smithsonian Institution Press, 2001), 18.

18. "Hollywood's Secret Star Is the Special-Effects Man," *New York Times*, May 1, 1977; "The Black Hole Casts the Computer as Movie Maker," *New York Times*, December 16, 1979.

19. For a casual, but undocumented, assertion about the shift in popular moviemaking from the 1970s to the 1990s, see José Arroyo, "Introduction," in *Action/Spectacle Cinema*, ed. José Arroyo (London: British Film Institute, 2000), x–xi. It is worth remembering, though, that films like *Jaws, Jaws II, Star Wars, The Exorcist, Moonraker*, and *The Spy Who Loved Me* were among the most popular movies of the 1970s.

20. On "theme park" films, see Scott Bukatman, "The End of Offscreen Space," in *The New American Cinema*, ed. Jon Lewis (Durham, NC: Duke University Press, 1998), 266; on "rootless, violent images," see Warren Buckland, "Between Science Fact and Science Fiction," *Screen* 40 (Summer 1999), 178. For the best overview of new special effects technology, see Richard Rickitt, *Special Effects: The History and Technique* (New York: Billboard Books, 2000). Other useful literature includes Stephen Keane, *Disaster Movies: The Cinema of Catastrophe* (New York: Wallflower Press, 2001); Yvonne Tasker, *Spectacular Bodies: Gender, Genre and the Action Cinema* (London: Routledge, 1993); Michelle Person, *Special Effects: Still in Search of Wonder* (New York: Columbia University Press, 2002); Brooks Landon, *The Aesthetics of Ambivalence: Rethinking Science Fiction Film in the Age of Electronic Reproduction* (Westport, CT: Greenwood Press, 1992).

21. See John Thornton Caldwell, *Televisuality: Style, Crisis, and Authority in American Television* (New Brunswick, NJ: Rutgers University Press, 1995), e.g., 64.

22. Caldwell, *Televisuality*, 152.

23. On network logos, see Margaret Morse, *Virtualities: Television, Media Art, and Cyberculture* (Bloomington: Indiana University Press, 1998), 74–80; the indignant newsman quoted is Charles Kuralt, "The New Enemies of Journalism," in *Fast Forward: The New Television and American Society*, ed. Les Brown and Savannah Waring Walker (Kansas City, MO: Andrews and McMeel, 1983), 95; also see Av Westin, *Newswatch: How TV Decides the News* (New York: Simon and Schuster, 1982), 51.

24. Douglas Merritt, quoted in Morse, *Virtualities*, 74.

25. Michael D. Murray, *The Encyclopedia of Television News* (Phoenix, AZ: Oryx Press, 1999), 140. For a good example of social science research, see Byron Reeves

and Esther Thorson, "Watching Television: Experiments on the Viewing Process," *Communication Research* 13, no. 3 (1986): 343–61.

26. See I. E. Fang, *Television News* (New York: Hastings House, 1972), 300–317; Ivor Yorke, *The Technique of Television News* (New York: Focal Press/Hastings House, 1978), 31–33, 84–91.

27. Kiku Adatto, *Picture Perfect: The Art and Artifice of Public Image Making* (New York: Basic Books, 1993), 2, 25, 62–67; Adatto, "The Incredible Shrinking Sound Bite," *New Republic,* May 28, 1990; Adatto, "Sound Bite News: Television Coverage of Elections, 1968–1988," *Journal of Communication* 42 (Spring 1992): 5–24; Thomas Patterson, *Out of Order* (New York: Vintage, 1994), 74–75, 159–61; Lawrence Lichty, "Video versus Print," *Wilson Quarterly* 6, no. 5 (1982): 52.

28. Frank Davidoff, "Digital Recording for Television Broadcasting," *Journal of the SMPTE* 84 (July 1975): 552; Thomas Battista and Joseph Flaherty, "The All-Electronic Newsgathering Station," *Journal of the SMPTE* 84 (December 1975): 958–62.

29. Elihu Katz, "The End of Journalism," *Journal of Communication* 42 (September 1992): 5–13.

30. On the background to MTV, see R. Serge Denisoff, *Inside MTV* (New Brunswick, NJ: Transaction Books, 1988); for analysis of the videos, see Patricia Aufderheide, "Music Videos: The Look of the Sound," *Journal of Communication* 36 (March 1986): 57–78; Marsha Kinder, "Music Video and the Spectator: Television, Ideology, and Dream," *Film Quarterly* 34 (1984): 2–15; E. Ann Kaplan, *Rocking around the Clock: Music Television, Postmodernism, and Consumer Culture* (New York: Methuen, 1987), 33–88.

31. Randall Rothenberg, *Where the Suckers Moon: The Life and Death of an Advertising Campaign* (New York: Vintage, 1995), 211–12; Jim Collins, "Appropriating Like Krazy: From Pop Art to Meta-Pop," in *Modernity and Mass Culture*, ed. James Naremore and Patrick Brantlinger (Bloomington: Indiana University Press, 1991), 201–23.

32. Rickitt, *Special Effects*, 33.

33. Caldwell, *Televisuality*, 152.

34. Robert Bellamy Jr. and James Walker, *Television and the Remote Control: Grazing on a Vast Wasteland* (New York: Guilford Press, 1996); on household ownership of remotes, see 1–2.

35. Walter Benjamin, "The Work of Art in the Age of Mechanical Reproduction," in *Illuminations: Essays and Reflections* (New York: Schocken Books, 1969), 217–51; Hadley Cantril and Gordon Allport, *The Psychology of Radio* (New York: Harper, 1935), 14–16; Jonathan Crary, *Suspensions of Perception: Attention, Spectacle, and Modern Culture* (Cambridge: MIT Press, 2000); Noam M. Elcott, *Artificial Darkness: An Obscure History of Modern Art and Media* (Chicago: University of Chicago Press, 2016).

36. See Marshall McLuhan, *Understanding Media* (London: Routledge and Kegan Paul, 1964); Pauline Kael, *I Lost It at the Movies* (Boston: Little, Brown, 1965), 9.

37. See Jon Lewis, *Hollywood v. Hard Core: How the Struggle over Censorship Saved the Modern Film Industry* (New York: New York University Press, 2000).

38. Lewis, *Hollywood v. Hard Core*, 192.

39. For an excellent discussion of the shift to videotape, see Carolyn Bronstein, "Have You Seen *Deep Throat* Yet?: The Growth of the Commercial Sex Industry in the 1970s," in *Battling Pornography, 1976–1986* (Cambridge: Cambridge University Press, 2011), 63–82; for estimates of porn video circulation, see Edward de Grazia, *Girls Lean Back Everywhere: The Law of Obscenity and the Assault on Genius* (New York: Random House, 1992), 583.

40. DeGrazia, *Girls Lean Back*, 578.

41. This is a textbook example of what Andreas Sudmann and Frank Kelleter call "serial one-upmanship." See Andreas Jahn-Sudmann and Frank Kelleter, "Die Dynamik serieller Überbietung: Zeitgenössische amerikanische Fernsehserien und das Konzept des Quality TV," in *Populäre Serialität: Narration—Evolution—Distinktion. Zum seriellen Erzählen seit dem 19. Jahrundert*, ed. Frank Kelleter (Bielefeld: Transcript, 2012), 205–24.

42. William Donnelly, *The Confetti Generation: How the New Communications Technology Is Fragmenting America* (New York: Henry Holt, 1986), 80.

43. "The Team behind Archie Bunker & Co.," *Time*, September 25, 1972.

44. Mary Leis Coakley, *Rated X: The Moral Case against TV* (New Rochelle, NY: Arlington House, 1977), 13. For a discussion of the emergence of conservative critics of TV, see Kathryn Montgomery, *Target: Prime Time: Advocacy Groups and the Struggle over Entertainment Television* (New York: Oxford University Press, 1989), 27–50, 154–73.

45. See Michele Rosenthal, *American Protestants and TV in the 1950s: Responses to a New Medium* (New York: Palgrave Macmillan, 2007), and Heather Hendershot, *What's Fair on the Air?: Cold War Right-Wing Broadcasting and the Public Interest* (Chicago: University of Chicago Press, 2011).

46. Steven Daly, "Blue Streak," *TV Guide*, August 2–8, 2003, 28.

47. On *National Geographic*, *TV Guide*, and the *Wall Street Journal*, see Vicki Goldberg and Robert Silberman, *American Photography: A Century of Images* (San Francisco: Chronicle Books, 1999), 224. See also Paul Martin Lester, *Photojournalism: An Ethical Approach* (Hillsdale, NJ: Lawrence Erlbaum, 1991); "Guide Puts Oprah's Face on Ann-Margret's Body," *Tulsa World*, August 29, 1989; "Going Too Far with the Winfrey Diet," *New York Times*, August 30, 1989.

48. Friedrich A. Kittler, "Computer Graphics: A Semi-technical Introduction," trans. Sara Ogger, *Grey Room*, no. 2 (Winter 2001): 32.

49. In the early 1950s liberal senator Millard Tydings was defeated after a "composograph" was circulated showing him standing with Communist Earl Browder, an event that never happened.

50. Stewart Brand, Kevin Kelly, and Jay Kinney, "Digital Retouching: The End of Photography as Evidence of Anything," *Whole Earth Review* 47 (July 1985): 42–50.

51. See, for example, Siegfried Kracauer, *Theory of Film: The Redemption of Physical Reality* (New York: Oxford University Press, 1960).

52. Roland Barthes, "L'effet de réel," *Communications* 11 (1968): 84–89; for examples from the *New York Times*, see "New Picture Technologies Push Seeing Still Further from Believing," *New York Times*, July 3, 1989, and Andy Grunberg,

"Ask It No Questions: The Camera Can Lie," *New York Times*, August 12, 1990; for examples in other mainstream media, see Jonathan Alter, "When Photographs Lie," *Newsweek* (July 30, 1990): 44–48, and Robert Mathews, "When Seeing Is Not Believing," *New Scientist*, October 16, 1993, 99–104.

53. Laura Mulvey, "Visual Pleasure and Narrative Cinema," in *Narrative, Apparatus, Ideology: A Film Theory Reader*, ed. Philip Rosen (New York: Columbia University Press, 1986), 198–209.

54. Kenneth Cmiel, "The Swirl of Image and Sound: The Latest Version of Antirealism," in *The Arts of Democracy*, ed. Casey Blake (Philadelphia: University of Pennsylvania Press, 2007).

55. Fredric Jameson, "Postmodernism and Consumer Society," in *The Anti-aesthetic: Essays on Postmodern Culture*, ed. Hal Foster (Port Townsend, WA: Bay Press, 1983), 125; Martin Jay, *Downcast Eyes: The Denigration of Vision in Twentieth-Century French Thought* (Berkeley: University of California Press, 1993), 546. (Martin Jay was Kenneth Cmiel's undergraduate thesis adviser at Berkeley.)

56. Adatto, *Picture Perfect*, 123, 171–72; Michael Rogin, *Ronald Reagan, the Movie* (Berkeley: University of California Press, 1988).

57. On the orphanage debate, see Kenneth Cmiel, *A Home of Another Kind: One Chicago Orphanage and the Tangle of Child Welfare* (Chicago: University of Chicago Press, 1995), 187–88.

58. See https://en.wikipedia.org/wiki/V-J_Day_in_Times_Square#Identity _of_the_kissers. More recently the photo has taken on new life as a document of a sexual assault.

59. James Curtis, *Mind's Eye, Mind's Truth: FSA Photography Reconsidered* (Philadelphia: Temple University Press, 1989), vii–ix; on *Migrant Mother*, see Robert Hariman and John Louis Lucaites, *No Caption Needed: Iconic Photographs, Public Culture, and Liberal Democracy* (Chicago: University of Chicago Press, 2007), 53–67.

60. Donna Haraway, "Teddy Bear Patriarchy: Taxidermy in the Garden of Eden, New York City, 1908–1936," in *Primate Visions: Gender, Race, and Nature in the World of Modern Science* (New York: Routledge, 1989), 54, 45, 27, 38, 30, 43. For a thorough critique of many of Haraway's claims, focusing on the progressive Boasian legacy of the AMNH, see Michael Schudson, "Paper Tigers," *Lingua Franca* 7 (August 1997): 49–56.

61. E.g., Judith Butler, "Endangered/Endangering: Schematic Racism and White Paranoia," in *Reading Rodney King, Reading Urban Uprising*, ed. Robert Gooding-Williams (New York: Routledge, 1993), 15–22, or Mike Mashon, "Losing Control: Popular Reception(s) of the Rodney King Video," *Wide Angle* 15 (April 1993): 7–18.

62. Walter Benjamin, "A Little History of Photography," in *Walter Benjamin: Selected Writings, 1927–1934*, ed. Michael W. Jennings, Howard Eiland, and Gary Smith (Cambridge, MA: Belknap Press, 1999), 2:507–30. Barthes's notion of the punctum was also important, and it probably owes something to Benjamin.

63. See Dudley Andrew, ed., *The Image in Dispute* (Austin: University of Texas Press, 1997).

64. Julia Keller, "Is PowerPoint the Devil?," *Chicago Tribune*, January 23, 2004.

65. For some polling data, see Daly, "Blue Streak," 34.

66. Lauren Berlant, "The Face of America and the State of Emergency," in *The Queen of America Goes to Washington City* (Durham, NC: Duke University Press, 1997), chap. 5; Evelynn Hammond, "New Technologies of Race," in *Processed Lives: Gender and Technology in Everyday Life*, ed. Jennifer Terry and Melodie Calvert (London: Routledge, 1997), 113; David Theo Goldberg, *Racial Subjects* (London: Routledge, 1997), chap. 4; Michael Rogin, *Blackface, White Noise* (Berkeley: University of California Press, 1998), chap. 1; Donna Haraway, *Modest Witness* (London: Routledge, 1997), 259–65; Shawn Michelle Smith, *American Archives* (Princeton, NJ: Princeton University Press, 1999), 223; Caroline Streeter, "The Hazards of Visibility: 'Biracial' Women, Media Images, and Narratives of Identity," in New Faces in a Changing America: Multiracial Identity in the 21st Century, ed. Loretta I. Winters and Herman L. DeBose (Thousand Oaks, CA: Sage, 2003), 301–22.

67. At the University of Iowa, a conference room in the English-Philosophy Building long sported black-and-white photographs of retired members of the English Department up through the mid-1980s. Graduate students sometimes called it the wall of patriarchy. Recent updates have yielded more diversity.

68. Ian Zack, "Deans' Pictures Open Debate in Virginia," *New York Times*, February 12, 1997, A15.

69. David Stout, "Clinton Backs Sculpture of Roosevelt in Wheelchair," *New York Times*, April 26, 1997, A16.

70. "F.D.R.'s Progressive Spirit Is Vote for Wheelchair," *New York Times*, April 26, 1997, 22; "F.D.R.'s Legacy of Hard-Won Goals Helps the Disabled Achieve," *New York Times*, May 5, 1997, A14.

71. But see Blynn Garnett, "Agreeing to Pretend," *New York Times*, April 26, 1997, 22.

72. Hariman and Lucaites, *No Caption Needed*, 128 ff.

73. Lynne Duke, "Red, White, and Blue, for Starters: Firefighters Memorial Sparks a Diverse Debate," *Washington Post*, January 18, 2002, C1.

74. Donna Britt, "It's the Actions, Not the Actors, We Will Remember," *Washington Post*, January 25, 2002, B1. Note that there were also differences in the two images. Rosenthal's Iwo Jima image showed no faces, only an anonymous chorus of military bodies united in national purpose; Franklin's 9/11 image showed three civilian faces united not by labor, but by the act of looking. See Hariman and Lucaites, *No Caption Needed*, 133–34.

75. See Lorraine Daston and Peter Galison, *Objectivity* (New York: Zone, 2007).

76. Compare the tyranny of framelessness in big data: see Mark Andrejevic, "'Framelessness,' or the Cultural Logic of Big Data," in *Mobile and Ubiquitous Media*, ed. Michael S. Daubs and Vincent R. Manzerolle (New York: Peter Lang, 2018), 251–66.

77. Shannon Barber, "Paul Ryan 'Selfie' with Young Republicans Backfires When Internet Notices One Very Telling Detail," *If You Only News*, http://www.ifyouonlynews.com/racism/paul-ryan-selfie-with-white-young-republicans-backfires-when-internet-notices-one-very-telling-detail/; accessed July 19, 2016.

78. Hariman and Lucaites, *No Caption Needed*, 119.

79. Milan Kundera, *Immortality: A Novel*, trans. Peter Kussi (New York: Grove Weidenfeld, 1990), 114–15.

Chapter Six

1. Clifford Geertz, "Blurred Genres: The Refiguration of Social Thought," in Geertz, *Local Knowledge: Further Essays in Interpretive Anthropology* (1979; repr., New York: Basic Books, 1983).

2. For more recent work in this spirit, see Naomi Oreskes and Erik M. Conway, *Merchants of Doubt: How a Handful of Scientists Obscured the Truth on Issues from Tobacco Smoke to Global Warming* (London: Bloomsbury, 2010), and Lucas Graves, *Deciding What's True: The Rise of Political Fact-Checking in American Journalism* (New York: Columbia University Press, 2016).

3. Kenneth Cmiel, "The Emergence of Human Rights Politics in the United States," *Journal of American History* 86 (December 1999): 1231–50.

4. See the excellent account in Ronald Bayer, *Homosexuality and American Psychiatry: The Politics of Diagnosis* (Princeton, NJ: Princeton University Press, 1981).

5. David Healy, *The Creation of Psychopharmacology* (Cambridge, MA: Harvard University Press, 2002).

6. Rael Jean Isaac and Virginia C. Armat, *Madness in the Streets: How Psychiatry and the Law Abandoned the Mentally Ill* (New York: Free Press, 1990). See also Maria Farland, "Sylvia Plath's Anti-psychiatry," *Minnesota Review* 55–57 (2002): 245–56.

7. David L. Rosenhan, "On Being Sane in Insane Places," *Science* 179 (January 1973): 250–58; Isaac and Armat, *Madness in the Streets*, 53–57. See also Roger Brown and Richard J. Herrnstein, *Psychology* (Boston: Little, Brown, 1975), 628–29, 680–81, for a discussion of the 1970s cult film *King of Hearts*, in which the inmates of an asylum prove to be more reasonable (and more fun) than the people outside.

8. See James H. Jones, *Bad Blood: The Tuskegee Syphilis Experiment* (New York: Free Press, 1981), Kennedy quotation at 214, and Susan Reverby, ed., *Tuskegee's Truths: Rethinking the Tuskegee Syphilis Study* (Chapel Hill: University of North Carolina Press, 2000), Proxmire quotation at 117.

9. Gary Edmond, "Whigs in Court: Historiographical Problems with Expert Evidence," *Yale Journal of Law and the Humanities* 14 (Winter 2002): 123–75; Mark Essig, "Poison Murder and Expert Testimony: Doubting the Physician in Late Nineteenth-Century America," *Yale Journal of Law and the Humanities* 14 (Winter 2002): 177–210.

10. See Carol Jones, *Expert Witnesses: Science, Medicine, and the Practice of Law* (New York: Oxford University Press, 1994); Daniel Farber and Suzanna Sherry, *Beyond All Reason: The Radical Assault on Truth in American Law* (New York: Oxford University Press, 1997); and Tal Golan, "Revisiting the History of Scientific Expert Testimony," *Brooklyn Law Review* 73, no. 3 (2008): 879–942.

11. Alice Echols, *Daring to Be Bad: Radical Feminism in America, 1967–1975* (Minneapolis: University of Minnesota Press, 1989).

12. Jorge Luis Borges, "John Wilkins' Analytical Language," in *Selected Nonfictions*, ed. Eliot Weinberger (New York: Penguin, 1999), 229–32.

13. David Ricci, *The Transformation of American Politics* (New Haven, CT: Yale University Press, 1993); for the same trend in the management of child welfare statistics, see Cmiel, *Home of Another Kind*, 185.

14. Cmiel, "Emergence of Human Rights Politics in the United States." See also

Peter Simonson, "Social Noise and Segmented Rhythms: News, Entertainment, and Celebrity in the Crusade for Animal Rights," *Communication Review* 4, no. 3 (2001): 399–420, and Lilie Chouliaraki, *The Ironic Spectator: Solidarity in the Age of Post-humanitarianism* (Cambridge: Polity Press, 2012).

15. Dorothy Lille, *A History of Information Science, 1945–1985* (San Diego, CA: Academic Press, 1989), 52–53, 84–92; Dennis Reynolds, *Library Automation: Issues and Applications* (New York: R. R. Bowker, 1985), 64–65.

16. William Ready and Tom Drynan, *Library Automation: A View from Ontario* (Halifax, NS: Dalhousie University, 1977), 1; Earl Joseph, "Twenty-First-Century Information Literacies and Libraries," in *Information Literacies for the Twenty-First Century*, ed. Virgil Blake and Renee Tjoumas (Boston: G. K. Hall, 1990), 8; also see Kenneth Dowlin, *The Electronic Library* (New York: Neal-Schuman, 1984); Daniel Carter, "The Library Charter: Is It Time for a Rewrite," *Library Journal* 106 (July 1981): 117; Gerald R. Shields, "The New Role of the Librarian in the Information Age," in *The Information Society: Issues and Answers*, ed. E. J. Josey (Phoenix, AZ: Oryx Press, 1978), 75l; and Kenneth Cmiel, "Libraries, Books, and the Information Age, 1945–2000," in *The Cambridge History of the Book in America*, vol. 5 (Cambridge: Cambridge University Press, 2014), 325–46.

17. Steven Epstein, *Impure Science: AIDS, Activism and the Politics of Knowledge* (Berkeley: University of California Press, 1996).

18. Marcia Angell, *Science on Trial: The Clash of Medical Evidence and the Law in the Breast Implant Case* (New York: W. W. Norton, 1996).

19. Jon Cohen, "The Duesberg Phenomenon," *Science* 266 (December 9, 1994): 1642–44; Epstein, *Impure Science*; Peter Duesberg, *Inventing the AIDS Virus* (Washington, DC: Regnery, 1997); Larry Kramer, "The F.D.A.'s Callous Response to AIDS," *New York Times*, May 23, 1987, A19.

20. Epstein, *Impure Science*, 118. For a more recent update, see Alice Dreger, *Galileo's Middle Finger: Heretics, Activists, and the Search for Justice in Science* (New York: Penguin Press, 2015).

21. Neil Harris, "Exhibiting Controversy," *Museum News* 74 (September-October 1995): 36–39, 57–58; Harris, "Museums and Controversy: Some Introductory Reflections," *Journal of American History* 82 (1995): 1102–10.

22. Mary Jo Arnoldi, "From the Diorama to the Dialogic: A Century of Exhibiting Africa at the Smithsonian's Museum of Natural History," *Cahiers d'études africaines* 39, nos. 3–4 (1999): 701–26.

23. Compare the *Historikerstreit* in 1980s Germany and the "history wars" in 1990s Australia.

24. See David Thelen, "History after the *Enola Gay* Controversy: An Introduction," *Journal of American History* 82 (December 1995): 1029–35. The entire special issue contains several thoughtful and rueful essays; Gingrich quotation from Richard H. Kohn, "History and the Culture Wars: The Case of the Smithsonian's *Enola Gay* Exhibition," *Journal of American History* 82 (December 1995): 1056.

25. David Thelen, "The Profession and the *Journal of American History*," *Journal of American History* 73 (June 1986): 9–14. See also Kenneth Cmiel, "John Higham: The Contrarian as Optimist," *Intellectual History Newsletter* 24 (2003): 134–38; Cmiel, "The Hidden Meaning of Blasphemy," *Intellectual History Newsletter* 20

(1998): 42–50; and Cmiel, "History against Itself," *Journal of American History* 81 (December 1994): 1169–74.

26. Joan Stephenson, "Medical Journals Turn Gaze Inward to Examine Process of Peer Review," *Journal of the American Medical Association* 278 (November 5, 1997): 1389–91.

27. See Andrew Abbott, "Publication and the Future of Knowledge," lecture to the Association of American University Presses (June 27, 2008), http://home .uchicago.edu/aabbott/Papers/aaup.pdf.

28. See Eliot Freidson, *Professionalism: The Third Logic* (Chicago: University of Chicago Press, 2000); and Nikolas Rose, *Powers of Freedom: Reframing Political Thought* (Cambridge: Cambridge University Press, 1999).

29. Elihu Katz, "Disintermediation," *Intermedia* 16, no. 2 (1988): 30–31.

30. Michael Warner, "The Mass Public and the Mass Subject," in *Habermas and the Public Sphere*, ed. Craig Calhoun (Cambridge, MA: MIT Press, 1992), 377–401, at 378, and Michael Schudson, "Trout or Hamburger: Politics and Telemythology," *Tikkun* 6 (March 1991): 47–51.

31. John Durham Peters, "Should Universities Be More Like Businesses? Some Businesses Are Learning to Be More Like Universities," culturedigitally.org/2015 /09/should-universities-be-more-like-businesesbusinesses/.

32. Fred Turner, *From Counterculture to Cyberculture: Stewart Brand, the Whole Earth Network, and the Rise of Digital Utopianism* (Chicago: University of Chicago Press, 2006).

33. Elihu Katz, "The End of Journalism," *Journal of Communication* 42, no. 3 (1992): 5–13.

34. Friedrich Wilhelm Nietzsche, "Truth and Lie in an Extra-moral Sense," in *Portable Nietzsche*, ed. Walter Kauffmann (New York: Penguin, 1954), 42–50, at 42.

35. See Kenneth Cmiel, *Home of Another Kind*, conclusion.

Postscript

1. Arthur Schopenhauer, *Parerga und Paralipomena: Kleine philosophische Schriften* (1851; repr., Leipzig: Brockhaus, 1874), 2:596.

2. See Garrett Stewart, *Bookwork: Medium to Object to Concept to Art* (Chicago: University of Chicago Press, 2011).

3. Mark B. Andrejevic, personal correspondence, April 4, 2016. His mother, Helen Bardeen Andrejevic, has since passed.

4. Margaret Schwartz, *Dead Matter: The Meaning of Iconic Corpses* (Minneapolis: University of Minnesota Press, 2015), 32.

5. I pursue this question in "History as a Communication Problem," in *Explorations in Communication and History*, ed. Barbie Zelizer (London: Sage, 2008), 19–34.

6. Josh Lauer, "Traces of the Real: Autographomania and the Cult of the Signers in Nineteenth-Century America," *Text and Performance Quarterly* 27, no. 2 (2007): 143–63.

7. See negotiations with his editor at William Morrow about the cover of *Democratic Eloquence*, Kenneth Cmiel Papers, Special Collections Department, University of Iowa Libraries, Iowa City, Iowa, box 3, "Democratic Eloquence— Contract" file.

8. Freud's original: "Wo es war, soll ich werden." I think I was there when Ken wrote this in the book, but it may be a memory trick.

9. James J. O'Donnell, *Avatars of the Word: From Papyrus to Cyberspace* (Cambridge, MA: Harvard University Press, 2000), 10.

10. Ibid., 70.

11. James Porter, "Homer: The Very Idea," *Arion: A Journal of Humanities and the Classics*, 3rd ser., 10, no. 2 (2002): 57–86.

12. Mark C. Taylor, *Altarity* (Chicago: University of Chicago Press, 1987), 308–14. See also David M. Levy, "Meditation on a Receipt," in *Scrolling Forward: Making Sense of Documents in the Digital Age* (New York: Arcade, 2001), 7–20.

13. See André De Tienne, "The Peirce Papers: How to Pick Up Manuscripts That Fell to the Floor," *Text* 10 (1997): 259–82, and Michel Foucault, "What Is an Author?" in *Language, Counter-Memory, Practice*, ed. Donald F. Bouchard (Ithaca, NY: Cornell University Press, 1977), 113–38.

14. See, for instance, Page DuBois, *Sowing the Body: Psychoanalysis and Ancient Representations of Women* (Chicago: University of Chicago Press, 1988).

15. See Michael Thompson, *Rubbish Theory: The Creation and Destruction of Value* (Oxford: Oxford University Press, 1979), and Gladys Engel Lang and Kurt Lang, *Etched in Memory: The Building and Survival of Artistic Reputation* (Chapel Hill: University of North Carolina Press, 1990), esp. chap. 9.

16. Ralph Waldo Emerson, "Self-Reliance," in *Selected Writings of Emerson*, ed. Donald McQuade (New York: Modern Library, 1981).

17. Mary McCarthy, "Editor's Postface," in Hannah Arendt, *The Life of the Mind*, one-volume edition (New York: Harcourt, Brace, Jovanovich, 1978), 2:241–54, at 250, 244, 247, 248.

18. Kenneth Cmiel, *Democratic Eloquence: The Fight over Popular Speech in Nineteenth-Century America* (New York: Morrow, 1990), 116.

19. The governing board of the New York Abortion Access Fund voted unanimously in May 2014 to not use *women* exclusively for those who are pregnant: "We recognize that people who identify as men can become pregnant and seek abortions." Michelle Goldberg, "What Is a Woman? The Dispute between Radical Feminism and Transgenderism," *New Yorker*, August 4, 2014, 24–28.

20. So much so that historian John Higham, in thanking Ken for an essay about his work, gently chided that he was still alive and didn't quite yet merit the past tense! See Cmiel papers, box 3, folder H.

21. E. A. Speiser, *Genesis: A New Translation with Introduction and Commentary* (New Haven, CT: Yale University Press, 1963), lxiv.

22. Jorge Luis Borges, "Pierre Menard, Author of the *Quixote*," in *Selected Nonfictions*, ed. Eliot Weinberger (New York: Penguin, 1999), 88–95.

23. Kenneth Cmiel, "The American Scholar Revisited," *Iowa Review* 19 (Winter 1989): 175–80, at 178.

24. See books by Karl Ove Knausgaard, Chris Kraus, Ben Lerner, and others.

25. See Alexander Starre, *Metamedia: American Book Fictions and Literary Print Culture after Digitization* (Iowa City: University of Iowa Press, 2015).

26. Ralph Waldo Emerson, "Friendship," in *Selected Writings of Emerson*, ed. Donald McQuade (New York: Modern Library, 1981), 214.

27. Published as "On Cynicism, Evil, and the Discovery of Communication in the 1940s," *Journal of Communication* 46, no. 3 (1996): 88–107.

28. Bette London, "Secretary to the Stars: Mediums and the Agency of Authorship," in *Literary Secretaries/Secretarial Culture*, ed. Leah Price and Pamela Thurschwell (Burlington, VT: Ashgate, 2005), 91–110.

29. Ibid., 106.

30. See Terryl L. Givens, *Wrestling the Angel: The Foundations of Mormon Thought; Cosmos, God, Humanity* (New York: Oxford University Press, 2015), 209–14.

31. I owe this point to Daniel N. P. Peters.

32. Florian Sprenger, *The Politics of Micro-decisions: Edward Snowden, Net Neutrality, and the Architectures of the Internet*, trans. Valentin A. Pakis (Lüneburg, Germany: Meson Press, 2015), 107.

33. George Eliot, *Middlemarch* (New York: Penguin, 1994), 475, 478, 479.

34. Ibid., 412.

35. George B. Handley, *American Fork* (Winchester, UK: Roundfire Books, 2018), 316.

36. See my "Recording Beyond the Grave: Joseph Smith's Celestial Bookkeeping," *Critical Inquiry* 42, no. 4 (2016): 842–64.

37. "Aktenarbeit ist Kampf gegen Entropie." Siegert, *Passage des Digitalen*, 79.

38. See Pierre Cassou-Noguès, *Les démons de Gödel: Logique et folie* (Paris: Seuil, 2007).

Index